Cherie Blair is a noted barrister and QC, specialising in human rights law. She is married to Tony Blair, the former Prime Minister, and lives with her family in London

SPEAKING FOR MYSELF

MYSELF

The Autobiography

CHERIE BLAIR

sphere

SPHERE

First published in Great Britain in 2008 by Little, Brown
This paperback edition published in 2009 by Sphere

A CIP catalogue record for this book
is available from the British Library.

ISBN 978-0-7515-4255-4

Typeset in Sabon by M Rules
Printed and bound in Great Britain by
Clays Ltd, St Ives plc

Papers used by Sphere are natural, renewable and
recyclable products sourced from well-managed forests and certified
in accordance with the rules of the Forest Stewardship Council.

Sphere
An imprint of
Little, Brown Book Group
100 Victoria Embankment
London EC4Y 0DY

An Hachette UK Company
www.hachette.co.uk

www.littlebrown.co.uk

To my mother Gale and my grandmother Vera

CONTENTS

My memory is not infallible, and this is not a history book. It is simply one woman's attempt to recollect her life – a memoir of someone who, for a time, had a walk-on part in history.

Cherie Blair
April 2008

June 2007

'OK, guys, that's it. Let's do the business.'

The time had finally come: our goodbyes had all been said, tears wiped away. At a nod from Tony, the custodian opened the famous front door with a little mock bow and the six of us trooped out into the June sunshine to face the cameras: Euan, Nicky, Kathryn, Leo, Tony and me, all six of us dressed in what my grandma would have called our Sunday Best, exiting that historic building to 'do the business' for the last time. I smiled, older and wiser than on the occasion of that first press call in Downing Street on that bright May morning ten years earlier, when we hadn't even seen inside our new home and anything seemed possible.

Although I hadn't wanted Tony to step down, I accepted that now was the right time to go, and with a renewed sense of purpose I kissed each of the children and saw them back into Number 10 where Jackie, our nanny, was waiting to take them to Chequers for our last family weekend there – the final tradition for the outgoing Prime Minister. Tony and I had first to go up to the constituency – he had decided to make a clean break, so needed to resign his seat as soon as possible in order that a by-election could be held before the summer recess.

All that remained was for the Rt. Hon. Tony Blair, MP for Sedgefield, Prime Minister of the United Kingdom of Great Britain and Northern Ireland, officially to deliver his resignation to the

Queen. As protocol decrees, while he was ushered into the waiting car by the door nearest the pavement – the principal seat, as it's called – I walked round to the other side behind the driver, closer to the waiting photographers shouting my name, and with the renewed frenzy of snapping came the sarcasm. 'Miss it, will you? . . . We'll miss you!'

The sunlight glinted on their long lenses and I thought, not for the first time, how threatening they were. How like weapons. I'd just said goodbye to all these people we'd loved and who'd loved us and I thought, Actually, I am going to miss all of them, but not you lot, no. So that's what came out. I couldn't help myself. 'Bye, I won't miss you!' And I laughed.

'You can't resist it, can you?' Tony said through clenched teeth as the door closed behind me. 'For God's sake, you're supposed to be dignified, you're supposed to be gracious.'

As the car swung out into Whitehall, I heard a helicopter overhead and suddenly I was filled with a sense of *déjà vu*. I remembered coming out of our house in Richmond Crescent in 1997, self-conscious in that red suit bought specially for the occasion, and hearing a voice shouting, 'Hey, Mum!' and looking up to see Kathryn and Lucy, her cousin, waving down to us from the top floor, and seeing the silhouette of a helicopter against the blue sky, and wondering what it was doing there, not realising of course that it was filming us. All our neighbours were out on the street to see us off, and all the way down to the Euston Road and on to the Palace the pavements were lined with people waving and cheering, and, overlaying it all, the sound of the helicopter pounding the air above our heads, the dark shadow that followed us all the way along the route.

Sitting in the back of the Daimler ten years later, Tony stony-faced beside me, I sighed. He could hardly claim to be surprised at my outburst. It wasn't the first time and it was unlikely to be the last – he even calls me his bolshie Scouser. Liverpudlians may be a tough, touchy and belligerent lot, but they have other qualities too. They are risk-takers, fiercely loyal and proud, who look after their own. They've had to: Scousers have always been outsiders, hence the humour. There's an old Liverpool saying: 'If you can't change it, take pride in it.'

As for the press and its relentless campaign to paint me as a grasping, scheming embarrassment, I knew, for all my faults, it was simply using me as a way of getting at my husband. I was born into a hard world, raised by strong women and I learnt to cope. The paradox was that in my work as a barrister and a judge – my chosen and hard-fought-for career – I spoke on behalf of other people and was used to being heard. Yet in this other life my voice had been literally unknown. As we drove down the Mall, I realised with a sudden surge of spirit that those constraints were no longer there. I had travelled a long way and learnt so much – the time had come, I decided, to speak for myself.

CHAPTER 1

The Beginning

The story starts in the early fifties when two young actors meet on tour in the provinces. As happens in such stories, they fall in love and are soon in the family way. When a daughter is born they are overjoyed and overwhelmed at one and the same time. Sadly, the strain of living in digs, short of money and short of work, and with a small baby in tow, proves too much. Thus, when their baby is six weeks old, they leave her in the care of the father's parents in Liverpool, and go off to the big city to seek their fortune.

The year was 1954, the baby was me, and I never grew tired of hearing how my parents met, of their respective childhoods, and, of course, how I got my unusual name.

My father, Tony Booth, fell into acting largely by accident. While doing his national service he conducted a prolonged flirtation with a colonel's wife. As she was heavily into amateur dramatics, he decided that this was the way in, as it were. And so the stage was set for the rest of his life. Although regularly complaining that the theatre was dominated by gays, this state of affairs presented him with plenty of opportunities in terms of the ladies.

My mum, on the other hand, took her profession a good deal more seriously. One year younger than my father, Joyce Smith had been born and brought up in Ilkeston, a mining village west of Nottingham.

Her mother, born Hannah Meer, remains something of an enigma.

Beyond her unusual maiden name and the fact that she was a local beauty with lustrous blue-black hair, I know nothing about her. My mum's father, however, was an extraordinary man, totally self-educated. Jack Smith first went down the pit at the age of fourteen as an ordinary miner, but was soon promoted to being a shot-firer – first into the mine at the beginning of a shift, armed solely with a miner's lamp, his job was to test for gas. By the end of his career he had made colliery manager.

From time to time we would go over to Ilkeston to visit my grandfather and I remember being terrified by the huge blue scar on his face. If you had an accident down the pit, he later explained, the wound could never be adequately cleaned of coal dust, which turned the scar tissue blue. Another thing that intrigued me was the amount of water he used to wash himself. He no longer worked underground by then, so had no need to douse himself in this excessive manner, but old habits die hard. He was still living in the house where my mother had grown up. The bathroom where Hannah would have scrubbed his back was still downstairs and toilet paper was still squares of newspaper on a hook.

Grandad Jack had always wanted to be a doctor, but as the eldest of eleven children this was impossible. The nearest he got to it was by joining the St John Ambulance Brigade and becoming involved with pit rescue. Later he gave lessons in first aid, using my reluctant mother as a guinea pig. He was a man of prodigious energy, active in the Labour Party and the Salvation Army; he also wrote poetry, and – towards the end of his life – obtained a degree from the Open University. He worked until he was eighty – long after the mines had closed, becoming a night watchman after he retired.

If that wasn't enough, he was also a football referee and ran athletics and netball clubs for young people, activities my mother would be obliged to join in with but always hated. What she enjoyed more was the youth club that he ran during the war. He was a considerable musician – there wasn't a brass instrument that he couldn't play – and, having trained up the boys and girls, he would visit old people's homes and hospitals with little shows, the musical accompaniment being provided by my mum on the piano, flute or violin.

She had an unusual education for the time, attending one of the first Rudolf Steiner schools, Michael House, which is still going strong on the edge of what is now Shipley Country Park. Everything about it was avant-garde. She began in 1936, at the age of three and a half. Music and movement – known as Eurhythmy – was central to its ethos. Michael House even boasted its own theatre and, from the beginning, my mum was always involved in school plays.

But then tragedy struck. Shortly after the war ended, the grandmother I never met died at the age of only forty-two. Although Hannah was a local lass, the Meer family wasn't close and no help was forthcoming from her sisters after her death. So on top of going to school, fourteen-year-old Joyce now had the house, her ten-year-old brother and her father to look after. Before leaving home early in the morning, he would ensure that the fire was lit, but that was the extent of his involvement in household chores. It fell to my mother to do everything else: shopping, cooking, washing, ironing, cleaning, not to mention scrubbing her father's back when he got home from the pit. Being a clever girl, the plan had been for her to stay on at school until she was eighteen and do her 'Matric', then the passport to university and beyond. But after a year of attempting to marry schooling and skivvying, Michael House suggested she leave.

Meanwhile, she had met a woman called Beryl John whose career on the stage had been cut short through illness, but who ran an amateur dramatics society and gave private lessons. How my grandfather could afford such an outlay I have no idea, but somehow he did. All went well, until out of the blue he announced he was marrying again, a woman whom my mother had never even met and knew nothing about beyond her name – Mabel. Not unreasonably, perhaps, my mum took complete umbrage at this interloper, and the day her father married was the day she packed her suitcase and left. It was as if when her stepmother came in at the front door, my mum left by the back. She never lived under their roof again. Encouraged by my auntie Beryl (as I later called her) my mum had applied to and had been accepted by the Royal Academy of Dramatic Art, better known as RADA, as prestigious then as it is now. She had also applied for a grant from Derbyshire County Council, but they turned her down – grants did exist in the 1950s, but drama schools were regarded with deep suspicion. In the end her father paid. Not because he thought it was a sensible thing to do, she believes, but through guilt.

At the end of her first year at RADA, needing money to see her through the holidays, not to mention the Holy Grail of experience, she jumped at a summer job with a touring rep. The Earl Armstrong Repertory Company was based in Yorkshire, a 'fit-up' company, run by a husband and wife team.

After one week of rehearsals, the company set out for Wales, and the newly named Gale Howard (Beryl John had planned to use Gay Howard for her own thwarted career) was soon playing romantic leads opposite a young actor from Liverpool with no training but charisma to burn. It proved a real baptism of fire. At one time, my mum recalls, they had thirty shows under their belts and had to do everything themselves: sewing costumes, selling tickets, making and painting the scenery, changing the sets. Performing was just the icing on the cake. If a larger cast was called for – and new plays were added all the time – there would be any number of keen amateurs, wherever they went, at no cost.

As the weeks ticked by, the stage kisses of the two juveniles became increasingly realistic. September arrived all too quickly, and a new term back at RADA was beckoning. Drama schools were all very well, but as any professional actor will tell you, there is nothing to match the real thing and Gale Howard never went back. More Welsh towns followed, and in one of them – history does not relate which – I was conceived; possibly in Rhayader, not far from Llandrindod Wells in mid-Wales. It would be nice to think so. Next to the theatre was a café the company used to frequent, run by the mother and grandmother of an eight-year-old girl so taken with the theatre that every night she would climb out of her bedroom window on the ground floor and persuade somebody at the stage door to let her in. After the show, Tony and Gale – at twenty-one and twenty barely more than kids themselves – would escort the little imp back home and pass her through the window, no one any the wiser. They became very fond of her. That Christmas found them back in Rhayader where the run comprised three pantomimes and one Christmas play. The name of the play is now lost in time, but the cast included two dogs called Schmozzle and Kerfuffle. In the pantos my mother played Cinderella, the princess in *The Princess and the Swineherd*, and one of the Babes in the Wood. The other babe was played by an ecstatic café owner's daughter, achieving her dream of appearing on stage, albeit with no lines.

By the end of the season my parents knew that my mother was pregnant, and when the Armstrongs refused to increase their wages, they had no option but to head back to London. The little girl was devastated that she was about to lose her new-found friends. My mum promised she would never forget her. If their baby turned out to be a girl, she said, they would even name it after her. And they did. Cherie.

Tony Booth and Gale Howard were married in Marylebone Registry Office, a decent six months before I was born. In the end it was all a bit of a rush: a job had come up at Castleford Rep and they were due to start rehearsals the next day. Their witnesses were the brother of the landlady my mother had had when she was a student at RADA and the registrar's assistant, a Mr Christmas. Afterwards, the landlady's brother took the newlyweds to the top floor of Lyons Corner House on the corner of Piccadilly Circus, where – to the strains of a string quartet – they celebrated with tea and cakes in preparation for the four-hour train journey to Yorkshire.

They were still in the north the following autumn, my father now with the Frank H. Fortescue Famous Players, and, according to my birth certificate, Cherie Booth was born on 23 September 1954 in Fairfield hospital, Bury, an event my father announced from the stage that evening to a rather bemused audience. His request for two weeks off to help with the new arrival, however, was turned down, so in true Tony Booth fashion he gave them two fingers. With no work forthcoming, and rent still needing to be paid, the young couple tucked their daughter into a basket padded with nappies and smelling of greasepaint, and boarded the train for Liverpool.

Crosby lies at the northern end of Liverpool, the Catholic end, where thousands, if not millions of Irish families disembarked from the ships that brought them from their homeland, convinced they wouldn't be staying longer than a few weeks – months at the worst – before they'd be sailing back across the Atlantic towards a new life in America. For some the dream came true, but for many it didn't. Instead of Manhattan's skyline, they had to make do with the Liver building and the cranes and derricks of the Liverpool Docks.

Crosby itself had aspirations. My paternal grandparents, Vera and George Booth, lived in a superior kind of terraced house in Waterloo, the poorer part of Crosby. Upstairs there were two and a half bedrooms (the half was a box room above the front door with barely enough room for a single bed), downstairs a front room (the 'parlour'), a back room (the sitting room), kitchen and a scullery. It was fully plumbed if basic. It was by no means a house to be ashamed of; indeed, they owned it. At the end of our road was a park where there were swings and a roundabout. This marked the demarcation line between Waterloo (terraced) and Great Crosby (semi-detached). Ferndale Road was the last of a grid of other 'dales', Thorndale, Oakdale etc., that all abutted St John's Road, our bustling shopping street, with its butcher and pawnbroker and grocers and barbers and second-hand shops, which seemed to me then to be the centre of the universe.

Like all the other houses in our street, Number 15 had a bay window, a small garden at the front and a slightly larger one at the rear made smaller by the presence of an old Anderson shelter left over from the war. Unlike the other yellow-brick houses in Ferndale Road, ours was painted cream and green, from the time when – so legend has it – my great-grandfather decided to show where his political allegiances lay in as ostentatious a manner as possible.

With the largest Catholic population in England, Liverpool has always been a highly politicised city. It prided itself on having no industry – that was left to lesser places like Manchester – no idle boast pre the Clean Air Act of 1956 when the industrial north was shrouded in smoke and washing was hung out only when the wind was blowing in the right direction. First and last it was a port, and Merseyside was thus built on transient labour where unemployment was the baseline. You helped your neighbour out today, because God help you tomorrow. In the years before Labour's general election victory in 1945 and the coming of the NHS and the welfare state, Liverpool's communities survived through networks of voluntary effort and the habit never died: helping out was not an option in our house. It was simply what you did, even if in doing so you went short yourself.

Fifteen Ferndale Road was a very Catholic household. My grandmother, born Vera Thompson, was an Irish matriarch of the old school, although Liverpool-born and with a rich Scouse accent. She had two brothers, Edgar and William, and by the time I arrived Uncle Bill was the proud owner of three small grocer's shops, an empire started by selling tea off a bike with a box strapped on the back. Vera's mother – my great-grandma Matilda, known as Tilly – came over with her family from County Mayo (or Cork, depending on whom you believe) on their way to America, the youngest of seventeen little McNamaras, but – like so many others – they got no further than Liverpool Docks. At some point she met my great-grandfather and that was that.

Her husband Robert Thompson's roots have been the subject of much family debate. The version my grandma told was that he was from Yorkshire, a young man from a family called Tankard who had dining rooms somewhere near Halifax, but who, after deserting in the First World War, hightailed it to Ireland where he changed his name to Thompson to escape detection. Another version is that he was simply another Irish immigrant who failed to get a passage to the promised land.

What is not in dispute is that he was a fiery character with a talent for horse flesh, drink and losing money. And he was a radical. In 1926 he had been on the Dockers' Strike Committee during the General Strike and this resulted in his being blacklisted by the Mersey Docks and Harbour Board. From then on he earned his money as a barber, sitting on an orange box outside the dock gates, shaving sailors and cutting their hair when they returned from months at sea with money in their pockets and an urge to spend it. Not everyone was willing to part with their cash, however, and my great-grandma would tell stories of how he'd end up accepting the strangest things in lieu, including a parrot that lived with them for years, and a monkey that she wouldn't let inside the front door. Eventually he opened his own barber's shop on the corner of Denmark Street in the area known as Little Scandinavia, whose narrow, cobbled streets – back-to-back houses with outside toilets – were to become my route to primary school.

Sadly, I never met him. Robert Thompson died in 1946 and my dad, who adored his grandfather, said the streets of Waterloo were lined with mourners from Ferndale Road as far as St Edmund's church when his coffin passed by.

On her husband's death, Matilda moved in with her daughter where the box room became her private domain. She remained there until she too died, when I was seven. She was the only person in the household who had a room to herself and yet in the years she lived there I can never remember her lifting a finger to help, although occasionally to show willing you might catch sight of her flicking a feather duster. Her major preoccupation was watching the comings and goings in the street below from behind her lace curtains. She was tiny, like a bird, grey-haired, but still with a hint of the fiery redhead she had once been. Her legendary temper, however, was still firmly in place. Nevertheless, she was remarkably tolerant when, dressed in my nurse's uniform, I would 'inject' her arm with a plastic syringe, and she was always a good source for a sixpence.

From the perspective of an imaginative young girl, my grandfather's antecedents had led far less exciting lives. They were resolutely English, with no unresolved mysteries – or so I thought then. My grandfather's mother's family had run a small fishing fleet out of Formby, while my great-grandfather's family were hill farmers from Westmorland. Nothing in our family is that straightforward, however, and after my grandad's death I discovered that in the First World War his father – my great-grandfather Booth – had been a pacifist and had gone to prison for it, later going to Mons as a stretcher-bearer where he had been severely gassed, while my great-grandmother's father turned out to be a famous smuggler who ran a protection racket on the side.

In contrast to the Irish branch of the family, George Booth, my grandfather, was never a great talker, though it didn't help that he was absent more often than he was at home. By the time I was living in Ferndale Road, this translated into ten days on shore for every six weeks away at sea. He was then the chief steward's writer on the MV *Auriel* that sailed from Liverpool to Nigeria, and his tales of the sights and sounds of Lagos brought Africa vividly to life. He only truly came into his own when playing the piano, which he did at every opportunity. My father claims he'd had to turn down a scholarship at the Royal Academy of Music in London when he was a boy, and that later he had been offered a job with the famous band leader, Geraldo. It may be true, but Grandad never mentioned it to me. He was much more than just a pub pianist, however. The piano stool was full of sheet music that he'd bought in New York on his sailings with Cunard. It's thanks to him that I can still sing most of the show songs of the fifties and sixties, though whether this is a good thing is another matter.

He was a gentle and sensitive man with the most beautiful, but tiny, copperplate handwriting. He hadn't been my grandmother's first choice of husband. Grandma would tell me how she married him on the rebound after 'the love of her life' – a Protestant – refused to convert. It was only then that piano-playing George made his move. He was a friend of her brother's and it turned out he'd been nursing this secret passion for years. Although the proposed marriage was frowned on by both sets of families, at the age of twenty-nine time was running out for Vera and she probably realised that the love of a good man was worth any amount of family tut-tutting. Love her he clearly did, though whenever he tried to kiss her in front of us, she'd push him away with a fond 'don't be so daft'. Only years later did it emerge that he wasn't a Catholic either. On paper, yes. He had converted – my grandmother would never have married him otherwise – but religion was nothing to him. He hardly ever came to church, but as he was away so much it didn't seem that strange and it wasn't as if the family didn't have enough priests to smooth its way into Heaven. My grandma's cousin, Bernard Harvey, was our local parish priest – one of Tilly's sister's boys. Then there were the Thompson brothers: with two out of his five children being priests, our great-uncle Bill held the moral high ground in the family. Father John was Dad's contemporary but Father Paul was only a few years older than me, and I can still remember the mystique which surrounded him on his visits from the seminary and how Grandma would insist that we girls keep our distance in case we corrupted him with our presence!

My relationship with the Catholic Church, although very important to me, has never been entirely conventional. It began with my baptism. Even though my parents had registered my birth in Bury, to a Catholic like my grandma, an unbaptised child was tantamount to a mortal sin. Luckily, she knew that her cousin, Father Bernard, would quickly rectify the situation and within hours of my arrival in Ferndale Road she had been to see him.

'So what would the little one's name be then, Vera?'

'Cherie.'

'What was that?'

'Cherie.'

'Is that it?'

'That's it.'

'Now, Vera, I don't have to tell you of all people that the Holy Church . . .'

He didn't. This was 1954, ten years before the Second Vatican Council. Services were still in Latin. Nuns were still fully veiled with habits that reached down to the ground, and Vera Booth knew only too well that a Catholic child could only be baptised with the name of a Catholic saint. Although there are over 7,000 of them, no amount of scanning unusual saints' names (and there are many) would have revealed a St Cherie.

A compromise was eventually reached and I was baptised Theresa Cara: Theresa being a bona fide saint, and Cara being the Latin for Cherie, which was probably Father Bernard's attempt at keeping the peace. At the same time, my grandma opened a savings account for me at Lloyds Bank, Waterloo, in the name, naturally, of T. C. Booth, which I used right up until 1997.

My mother, needless to say, had no voice in these decisions. Although she came from a religious background herself – her father was a Salvationist and she'd gone to Sunday School as a child – she claims she was quite happy for me to be baptised a Catholic, having no strong feelings one way or the other. There may have been another reason for her acquiescence, however. Locking horns with one of the most formidable women on the planet was not something anyone would do voluntarily – particularly if they were now living under the same roof. Nobody messed with Vera Booth.

People who lived through the depression never entirely forgot it. Make do and mend wasn't some green-friendly exercise for my grandmother, it was the result of years of draconian economy. For the decade preceding the war, my grandad had virtually no work. Trade between England and America was at a standstill. No ships, empty docks, work only for those who knew somebody who knew somebody else. In those circumstances the women became the bread-winners. My grandma did anything she could, cleaning the houses of the well-to-do who lived in nearby Blundellsands – only a short distance away geographically, but light-years from Crosby in terms of money and horizons. Her world was divided between the rich and the poor – and we were definitely the poor.

Before she married, she had worked in a draper's in Blundellsands, called Pullers of Perth, and she would tell the story of how one day a young woman came in with a new baby. My grandma could never resist a baby and after chucking him under the chin she asked what he was called.

'Anthony' came the answer, pronounced with a soft 'th', rather than a 't'.

'Oh,' she said. 'I love that name. If I have a little boy I think I'll call him Anthony.' She said she would never forget the expression on the woman's face. A 'people-like-you-don't-have-Anthonys-like-my-Anthony' expression. My grandma remained class-conscious all her life and continued to believe that there was one law for the rich and one law for the poor. When my dad was about ten, he came down with scarlet fever and – as happened in those days – was sent to an isolation hospital where his mother could only look at him through some kind of window. When he was eventually allowed home, he asked her why she had never been to visit his bedside. 'Because it wasn't allowed,' she said. Then he told her how the boy in the next bed had had regular visits from his parents: a boy who came from Blundellsands. I don't know how long my dad was in there, weeks certainly, if not months, and it undoubtedly affected him. I also think it affected my grandmother's attitude to him as she felt so guilty that she had simply accepted what she'd been told and hadn't insisted on seeing him. And while Grandad never forgave my dad for abandoning my mother (years later, of course) my grandma could never bring herself to cut him off entirely.

When I was growing up, my source for stories of my father's early life was my grandmother, because by the time I was old enough to savour and enjoy them he had completely disappeared from our lives. He was born in 1931 and named, of course, after that superior baby in Blundellsands. Then came my auntie Audrey in 1935, and finally my uncle Bob who was born during the first Luftwaffe bombing raid on Liverpool in May 1940.

With the outbreak of war everything changed. For a start, suddenly the docks were alive again. The merchant navy was desperate for men to work the Atlantic convoys and so that's what Grandad did. Dangerous though it was – more merchant seamen died than in the Royal Navy – it was work, and it was patriotic. In fact, it was no safer to stay in Liverpool, where the docks were a prime target for the Luftwaffe, peaking in May 1941 with a week-long blitz, when 4,000 people were killed, 10,000 homes were destroyed and 70,000 people were made homeless.

War or no war, my dad was growing up. In 1943 he got a scholarship to St Mary's College, a Catholic grammar school run by the Christian Brothers, about half a mile along the Liverpool Road into Crosby proper. He was clearly destined for great things. St Mary's boys were famous for going into the Church and the University (its alumni include John Birt and Roger McGough). My grandma had secret hopes for the latter, she later confessed. Perhaps to square her conscience for this sinful wish, the young Tony Booth was forced (his words) into being an altar boy, a role in which he continued until he was eighteen.

An academic future was not to be his, however. Shortly after my grandad returned from the war in 1946, he was hit by a crane and plunged eighty feet into the hold of a ship, breaking his pelvis. He was lucky not to have been killed. His pay was stopped immediately and he was off work for nearly two years. Through the union he was eventually awarded compensation but as soon as he was fit enough to go back, Cunard's response was to lay him off.

In the days following the accident my grandma did everything she could to find a job herself, but nothing would pay enough. Eventually she had to accept the inevitable and my father left St Mary's. It wasn't that there were fees to pay; it was simply that the Booth family now had five mouths to feed, including a seven-year-old (Bob) and a twelve-year-old (Audrey), and no money to do it with. So at fifteen my dad began working on the Cunard trans-atlantic route – eventually getting an office job at the US consulate in Liverpool – although it was too late for my father and my grand-mother's aspirations.

I remained with my grandparents for about two years following my arrival as a babe-in-arms, my parents coming and going as work allowed. At one point they did a summer season in Blackpool, close enough for them to come down to see me at weekends (which meant Sunday to Monday). Sometimes my mother stayed with me in Crosby, but usually not, and I certainly never travelled with them. I was left with my grandma, my mum now says, because she wanted me to have continuity, 'a steady place', though I suspect she already knew that to keep my dad, she'd have to stick to him like glue. And of course she wanted to be with him: he was witty and handsome, and she was in her early twenties and in love.

By late 1956 my father found the beginnings of fame, if not of for-tune, with *No Time for Sergeants*, which ran for eighteen months in the West End, and by the time my sister Lyndsey was born, he and Gale (as my mother is always called) were living in a settled way in a large Victorian house in Stoke Newington, north London. When Lyndsey was about three months old, my grandparents took me down to meet her.

On arrival, my grandma went straight to the nearest Catholic church and arranged to have the baby baptised the following day. The only Catholic my mother knew – an actress living in the house whom they had met in Llandudno – was roped in to be Lyndsey's godmother. This duty done, my grandparents left, at which point I discovered the hideous truth: I wasn't going with them. According to my mother, my grandma's last words to me as she and Grandad left the house were, 'You're going to live with your mother now. You'll probably never see me again.'

I was inconsolable: kicking and screaming and generally expressing my anger and distress in the only way I could. The woman I called 'Mama' had gone for good. What it must have been like for my poor mother, I can scarcely imagine, overcome as she no doubt was with guilt and remorse, and possibly even jealousy. As for my grandmother, traumatic as it was, she had clearly fuelled my dependence on her and so exacerbated my sense of abandonment. Later, when we were all happily (from my perspective) back in Crosby, she would repeatedly tell me how she could never listen to 'I Could Have Danced All Night' – the Julie Andrews classic from *My Fair Lady* – without crying, because it had been playing on the radio when her 'baby' had been taken from her. My mother now describes her mother-in-law's behaviour as 'naughty'. I might be tempted to use something stronger, but I was always my grandma's little girl – her fourth child – and cannot bring myself to condemn her.

I stayed in Stoke Newington long enough for photographs to be taken of the toddler Cherie looking bemused in Clissold Park, her baby sister propped up in her pram beside her. The photo is of poor quality but the general impression is not a happy one, and I think that was probably the case. It couldn't have helped that my parents were living in what was essentially a student house with rented rooms and no real structured family life. My dad would come home from the theatre late at night and inevitably I'd be woken up, and I have a vague memory of another flamboyant couple in the acting line, blessed with an equally cavalier attitude to children and their needs. Apart from my mother – whom at this juncture I really barely knew – the most stable presence in the house was my auntie Diane –

not a real aunt but my mum's friend, to this day. She lived in the basement with another girl, both of whom were studying design at the North London Poly, as it was then known. To make ends meet, my mum spent hours packing sherbet fountains during the day. In later years I could never bring myself to eat them; the smell alone was enough to bring back twinges of anxiety.

Christmas passed. (The only Christmas I ever missed having with my grandma until she died. I never missed a birthday.) Then spring. I imagine they'd been hoping I'd settle down, but I didn't. For the previous two years I had been the apple of my grandma's eye and now I was just one of two little girls competing for affection. There is no doubt that, for all my grandmother's iron will, I had been horribly spoilt. That summer my auntie Audrey – my father's younger sister whose room I had shared when I was first living in Ferndale Road – married her young man, and we all came up to Crosby for the wedding. I was her bridesmaid in a pale blue dress with puff sleeves, white shoes and white socks, and a little coronet of flowers round my head. Then, shortly before Christmas, my dad's show closed and, having no means of paying the rent in Stoke Newington, our little family returned to Ferndale Road. Even now I can remember the joy of finding myself, once again, sharing my grandma's bed.

It is only once I returned to Ferndale Road that my own memories really begin, starting with the smells: my grandad's Senior Service cigarettes; the condensed milk he used to sweeten his tea; coal burning in the grate; hair drying in front of the fire. Then the animals. In addition to the various humans in the house, we once had a cat and always had dogs: Alsatians all called Sheba; and Quin, a poodle; plus sundry white mice and tortoises. In those days nobody connected the pets with my frequent asthma attacks. I remember listening to *Two-Way Family Favourites* on the wireless, which my Grandad had linked from the sitting room to the kitchen so that grandma could listen while she was cooking the Sunday dinner. I remember the circular ashtray where the cigarette stubs disappeared when you pushed down the plunger. Lino that curled up at the edges. The gas meter behind the front door which we fed with shillings: as a treat, I'd drop them in and Grandad would turn the knob.

For the next eighteen months my father worked in various theatres around the north, based with us, but in reality only visiting at weekends. It was during this time that he first played opposite Pat Phoenix, then an unknown young actress called Patricia Dean, who would later become such an important person in his life – and indeed in mine. Whether they had an affair at the time – as he claims they did – I don't know. It's possible: temptation and my father are old bedfellows.

The only time he actually lived with us was when he did a season at Liverpool Playhouse, but when that came to an end he headed back to London. Realistically it was the only place he could forge a career. Once he'd found somewhere to live, he told my mum, then we'd join him. It never happened.

CHAPTER 2

Growing Up

I remember clearly coming home after my first day at school, turning the corner into Ferndale Road past the chemist, and seeing Lyndsey and her friend Suzanne waiting for me by our gate, and running up to them, feeling so grown up, and telling them all about school and how exciting it was.

School was naturally St Edmund's Catholic Primary, where my father, Auntie Audrey and Uncle Bob had all gone before me, and which was attached to St Edmund's church where Father Bernard Harvey, my grandma's cousin – the one who baptised me – was the parish priest.

I suppose that for the first day or two I must have been taken to school, but from then on I would go on my own and later took Lyndsey with me. Hand-in-hand we would walk or skip down St John's Road, past Ronnie the cobbler, who had been at school with my dad and who'd always say hello. Further along there was the pawnbroker's on the corner with its three gold balls, and the window made entirely of black glass that came down to the pavement. If you pressed your nose to the glass and raised an arm and a leg, you looked as if you were flying. Then up over the railway; if a train was coming we would stand on the Meccano-style footbridge and shriek as the steam billowed round us, lifting our skirts and warming our bare legs in winter. It was a level-crossing, but we rarely walked across the track, because of the terror of knowing that at any minute

a train could come roaring through, though we were happy enough
to swing on the great white gates. On the far side lay Little
Scandinavia, a network of narrow streets and passages, known as
'entries', running between the back-to-back houses with their outside
toilets, which were a short cut to school. Still cobbled, the game of
never stepping on the cracks was far more challenging here than on
the hop-scotch pavements of Ferndale Road. In the middle of this
labyrinth, the rag-and-bone man kept his horse. At Crosby we had
dunes – miles and miles of them – you could even see the sea from
my classroom window – but this was the nearest we got to the country, so whenever the old man wasn't around we would clamber up
and peer over the wall at this poor horse. If the old man found us,
he'd yell abuse and we'd scramble down, scraping our knees on the
brick then rubbing them better with lick. Another game was breaking empty milk bottles. Stacked up like skittles, all you had to do was
pick one up, drop it, then run down one of the entries before the
aproned housewives could reach the door. One morning, my friend
Margot and I were spotted and I'll never forget the shame of having
to stand in front of the whole school while our hands were rapped
with a ruler. On the way home we might stop at my uncle's shop, a
grocer's-cum-sweet shop, and buy a halfpenny chew or my favourite
sports mixtures. We had to pay: Uncle Bill was far too canny a businessman to give anything away, even to us, although he used to have
these little cereal packets for display purposes, and when he changed
the window he'd let us have them to play shops.

It's all gone now. Denmark Street, Sweden Street and Norway
Street – Little Scandinavia was knocked down in the sixties. Now it's
open space. Even the old infant school has gone, part of what are
now playing fields for the main school.

As soon as I was old enough, I'd be sent out on errands – 'messages' as they were called. Number 15 was only a few houses up
from St John's Road. You could get anything there, from a mouse-
trap to a haircut, from a quarter of pear drops to an ounce of
tobacco or a bottle of stout. Not that I was sent for any of these, but
the sheer variety of shops turned the short walk to the butcher's or
the baker's into an adventure. Everything was weighed out: sugar,
flour, bacon, even at the Co-op. I can still remember our Co-op divi-
dend number: 74101.

Then there were the messages that Grandma made us memorise

and had to be delivered word perfect. 'Four nice, lean lamb chops, please, for Mrs Booth.' And God help either me or the butcher if they weren't. The question for the baker was: 'Is it fresh?' If it turned out not to be, then woe betide. I'd be packed off back with the stale loaf, where my line would be 'Mrs Booth is not satisfied.' There was a wonderful occasion (in retrospect) when my poor sister was sent to get one 8-pennyworth and one 6-pennyworth bag of chips and she returned with eight 6-pennyworth bags . . . the chip shop was quite a walk – the other side of the railway line in Little Scandinavia – but she was sent back with all the chips growing colder by the minute, crying all the way, to get the money refunded *and* the correct order. 'Mrs Booth says you know it couldn't possibly have been eight 6-penny bags . . . and she wants them taken back.' And they did. Grandma would have been up there like a bat out of hell if they hadn't. Poor Lyndsey. The humiliation was total. Although she was small, comfortably plump and generally unremarkable physically, Vera Booth was a force of nature, a one-woman tsunami. Her actions were prompted by a strong sense of justice and she was the source of advice and support not only to her family but neighbours too. Even so, everyone from family to shopkeepers quailed before her.

Life could not have been easy for my mother. From the beginning her mother-in-law made it clear that, grandchildren or no grand-children, we would have to pay our way, and what did Gale intend to do? If either of them had expected my dad to support his family, they were mistaken.

One morning my mother was frogmarched across Waterloo into Seaforth, about two miles to the south. The destination was a fish and chip shop and it was the hours she had negotiated that particularly appealed to Mrs Booth. Our mum would have time to get Lyndsey and me up and breakfasted and ready for school before setting off on the bicycle which was found from somewhere. She then worked behind the counter from ten o'clock till two – Grandma gave us our lunch – but she'd be back in Ferndale Road in time to give us our tea; then she was working again from four until six, then home to get us ready for bed, then back on the bike ready for the final stint from eight till midnight. All for a princely £4.10s a week. There was no way out. It was a question, my mum now says, of: 'You're in my house, you do as I tell you.' It wasn't that Mum was treated any worse than anybody else, and Vera was just as tough on herself, but she had come up through a hard school. But she also knew that Gale didn't have a mother and, as much as she could, she treated her as she would her own daughter.

It's hard to imagine what working at the Seaforth chippie must have felt like for my mum. Only a few years earlier Gale Howard had been a rising star at RADA, glamorous, accomplished – Jackie Collins had been one of her contemporaries – a young woman who seemingly had the world at her feet, and now here she was serving penny packets of cod and chips and saveloys to drunken sailors who must have felt their luck was in at being served by such a beautiful young woman. I can just imagine the leers she would have got late at night. How long she suffered it, nobody remembers now. Months certainly. Luckily salvation was at hand in the shape of Auntie Diane, her friend in Stoke Newington. Since qualifying as a designer, she had started work at Selfridges as a trainee buyer. Selfridges was part of the Lewis's group – in fact it was owned by Lewis's, which had its flagship store in Liverpool. Lewis's had originally been Liverpool's premier gentlemen's outfitters and Diane managed to get her friend on to their graduate trainee scheme or, rather, she got her the interview, but it was my mum who got the job.

Whereas an ordinary shop assistant's wage was £7 a week, my mum went straight in on £11, nearly three times what the fish and chip shop was paying her. Every week from then on she gave half of whatever she earned to her mother-in-law. In addition, she continued to do the washing and the ironing – although the job meant that we soon got a top-loading washing machine, rather than hand-washing and using the mangle to squeeze out the excess water as before. Naturally she also bought our clothes: another plus of working for Lewis's was that she was entitled to a discount, which increased the longer she worked there. The bicycle was dispensed with. From now on my mum took the bus to work, which went from the end of St John's Road straight down the Liverpool Road, and got off at the stop outside Lewis's. Then she did a full day's work, followed by the bus back in time to put us to bed. As for her own life, she put it on hold. For a while she kept nursing the hope that her husband would come back, but he didn't. The money stopped, the visits stopped. There were no more telephone calls, or none that I remember until the fateful one.

It was April 1963. The Easter holidays. I was eight and Lyndsey was six. As a special treat, mum had taken us to see *Summer Holiday*, Cliff Richard's new film, which was about a bus conductor (Cliff) who takes a London bus all the way to Greece for a holiday. We didn't often go to the pictures and I'd been looking forward to it ever since I'd heard it was coming to Crosby. I was already a fan and had a poster of Cliff pinned on my bedroom door. When we got back, Lyndsey and I were packed off upstairs to bed and banned from coming downstairs. Instead we played one of our favourite games called 'policewoman's training', which started because my grandma was always obsessed that burglars were about to come in and steal our non-existent worldly goods. It involved creeping downstairs, touching the front door and rushing back up again, before our mum and Grandma, who would be watching television, could hear the squeaky floorboards. The rules were no noise and no giggling. Sometimes I'd lift Lyndsey on to the banister and give her a little shove so that she slid down to the bottom. On one occasion my hands slipped, so instead of putting her on the rail I pushed her right over and she plummeted down into the hallway. It wasn't a question of not giggling – there was a sudden scream from downstairs and Lyndsey was bawling out at the top of her voice: 'Cherie tried to kill me!'

They were so relieved that no great harm had been done – Lyndsey was only winded – that neither of us was punished, but I can still remember hiding behind my grandma's bedroom door, shaking with fear. Except when Grandad was at home, I always slept in my grandma's bed, while Lyndsey slept in our mum's. In fact, they slept in the same saggy double bed right up until Lyndsey left home.

So on this particular Thursday night we were playing policewoman's training, when the phone rang. Scuttling hurriedly back upstairs, I crouched outside the bathroom as my mum came into the hall and picked up the phone. She didn't seem to say anything at all, apart from 'Hello' at the beginning. Then, suddenly, she began to cry. I had seen her cry before but nothing like this, and it was somehow worse because she didn't say anything to explain it. Then my grandma came out and started hissing – still trying to keep her voice down – things like, 'How could he . . . it's absolutely unforgivable . . . as for the *Crosby Herald*', and putting her arm round my mum, which was another thing she didn't usually do.

Eventually they went back into the front room and I just sat there on the landing, feeling my eyes prick as if I was going to cry. Eventually I found Lyndsey and told her that something terrible had happened, but I didn't know what.

The next morning at breakfast everyone was quiet. My mum had obviously been crying all night but nothing was said.

'Why don't you two run along to the park?' Grandma suggested.

So we did. The park was just at the end of our road. It was a lovely sunny April day and you could always find somebody to play with. I remember Lyndsey took her skipping rope and there was some discussion about whether we needed woollies or not.

As soon as they saw us coming, other children began staring and whispering. Finally I got up the courage to say something.

'What is it?' I asked one of my friends. 'What are you looking at me like that for? What's happened?'

'You should know,' she said, and shrugged and looked down at the ground. Then a group of boys started giggling and chanting my dad's name.

'Tony Booth, Tony Booth, Tony Booth!'

Even though he hadn't lived there for years, everyone in Crosby knew who my father was. He was on the telly!

And then it all came out: the *Crosby Herald* was published on a Friday, but the first edition appeared the night before and that week, on the announcements page, top of the list, was the following:

BOOTH, Anthony, late of 15 Ferndale Road, Waterloo, and Julie née Allan proudly announce the arrival at the London Clinic of their daughter Jenia, a half sister for Cherie and Lindsay.

We had no idea. My mum had no idea. My grandma had no idea. Crosby had no idea.

It had generally been accepted in the family that my father had abandoned us, and by then Mum knew he was seeing someone else: she was even considering giving him a divorce. But when the new woman, Julie Allan, decided to force her hand with this announcement it backfired spectacularly. Divorce was the one thing Mum could withhold.

It is difficult to overestimate the humiliation – to my mother, to his mother and, of course, to us, his children. This was 1963, in the heart of Catholic Liverpool. People didn't get divorced, or if they did they didn't talk about it. Girls who had the misfortune to get pregnant were sent away to convents to have their babies who were then offered for adoption. As for 'single-parent', it was a term that hadn't yet been invented. To blazon your sins to the world by placing an announcement in the local paper that everybody would read was a crime against society, against the Church, against everything that any decent-minded person stood for.

And he hadn't even spelt Lyndsey's name right.

CHAPTER 3

Girlhood

My uncle Bob was only fourteen when I arrived at Ferndale Road and in many ways he was more like a brother than an uncle. He was everything a big brother should be: handsome, brave, teasing, rebellious, fun. Football was his big thing and at one point he even played for Tranmere Rovers, now a First Division club, but then barely scraping into the Third. They were based just across the Mersey in Birkenhead.

When Lyndsey and I were about four and six respectively, we came down with chickenpox, and on this particular Saturday, Tranmere were playing away. So Uncle Bob took the coach to wherever it was with the rest of the team, but by the time they arrived he was covered in spots! Consternation . . . The match was cancelled and the whole team put into quarantine. Lyndsey and I being the only members of the household he could no longer infect, he was moved in with us. To pass the time he regaled us with made-up stories about Ena Sharples, the resident busybody and battleaxe of *Coronation Street* that had just started on ITV, already a huge success and in which my dad even had a small part. Bob was always a wonderful storyteller and I have no doubt, knowing him as I do now, that his tales were completely scurrilous. He was irrepressibly naughty, lifting us up on the wardrobe and getting us to jump down on to the bed. First came the terror and then the squealing, then the demands for 'more, more!' Uncle Bob was what grown-ups would call a really bad influence, but we thought he was wonderful.

In 1961, when I was not quite seven, my great-grandmother passed away. She had gone a bit bonkers towards the end, wandering round the house saying, 'When I die I'm going to haunt you!' – not in a malevolent way – she thought it was quite funny. At least it meant that Bob finally got to have a room of his own. Until then he'd had to sleep on a camp bed wherever there was floor space. What he did have by this time, however, was a car. And what a car! It was a Triumph Roadster, all sparkling chrome, shiny gold curves and leather seats – old-fashioned looking even then. For some reason Grandma was away visiting friends when Bob had his twenty-first, which coincided – luckily – with a time when Grandad was at sea.

The afternoon of his birthday Uncle Bob drove around the streets of Waterloo, with the roof down and a megaphone – last used in the 1959 election – shouting out: 'There's going to be a party!' The house had never seen anything like it, and neither had I. I remember thinking Grandma would go mad when she found out. It was a lovely May evening, every window and door was open and the house was swarming with people. Music was blaring out into the street from Bob's portable gramophone, and the furniture rattled with the pounding rhythm of 'Come On, Baby, Let's do the Twist'. Later on Elvis was asking, 'Are You Lonesome Tonight?' Well, we weren't, that's for sure. And neither was my mum. For once she was having a bit of fun too. After all, she was not even thirty herself. All the rooms in the house were full to bursting, including mine, which was actually Grandma's, with girls in high heels sprawled out on the beds, on the floors, on the windowsills, smoking cigarettes, drinking, though what I can't imagine. And Lyndsey and I had our eyes out on stalks. There seemed no end to their laughing and giggling. All they wanted to do was talk about our uncle Bob. Isn't he handsome! Of course, I had to agree. Even if he did wear glasses, he was tall, and slim and athletic with floppy dark hair. He was definitely the local heart-throb.

The car wasn't only used for impressing the opposite sex. If we were very good, then he'd take us out in it. One particular trip to Chester Zoo I shall never forget. Bob and his girlfriend were in the front, while Lyndsey, Mum and I were in the back. It was really only a two-seater, but the back pulled down like a boot to reveal what he called the dickey where in a normal car you might put the luggage. It was a miniature backseat that even had its own separate windscreen, parallel to the one in front. All went well until the heavens opened on the way back, and Uncle Bob was so worried about the leather getting spoiled that he stopped the car and closed the boot up as far as it would go with us in it. Lyndsey and I thought it was hilarious. To be squashed in the back of this speeding car was such an adventure. However, my poor mum, bent double all the way back to Crosby, was none too amused.

Shortly after the painful business with my father, and the announcement of Jenia's birth, Uncle Bob left home. He too had decided he was going to be an actor and had taken up a place at the Central School of Speech and Drama. All at once the house felt very empty. The sole advantage was that I was given his room, but I would gladly have done without it to have him back again.

I was becoming a disturbed little girl. Children can be horribly cruel to anyone they sense is vulnerable or different, and I can remember standing in a corner of the playground with taunts ringing in my ears of the 'you're-not-a-proper-family, your-dad-doesn't-love-you' variety.

Newton's Third Law of physics tells us that for every action there is an equal and opposite reaction, and mine was to fight. I pulled hair. I punched. I bit. Friends stopped knocking at the door to ask if I could go out to play. Whether this was their own decision or their parents deciding that the Booths weren't the kind of people they wanted their kids to mix with, I don't know. The effect was the same. I remember going down to the swings in the park, swinging as high as I could, my legs pumping away, wishing that a rope would break and like Katy in *What Katy Did*, I'd come crashing down, break my neck and spend a lifetime as a cripple, and then they'd be sorry.

During those dreadful months, reading became my refuge. Although my grandmother had no education worth the name, she had always been a great reader and would pass on books she thought I might like, books that were far more sophisticated than a ten-year-old in those days would usually have access to, though by then I had read my way through all the children's books in the local library. One of her favourite authors was Daphne du Maurier, and in

Frenchman's Creek and *Jamaica Inn* I could escape from the misery of the playground to nineteenth-century Cornwall and beyond. It was thanks to her that I discovered *Wuthering Heights* and fell in love with Heathcliff, Emily Brontë's dark-skinned orphan from Liverpool. Luckily, Mrs Savage, my class teacher, was a woman of both sensitivity and sense; not only did she arrange with the library to bend the rules and let me borrow adult books, but as the summer term drew to a close she spoke to my mother and suggested that the following September I went up a year. I was bored, she said. It was no wonder I was getting into trouble. It was simply that I wasn't being stretched.

I remember my mum sitting on my bed that night, holding my hand and telling me what had been decided – and yet warning me at the same time.

'Now remember, Cherie, you're going to be with children a whole year older than you, and it's going to be difficult.'

Even so, it seemed as if I had won some sort of small victory and my recent experience of trial-by-taunt only served to strengthen my resolve. I was, as my grandma used to say, 'contrary'. If my mum was saying it would be difficult, I'd show her she was wrong. I was determined to prove that it wouldn't make a difference. I succeeded. At the end of the year, my final year at St Edmund's, I came top of the class and I remain convinced that it was the prompt action of this caring and far-sighted teacher that stopped me going completely off the rails.

The only thing that really suffered through missing a year was my handwriting. In order to catch up, I'd have to do extra arithmetic while the others in the class were having handwriting lessons. As a result, it is still absolutely terrible and my grandad would be appalled. By the time I was at secondary school, I was writing too fast to worry about what it looked like, and by then it was too late for remedial treatment.

That last year at primary school was a magical time for me. My class teacher, Mr Smerdon, was one of those charismatic teachers you never forget. He had been a fighter pilot in the war and would devote hours recounting his experiences, and however unconventional the teaching it certainly did me no harm at all. A larger-than-life figure, he had theatrical aspirations and would occasionally disappear to London for auditions. He was also in charge of the school choir of which I became a very enthusiastic member, and we even made it to the International Eisteddfod in Wales. He became a significant male figure in my life, the sort of man my father might have been if he had not left home for the bright lights.

Now that we didn't have Bob to take us out, Grandma decided we needed a car of our own. So in 1964, in an uncharacteristic act of generosity and folly combined, she bought a Mini. I can still remember the number plate: ALV 236B. She had no intention of driving it herself: this masterpiece of modern engineering and design was for Grandad. He loved that Mini and was ridiculously proud of it. Didn't I realise that Stirling Moss even drove one? There was one small problem, however: Grandad couldn't pass his test. I don't know how many times he took it, but he always failed. It didn't stop him driving, although never very far. He and my grandma would take us down to the sea front where Lyndsey and I could play on the beach while they watched the great ocean liners – like the *Queen Elizabeth* and the *Queen Mary* – make their stately way from the docks to the open sea. Grandad had retired by this time, due to his bad heart, but the sea and ships were still in his blood.

Otherwise life in Ferndale Road continued much as usual: my mum went out to work and Grandma stayed at home. Mum did the washing and the ironing while Grandma did the cooking. She was what was known in those days as a plain cook, but a good one. The menu never varied. Sunday: roast shoulder of lamb. Monday: left-overs. Tuesday: Scouse – a mutton stew with potatoes cooked in with it. Wednesday was baking day and we'd have steak and kidney pudding, and apple pie – nobody could make pastry like my grandma. Thursday was the 'four nice lean chops' I'd learnt to ask for. Friday was inevitably fish and chips, and Saturday was mince. And so it continued, week-in week-out. We rarely had chicken which, in those days, before factory farming, was expensive. Shoulder of lamb was cheap (if bony), because it came in, frozen, from New Zealand and the great Sunday treat was gnawing the sweet meat off the bone. I will never forget my grandma's mortification when, right in the middle of Mass, my cousin Catherine, Auntie Audrey's little girl, shouted out, 'Grandma, are we having bones for dinner?'

Sunday Mass was an important ritual. It wasn't simply our weekly appointment with God; it was the weekly get-together of the various branches of the family. The only person who didn't participate was my mother, although she'd always come to the big celebrations, like my first Holy Communion or Easter. Whatever the current crisis, standards had to be upheld, so you would always dress up in your best coat and hat. When I was very young, Mass was entirely in Latin, even the gospel readings. Then, as the Second Vatican Council began to take effect, the gospel at least was in English, though sung High Mass remained in Latin. But it had the advantage that I can now understand the service wherever I am in the world.

During the years immediately following the discovery of my father's other family he kept in touch with his mother sporadically, but rarely came home. There came a point when my mum became a more important part of the household than he was. My grandad was especially fond of her and he consistently refused to have anything to do with my dad.

From time to time Uncle Bob would see him in London, however, and I remember on one visit back to Liverpool, he showed me a photograph of my dad smiling broadly with a toddler and a new addition: Jenia and Bronwen, who had been born only a year later. I must have been upset – I can't imagine that I wouldn't have been – but whether I kept it hidden at the time I can't now remember. As to why Bob showed it to me, who can tell? Perhaps he thought it was a way of easing me in gently.

Over the next ten years or so, I saw my father only rarely. The first time I was in the top form at St Edmund's. Crosby Baths was a state-of-the-art indoor swimming pool recently built on wasteland behind Crosby beach. St Edmund's being just down the road, our class had been learning to swim. I have always been very uncoordinated physically and was as hopeless at swimming as I was at riding a bicycle – something I still can't do. Nevertheless, at the end of term there was going to be a gala and for some reason my dad came along, ostensibly to see me compete.

When he arrived there was pandemonium. The pilot for *Till Death Us Do Part* had just been shown and had become an instant hit. Tony Booth would soon become one of the most recognisable faces on television, and playing a left-wing, working-class Scouser – a character based by the writer Johnny Speight on my father himself – made him a near-god in left-wing, working-class Liverpool. While everyone swarmed about him, I felt non-existent.

My father is not one of nature's diplomats and over the years, whenever he was interviewed in the newspapers, it was always his current daughters he talked about. At the time of the Crosby Baths gala, it was Jenia and Bronwen. Later their place would be taken by his next batch, Sarah (later known as Lauren) and Emma. I pretended I didn't care. But I did.

The only time I saw him at home was after my grandad died in September 1968. The death certificate said heart disease, but he'd been going downhill for some time because of his smoking. The heart got him before the lung cancer did.

Until I inherited Uncle Bob's bedroom, I'd had an ambivalent relationship with my grandad. Of course I loved him, but whenever he came back from sea I'd be ousted from my place in Grandma's bed, obliged instead to sleep on a camp bed in my mother's room which she continued to share with Lyndsey.

But my resentment was always short-lived. Who could resist someone who played all your favourite songs? The first Sunday back on shore, our front room would be filled with aunts, uncles and cousins for a singsong. Grandad would always start with 'Thank Heaven for Little Girls', dedicated to Lyndsey and me; then one song would flow into another, with people asking for their favourites, and we'd all join in – Broadway musicals mainly: *My Fair Lady*, *South Pacific*, *West Side Story* and, best of all, *The Sound of Music*. There was a time when I knew every single word.

Grandad was not without vices: the first was horses – he was always trying different 'systems' but he never seemed to win. The second was smoking: cigarettes were cheap at sea and he would get through forty untipped Senior Service a day and he coughed his guts out in the last few years before he died. As a result I have never touched a cigarette in my life. His third vice was drinking. Not alcohol: his weakness was for very strong tea sweetened with lashings of condensed milk, which also came in handy for sticking tiles on the wall in the bathroom whenever they fell off, a regular occurrence.

Grandad's funeral was the first that really affected me. I'd only been seven when my great-grandma had died, and Mum had decided I was too young to attend. I wasn't unused to the rituals of Irish death, however. As my grandma's favourite, I'd gone to any number of wakes when the various members of the Thompson clan returned to their maker. But Grandad was Grandad and I was completely devastated. His body was laid out in our front room and, despite my mother's protests, I insisted on seeing him.

So there we all were in church, red-eyed and sombre, waiting for the service to begin, while I tried not to stare at that horrible shiny coffin where I knew his poor old body was lying, wondering what was going to happen to him when it was put into the ground, wondering how long he would have to stay in purgatory, whether God would have mercy on his soul and let him go straight up to Heaven, when there was a sudden clattering and banging of the door and the thud of heavy footsteps crashing down the nave. And there was my dad, barging through the ranks of other family mourners to get to the front. It was four years since I had last seen him at the Crosby Baths, and I clearly remember my fourteen-year-old self sitting there thinking, What is *he* doing here? It wasn't just outrage that he couldn't even turn up at the right time. My concern was largely for my mum and what she would be feeling. I had reached the age when I was beginning to understand the wider implications of what he had done, specifically what it meant to her. Ironically, although he had abandoned us, he never ceased to be a presence in our lives. My sister and I were very much part of his family in which he was a central, if absent, figure, whereas we were not really part of my mother's family at all. When we were small I think my grandma nurtured my mum – who was, of course, motherless – but as we grew older friction developed along the more traditional mother-in-law/daughter-in-law lines about the best way to bring us up.

There was never any question of where I would go after St Edmund's, always assuming I passed the Eleven-plus – which, given I was taking it a year early, was an optimistic assumption. Although in 1964 Britain had elected a Labour government, it would take many years for changes in the education system to be implemented and, at that time, where you went depended on academic ability. In Crosby we even had a public school, Merchant Taylors' – Church of England – with separate schools for girls and boys, while Catholic boys had St Mary's College (my father's alma mater) and Catholic girls had Seafield Grammar. Just as St Mary's had been run by the Christian Brothers, so Seafield was run by nuns, a French order, the Sacred Heart of Mary.

Seafield was a direct-grant school – a mix of girls, some paid for by the state, the rest paid for by their parents. Not everyone had even taken the Eleven-plus, so, in fact, there was a wider range of ability than is often supposed.

St Bede's was the Catholic secondary-modern school but there was never any question that I would go there. My grandma was determined that I would make something of my life academically. Fate had thwarted her ambitions for my father, and she wasn't going to be done out of it again. In addition, Seafield pandered to all her notions about class. Snobbery was endemic. I remember, much later, when I was in the sixth form, bumping into a teacher in my road, and the teacher – a nice woman – looking concerned.

'Oh, Cherie,' she said, 'whatever are you doing here?' I think she thought I was lost. Shame-faced, I had to confess that this was where I lived. Our area of Crosby – Waterloo – was very definitely the wrong side of the tracks.

Although no fees were involved for the scholarship girls (as those of us who passed our Eleven-plus were called), there were other, hidden expenses, specifically the uniform. While St Bede's had a badge that your mum could sew on to your jacket, Seafield boasted a navy blue blazer with the school crest embroidered directly on to the pocket. It was expensive, but you had to have it. Then there were the hats: for the first three years you had a round velour hat for winter and a boater for the summer. In the fourth and fifth form, the winter uniform was a blue beret with a blue tassel, and in the sixth form you had a blue beret with a silver tassel. Then there were indoor shoes and outdoor shoes and, as every parent knows, feet grow at an alarming rate. From the seventy pupils in my year at St Edmund's, only three girls got into Seafield Grammar. There was another girl who got in but her parents couldn't afford the uniform so she didn't go. She went to Manor Park, the mixed, non-denominational grammar school. It was the same story for the boys at St Mary's.

When Lyndsey followed me to Seafield three years later, she inherited my old blazer and a new one was bought for me. On her first day at the school, she was singled out by the headmistress. 'Why are you wearing this shabby blazer?' she demanded. Poor Lyndsey said later that she stammered and blushed and wished the ground would open up and swallow her. The truth was, of course, that my mother couldn't afford to buy two, even though she got a discount – Seafield's school outfitters being Lewis's.

*

After a couple of years in various departments in Lewis's, my mum had eventually transferred to the travel bureau and there she found her niche. It had the best position in the building, on a mezzanine between the ground and the first floors, in a corner a little apart, directly under the huge Epstein bronze celebrated in the chorus of 'In My Liverpool Home'.

> *In my Liverpool home*
> *We speak with an accent exceedingly rare*
> *And meet under a statue exceedingly bare*
> *If you want a cathedral we've got one to spare*
> *In my Liverpool home.*

By the late sixties, after years of being little more than an embarrassing joke, Liverpool had become the centre of the universe. Although I had been too young to go to the Cavern and see the Beatles, nonetheless we were all very proud to be Scousers. It wasn't only the Beatles; there were the Searchers, the Swinging Blue Jeans, the Merseybeats, Cilla Black and Gerry and the Pacemakers and dozens more, now forgotten. By the time I was old enough to go out on my own, however, I was more into folk. Together with my friend Cathy Broadhurst from Seafield, I had learnt to play the guitar and we would do versions of traditional songs that the Spinners were bringing to a wider audience. They were a home-grown band who had revived 'Scarborough Fair' long before Simon and Garfunkel recorded it. The Spinners became famous for songs about Liverpool like 'Maggie Mae' – the original one about a Liverpool sailor and a prostitute, nothing like the later Rod Stewart version. And, of course, 'In My Liverpool Home'.

> *I was born in Liverpool, down by the docks*
> *Me Religion was Catholic, occupation Hard-Knocks*
> *At stealing from lorries I was adept,*
> *And under old overcoats each night I slept.*

Once I was a Seafield girl, I no longer saw my friends from primary school who had gone to St Bede's. It wasn't that I was hostile to them; they were hostile to me. I was now 'posh'.

It took me time to settle down. The regime was comparatively strict. Although the majority of teachers were not nuns, the nuns ran the school and lived in the convent attached to it. There was one part of the building that was completely out of bounds because it was where the nuns had their cells. Skirts had to be a regulation two inches above the knee, though of course as we got older we got bolder and were always hoiking them up. The moment you got into school you had to change your outdoor shoes for indoor shoes and there was no running in the corridors. The nuns used to keep the oak floors polished like mirrors and heaven help you if you transgressed.

The worst aspect of life at Seafield was the school dinners. At St Edmund's I had been close enough to go back home at midday. Seafield, however, was a good twenty minutes' walk away. By the time I got home it would be time to go back. Was the food at Seafield really so terrible? It's hard to know. Dire tales of congealed gravy, gristle and boiled swede are commonplace among my generation. The truth is that I'd only ever had my grandma's cooking and she encouraged me to think that nobody else could meet her high standards. Faced with this dilemma there was only one solution: I didn't eat.

I had always been what in those days was called 'painfully thin', and the first sign that something was amiss was an asthma attack. It was then that the doctors decided I was malnourished. I could not go a whole day without food, they said, no matter how good a breakfast I had. Something had to be done. By chance, my auntie Audrey lived only about fifty yards from Seafield, on the opposite side of the road. She had moved there when she married. As her third baby Robert had just been born, she was at home during the day and she agreed to give me lunch. This arrangement continued until I was fourteen, when Auntie's husband, my uncle Bill, was promoted to bank manager, at which point they sold their house and moved to Warrington in Cheshire.

Over those three formative years Auntie Audrey and I became very close. I even started my periods at her house. Back then this was still considered something shameful and not to be discussed, but thanks to her, I was spared all of that. Although never academic, she had always been politically aware, and while I was used to my grandad and the other men in the family talking politics – not to mention tales of my high-profile father – women largely kept out of these conversations. In retrospect, I think it likely that I owe my early interest in politics to her. Whatever the trigger, by the time I was fourteen when asked what I wanted to be when I grew up, I would answer 'Prime Minister!' Whether it was simply the Smart Alec reply of a teenager who wanted to impress, I no longer remember. What is in absolutely no doubt, however, is that in 1970, at the age of sixteen, I was committed enough to join the Labour Party, helped by the encouragement of one of my teachers, a Mrs Speight.

CHAPTER 4

Convent Girl

As far as academic progress was concerned, although I was always in the top stream, I was never first in the class until I reached the sixth form. I was useless at languages so, until I could drop them, they always pulled me down. Looking back, I realise this was a mistake as – unusually for the time – I had every opportunity to get practical experience.

Right from when we were small, Lyndsey and I had always gone away on holiday. With hindsight I know that it was the one chance our mum had of having us to herself. Otherwise there was no ostensible reason to leave Crosby. With its sand dunes and a beach that went on for miles, it was more than enough for anyone. I would spend the whole day there if I could. There were no worries about sunburn back then, and every summer I would go as brown as a nut. If Crosby palled, there were always day trips: picnics on Hilbre Island on the other side of the Wirral peninsula with the excitement of being cut off by the tide and watching seals playing on the rocks. Then there was Rhyl, in North Wales, where the Derbyshire miners had a holiday camp and, every summer, Grandad Jack would go there. Ilkeston was comparatively difficult to get to without a car, and my mother never learnt to drive, so visiting him in Wales was the easiest way for us to see him. For us girls, Rhyl was like heaven because it had slot machines and a swimming pool.

Butlins in Pwllheli suffered our visits more than once. For Mum, it must have been a godsend: a heated outdoor swimming pool for when it wasn't raining; and a roller-skating rink for when it was; and of course shows and competitions with the Redcoats, not to mention the fun of being in our own little wooden house.

Once my mother was firmly ensconced in the travel department, however, our horizons broadened. As a matter of routine, counter staff were encouraged to take advantage of the subsidised travel offered by companies whose holidays they were selling, this being particularly important for new destinations. So while Mum would go free, Lyndsey and I would tag along for a nominal extra cost.

My first taste of 'abroad' was a coach tour to Spain when I was around twelve. It was right at the beginning of the package-holiday era, when the Costa Brava was still relatively undeveloped. On the way down through France, bunks came down from the roof for us to sleep on and I was horrified by the toilets we had to use when we stopped, which were hole-in-the-floor affairs. To someone brought up with Grandma's near-holy attitude to toilet cleanliness, it was a salutary lesson. When we eventually reached Calella – then no more than a fishing village – I remember being astonished at seeing oranges and lemons growing on the trees and having fresh juice to drink instead of squash.

The following year we went to Italy, to a village on the coast just across the border from Nice in what I now know is Liguria. This time we flew, and the whole thing seemed incredibly glamorous and exciting. I loved it, and still do. Our next trip was even more exotic – to Romania. As this was shortly after Grandad died, my mum felt obliged to take Grandma with us. I had never seen her so unnerved. First time out of England, first time in a plane, first time hearing foreign voices and, as for the food . . . Romania was still a communist country and we had been advised to take tights as presents for the chambermaids. We flew into Bucharest, but we were mainly based in a down-at-heel resort on the Black Sea. As part of my mother's research, we visited a health spa, which was the big thing over there, where the treatment consisted of being entirely covered in mud. It was all very un-English. It might not have helped my languages but it certainly gave me a fascination for the wider world.

By this time my social life revolved around the Young Christian Students (YCS) – the best chance a good Catholic girl had of meeting a good Catholic boy, which – for Seafield girls – meant boys from St Mary's. Although the two schools faced each other across Liverpool Road, opportunities for getting to know each other were extremely limited. Hanging round the bus shelter rarely did the trick – and debating only really got going in the sixth form. I joined the YCS at the same time as my friends, Cathy Broadhurst, Cathy McNabb, Maureen Dacey and Jackie Maddox, who affected to be scandalised when, aged about fifteen, I began going out with a boy in the year below me, called Patrick Taaffe. In fact there was not much difference in our ages – I was still a year adrift.

Patrick was a doctor's son and his father was a GP on the Scotland Road which in those days was the roughest part of Liverpool 8. By coincidence, the other partner in the practice was Dr Attwood, whose son David I subsequently went out with, but I met him quite independently.

The Taaffes were the first middle-class family I had ever come across and they lived in a detached house in Blundellsands, complete with drive, conservatory and garage. They also had a holiday cottage in Dolgellau, near Barmouth in North Wales, and during the two years Patrick and I went out together they would take me with them at weekends. It was another world. It was the first time, for example, that I had seen a Rayburn in a kitchen.

Patrick's mother Meriel was a nurse and she became very fond of me. (She and her husband even came to my wedding.) 'You remind me so much of me when I was your age, Cherie,' she would say rather wistfully. She was a really bright woman who, although she would never admit it, had not fully realised her potential and I think she wanted me to realise mine. Later, when the time came to think about university, it was Meriel who came up with the idea that would change my life.

'You're good at debating,' she said. 'You're good at drama, have you ever thought about becoming a lawyer?'

After my O levels were over, Dr Taaffe gave me a job at the surgery helping out the receptionist over the summer, and occasionally he would give me a lift home after work. On our way back he'd usually have one or two visits to make and, rather than wait in the car, I'd go in with him. It was the first time I had come across this level of poverty and I was shocked. No inside toilets. Dirty. Damp. Depressing. Sometimes old back-to-backs. Sometimes tenements.

Mould everywhere. And too many children, the mothers hollow-eyed and worn down by everything.

'You cannot imagine what they're like,' I would tell my grandma after Patrick's father had dropped me off.

'Oh, but I can, young lady. We didn't always live in this kind of luxury, you know.' Where she grew up, she said, the doors opened straight on to the street. There weren't even pavements. The only people who lived there were fishermen and dockers. 'Fishwives' she called them. Living in those conditions, it was all they could do to feed their kids and keep them clean. Never mind anything else.

The central pillar of the YCS was community work. In the late sixties, inner-city Liverpool was being torn down and people were being moved out to new suburbs. Even then it was obvious that the policy was a disaster. Whoever was in charge had forgotten that a community needs more than flats and houses; it's like a body with limbs but no heart. These new towns had been built with no social facilities. No surgeries, no cinemas, no pubs, no bus links, nothing. They were just dormitories. The residents were completely isolated.

The nearest of these to us was Kirkby, a few miles to the north-east of Crosby, and during that summer the YCS ran a summer school and playing-field project – a whole range of activities for the kids to do during the holidays. We were based in one of the local primary schools. It was a twenty-four-hour project and we slept on the floor in sleeping bags. On one level, of course, it was fun. I'm sorry to say that we probably wouldn't have done it with such gusto if it hadn't been. But I ended up feeling really shocked because, whatever else you might say about where I lived, it was, at least, a real community. These new towns were not and the people being moved out knew it.

One of the songs our folk group used to sing expressed it much better than I ever could:

> *A fella from the Council, just out of planning school,*
> *Has told us that we're being moved right out of Liverpool.*
> *They're sending us to Kirkby, to Skelmersdale or Speke,*
> *But don't wanna go from all we know in Back Buchanan*
> *Street.*

The verses continued documenting the life of old Liverpool. No bathrooms or hot water certainly, but real communities for all that. The result of this experiment in urban cleansing was vandalism, crime and corruption. We did what we could, but it was like spitting in the wind.

The alternative to working in the community – which needed a commitment of at least two weeks – was a week of spiritual reflection, and the following summer I went to one such in Rugeley, near Lichfield in Staffordshire. It was 1971, and peace and love were breaking out all around and the YCS retreat was no exception: there was a lot of scurrying about in the dark while more saintly souls sang songs round the campfire. In the hours of daylight the debate was as much political as spiritual. But as revolutionaries went, we were pretty tame. Nonetheless, we saw ourselves as part of the sixties workers-of-the-world-unite kind of movement. It was all vaguely left-wing Christian socialism.

Until now, the only boys I'd met through the YCS had gone to St Mary's. However, the boy I had been scurrying around with in Rugeley lived in Leeds, a distance that required a certain amount of ingenuity to keep the romance going. His name was Steven Ellis and he was the national secretary of the YCS, so my friends were dead impressed. We could write to each other, but that took time. Best was the telephone but, in those days, it was still very expensive, particularly long distance, and when it came to making calls, Grandma was very strict. She had a specially designed moneybox on the hall table next to the phone, which said 'Phone from here when 'er you will, but don't forget to pay the bill'.

As long as you weren't the one doing the phoning, you could talk as long as you liked, so Steve and I developed a wonderful scheme though, with hindsight, scam would be a more appropriate description. It was extremely simple. Steve would ring from a call box – his family didn't have a phone – I'd answer it, then close the door to the hall. This was considered perfectly reasonable behaviour if your young man was phoning you. Grandma would think, That's all right, it's on his bill, and she'd carry on watching *Coronation Street* or whatever it was. Then, very quietly, I'd put down the receiver and dial him straight back – and nobody any the wiser!

After a few months of this, as I saw it, mild deception, the inevitable happened. A phone bill arrived. A very substantial phone bill. My grandmother went berserk: the bill for that one quarter exceeded the total of the previous year and she just couldn't account for it. It had to be a mistake, she said. So naturally she called the GPO to give them an earful.

'There's been a mistake,' she said.

'I'm afraid not, Mrs Booth. There's no mistake.'

She wasn't taking this lying down. They said they would send her a breakdown to clarify matters.

'I don't understand it,' she said, one evening when my mum got back from work and the breakdown had arrived.

'There seem to be a lot of long-distance phone calls. We don't make long-distance phone calls,' she muttered as she scrutinised the letter. Not that it contained very much. In those days individual calls weren't itemised. The statement was broken down into totals: local, long-distance, or foreign, but that was as far as it went.

'I mean, what are all these trunk calls? Have you made any trunk calls, Gale? I know I haven't. How often do you call your dad in Ilkeston?'

Suddenly it dawned on me. I genuinely hadn't realised just how much my little chats across the Pennines were costing and I knew that if I didn't own up, the blame would fall on my mother. I had no choice. To say I got a tongue-lashing is putting it mildly. My grandmother was furious. There was no way she was going to pay, she said. So what was I going to do about it? There was nothing I could do. I couldn't pay because I didn't have any money. In the end it was my poor mum who had to foot the bill, but at least she wasn't blamed. There were no more phone calls after that.

If my relationship with Steve was to continue, hitch-hiking was the only answer, and in fact it proved so successful that from then on I hitched all over the country. When the M52 (as it was originally known) opened in 1973, I was among the very first to benefit from it, standing on the slip road on that historic day with my thumb out, hitching a lift to Leeds.

At A level I did history, geography, economics and general studies. By this time the nuns knew that I was going to do well, though they didn't see fit to communicate the good news to either me or my mother. At the final prize-giving, she was shocked and acutely embarrassed – though I'm not sure in which order – to discover that I had won all the prizes except religion. As I kept going up to the dais to collect the various awards, my mum was falling under the seat with embarrassment, she says. Before this, the only prizes I had won since I'd been at Seafield were for history – for coming top in the O level – and in the third year for a project I'd done on historical costume, lavishly illustrated with cards collected from packets of PG Tips. (For that I was given *The Age of Baldwin* – not a choice, it must be said, to inspire a budding thirteen-year-old historian.) My reports had been nothing exceptional, and as for parents' evenings, when in the normal course of events you might expect a bit more depth, the nuns would tell her nothing beyond the fact that they couldn't read my handwriting and it was a shame she hadn't done something about it earlier. Why did they treat her like this? Because she didn't have a husband. For all their lip service on independence and individuality, when it came to it they were the same as everybody else, and my poor mother, who had given up her career, and worked hard all her life to do the best she could for us, was treated with disdain.

Meriel Taaffe couldn't have known how well her idea of the law would be received back in Ferndale Road. My grandmother had always been an admirer of strong and independent women who had made a mark on the world and Rose Heilbron, the most famous defence lawyer of her generation, fulfilled all these criteria. She was a true pioneer. The first woman to win a scholarship to Gray's Inn. The first woman to become a King's Counsel. The first woman silk to defend the acccused in a murder trial – a case conducted in her home town of Liverpool. The first woman judge to sit at the Old Bailey. If that wasn't enough she was also beautiful and by the fifties, with dozens of murder trials to her name, she had become a celebrity in her own right, to the extent that a television series was based on her. Called *Justice*, it starred Margaret Lockwood. As Rose Heilbron was married to a Liverpool doctor, she continued to practise on the northern circuit, with chambers in Liverpool, and from time to time my grandmother would go down to watch her in action at the Crown Court – when trials were still conducted in the baroque splendour of St George's Hall – and come back full of it.

At my grandmother's instigation, I too had watched Margaret Lockwood dishing out justice on TV in her wig and gown, and, when the idea of the law was first raised by Meriel Taaffe, that was the image that shot into my mind: I could be another Margaret Lockwood!

The big question in the upper sixth was which university? No one in either the Booth or Thompson families had ever done such a thing, so I had no one to advise me. The LSE, I remember, was the last one on the list of five, put there in part to annoy the nuns who considered I had rebellious tendencies anyway – in the early seventies the LSE was seen as a hotbed of revolution. Another of my choices, I remember, was Durham. At the previous year's YCS camp I'd become friendly with a girl who lived in Whitley Bay. I'd like to catch up with her, I told my mum, and I could go there on my way back from the interview and stay the night.

As Durham is a collegiate university, you apply to an individual college rather than a faculty and my interview was with Trevelyan College, then a women-only establishment. It seemed like a good idea at the time, but within two minutes of arriving, a sentence was running through my head, refusing to go away. 'This is a really bad idea.' I had just spent seven years at an all-girls' school and here I was talking about spending another three years in yet another all-girl institution. I must be mad. I did the interview and left.

As for Whitley Bay, I never got there. Instead I took a train to Leeds where Steven met me at the station, which had been our plan all along. He had a very indulgent grandmother who, very sweetly, let us stay the night in her council flat. To this day my mother pretends she didn't know what was going on.

The relationship eventually fizzled out. Steve was a bit of a ladies' man, anyway, so it was probably all for the good. In the meantime there was Pete Clark to keep me going. Pete was one of the left-inclined YCS guys, though we had really got to know each other through the debating society at school. He was also at St Mary's. My recent experience in hitch-hiking proved useful and we would do that old trick of the girl standing in the road, and only when a car pulls up does the guy come out of hiding. It never failed. In this way, within little more than an hour of leaving Crosby we'd be in the Lakes with a glorious day of walking in front of us.

Next stop the LSE. Many of my Liverpool contemporaries considered London to be one step short of hell. But to me it wasn't that off-putting. My dad lived there. Uncle Bob lived there. My mum went to London regularly for her work. So when the LSE made me an offer, I didn't wait to hear about the other places I'd applied to. I accepted straight away.

As for the nuns, they continued to disapprove. They didn't understand why I couldn't have stayed in Liverpool or, if I really wanted to spread my wings, then Manchester was very good. 'Lots of Seafield girls go there,' they said. Exactly.

'You know, Cherie, you could be a good leader, but you're very headstrong. If you go to London, then you had better be careful.'

They didn't have high expectations of me, and who could blame them? I wasn't even a prefect, so never came within a mile of being head girl. Discipline was all about getting girls to wear hats when they left the grounds. I hated my hat and did everything I could to lose it, so there was no way I was going to make anyone else wear one. During my time in the sixth form I set a world record for late marks. I wasn't that keen on assembly and often wouldn't bother to turn up until it had finished. The nuns turned a blind eye simply because they recognised my academic potential and, long before league tables became such a hot potato, that kind of thing mattered more than hats.

I'd always had holiday jobs. The first had been with Dr Taaffe in the summer of 1969, but as soon as I could I went to work at Lewis's, for all the obvious reasons. The summer of 1971 they put me into baby clothes – about which I knew absolutely nothing, although like my grandma I have always loved children, so it couldn't have been better. The following summer – as soon as I'd finished my A levels – I started in the school outfitting department, about which I knew considerably more, particularly hats. On the same floor, just along from me, was gents' outfitters, where I couldn't help catching the eye of another student who looked equally bored. The eyes were blue, and he was slim and dark, with hair considerably longer than St Mary's boys were allowed. He even had a cute-looking beard! With his John Lennon glasses and well-cut clothes, he was the last word in trendiness. We started taking breaks at the same time and would chat over a coffee in the canteen. His name was David Attwood and he was two years older than me and at Liverpool University reading law. His father was a GP who worked in Scotland Road, in the very same practice as Dr Taaffe, and like the Taaffes, the Attwoods lived in Blundellsands. With all these coincidences we had plenty to talk about.

Towards the end of the summer Mum took us off on our annual holiday, this time to Ibiza, when it was just an ordinary holiday island, with none of the hard-drinking, hard-dancing reputation it later gained. Imagine my surprise when who should I see on the beach but my fellow flirt from gents' outfitters! He was there with a group of friends from university. It was the perfect holiday romance: sun, sea, sand and . . . sangria. As for my mother, she was putty in his hands.

I was due to leave for the LSE at the end of September but David and I made full use of the few weeks still left to us back in Crosby. The weather was still lovely and the evenings still long. Plenty of opportunities for walks along the dunes, where romantic sunsets were two a penny, and we were never not in the mood.

The one fly in this romantic ointment was the Blundellsands/ Waterloo divide. With the Taaffes it had never been a problem, but although David's mother had always been fine with me, he thought it prudent to play safe. He told her only that I lived near Merchant Taylors', the smart Protestant school that is a Crosby landmark, which wasn't entirely a lie. This had practical implications, however. The Attwoods were always very kind, Mrs Attwood particularly so, and she wouldn't hear of my walking home after dark and would insist on giving me a lift home.

'So where shall I drop you off, Cherie?'

'Oh anywhere near here will be fine, thank you, Mrs Attwood.'

'I'd much rather see you to your door—'

'Please, this is just as easy . . . quicker in fact. I'm just by the park.'

The car would slow down and I'd be out and off within seconds, heading in entirely the wrong direction, waving my thanks wildly. Yes, we did live by the park. But the other side. One side was acceptable, the other wasn't.

Eventually she found out and, just as David said it would, all hell broke loose.

CHAPTER 5

Student Life

On 24 September 1972, the day after my eighteenth birthday, my mum and I took the train from Liverpool Lime Street to London Euston. The night before, I'd had a combined birthday and farewell party with a few of my YCS friends at home and made a little speech saying how I owed everything to my mum – sentiments which were overtaken by my embarrassment as she burst into tears when the time came to leave me at the hall of residence. But this was it. The first day of the rest of my life.

Term didn't start till the following week, but freshers came earlier to get the hang of things. As the first in my family to go to university, there were a few basics that I hadn't considered – like where I was going to live. Although the authorities had found me somewhere in the short term, another solution was needed for the rest of the year, they explained. I was sent to an address in Pembridge Villas, Notting Hill, which turned out to be a lodging house for the Digby Stuart Teacher Training College – run by the nuns of the Sacred Heart: dormitory accommodation and in by ten. I could just imagine what they must have thought: good Catholic girl, barely eighteen – a convent is the very thing. Well, they thought wrong. I was not going into a convent. I did not want to be a good Catholic girl. I intended to put all that behind me and have a bit of fun. I went straight back to Passfield Hall, the halls of residence in the heart of Bloomsbury, where I'd been staying till then, and somehow, after a pleading that would not shame a defence counsel in a murder trial, I was squeezed into a room with two other girls: Caroline Grace and Louise Oddy, both of whom were also reading law.

A law degree in itself doesn't qualify you to do anything professionally speaking. Whether you become a solicitor – the first port of call for a member of the public – or decide to practise as a barrister – retained by a solicitor to put their client's case before a court or to give a legal opinion before it gets that far – you need at least a year's further study and then practical on-the-job training after taking your degree before you are of any use to anyone.

There are six core subjects common to all universities that offer law degrees in the UK: contract, tort, constitutional and administrative law, criminal law, trust law and land law. These are covered in the first two years. In the third year, you start to specialise. Standard options will include subjects like company law, family law and tax law, but the LSE offered a far wider range than most universities and, in the end, mine was a very eclectic set of options.

By the end of the second year I knew I didn't want to be a commercial lawyer, so company law or the more focused commercial law were out. Civil liberties and human rights were then a half-option, and I took tribal law as another half-option. (This was mainly taken by Commonwealth students but I found it fascinating.) Another reasonably unusual choice was history of English law. This went back to Henry II and the Assizes, and we learnt about entail, about how to protect family wealth – not only a central subject in Jane Austen's novels, but highly relevant today in many African and Arab countries. Most importantly, as it turned out, I chose to do employment law which wasn't recognised as a speciality at that time – it was then called labour law. The LSE was one of the few places that taught it.

Industrial relations had reached a critical stage in Britain in the early seventies. In order to combat inflation, the Conservative government had put a cap on pay rises, yet with prices showing no sign of levelling off the unions began to flex their muscles in the only way they could. When the miners went on strike, fuel stocks began to get dangerously low and, during the first months of 1974, the government put the whole country on to a three-day week in order to limit consumption of electricity.

The LSE differs from all other English universities in that it has always been political. Although now part of the University of

London, it was originally set up at the end of the nineteenth century by Beatrice and Sidney Webb – founders of the Fabian Society – who believed in advancing socialist causes by reformist rather than revolutionary means. Its full name is the London School of Economics and Political Science, and the Fabians envisioned the LSE as a research institution that would focus on the problems of poverty, inequality and related issues. Certainly in the seventies, this ethos remained at the heart of the place – one of the reasons I'd decided to go there. Instead of teaching law in order to churn out solicitors, the LSE saw the subject more in terms of its impact on every area of political and economic life. And this was the kind of work I saw myself doing – helping in the more politically relevant areas where traditionally ordinary people had been short-changed by lawyers.

In fact, during those first few years in London I didn't involve myself much with politics. Students at the LSE were still living in the aftermath of 1968 when it had been the epicentre of student revolt in Britain. In 1971 the then Prime Minister Edward Heath had raised hackles by expelling the leading East German student leader Rudi Dutschke, and the LSE had become the focus of dissent for the whole country. Most of those involved were the public-school crowd – well-meaning but who indulged in romantic notions of what it meant to be poor. I knew only too well but I was in too much of a hurry to get on in the world to waste my time on fashionable student politics. There was a Labour club, but I wasn't active. Among those who were, however, was Glenys Thornton – now Baroness Thornton of Manningham. She and her husband John Carr were both in Passfield Hall; like me working-class kids who came from the north, though we were definitely in the minority. We became friends, and so I'd go along to support them, but at the time it was little more than that.

That first term David Attwood came down from Liverpool a couple of times to see me, but sharing a room with two other girls didn't leave much scope for romance. Things weren't much easier when I got back to Crosby. He would borrow his mother's car and we'd park on Marine Road where street lighting was at a minimum. The sand dunes were still there, of course, but December on the banks of the Mersey is cold and no amount of youthful passion can cope with near-zero temperatures.

I'd been so looking forward to coming home that I hadn't realised how quickly I'd got used to my new life. My family were inordinately proud of me but knew nothing about universities, hadn't a clue about what I did, what any of it meant. As for the law, with its arcane vocabulary, that was a foreign country. It was as if a chasm had opened up between us, a split in the earth that could only grow wider.

I began to see how unworldly they were. At Passfield Hall I'd have a shower every day. At Ferndale Road we'd have a bath once a week, because hot water was heated by our coal fire in the sitting room. Lyndsey and I would go first, and then my mum and grandma would use the same water, with a kettle or two added to keep it hot. Meanwhile, we'd wash our hair and sit in front of the fire and let it dry. It we needed a heater upstairs – for example if someone was ill – there was a paraffin stove and I can still remember that smell.

That Christmas David took me out to my first-ever restaurant – the Berni Inn steak house in Southport, a few miles up the coast, the height of sophistication in 1972. I can remember even now what I had: prawn cocktail, followed by steak and some sort of ice-cream, and to finish, an Irish coffee. I imagine there was wine or even possibly a schooner of sherry. I arrived back home in a state of near bliss, swiftly dented by my grandma's 'a waste of money, when it could have been spent on good home cooking'.

On New Year's Eve, David took me to a party given by student friends of his in Liverpool and we stayed out all night. When we eventually got back my mum was fine about it. I remember her saying that she hoped I'd been careful . . .

That afternoon there was a knock at the door. It was David's younger brother, Michael. I was upstairs.

'Cherie, there's someone to see you,' my mother called. I peered down to see Michael standing on the step looking cold and miserable. I immediately sensed something was wrong. Michael had never been to our house before.

'What's wrong? Is David OK?'

'He's OK. But—'

'You'd better come in,' I said. 'You'll catch your death standing out there.' He was a nice boy, about sixteen, and he and I had always got on.

'David says to say he can't come—' he began.

'I wasn't expecting him—'

'No, you see . . . what I mean is . . .'

It turned out that David's mum had gone bananas, just as he'd predicted. Although he'd denied that anything had 'happened' she was not convinced. If he continued to see me, she said, his allowance would be cut off, which would mean an end to his university career. She had already been telling him that she thought I was after his money, and, in her eyes, making him stay out all night showed my motives were strictly dishonourable.

'He says to tell you that he'll have to lie low for a few days, give her a few days to calm down, but you shouldn't try to call him.'

There wasn't a lot I could say, except to reassure Michael, but even so it was upsetting. I had always liked their mother. 'Don't worry,' I told him. 'It'll be all right, I know it will.' And I stood at the doorstep and watched him walk back down Ferndale Road towards the park

Later that night, we were watching TV when the phone rang.

'That'll be for you, Cherie,' Grandma said with a nod of her head.

I sighed. The idea that I wasn't good enough for Mrs Attwood would drive her mad. I didn't rush to get it. It wouldn't be the one person I wanted it to be.

I was wrong. I felt a rush of blood to my head when I recognised David's voice.

'I thought you weren't going to call,' I said.

'I had to . . .' he paused. 'Something awful's happened.' Gradually I began to make sense of what he was saying. It was Michael, his brother. About an hour after he'd been to see me, he had collapsed playing golf. They'd taken him to hospital and found that he had an enlarged spleen. Leukaemia. Our little local difficulties suddenly seemed unimportant.

From then on there was no more talk about splitting us up. I didn't see Mrs Attwood before I went back to London. When I was next in Crosby she barely noticed I was around. There were more important things in life than worrying about whether David was involved with the right kind of girl.

Nine months later Michael was dead.

The funeral was really shocking. When somebody young dies like that, it is heartbreaking. I had been to family funerals before, and Grandad's had been painful for all sorts of reasons. But even

Grandad, important as he was, had been old. This was entirely different. The church was full of boys from St Mary's – sixteen, the same age as Michael. The same age as Lyndsey. For Dr Attwood it was terrible. You could sense what he was feeling just by looking at him. There he was, a doctor, and he couldn't even save his own son.

It was around this time that I renewed contact with my dad, perhaps for the same reasons – the sense that life is too short to hold grudges against the people you love. My grandma had always wanted me to keep in touch with him and, in her own way, so had my mother, though her feelings were obviously more complicated.

Following my grandad's funeral, things had begun to thaw a bit between my parents. By then, my dad's relationship with Julie Allan, Jenia and Bronwen's mother, had ended. His drinking had finally become too much for her and she had disappeared to America, taking her daughters with her. Her father was a successful Canadian screenwriter, who she knew would provide both practical and emotional support for his grandchildren. From my mum's perspective, this made things easier. For my dad, however, it was devastating. He didn't see them for years.

When I was about eleven my dad started writing to us. He also sent books. The first one I remember was a leather-bound *Pride and Prejudice*, which I fell in love with. Most, however, were rather more radical or eccentric in nature. I particularly remember *The Female Eunuch* by Germaine Greer and later *The Doomsday Book: Can the World Survive?* by Gordon Rattray Taylor. (I got off lightly. He sent Lyndsey *Portnoy's Complaint*.) *The Doomsday Book* was an early broadside on the environmental disaster that was about to be unleashed on the world. Not surprisingly, with books like these, I found plenty to write back to him about, and so a relationship between us gradually developed. Not so with Lyndsey. She never replied. Being so close to our mother, I think she always felt his betrayal more acutely than I did. I was more inclined to think of him in the same way as my grandma, more as the Prodigal Son. As Dad always says, when it comes to his funeral 'Lyndsey will be the one dancing on my grave'. I'm convinced that this disparity in our early experience is the main reason my relationship with my father continues to be more forgiving than Lyndsey's.

My father was now famous. *Till Death Us Do Part* had become one of the most popular comedy series in British television history. It ran from 1966 through to 1975 and the 'Scouse Git' was recognised everywhere he went. As a prominent Labour supporter Tony Booth had even been invited to Downing Street by Harold Wilson, which made me immensely proud. And he was the living embodiment of the Scouse Git: when he wasn't chivvying left-wing politicians, he was haranguing Tories.

In 1970 he was back in the headlines again as one of the original cast of *Oh! Calcutta!*, an 'erotic review' in which the whole cast, male and female, performed naked. The mix of serious, if explicit, writing and full-on nudity was described by critics as ground-breaking. Cringe-making would have been my verdict. Not that I ever saw it. After an initial six-week run at the Roundhouse, it transferred to the Royalty Theatre, just behind the LSE. Luckily for me, by the time I was a student he had left the cast, but every time I walked past those huge posters – flags and books in appropriate places – I winced.

My father's potential for embarrassment proved endless. In 1974, in my second year at the LSE, he co-starred in *Confessions of a Window Cleaner*. This was like an X-rated version of a *Carry On* film. Or so I've been told. Needless to say, I didn't see this either. My grandma wasn't going to pass by the opportunity of seeing her errant son, however, and when it came on at the Waterloo Odeon she informed the box office that she was the star's mother, demanded a free ticket and got it! She told me afterwards she couldn't see what all the fuss was about.

It may well be as funny as he claims – it was certainly a huge commercial success and led to several more *Confessions of* films – but each one would be the source of acute misery for me. Jibes by fellow students were the least of it. Most children find their parents' sexuality faintly disturbing. But for it to be so public was difficult to handle. The paradox is that, at the same time as being appalled, I was immensely proud of my father, even then. Proud of what he'd achieved in his chosen profession, proud of his forthright views on politics, proud that I was his daughter. He was a highly intelligent, witty man who could run rings around anyone he chose to.

Successful though he was in the public perception, in private his life was a complete disaster. After Julie Allan left him, he had started drinking even more heavily and smoking cannabis – another reason my mum was nervous about my seeing him. By now he had fathered two more daughters. Their mother was Susie Riley, whom my dad had met when reeling from Julie's departure.

Even though I had no very positive feelings about her at the time, Julie was a good woman. She had been acting with Joan Littlewood's company at the Theatre Royal Stratford East when my father met her, and she went on to become a successful writer and producer. Susie was a model and my father now describes their relationship as 'mutually ruinous'. Adults must be responsible for their own actions, but when there are children involved the results can be devastating.

By the time I met them, Sarah and Emma were perhaps five and two, and I would regularly go to the flat in West Heath Road, Hampstead, to baby-sit. It was not good there. There were times when they had to get themselves up and dressed. There was no structure in their lives. Even if I hadn't planned to, I'd stay the night. I felt I couldn't just leave these so-called parents in charge of my half-sisters. Having woken the girls up, they would then take no further notice of them.

Although I didn't analyse it at the time, I suspect this was one reason I never got involved with drugs myself, though there were plenty of them around. I don't even remember being tempted, but if your father is behaving like that, it's guaranteed to put you off. Who wants to look that stupid?

As far as Sarah and Emma were concerned, I did what I could when I could, but an instinct for self-preservation kept me at a reasonable distance. The only stability in their life was provided by Susie's parents, who would take the girls at weekends and give them some love and affection.

At the end of my third year, it was clear that I was going to get a good degree, so my tutors were encouraging me to do my BCL (Bachelor of Civil Law), the MA of law. Student life had its advantages and so I thought, Why not? It was May 1975 and I was still only twenty.

I took the train up to Oxford and walked from the station to Wadham College, which had links with the LSE. It too was a radical college, the first of the historically all-male Oxford colleges to take a woman undergraduate – 1974 had been the first year women could be admitted at all levels. I had never been to Oxford before, or seen anything like it. The LSE looked like a bank. This was quite different. Everywhere you looked there were quadrangles and court-yards, pillars, statues, cupolas and towers, all built in golden limestone.

At Wadham I was interviewed by Ian Brownlie, professor of international law, who later advised President Carter on the Iranian hostage crisis in 1979. All appeared to go well. Although he couldn't tell me if I would be accepted, his demeanour towards the end of the interview tended to suggest it. He had one final point to make before I left.

'Even if you are planning to be an academic lawyer, you need to have a professional qualification,' he explained. In other words I either had to be called to the Bar – to become a barrister – or do a six-months' solicitors' course followed by two years' Articles. He didn't see this as a problem, however. 'You can quite easily do your Bar Finals while you are here.'

The Bar Finals, as a professional rather than an academic qualification, are taken under the auspices of one of the four Inns of Court, the professional associations to which all barristers and judges belong.

It was one of those English summer afternoons in Oxford that foreign visitors always hope they'll experience. Exams must just have ended and everywhere you looked there were undergraduates celebrating, champagne bottles clutched by the neck, young people sprawling on any available patch of grass, perching on walls and balustrades. They might have been the same age as me, but that was the only thing we had in common. Worst were the accents, which I couldn't bear. Would it get any better once I got there? My grandma had been ecstatic when I told her I was going up to Oxford for an interview. It meant much more to her than the LSE. I felt decidedly uncomfortable and there was this voice in my head saying: 'This isn't the place for me.'

My interview was successful. Within a week I had a letter offering me a place at Wadham to do my BCL. By the time it arrived I'd already written to each of the Inns of Court, asking for an application form for membership. How I was going to pay I had no idea. The cost of joining alone was £75 – a month's wages for my mum. In addition, the arcane rules obliged you to eat a certain number of 'dinners' per term. That was only the beginning. Once I'd been accepted by an Inn, I would have to pay for the Bar exams.

All four Inns of Court duly replied, and one – Lincoln's Inn – included an application for an entrance scholarship. Naturally I filled it in, and to my astonishment I got it . . . No £75 to pay, and all my dinners free! This was the first time I thought, Wait a minute: why would I want to be an academic lawyer when I could actually do the real thing? As a barrister I could make the law. I wouldn't have to write about other people making the law. All at once, everything became clear.

I turned Wadham down. No regrets, only relief. Not till years later did I discover how furious they had been. To be accepted and then say no was unheard of and, for several years after that, Wadham refused to take any LSE graduates to teach them a lesson – or so legend has it. Of course I should have written to Ian Brownlie to apologise – and given my reasons. But I didn't. I was so naive it didn't even cross my mind.

The next stage was working out how to survive the following twelve months. During my three years at the LSE I'd had a full grant, which meant I was better off than many middle-class students, like David, whose parents weren't always able to top up whatever grant they got. This happy state of affairs was about to stop.

Grants for undergraduates were mandatory in those days, but post-graduate and other professional courses, such as Bar Finals, were not similarly funded. I applied to Lancashire County Council and was awarded a discretionary grant that covered the fees. But how I could afford to live was another matter. I decided I needed to get some work to fund myself. Somebody suggested I could lecture, so I applied to the Polytechnic of Central London and was accepted. Apart from my age, my credentials were good: by then I knew that I had got a First.

At that time the Central London Poly, as it was known, offered a wide range of external degrees, which is how I found myself teaching tort, trust and land law at the same time as I was having to do these same topics myself for Bar Finals. Clearly I had already done them for my degree, but for the professional qualification they were approached from a practical perspective. Because the Poly wasn't involved in setting the papers, I had to cover the full curriculum – more than I had done originally – as I could never be sure on what areas my students were going to be questioned.

I had such admiration for those students. They were all holding down full-time jobs, yet were so determined to qualify as lawyers that they gave up their free time for years to get there. And there was I, just turned twenty-one with no responsibilities, no one to consider but myself.

My twenty-first birthday had proved a milestone in more ways than one. I was taken to dinner by my father somewhere in Soho, the first time he had ever taken me out anywhere and the first time I had ever been somewhere in London that wasn't a Spaghetti House. Whenever he and I had met up previously, we'd have a Chinese take-away, always one of my favourites. He wanted this evening to be memorable, however. And it certainly was. It was French and all very chic. He was obviously a regular, and when he announced me as his daughter I was subjected to a flurry of hand-kissing. We started off with snails and it went on from there. At the end I was violently sick. Whether it was the snails or the unaccustomed quantity of wine, I am in no position to judge.

As an undergraduate, I had been lucky enough to spend three years in halls of residence, but 'home' was now a hideous bedsit in Weech Road, West Hampstead. The one time my grandma came down to see me – bringing some pots and pans she thought I might need – she cried her eyes out, because she thought it was so awful. For her, cleanliness was everything. I can see her now, peering round the bathroom door and nearly having apoplexy. London water is notoriously full of iron and the combination of lime-scale and rust made everything in the plumbing line look disgusting. Elsewhere it was the usual thing for those days: dirty lino; peeling paintwork; windows you couldn't see out of; meters for electricity and gas, in which you'd put a shilling and which would always run out at the worst moment. A geyser for the bathwater, which spluttered and gave out noxious fumes, and a pilot light that was always going out. I shared a couple of gas rings on the landing with another girl and I didn't even have a fridge. Anything that needed to be kept cold I kept on my windowsill.

At the LSE there had been a fair sprinkling of women, but the Bar was still overwhelmingly masculine. That year was the first time the number of women at Lincoln's Inn had exceeded 10 per cent. During the formal dinners at Lincoln's Inn a group of us tended to sit together and I was the only girl. Peter Farrell was a St Mary's boy, who had read law with David at Liverpool, as had David Robinson, who in turn had been to school with Bruce Roe. John Higham – now a QC – also came from Crosby, though he wasn't Catholic, but had been at Shrewsbury. I was beginning to learn that the world was a small place, particularly the Bar.

Unlike most of the boys I had met reading law at the LSE, my next boyfriend was not the product of a public school. I hadn't been look-ing for anyone, John just happened along, and then it became more serious. He was the son of a solicitor who, out of principle, had sent all his children to the local comprehensive.

Although David and I were still seeing each other when I went back to Liverpool, it's hard to keep a long-distance relationship going however much you want to. Even at the LSE I'd had the occa-sional London boyfriend, though nothing serious. At least in Passfield Hall I'd had plenty of companionship during the week and at the weekends I'd either go back to Liverpool or David would come down to London, and of course there were the holidays. Everybody thought we would get married, including my mum. But once I moved to Weech Road I was much lonelier. I didn't have the ready-made social life offered by a hall of residence, especially one in central London, and my bedsit in contrast was drab and depressing and miles away.

Having lost my grant, I was worse off than I'd ever been and couldn't afford to go home as regularly as I'd done before. As David was now doing his Articles, he had less time to come down to London. It's hard keeping up the excitement when you don't see each other for weeks, hiding frustrations, not wanting to talk through important things on the phone in case a wrong word, a pause in the wrong place, can't be put right by a look, a squeeze or a kiss. Conversations in hallways with people coming and going every few minutes can be strained, and in the seventies long-distance phone calls were expensive, the money going into the box at an alarming rate. Messages can easily go astray, and regularly did. There were no such things as answerphones then. Letters offered more scope but romantic ramblings written at one in the morning don't always read well at nine o'clock on the top of a bus when you're late for a lec-ture. In a sense, my double life was a situation I just drifted into and it meant nothing. John was fun and he lived in a nice student flat but I always made it clear that I was committed to David.

*

Halfway through the year I was advised to start looking for a pupil-lage. These days there is something called the Bar Vocational Course (BVC), which instructs students on the practical aspects of being a barrister: advocacy, drafting, client conferences, criminal litigation, sentencing, case preparation and analysis – the day-to-day stuff of a barrister's work. In our year we had just started to do practical exer-cises, as they were called, where we were taught the techniques of drafting opinions and court documents, but it was only a minor part of the course. The main way of learning to be a barrister then, and even now, is by watching and helping an experienced junior barris-ter – known as the pupil master. In those days this was very much a hit-or-miss affair. Some pupil masters took their teaching duties seri-ously, others saw their pupils as unpaid skivvies. The system still continues, but in a far more regulated form, both in how pupils are taught and how they are selected. They are also paid for what they do, albeit not a lot.

One of the pluses of having a split legal system (one which encom-passes both solicitors and barristers such we have in Britain) is that barristers can – and usually do – specialise. A small firm of solicitors can thus call on very specific expertise when they need it; they don't have to have it in-house. Of all the specialities, commercial law is the most lucrative but I had already decided it was not for me. In the end I opted for employment law; I thought it would be intellectually challenging. It was just starting to kick off as a result of the Industrial Relations Act brought in by the Conservative government in 1970. This was the first time that anyone had actually formalised employment law: until then it had been a sub-branch of contract and the law of master and servant – those were the terms that were then used. It was only at somewhere like the LSE that we even talked about workers or employers and employees. Edward Heath had also set up the National Industrial Relations Court, designed to limit the power of the trade unions. People were being sent to prison – the Pentonville Five was the most high-profile case – so it was a really hot topic. In fact the NIRC was abolished in 1974 by the incoming Labour government, so it fell firmly within the area of law that inter-ested me: people and politics. From a career perspective it had one overriding advantage: it was all very new, so there was a real short-age of people doing it.

Professor Grunfeld, who had written the textbook on redundancy payments brought in by the Wilson government in the late sixties, had taught me employment law. When I consulted him on pupillage possibilities, he told me that there were very few practitioners holding themselves out as employment lawyers, and only three names he could recommend. I can now only remember two: Alan Pardoe and Alexander Irvine, always known as Derry. Both of them offered me a place so I was in the extremely fortunate position of being able to choose.

At that time Alan Pardoe – now a judge – was in a more conventional set of chambers which mainly did commercial law. His interest in employment law was little more than a niche, he explained. Alan himself was guarded and charming – a traditional kind of barrister. Derry was anything but. Even then he was larger than life: overweight, bullish, blunt. He gave me this line that he was a down-to-earth, working-class boy who'd gone to Glasgow University and somehow ended up at Cambridge. In many ways I understood where he was coming from. As you shadow your pupil master for a year, the relationship is vitally important. These are the people who will form the core of your professional life. If things go well, then your hope is to be taken on – given tenancy, as it's called – in the same set of chambers, so developing a good personal relationship is crucial.

The interview didn't start well.

The first thing he said was: 'Why are you wearing that dress?'

'What's wrong with it?' I asked. I had bought it in the January sales from the Liverpool branch of John Lewis, George Henry Lee. It was dark blue with a Paisley pattern, and I had been rather pleased with it. I was very thin in those days and as it was ruched round the waist it made the most of my not-very-curvy figure.

'Don't you know lady barristers are supposed to wear black and white?'

I remember thinking, What a nerve! It's all right for you with all your money, but this is the only smart dress I've got and I have to wear it for other things besides being interviewed by pompous barristers.

What I actually said was: 'Well, this is the only decent dress I've got and I bought it especially for interviews. So sorry it isn't black.'

It clearly did me no harm, however, as he offered me a pupillage there and then, or as he actually put it: 'OK, you can start in July.' It would never happen like that now. Derry himself had been a lecturer at the LSE so he knew that a First from there meant something. These days, pupils are taken on by a committee – members of chambers – and it's no longer down to an individual barrister's whim.

'By the way,' he said. 'I'll waive the fee but my clerk might want his ten per cent.'

It was only his little joke, but I remember my heart starting to race. In those days they were still in theory entitled to charge a pupillage fee, which was 100 guineas.

'And just one more minor thing,' he added, as I was leaving. 'I've half promised this place to somebody else, some fellow from Oxford.' Then he paused and gave me a broad smile. 'But don't you worry about that. I'll get rid of him and I'll take you instead.'

As well as offering entrance scholarships, Lincoln's Inn also had major scholarships that were intended to help fund the year of pupillage. Charging for the privilege might have been abandoned, but you weren't paid and you still had to live.

Once again the blue Paisley dress was dusted down and on the appointed day I found myself in the anteroom sitting next to another scholarship hopeful. His suit was far less suitable than my blue dress, I decided, being made of some kind of tweed, an old-fashioned thing complete with turn-ups. He was obviously a public-school type and equally obviously had just had his hair cut. He was looking very shorn. As there were only the two of us sitting there, I decided to break the silence.

'I think we must have names close to each other,' I said by way of introduction. 'My name's Cherie Booth.'

'Then I'll be going in before you,' he said. 'Tony Blair.'

He smiled, a wide broad smile. His voice wasn't as public school as I thought it would be from the appearance. There was a slight accent I couldn't place. Only later I realised that it was a hint of Scottish left over from his time at Fettes College, which is just outside Edinburgh.

We talked for a few minutes until I asked him whether he had got pupillage yet.

'Yes, thank goodness. Two Crown Office Row. Derry Irvine. What about you?'

For once in my life I was speechless. I was about to say something, when he was called in.

CHAPTER 6

Brief Encounter

In the spring and summer of 1976, I spent most of my non-teaching hours in Lincoln's Inn library. While everyone else took a break at lunchtime, I stayed in: reading, making notes and eating my sandwiches. Even with the money I got from the Poly, I had to eke things out and every week I would buy a loaf and a little round box of Kraft Dairylea with its six triangles of processed cheese wrapped in silver foil. I would keep them out on the windowsill and make up one sandwich every day, the cheese getting softer and softer as the summer built up to a heat wave. It was all I could afford.

Although I didn't know it at the time, my lunchtime eating habits were being watched.

'You know, Tony Blair quite fancies you,' an odd, but clever chap called Charles Harpum told me one evening as we were dining in the Great Hall – one of the obligatory twelve dinners – the only times I would have what my grandma would call a proper meal.

'How could he? I don't even know him.'

'Well, he thinks he knows you.'

A few days later I heard the same thing from Bruce Roe.

I wasn't interested. I already had a boyfriend. In fact, I had two: David in Liverpool and John in London. John knew about David but David had no idea about John. It might seem odd that a girl with my Catholic upbringing was being so flighty. But it's like contraception: most Catholics use it as much as anyone else; otherwise we'd all have families in double figures. You can always go to confession, though I have never confessed to fornication. Perhaps one day in my old age I will: 'Father, forgive me. I am trying to be sorry for it, but I still find it quite difficult!'

Nor did it seem that terrible then. We were living in different times, post the pill and pre-Aids.

The summer after Bar Finals, John and I had even managed to go away on holiday. We had a week in Corfu which, in those days, was totally unspoilt. When it was over, I went back to Liverpool and had another holiday, this time with David and my mum. My mum had become very fond of David and there was an assumption by both families, his mother included, that he and I would marry.

Over the autumn of 1975 I had given it long, hard thought. David had always planned to be a solicitor. He was now doing his Articles and was expecting me to go back to Liverpool once I'd done my Bar Finals. But if I did, then I would have to join the Northern Circuit and that would be the end of a London-based career. By this time I realised I didn't want to do criminal law so I was looking for a civil chambers. I did contact several in Liverpool, and I went to see one, but they didn't make me an offer. If they had offered me a place it would have been more difficult to turn it down, but my instinct told me that if I really wanted to do employment law I wasn't going to be able to do that in Liverpool; it would be much more general practice. In fact, I might never do any employment law at all, because when I had raised it at the interview they didn't seem to know what I was talking about. With Derry I knew that I could. It was something I knew I was good at, something that I was interested in, so I decided I would take his offer.

I finished my exams at the end of June, and the following Monday I started work with Derry. Most people didn't begin their pupillage till the results were out and they'd officially been called to the Bar – but there seemed little point in my going back to Liverpool. Why look for a job up there when I could be getting on with it down here?

Derry's chambers – as barristers' offices are called from the days when they lived in them – were in 2 Crown Office Row, a Georgian terrace in the area of London known as the Temple, between Fleet Street and the Thames. It had been bombed during the Second World War and had been rebuilt in an approximation of the original style but with the addition of a lift. There were no computers, no typewriters even, except in the clerks' rooms. In the squares outside, bat-winged barristers still flitted round and gathered in corners, carrying piles of paper tied with pink tape like parcels. Only the occasional ringing of a telephone would remind you that you were living in the twentieth century. Barristers were referred to as Mr (or in my case Miss) by the clerks, while we called them by their Christian names, even if they had been in the job all their lives and earned more money than a successful silk. The chief clerk was called David. His formidable wife Cassie would do the books – one of the few women you saw regularly around the building. There were about sixteen tenants in the chambers, of whom two were women, but their practice wasn't deemed as good as the men's because commercial solicitors – where the big money lay – would never take them seriously.

Seniority at the Bar is measured in the number of years since you were first called. Chronological age is irrelevant. Derry was a relatively junior member of chambers – probably only about eight years' call – but he was nevertheless a big player. He had started out as an academic, which was how he managed to take on two pupils, although I didn't find that out till much later.

About three weeks into July, the Bar Finals results came out and by nine o'clock I was already at the Council of Legal Education in Gray's Inn. There was a board up and people were several deep trying to find their names, which were listed alphabetically. I found Blair, A. nestling in the Third Class section, but no mention of Booth, C. at all.

I was standing there feeling bewildered – could I really have failed completely? – when Charles Harpum came up, the strange but very clever chap who had told me that Tony Blair fancied me, an 'old fogey' before the term was coined. He was a high-flyer who'd got the top First from Cambridge; not exactly a friend, but I used to dine with him in Hall quite regularly and we would talk for hours on the law.

'Well, Cherie, I must congratulate you,' he said, with an odd expression on his face.

'It would be nice if I could just find my name,' I replied.

'You don't know?'

'Know what?'

'You've come top.'

He grabbed my shoulder and propelled me towards the end board where the top names had been put. These weren't alphabetical at all. And there it was, Booth, C. The first on the list. The blood, which had previously descended into the pit of my stomach, came surging up to my face. I could feel myself going bright red. The irony was that everyone had assumed it would be Charles Harpum who'd come top. He would have fitted the pattern: public school, Cambridge etc. And now, here was me, the grammar-school girl from Liverpool and the LSE.

I ran all the way to Crown Office Row to tell Derry. Next thing he was crowing to everyone about how clever he was to have discovered this pupil who was so brilliant. Somehow or other it was his achievement. It wouldn't be the last time that somebody else's success would miraculously turn out to be Derry's.

Kudos is one thing, but for me there was a distinct practical advantage in coming top: I became the first recipient of the Ede & Ravenscroft Prize. Ede & Ravenscroft is where you get your wig and gown and, as these were an essential expense, I'd already had my head measured for my wig and been fitted for the gown, though I still had no idea how I was going to pay for them. Now I wouldn't have to, because they were my prize. In addition, I got a black and gold wig box, with my name printed in gold letters, which I certainly wouldn't have bothered buying. Also a blue bag with a drawstring with my initials embroidered in white, which was traditionally used for carrying robes, although in truth I have only ever used it for laundry.

The ceremony took place a few weeks later and David came down with my mum and my grandma. Because he was being called at the same time, John was there as well, but knowing what the situation was he kept well out of the way. I had invited my dad but there was some crisis, not entirely unexpected, and he couldn't come. In many ways I was pleased. I didn't want any unhappiness for my mum. It was all thanks to her that I had got this far.

A week or so before the swearing-in, I'd been asked to provide details as to how I'd be introduced. The form asked for father's name and occupation. I crossed it out and wrote my mother's name and occupation: I wasn't going to have her stand there and hear me being called to the Bar as the daughter of Tony Booth when actually she was the one who had made all the sacrifices. My father had done bugger all to get me to this point. The powers-that-be raised a few eyebrows, but I was insistent. So at the moment I was admitted, the voice intoned: 'Cherie Booth, daughter of Gale Booth, travel agent.'

As valedictorian I had to give the valedictory address. Traditionally, Lincoln's Inn has always taken a large number of Commonwealth students, including many who have gone on to become chief justices of their countries, so the only instruction I was given for the speech was that I acknowledge them and say how pleased we were that the link via the Common Law would continue through our generation.

My one regret was that, as valedictorian, I had to sit next to the head of Lincoln's Inn, known as the Treasurer who, at that time, was a boring circuit judge from the Old Bailey, and so I missed out on sitting next to Lord Denning, Master of the Rolls, and the most famous judge of his generation. I would love to have had the opportunity to talk to him, particularly as he was vociferously anti-women at the Bar, even though his stepdaughter Hazel Fox was herself a barrister. He wasn't the only one to think like that. It was very much the prevailing attitude.

I didn't have a holiday that year but just did my best to make myself part of the furniture in Derry's room on the first floor of 2 Crown Office Row. Derry's pupils soon learnt the meaning of the term 'devil'. It meant doing your pupil master's work for him. He would then check it, sign it and from then on it was his. Derry used all his pupils to devil.

Chris Carr, his pupil immediately before me, and one of my tutors at the LSE, devilled all Derry's commercial stuff. I did the rest. He started me out on some minor things, but once he realised that I knew my employment law, I would write his opinions for him and he would sign them off. With Derry, you wrote it all out in longhand, double-spaced, leaving big margins. He would then correct it before sending it off to be typed.

Although pupillage was only supposed to last for a year, in those days young barristers would stick around as 'squatters' until they found a tenancy. There was plenty of small case work they could do even if they didn't have a permanent place. Legal Aid was expanding then and new chambers were starting up all the time. They weren't necessarily very good chambers, but with Legal Aid you could make a living.

For all his faults, Derry was an extremely good teacher. He was very strict but he gave you one-to-one tuition, going through it word by word. He was obsessive about style and about not splitting infinitives. He kept telling me he thought I was probably dyslexic. The reason I hadn't been diagnosed, he decided, was because my handwriting was so bad nobody had noticed how atrocious my spelling was.

In order to pass off his pupils' work as his own, he needed them to clone his style. I have never forgotten what I learnt from Derry. When it came to an affidavit, for example, he told me you must never forget that you need to tell the story. The technique of pleading and the technique that I use in my opinions to this day is based on what he taught me.

While Derry's written style would serve me well, as an advocate he was distinctly aggressive – hardly the ideal template for a twenty-two-year-old lady barrister. But how, as a woman, do you develop a style in a man's world when what works for a man is regarded as inappropriate in a woman? Once I became a pupil, I saw how few women there were, and thus how difficult it was to find female role models. Most chambers still had women-need-not-apply attitudes, and, during the time I was a pupil with Derry, I never once saw a woman advocate. The perception of women barristers was almost entirely negative: there were those who had left because of children or because they had failed to build up a practice. Even after I began practising on my own, it was very rare to come up against other women except in the occasional family case. Those I did come across tended to be beginners like me.

Working with Derry wasn't all sweetness and light, however, particularly working in the same room, as only I did. He would make very offensive personal remarks – particularly in the summer when it was hot – coming into the room, and remarking: 'This room smells. I'll open the window.'

John used to tell me that I'd start shouting in my sleep: 'You can't speak to me like that.' Not that I would have dared say that to his face.

One of my friends at the LSE had been Veena Russell. She had originally trained as a ballet dancer at the Royal Ballet School but, having grown too tall, had moved to the LSE to do law at the same time as me. She was extraordinarily beautiful. Her parents were

South African Asians and they still lived in Durban. They were quite well off but weren't allowed to take money out at that time, though somehow they had managed to buy a flat in St John's Wood, where Veena lived. At the LSE she had fallen in love with a Welsh barrister and their wedding was that summer. As she had managed to get pupillage in Cardiff, the flat would be empty from September, she said. Her parents came over from time to time so it couldn't be rented out. She needed somebody to house-sit and would I be interested? Overnight my life changed. Goodbye bedsit, hello luxury – certainly by my standards. My own bathroom. And a fridge. All I had to do, she said, was pay the bills. There was a double and a single bedroom. The double was kept for Veena or her parents when they arrived from South Africa. I moved in that September.

If Veena was beautiful then her mum was exquisite. She was still only in her forties, and, when they came to stay, I would find myself just gazing at her. It was doubly shocking somehow that it was through the Russells that I first experienced racial prejudice. Veena's dad had come over on business on his own and one evening suggested he take me out to dinner.

'I know a very good restaurant in Willesden Lane,' he said.

I remember sitting on the bus together with this kind, intelligent, cultured man and then realising that everyone was giving me dirty looks. He didn't even seem to notice and then the penny dropped. They were looking at me. Here was I, a white girl, with this handsome, older Indian guy. I could feel the hatred blazing from the passengers' eyes like sparks from a ray gun in a children's comic. It was the first time I felt just an inkling of what it must be like to be discriminated against on the basis of skin colour.

To some degree, as a Catholic and a Scouser, I was used to feeling like an outsider, but my sense of apartness didn't cause people on the top of a bus to stare at me. In working-class London race prejudice was still rife. *Till Death Us Do Part* was not written in a vacuum. The character of Alf Garnett rang all too many bells – one reason it was so successful. It wasn't that long since there'd been signs up saying, 'No Blacks, No Irish, No Dogs' in boarding houses following the first wave of post-war immigration. The first Race Relations Act was passed in 1965 and then in 1976 Labour brought in a new Race Relations Act, which stopped discriminatory advertising and established the Commission for Racial Equality. But just a month or so before I was called to the Bar, there were riots at the Notting Hill Carnival, which was itself set up in the wake of the Race Riots of 1958.

My pupil master was already known as a formidable brain and an aggressive advocate. I saw this at first hand when I witnessed a clash of the titans: Derry took on a trade union case and, against him, representing the government, was Tom Bingham, then a QC, who later went on to became the Lord Chief Justice and Senior Law Lord. Although both were brilliant advocates, in their methods they were chalk and cheese. Derry was like an attacking rhinoceros. Tom Bingham, on the other hand, was like a snake, smooth, charming, almost hypnotic, who would then suddenly strike, exposing the weakness in the other side's argument without ever raising his voice. Bingham subsequently became my role model. As a woman I could never have been as aggressive an advocate as Derry Irvine. I would have been accused of being shrill, and it would certainly have put off judges, who were not sure about women in the courts anyway. But just as men like Tom Bingham could succeed at the Bar through subtlety rather than aggression, so could women advocates by developing a softer but equally effective style more in tune with the modern style of advocacy.

As befitted his heavy workload, Derry's room on the first floor was larger than most and dominated by a huge partners' desk at which he sat with the window behind him. My much smaller desk was facing him, and the wall between us, opposite the door, was lined with books. Behind the door was a table stacked high with briefs, piles of A4 paper tied with pink cotton ribbon, which he would allocate. Above my head was a large oil painting that Derry would stare at when he was thinking. He was a collector of art and to one side of his desk was a sketch of a baby given to him by the artist Philip Sutton, who drew it when Derry's first son David was born about a year before I arrived.

Sometime in October a familiar face peered round Derry's door.

'Hi,' the newcomer said, not noticing me sitting at the desk opposite the window. 'Just to say I'm here.' He was clutching an old briefcase and his hair was looking considerably longer than before.

'Ah, yes. Tony,' Derry said. Then he waved a hand vaguely in my direction. 'Cherie Booth, Tony Blair. You see, Tony, I've got two of you, and I'm afraid young Cherie here beat you to it. I'm putting you upstairs.'

And that's where he stayed.

Tony had got his pupillage in the time-honoured way of a personal introduction – how it was done then. Before a stroke ended his
career, his father had been a barrister in Newcastle and his older
brother Bill was already in practice in a more commercial set of
chambers in the Middle Temple.

It is tempting to think it was Derry's politics that attracted both
Tony and me to his chambers. He had stood for Hendon North as
the Labour Party candidate in 1970, but it was a lost cause.
Although many barristers become politicians, the Bar is curiously
apolitical in the everyday sense. The law is concerned with how
effective you are, and your standing within the profession, not what
your politics are, though there was never any doubt that I considered
myself a person who was on the side of the workers.

Inevitably, as Derry's two pupils, Tony and I spent a good deal of
time together. Apart from anything else, I needed to keep an eye
on my rival. It was unlikely that Derry would see both his pupils
accepted as tenants. I needed to persuade him that, of the two of us,
I was the better bet. Tony and I went out on cases together where
there's always a lot of hanging around, and he would regale me with
stories about his recent time in France with Bruce Roe. After Bar
Finals they'd gone to Paris and worked in a bar. Then, with the
money they'd earned, they'd gone round the Dordogne and the
Languedoc. He'd tell me about his love life. He didn't have a permanent girlfriend at the time, but I'd hear about the debby types
who had flats in Fulham and were always asking him out. There was
one girl, I remember, who kept calling him up and he wasn't that
keen. Eventually he said yes to some party she'd asked him to, and
when he got there it transpired that he was the only guest . . . As his
in-house agony aunt, what did I think it meant? In all seriousness, I
would give him advice. A girl he'd gone out with in France had got
in touch and was talking about coming to see him in London. What
did I think? He knew about my London boyfriend, as indeed did
Derry, because occasionally 'the worm', as they called him, would
turn up at chambers. Derry was particularly disapproving, but then
he was by nature proprietorial. I didn't dare tell them about my
Liverpool boyfriend.

John and I would usually go over to his flat in Blackheath.
Although it was quite far out of central London, I had a weekly bus

pass that gave you various perks. One was that at weekends a friend could go free. So that year John and I went everywhere by bus. We'd go down to Plumstead Common or right to the end of a line and explore wherever it led. That was our entertainment.

That Christmas John and his flatmate decided to do a Christmas dinner. John volunteered me as cook. Even then I enjoyed cooking, and the chance to do something properly, as opposed to frying up bacon pieces on a gas ring on a landing, was something to look forward to. The oven wasn't big enough to roast a turkey so we had chicken. I was told I could invite someone, so I thought I'd ask Tony.

It was a proper Christmas party with games. One involved putting a balloon under your chin and passing it along. As Tony didn't know any of the other guests, he'd been put next to me, and so we were doing this passing the balloon and I suddenly thought, Hang on a minute . . . I don't know what it was. Perhaps the smell of his skin, something so fleeting, a little flicker, but definitely there. Until that moment it had genuinely never crossed my mind that he was anything but a rival.

The truth, I began to realise, was that he was a very good-looking young man, tall and slim, yet broad in the shoulders. A really strong body. The short back and sides he'd had when we'd first bumped into each other had grown out into an unruly mess, and his hair curled down over his collar in a way that made me want to twist it round my fingers. As for his eyes, which I'd barely registered before, they were a clear penetrating blue, penetrating because they seemed to see right through me, to the extent that I could feel a blush rise up from some uncharted part of me and flood my face.

Towards the end of term, as it's called, Derry decided to take us out for our Christmas dinner. It wasn't an office party as such – there weren't enough of us for that – it was just Derry being Derry. He loved being expansive. The table was booked for twelve thirty at Luigi's in Soho – a favourite haunt of Derry's – one of those Italian restaurants where they had photographs of famous people on the walls. The lunch went on and on, with Derry pontificating on the state of the world. I remember four o'clock coming and going. Derry ordered another bottle – and another. Anyway, by ten thirty we were still there. A lot of drink had been drunk. The remains of the food had been taken away and there was me in the middle of these two men, one of whom – Derry – was decidedly inebriated, the other of whom – Tony – was decidedly amorous. I knew if I said it was time I went, Derry would leap up and I'd have to take a taxi with him. He lived at the top of Abbey Road, a stone's throw from me at Abercorn Place. Tired though I was, I decided to sit it out until Derry went home on his own. Eventually he did. Then Tony and I took the bus in roughly the same direction: he was living in Primrose Hill with three of his friends from Oxford. It was a double-decker and we went upstairs. It was completely empty and by the time we got off we knew each other better than when we'd got on. And even better the next morning.

The next day Tony came downstairs from the attic annexe for the usual morning conference. As chief pupil, I always sat next to Derry, while Tony sat at my desk opposite. He claims – and I don't believe this at all – that I spent the entire time winking at him.

So that left me with three men in my life. Tony knew about John but not about David. John knew about David but not about Tony, and poor David fondly imagined I was living a quiet life of hard work in dreary London, enlivened by occasional visits to Liverpool. Oh dear.

Inevitably, as the months ticked by, my thoughts turned to the chances of my getting tenancy. One of the things Derry kept repeating was that the Bar was a tough place for a woman. Also he thought that, of the two of us, I was the political animal. It was completely the reverse, as Tony was never really as committed to the law as I was. I was just much more open about my political affiliations. When I was living in Weech Road, I had joined the local (West Hampstead) Labour Party and was their nominee governor at Quinton Kynaston School. This was common knowledge in chambers. In fact Tony was already a member of the Wandsworth Labour Party but he kept it quiet. There were also pragmatic reasons for Derry going for Tony over me. Because he was focusing on commercial law, he could be more useful, as it brings in much more money than employment law, and Derry was keen to build up the commercial side of the practice. I was just the Leftie who did that other stuff. I was also naive. Ironically, I hadn't the least idea how to think politically.

There were other names in the hat as well as Tony's and mine. Not every pupil master can get their pupil accepted every year – there simply isn't the room.

Meanwhile, the politics of chambers began to hot up. While my position as chief pupil was not in dispute, being constantly in Derry's company had its disadvantages. Up on the top floor Tony was sharing a room with two junior members. This put him in a much better place to network, while I was downstairs with my nose to Derry's grindstone.

Upstairs from us – on the second floor – was another set of chambers, and up on the third floor – originally the servants' quarters, I suspect – next to where Tony worked, this other set also had an annexe. One of the junior tenants in this room was a guy Tony knew from Scotland. They had become involved – if that's the right term – over a girl called Amanda Mackenzie Stewart, the daughter of the chair of governors at Fettes. As an experiment, the governors had decided to allow one girl into the sixth form and Tony had set his cap at her. But after some behind-the-bike-sheds-style romance, she went off with this boy from another school, and that was Charlie Falconer. By the time we were all ensconced in Crown Office Row, any bad feeling between the two former rivals was forgotten and, a year or so later, when Charlie was doing well enough to buy a house in Wandsworth, Tony went to live there with him.

I liked Charlie from the beginning. He was personally disorganised in an endearing sort of way, one of those jolly people who are always smiling. If you sat down next to him at a dinner party he would get your entire life history out of you in five minutes, including all your deepest secrets, because he's charming and he's interested. He knows everything there is to know about 1960s pop, including all the words to the most obscure B-sides to singles. He couldn't really sing himself, so he'd give me the words and I'd do the singing.

I had always been the kind of girl who would put her hand up in class because I knew the answer, and I have never lost that keenness, although I know it can be very irritating to people round me. It might not have mattered in school, but it was beginning to matter now.

Tony was working on one of Derry's commercial cases. We'd gone up to do the hearing before the Master of the Rolls, Lord Denning, and I had only vaguely looked at the papers because I wasn't really involved. We were all sitting round talking about it, and I suddenly had a brainwave. 'But surely,' I chipped in, 'the answer is such-and-such.'

Then Derry said, 'Oh, that is a good idea.' And I was right. But it didn't go down terribly well with everybody else. I was just a pupil and pupils should know their place.

On another occasion Derry was conducting a case with the then head of chambers, Michael Sherrard, QC, and I sat in on a conference with the client, and Michael Sherrard said something that I knew was wrong.

So up comes Miss Know-All: 'But it isn't that!'

Michael Sherrard never forgave me, not a good situation to have with a head of chambers. Forever after, he had me down as that chit of a girl who had embarrassed him. I never intended to. It just hadn't occurred to me.

In many ways I *was* just a chit of a girl. I was twenty-two but I looked twelve. I had the waif look before it was fashionable. I hadn't got that public-school nous that the majority of my peers had, male and female. I had never been taught the meaning of the phrase 'discretion is the better part of valour'. In other words, when to keep quiet. The nuns must have mentioned it, I suppose, but I had clearly taken no notice.

It was increasingly obvious that, in terms of getting a tenancy, my major obstacle was gender: I was the wrong sex. That year only 16 per cent of those of us called to the Bar were women. The year before it had been 9 per cent and the year before, even fewer. Yes, the percentage was growing, but attitudes among senior barristers – the people who would decide who got tenancy – were not. A set book in my first year reading law was *Learning the Law* by Professor Glanville Williams, QC. In the 1973 edition he warned of the difficulties of women succeeding at the Bar. 'Practice at the Bar is a demanding task for a man,' he wrote. 'It's even more difficult for a woman. It's not easy for a young man to get up and face the court; many women find it harder still. A woman's voice does not carry as well as a man's.' His advice to young women was 'become a solicitor'.

I will never forget how, shortly after I was called, an entire robing room full of men fell silent in shock and horror when it dawned on them that I was going to go in there and change into my wig and gown along with the chaps.

In many ways Derry was no different from the rest. But he had taken me on, and he had already got considerable mileage out of having miraculously discovered the top law graduate in the country. I had also seen how he pushed his former pupils and found them tenancies. He was someone who honoured his obligations. I would have to trust to that.

CHAPTER 7

Tenancy

I have always been very protective of my sister. Our early childhood was so disjointed, and the betrayal she felt when our father disappeared from our lives hit her far more than it did me. Even though I was only two years older, I knew it was somehow more difficult for her. My friends at school accepted that wherever I went, Lyndsey went too. Having someone two years younger tagging along wasn't what girls of our age might ideally have wanted. It was as if she wasn't going to risk being separated again. When I made my first Communion, like all the little Roman Catholic girls before me down the ages and across the globe, I wore a white dress. Lyndsey was so distressed at not being part of it that my mum got her one too. Lewis's knew what our circumstances were and always let Mum have the pick of things at sale time. When Lyndsey eventually left school, no one was surprised when she decided to read law, which she did in Cardiff, at UWIST. David's sister was working there as a town planner, having just graduated from the university. Lyndsey started there in 1975 and, every so often, David and I would drive down to see our sisters.

Once both Lyndsey and I had left home, there was no further reason for our mum to stay in Ferndale Road. It's one thing living with your mother-in-law when you have no real option, but Grandma was now well into her seventies and my mum was more or less looking after her. As it turned out, she wasn't the one to make the eventual decision. One day, when my mum got back from work, Grandma made her sit down. There was something she wanted to say: 'Now, Gale, have you thought what you're going to do when I die?'

'Whatever do you mean?'

'Well, when I die, this house is going to be sold and divided between my three children, so what's going to happen to you?'

My mum says that's when alarm bells started to ring, so she called the council and applied for a flat. An assessor came round to Ferndale Road and my mum said that that night she just wept. She had suddenly seen the reality of her situation through outside eyes. She owned nothing. Nothing beyond what was in her wardrobe. Even though by this time the bed she shared with Lyndsey was sagging and everything was falling apart, Grandma hadn't let her have anything or buy anything. The only thing Grandma *had* let her buy was a television from Lewis's and, of course, she left that there when she moved out.

Because she still had one daughter in full-time education, my mum was given a two-bedroom flat in Seaforth, down by the docks in a pretty rough area, not far from the fish and chip shop where she'd worked all those years before. The flat was on the sixth floor and was actually very nice, with lovely views out across the sea. I stayed there that Christmas, but it never felt like home.

One afternoon, shortly before the New Year, the phone rang. My mum answered it then passed it to me with an odd expression.

'It's for you,' she said.

Much to my surprise it was Tony. He had vaguely suggested that, as we would both be in the north, sometime over the holiday I might go over to his father's house near Durham. Now he was calling to see what was happening. I said OK.

'Who was that?' my mum asked, accusingly. 'No one from round here, in any event. Not with that voice.'

'Tony Blair. You remember. Derry's other pupil. You met him at the ceremony.' And she had. While I'd warned John to stay well clear, I'd had no qualms about introducing Tony to her as, back then, he was only the rival.

'I don't remember.'

'Well, you did.'

'So what did he want then?'

'He wants me to go over there.'

'Where?'

'A village near Durham. Where his dad lives. His sister is there and he thought I might like to meet her. She's reading law at Oxford.'

She was definitely suspicious. I knew that David had promised to come over and help paint the flat.

'I told him I'd go.'

'I heard. Well, you know what you're doing, I suppose.'

'I'll go on my way back to London.'

'Just don't you forget, Cherie, an accent like that is as much of an accent as a Liverpool accent.'

Even though I hadn't been staying with Grandma, I'd still managed to see a lot of her that holiday. Mum's moving out had obviously upset her, even though she was the one who'd instigated the whole thing. For me, it brought back all the old confusion: the two-way pull between my grandma and my mum.

Because there was little to occupy her now in Ferndale Road, Grandma had taken to going to the chandlers on the corner and minding the shop. It sold things like disinfectant and general knick-knacks – all very cheap – so I would often stock up before going back to London.

The morning I set off for Durham I went to say goodbye to her and she came along to the chandlers where I bought a bottle of disinfectant, some cheap bleach and some toilet rolls, enough to fill a carrier bag, which I stuffed into my holdall.

All went well till I arrived at Durham, when the carrier fell out of the holdall. As if that wasn't bad enough, Tony wasn't there to meet me, and he'd promised he would be. I was so irritated that I thought I'd take a taxi and go straight there. So I got in this cab, reeking of cheap disinfectant, and gave the driver Tony's dad's address. Just as we pulled away, I saw Tony getting out of a car behind me. I was so cross that I said nothing to the taxi driver. But Tony must have seen me get in, because, as we drove along, my driver kept saying, 'There's a fella behind as keeps flashing his lights.' I told him to carry on. I thought, I've put myself out for him so he can bloody well lump it.

We both arrived at the same time. It wasn't a great start, admittedly, but at least I had the moral advantage. And he paid for the taxi.

I don't know now what I'd been expecting but the house wasn't remotely grand. In fact, they hadn't been there long. I knew a bit of the story already, and it was really tragic. When Tony was only ten his father had had a stroke. He'd been a lecturer in law at Durham University and a part-time barrister in Newcastle. He had been planning on going into full-time practice as a barrister when it happened, with a view to becoming a Tory MP. Then, a little over ten years later, Hazel – Tony's mother – had died of throat cancer. They had always talked about moving to Shincliffe village, and finally, after all the setbacks, had found this house which they really liked. But Tony's mum had never moved in, so it was all very sad.

Only a few hours before, I had been in Ferndale Road and now I was here. I surprised myself at how easy it was to move from one world to the other. Something I could never have imagined doing even a few years before.

All five of us were 'legal'. Leo, Tony's father; his brother Bill, who had a commercial practice in the Middle Temple; Tony and I, of course; and Sarah who was then at Oxford – following both her brothers – reading law, though not entirely happy with it as I soon found out. Looking at the line-up of Blairs in the kitchen, I was surprised at how tall Tony appeared in comparison with the others. He's a good six foot while both his father and Bill were almost six inches shorter, as indeed was Sarah.

She and I immediately hit it off. Leo turned out to be fairly right-wing, so he would come out with something completely outrageous. I would inevitably rise to the bait, then Sarah would join in, the pair of us taking the feminist stance. But it wasn't just women versus men. I never forgot that Tony was my rival and I was trying to counteract this effortless idea that anyone who wasn't from public school and Oxbridge didn't cut the mustard.

I can't imagine what his family made of this rather odd girl who, having stunk the kitchen out with the smell of cheap disinfectant, proceeded to harangue their father about why women are as good as men, while his sister cheered on from the touchline. My mum, having trained at RADA, had always spoken well herself, which served to temper the Scouse that was all around us – though no one could doubt that I was a northern lass. In addition, the nuns saw to it that we had elocution lessons. Those things were important if you were going to get on in life.

The moment Tony and I were back in chambers, Derry started a big case. Unusually for him, it was a criminal case concerning a huge scandal in Singapore. Derry was representing the Singapore government, who was trying to extradite a number of British businessmen to stand trial for fraud. The two key individuals involved were Jim Slater, the main protagonist, represented by a famous criminal barrister, and Dick Tarling, managing director of Slater Walker's Singapore subsidiary, represented by Michael Burton, fellow tenant of 2 Crown Office Row. The case was being heard at Horseferry Road Magistrates' Court and Tony and I obviously went along. Our job was to see that Derry had what he needed on the day, passing him the necessary papers, taking notes and the rest of it. The court was just along from the Tate Gallery, so every lunchtime Tony and I would go there, and it was then that he really began to open up.

He talked to me about his mother who had died only the previous year, just two weeks after he left university. Also about religion, which was obviously very important to him. He told me how he had been confirmed during his time at Oxford. Although the Blairs were not a church-going family, the two boys had been sent to the Chorister School attached to Durham Cathedral. His father wasn't a believer, however. Perhaps this was why Tony wasn't confirmed earlier.

At Oxford he had met an Australian priest called Peter Thomson, studying theology as a mature student. Their discussions were all about liberation theology: Christ as a radical and how it all fits in and resonates with socialism. It was exactly what had inspired those camp-fire debates with the YCS. We had both read John Robinson's *Honest to God*, for example.

Even at that very early stage in our relationship, Tony and I would spend hours talking about this kind of thing, about God and what we were here for. I don't think it would be too strong to say that it was this that drew us together. This and the fact that he had just lost his mother. He was incredibly honest and open about his feelings, which was unusual in a man at that time. He had very confirmed views on marriage, for example. He genuinely thought that two people could be together for life. Having seen what had happened to my mum, it seemed like a wonderful thing to aim for, though I wasn't sure that men were up to it. I certainly wanted it to be true, not least because I had seen for myself how damaging a wandering male can be to his family and his kids: by then my father had six daughters by three different women – those that we knew about anyway. Yet when Tony talked about love and fidelity, there was no sense that these were anything more than general conversations. He always kept me guessing in that department, which I found intriguing and not a little challenging. What I really admired was his honesty and his desire to get to the heart of things and his belief that we were here for a purpose. I loved talking to him and, on the odd occasion when we couldn't have these lunch breaks together at the Tate, I felt as if something was missing.

By now he was introducing me to his friends as his new girlfriend, and I'd be saying, 'I'm not sure I am your new girlfriend', but I liked his friends.

The house where he was living in Primrose Hill was owned by the mother of a guy he'd known at Oxford, called Marc Palley. The family was originally from Rhodesia where Marc's MP father was described by Ian Smith as a 'one-man opposition'. His mother Claire Palley was a law professor at Oxford, as vociferous as her ex-husband in terms of African emancipation and an extremely formidable woman, though not a very motherly one. Marc lived in one of the flats with his girlfriend Bina (short for Sabina), while Bina's brother Dave – who had also been at St John's – was in the flat below with Tony and another St John's friend, Martin Stanley. They were all quite posh but, surprisingly, I liked them. At the LSE I had avoided anybody like that. I can remember the first time I met Marc, and him saying to me, 'Oh, Tony's been talking about you – you're not like his usual girlfriends. He usually wears his girlfriends like a flower on his lapel.' At the time I thought this was a dig at my not being a debby type, but later I realised it was meant as a compliment, meaning that I wasn't just a pretty face.

Once his Oxford friends had given me the thumbs-up, it was the turn of his school friends. He was really wooing me now. One weekend he wanted to take me to Reading where Ian Craig – a friend he'd been with at Fettes – was reading agriculture. In order to do so, I'm afraid I told John that a friend from the LSE had been dumped by her boyfriend, so I had to spend the weekend propping her up.

It was around this time that I first met Geoff Gallop and his wife Beverley. Geoff, who would later become Premier of Western Australia, was a couple of years older than Tony, and they first met at St John's when Geoff was a Rhodes Scholar, studying PPE. He had been in the International Marxist group at the time, and it was Geoff who had introduced Tony to left-wing politics. It was also Geoff who introduced him to Peter Thomson, who had rekindled Tony's interest in theology, so he was a very important figure in Tony's life. When I met him, Geoff had just arrived back in Oxford to do a Ph.D. I was totally captivated by him. I'm a real sucker for intellectuals, and not only is he a really bright guy, he is also one of the kindest and funniest people I know.

Although John had been to Cambridge, I just didn't seem to have the same kind of conversations with his friends. By now he was even more in evidence than ever, always wanting to come to the flat, and generally being over-keen and clingy. He must have sensed I was losing interest. He certainly felt that there was something between me and my co-pupil but he didn't know what. I was beginning to feel very uncomfortable about the whole thing.

And then there was David.

The previous summer, David's sister had married her Welsh solicitor boyfriend, and it was just as you'd imagine a wedding at Blundellsands to be: morning suits, frocks, hats, the marquee, the flowers, the champagne. Already I must have known it wasn't going to work because I did everything I could to stay out of the photographs. Nothing to do with Tony – I barely knew him then – nor even to do with John; it was simply that – although compatible in so many ways – David and I disagreed politically. He was definitely a Conservative and I was definitely not a Conservative. Although we had never really talked about politics, it was a fundamental difference between us and it mattered. What made it so difficult was that I was very fond of him and we had a connection, a quite deep connection that went back a long way.

The wedding was lovely. As for David's mother, she had long forgotten my lowly origins and did her best to have me standing next to him for the photographs, while I did my best to stay out of them. By now she and I were definitely friends and I felt bad not joining in, but I'd decided it was more politic not to feature too prominently, because I didn't want to cause lasting embarrassment to the future Mrs Attwood who I knew by then wouldn't be me.

Over that Christmas I had tried to tell David, coming out with things like, 'There's no future in this.' Basically I was a coward and I didn't have the heart to do what I had to do and it didn't help that he and my mother had become so close. She'd met somebody in Canada on one of her trips abroad and had begun to think about the future – even talked about emigration – and David was now helping her get a divorce based on over five years' separation.

Then one evening, sometime that spring, out of the blue David turned up on my doorstep at Abercorn Place. I'm not sure I ever knew what prompted it, but he arrived, knocked on the door and John answered with a shoe in his hand. Mine. He was one of those breed of men who enjoys cleaning shoes. And at that point David realised that was it. He was very upset and left immediately.

My mum could barely bring herself to talk to me. David had gone back and poured out his heart to her. Not surprisingly, she was really angry, and was probably right to be. There is no doubt that I behaved very badly. I don't regret many things in my life, but I do regret how I treated David. I had known for some time that we weren't going to walk off into the sunset together, yet I couldn't find the courage to tell him. I know that he found it hard to forgive me, and I don't blame him. Fortunately, young people are resilient, and two years later David met and fell in love with a friend of my sister's, and they are now married with two daughters. I am happy to say that a few years ago David and his wife came to see us in Downing Street. So, at some level, anyway, I hope that I've been forgiven.

After this incident, of course, John thought he was in the ascendant, and it just seemed easier for him to go on thinking that. Once again, cowardice got the better of me, although the more time I spent with Tony, the less I wanted to be with John. The situation was complicated by the fact that Tony and I were still rivals, and would be until the question of tenancy was settled.

Sometime that spring Derry had asked me and Tony to dinner at his house. He didn't often ask his pupils to dinner, but I think someone else had dropped out.

Among the other guests was a painter called Euan Uglow. He was about the same age as my father. A small, wiry man with a neat moustache and a very eclectic dress sense – whatever the weather he always wore sandals, for example – but he was undoubtedly charming, intense and quietly spoken, with the manners of somebody from a previous age. He told me that he was always on the look-out for models, and would I like to sit for him? He knew enough about the Bar to know that pupils were always in need of extra cash. The standard fee, he said, was £3 an hour so I thought, Why not? It wouldn't take very long, I surmised, and I was always one for new experiences. I said OK and he said he would give me a call.

So one afternoon, when nothing very much was happening at chambers, I went along to his studio in Battersea. I had no idea when I went there that he was one of the most important figurative painters of the last half of the century. The pictures in the studio were mostly of women.

'I'm currently doing two paintings of a standing nude,' he explained. 'One is of a blonde girl and you're going to be the dark girl. Here's the one I've already started.'

The blonde girl was looking left and she was wearing practically nothing.

I was going to be facing the other way, he said, and then handed me what he called 'a blue dress' that he wanted me to wear. It had never occurred to me when he said come and sit for him, that I would be expected to pose naked. Or as good as. What could I say?

'Fine.'

The blue dress turned out to be just a piece of material he had stitched together, almost like a hip-length waistcoat. It was completely open down the middle. The pose he wanted was very straightforward. I had to have one leg out in front and the other behind, as if I had been caught in the middle of a stride.

In order to keep me still and engaged, he would put pictures of paintings he admired in front of me on another easel, then talk about them. The minuscule amount I do know about art was taught to me by Euan Uglow.

A barrister's work, particularly in the first few years, is very hit or miss, so when I didn't have anything on, I'd ring up and say, 'Can you fit me in?', and then I'd go round to his studio. Or I might be at the magistrates court just down the road in the morning and, when that was finished, pop over to the studio where he'd give me lunch and talk about what he was doing and why, about the system of plumb lines he used, and how the light changed, and its effect on my skin and my stomach, and how he saw the different colours. Over the many months I posed for him, we became very fond of each other. Neither of us had much money so we agreed to make each other Christmas presents. I gave him two tea cosies which I religiously knitted in two very different patterns. He, in turn, made me

Mum and me in the park at the end of our road in Waterloo. My dad took the picture.

1960. A St Edmund's school photo. Grandma had a thing about bows, the fancier the better as far as she was concerned.

My parents met on tour with a small theatre company. Here the two young ingenues star in *The Princess and the Swineherd*.

Lyndsey (centre) and me with Mum, Grandma and Grandad on holiday at Butlins, Pwllheli. Until we started going abroad, Mum rarely managed to escape her parents-in-law.

1961. My first Communion. Lyndsey hated to be left out, so she was dressed the same.

The back garden at 15 Ferndale Road with our cousins. Lyndsey with Robert, Christopher next to me and Catherine swamped by our poodle Quinn.

A rare trip back to my old school, aged fourteen, in Girl Guide uniform. I'd been asked to help out at the church fête.

Tony and me in Crown Office Row, the chambers in which we were both pupils.

Christmas 1979 with Lyndsey and my mum at her house in Oxford, a few months before our wedding.

The happy couple, even more windswept than usual.

Classic photo of the bride's family: Auntie Audrey, Uncle Bob, Mum, Lyndsey –
Tony and me – my grandma, Uncle Bill and my cousin Catherine.

May 1982. The candidate for Beaconsfield, his wife and the campaign team. A lost cause from the start.

January 1984. Picture taken for the local paper only hours after Euan's birth. I managed a smile thanks to a rubber ring.

France, August 1994. Our trip to persuade Alastair to join Tony's team. From left: Neil Kinnock, Tony pushing Grace (Campbell), Alastair with Rory, and Glenys with Kathryn.

Peter Mandelson, Euan, Nicky and Tony with Kathryn. Peter was a regular visitor to our house in Richmond Crescent.

Tony and Euan climbing in the Pyrenees – something we did every summer when staying at Maggie Rae's house in France.

Kathryn, Tony and me on the stairs at Myrobella. My first experience of publicity – this accompanied the profile by Barbara Amiel.

Nicky and me on holiday in France.

a miniature lectern with a marble base. It was too heavy to take to court, but I still have it.

I really loved him. He was such a gentle, intelligent man with a lovely smile. After about eighteen months – or even two years – I realised that I just didn't have the time to continue. Also Tony had begun to query why I was spending quite so much time with this man . . .

I found it really hard to tell Euan that I had to stop, but in the end I said that I didn't feel it was fair on him. I was thinking, He makes his living like this, and he's wasting time on me when actually he could be doing a painting of somebody else. He told me not to worry and that he'd get another dark model to take my place. He had never got round to doing my face, though you can still see it's me. I think he did try to get a replacement, but it didn't work out, so he decided to leave my painting unfinished. It still exists somewhere, but where I don't know. I would love to have it, of course, but his paintings are very valuable, even more so now that he's no longer alive. He died in 2000 and I was very proud to go to his memorial service.

During the first few sessions I remember standing there, desperately trying to hold the pose and thinking, What on earth am I doing this for? But at the same time it went through my head that one day I might want my children to know that I wasn't such a dull-o, bluestocking, goody-two-shoes after all.

In all the time I was going to Battersea to model for Euan, Tony never knew that I was posing nude. I certainly never told him. There came a point when I think Derry hinted at it. Possibly Derry had seen it as a work in progress. I don't know. Either way, Tony was very uncomfortable with it. He still is.

Meanwhile, the business of what was to happen when my pupillage came to an end was like a nagging headache that, no matter how many aspirin you take, won't go away. A set of chambers is a bit like a family. Different members have different roles and contribute in different ways. The tenants doing commercial work were earning huge amounts of money, a percentage of which they would pay as 'rent'. Given that their financial contribution was higher than anyone else's, they wanted more of a say about who came in. On the other hand, those doing crime and family law were saying, 'We're providing a good service. You commercial boys are forever insisting we take on your pupils and yet we also need people to do our work, and the people who come via you don't want to do our work.'

So that spring of 1977 there was an internal power struggle going on in 2 Crown Office Row. The last four or five pupils who'd been taken on had all been Derry's, and Michael Burton, who had a highly paid commercial practice, was saying that it was his turn now. Like Derry, he was an up-and-coming junior who would take silk very shortly, so some of it was him simply flexing his muscles.

One evening in late spring Derry took me out for a drink and said that, in his view, he couldn't get both Tony and me taken on and that obviously, since one of us was a girl, it would be easier to get the boy taken on. Not that he could guarantee Tony would get it either, because Michael Burton was pushing hard for his pupil, he said, but at least Tony would stand a better chance. As for me, what he proposed was to find me somewhere else.

Of course I was hurt. It was the first time I had ever been discriminated against because of my gender and it was hard to accept that I was being pushed out simply because I wore a skirt. But at the time I just thought 'that's life'. I wasn't on a crusade.

He put me in touch with Freddie Reynold, whose chambers were in 5 Essex Court. As luck would have it, Freddie and I got on instantly. He came from a family of immigrant German Jews and was about the same age as Derry, whom he had got to know through doing work for the same trade union solicitors that Derry worked for. Freddie himself did a lot of trade union work, which was another reason Derry probably thought the arrangement might work – he had me down as a committed Leftie. Of course, tenancy was not in Freddie's gift. The decision would ultimately rest with the head of chambers. But David McNeil, QC, was somewhere in the north of England . . . So Freddie basically said yes.

When Chris Carr heard what had happened, he couldn't believe it.

'Listen, Cherie. You are much better qualified than Tony. You are mad even to think about moving. You must stay on and fight for your place, because you deserve a place.'

Maybe. But then there was the whole romantic complication, which neither Chris nor anybody else in chambers knew about. Although I wasn't about to admit it even to myself, the truth was that I was in love with my witty, charming yet vulnerable rival and the last thing I wanted was to jeopardise that, even subconsciously.

As for the battle of 2 Crown Office Row, in the end Michael Burton didn't get his pupil taken on, while Derry, the more senior, got his nominee, that is, Tony.

Chris Carr gave me the right advice really: I should have stayed and fought. But I could so easily not have got tenancy. Then what would I have done? Hung around like the other squatters for another six months, and then another six, living on whatever crumbs Derry and others decided to throw my way? Put Tony into the equation and it was a real mess. At least once Freddie had said yes, then I was a tenant. A tenancy in those days meant you were there for life. In the end, of course, I didn't stay in Essex Court for life, but I was in. I knew where I was, and I could start dealing with my debts and generally begin making a contribution to my family.

Lyndsey was in her last year at Cardiff and had applied to do her solicitors' exams at the College of Law in Chester. This was deemed a post-graduate qualification and Lancashire County Council had just stopped giving discretionary grants, so we had to find another way for Lyndsey to pay her fees. Now that I was a tenant I could borrow money, so I could I help her, and that's what I did.

CHAPTER 8

Romance

Moving from 2 Crown Office Row into 5 Essex Court was like going backwards in time. The lower floors had generous-sized rooms but the upper floors were pure servants' quarters, all creaking floors and ill-fitting windows. In other words, nothing much had changed since it was first built. The wards in Jarndyce would certainly have recognised it and Mr Tulkinghorn would have felt quite at home. We even had gas lamps outside which were lit every night by the porters in the Inn. I had a room in the annexe which I shared with Malcolm Knott, a former solicitor who had come to the Bar after having his own firm in north London. He was meticulously tidy and I was not, but he put up with me, even selling me his own small Victorian writing desk and buying himself another larger version.

So there I was, twenty-two years old, no longer anybody's pupil, but a tenant in my own right, able to take my own cases and give opinions under my own name. I may not have been the lowest of the low (a pupil) but I was at the very bottom of the chambers' ladder nonetheless. On the top rungs are the silks (QCs) then come junior barristers of many years' call, descending to the likes of me. In those days the head of chambers was not elected – he was simply the most senior silk. Judges have to leave once they are appointed to the Bench – which is how room is made lower down the ladder for new tenants.

Like any young barrister, my work came primarily through the clerk who, in those days, operated much like an agent, taking 10 per cent of each fee – a fee which he would also negotiate. Solicitors would go to a particular set of chambers because they offered the expertise they sought for that particular case. As always at the English Bar, the cab-rank system applied. Then as now. If the requested barrister can't do the job, it's passed on to somebody who can (usually lower in the hierarchy) within the same set of chambers. This cab-rank system also dictates that you can't turn down a case because you don't like the look of it, whether it offends your politics or your sensibilities – like rape, for example. You can only turn down a case if you are otherwise engaged. There are no exceptions. In this way a young barrister builds up a practice by taking on cases that somebody else can't do and, of course, broadening his or her experience in the process. I was very lucky. The most junior tenant until I came along was a talented advocate called Charles Howard – now a family law QC – who was already building up a good practice among the burgeoning group of left-inclined legal-aid solicitors. Charles and I became firm friends and, when he was not available, he would recommend me, and in that way my practice too began to develop.

Number 5 Essex Court was unusual in that the majority of its silks – its high earners whose income basically kept chambers going – were based in Manchester and Liverpool and hardly ever came down to London. The entire set-up had been masterminded by the chief clerk, Ronnie Lynch. He was of the old school with a real eye for talent. Freddie Reynold and Alastair Hill had been the first two London-based juniors to join. Freddie was of the same generation as Derry and, like Derry, soon after I arrived, he took silk himself. As the other juniors were mainly doing general common law, Freddie had felt he needed help with his trade union clients, which is to say employment law, so I suited him perfectly. By the time I joined there were about twelve juniors of different calls, and about five or six northern silks, most of whom we barely saw, but all of whom were class acts. The most well known of these was George Carman, who first came to national prominence in 1979 when he successfully defended Jeremy Thorpe, the leader of the Liberal Party, on a charge of murder and then became famous as a libel lawyer, known for his celebrity clients.

Needless to say, I was the only woman.

In practical terms I was living on what the barristers above me couldn't do, so I had essentially a general common law practice in which I'd do crime, family law and personal injuries, as well as any employment law passed on by Freddie. Meanwhile, I continued to work as a devil for Derry. Devilling is quite an accepted practice at the Bar, so I made a reasonable income being Alexander Irvine and giving opinions in employment law. From time to time Derry would introduce me to the solicitors who had instructed him and sometimes they would send me small work on my own account. This was how I managed to maintain my employment law connections, though not as well as if I'd stayed on at 2 Crown Office Row.

In the main I did very lowly stuff. The first case I did was a bail application at Bow Street. I was ill-prepared; there were no papers. I was simply instructed to appear and ask for bail. 'Counsel will do their best' was the basic instruction in those days.

So I turn up, get there at ten o'clock, and am standing outside the court and everyone is milling about, as they do. There are dozens of cases listed every day. There are defendants, witnesses, barristers, solicitors and everyone in between. They all look much the same – solicitors in suits, barristers in gowns, even the defendants and witnesses are in their Sunday best. And there am I calling out my client's name: Mr Bloggs? Going up to likely looking strangers who still seem to be unattached. Then it suddenly occurred to me: Mr Bloggs is not going to be standing outside the court because he's getting a bail application, which means he's in the cells.

So I hurtle down the stairs, and get to the door just in time for them to call Mr Bloggs up for his bail application. I can't remember now whether he did or did not get bail, but it was nearly a complete disaster. I could still have been standing there. On another occasion, early in my career, I had a guilty plea, this time at Highbury Corner Magistrates' Court. Despite my impassioned eloquence that he be given a second chance, my client was sentenced to imprisonment and on his being sent down into the cells, I went down with him because that's what you do. The sentence was lenient, so I had to tell him that it wasn't too bad really. After saying goodbye, I went into what I thought was the lift. I pressed the button to go up and when it stopped, got out, looked round and realised that I wasn't where I had expected to be. I was in a room with two doors on either side and nothing else. Behind me the lift door closed and I heard it rumble back down again. At the same moment everything went black.

I had no idea where I was and could see nothing. First I groped round the sides of the lift, looking for a button. Nothing. I groped round the room, looking for a light switch. Anything. Then I started banging, on the walls, on the lift door, shouting. And I remember thinking, I'm going to die! They are going to find my body and my mum will be so upset . . . They'd find this skeleton in the corner, identifiable only by her briefcase. A promising career tragically ended.

Suddenly I heard the lift rumbling up again. The doors opened and I practically fell into the arms of two court officials.

'Now then,' said one. 'You're all right, Miss. Got yourself trapped between court one and court two, that's all. You were making such a racket up here, they had to suspend the sitting in court two!'

Having got me back down to the cells, I then had to make a grovelling apology to the magistrates, before sneaking ignominiously away.

The lift I had taken was the prisoners' lift and I'd ended up in a holding room between the two courts. Obviously these doors were kept locked, with only prison officers having the keys into the dock.

As 5 Essex Court was in the Middle Temple, we would generally eat in Middle Temple Hall and use the Middle Temple library, whereas in Crown Office Row they tended to go to Inner Temple and use the library there. Yet somehow or other Tony kept coming to the Middle Temple library, whereas I started avoiding the Inner Temple library where boyfriend John would often be found. Also, because I was still devilling for Derry, I would regularly find myself going back to Crown Office Row.

As far as Essex Court was concerned, John was my boyfriend. John, meanwhile, was always aware that Tony was around. He knew that we sometimes went out, but he didn't know how far the going out went and he was very keen that the going out stopped.

One Saturday afternoon John was round at Veena's flat. It must have been sometime in October. Suddenly there was a knock on the door. The flat was on the fifth floor of a thirties block, so whoever it was had taken the lift up then walked down the corridor.

I don't remember what I was doing. I just remember the knock on the door, and a voice saying, 'It's me.'

Tony.

I remember watching as John walked over and looked through the spy hole. Next I heard the click of the lock as he turned the key. Not to open it, to lock it. I remember looking at him aghast. He was leaning on the door and had his head in his hands. Somehow it was terrible.

The knocking continued. John shouted at him to get lost, but Tony wasn't budging. If he hadn't known it before, he knew now that John was there. He knew that I would never turn a lock against him.

'Cherie? What's going on? Just let me in. I promise you that whatever else happens, I will never keep you against your will.'

This was my home. It may not have been my flat, but it was my home.

So I thought, OK. I got up and walked to the door, turned the key and opened it. Tony, his eyes blazing, came in.

'Right,' said John immediately. 'You've made your choice. I'm off.' And he picked up his bag and left.

There was no showdown. No saying you must choose one or other of us. John had never been one for the melodramatic. He was always calm. In fact, they both were.

But he was right. I had made my choice.

John should have been the more comfortable choice for me because he was a comprehensive-school boy, and he was clever and kind and all those sorts of things, but I was probably the dominant one in the relationship.

I was not the dominant one in my relationship with Tony. There was no way that Tony was going to be dominated by me, but nor was I necessarily going to be dominated by him. It was much more of an equal thing, so much more challenging.

My friend Felicity always says, 'You can see why Tony wanted Cherie, but we're not quite sure why Cherie agreed to take Tony!' Perhaps she considered that he needed a working-class girl to give him working-class credibility. But she couldn't understand why I needed a charming public-school boy when my principles were so clearly to the left.

Politics and religion certainly played a part. John wasn't interested in politics although he would have described himself as left of centre. David was far from left of centre, but he was a Catholic. He would have represented the safe choice, of going back to my home town and doing OK, but never really being able to spread my wings. Tony might not have been Catholic, but religion was more important to him than to anyone I had ever met outside the priesthood. In terms of politics, we might not always have agreed on the details, but we were never that far apart.

Over the years I have thought about what made me choose Tony. It was partly chemistry – I fancied him rotten, and still do – but partly because I thought even then that he had something. Behind the charm there was a steely quality to him. Frankly, he fascinated me as I had never met anybody quite like him before, not somebody who could give me a run for my money.

Life with the others would have been easier, but in the end not so challenging. Foolish girl – to think how simple my life could have been . . .

There turned out to be a curious symmetry between Tony's family history and mine. His paternal grandparents were actors – in this case music-hall performers – who met on tour in the north of England. In 1923, in Yorkshire, a son was born: Tony's dad. A week or so later they arrived in Scotland and decided – no doubt for all the right reasons, just like my parents – that the life of a travelling player was no life for a baby – particularly, in their case, one born out of wedlock. So their baby was fostered out to a Glaswegian electrician and his wife, James and Mary Blair. The little boy's parentage was acknowledged in his new name: Leo Charles Lynton Blair. Charles for his father (born Charles Parsons) and Lynton for his father's stage name, Jimmy Lynton – which strikes me as a bit hard on his mother, who got precious little thanks for her contribution. For the record, her name was Mary Wilson, née Bridson, stage name Celia Ridgeway. When Tony was christened he inherited those same two middle names. Although Leo's birth parents eventually married and desperately wanted their only son back, Mary Blair refused to relinquish her clearly much-loved adopted child. If you're looking for a parallel there, think no further than my grandmother.

Another thing Tony and I have in common is ambition. We are both driven. It has been suggested that Tony needed to accomplish what his father couldn't as a result of his stroke. I certainly felt the need to make it up to my mum and grandma for their disappointments. My mum's father, Grandad Jack, had extraordinary ability, but he was born in the wrong place at the wrong time. As for my dad, for all his charm, wit and innate intelligence, he didn't really do his mother proud. Not that she wasn't proud of him. On the contrary, she was immensely proud of him. And with reason: he was a very talented actor. Sadly though, he never really reached his potential. Perhaps his charm was his undoing. In a sense, Tony is charming like my dad. But in the end, Tony has the steel my dad lacked.

Did I see in Tony the man my dad might have been if he'd had that steel? No. That person is me. As my dad always says, 'My mother will never be dead as long as you're alive.'

My mum never got to Canada – the romance fizzled out. In November 1977 she moved down to Oxford. The travel bureau of Selfridges' Oxford branch was in some kind of trouble and head office asked her to sort it out and then take over the management. When I was at the LSE she had been brought in to troubleshoot at Selfridges in London and they had offered her Oxford then, but she'd turned it down. Lyndsey was still at school; Mum had left a daughter once and she wasn't about to do it again. Only now, with both of us having left home, and Lyndsey set to come to London to do her Articles, did she feel she could think of herself. It would be a promotion – at Lewis's in Liverpool she was deputy manager – and with the increase in salary it also meant she could buy a small house. As she said to me at the time, 'Well, I either stay in Liverpool for the rest of my life or I take this one chance to move nearer you and make a better life for myself.'

She kept the Seaforth flat on for a few months so that Lyndsey had somewhere to go at weekends from Chester, but basically she said goodbye to Crosby where she had lived for over half her life. Lyndsey had made it clear she wasn't planning to stay in the north, and so with both of us in London, it made sense to move south. With us both on our way, she could finally get herself some sort of financial security. God knows she'd waited long enough.

In the spring of 1978, her finals over, Lyndsey came down to London. Through one of the trade union firms of solicitors Derry had introduced me to I was able to help get my sister an articled clerkship. It didn't pay much, but thanks to Veena's flat, she could stay in Abercorn Place for nothing.

Late one evening, shortly before Derry took silk that Easter,

Lyndsey and I were in the flat when who turns up at the door but my former pupil master. He'd quite often drop in on the way home, Abercorn Place being only a few yards off his route. On this occasion he was very drunk.

'For God's sake,' he slurred, 'you've got no drink in this place!' I could hear him in the kitchen poking round in the fridge and anywhere else he could think of. He was right, we hadn't. Good, that meant he would soon go. But then disaster.

'Aha! What's this? Oooh, yes. Very nice. Thought you could fool old Derry, did you?' For a moment I couldn't think what he was talking about and then I remembered. Oh no.

A year before, at the dinner party at Derry's where I'd met Euan Uglow, Tony and Euan had had a bet. Something about Fauvism. Tony turned out to have been right, and he had won this exceptionally good, exceptionally old, exceptionally expensive bottle of wine. There had never been an occasion special enough to drink it, so I'd been looking after it all this time. I had put it in the broom cupboard, not to hide it but simply because it was the coolest place in the flat.

I jumped up from the settee, but it was too late. By the time I got to the kitchen, I'd heard the squeak and pop of the cork and he was pouring it out, heading back towards his 'Liverpool lovelies'.

Lyndsey and I were by now hysterical. The flat was small and Derry was big, blundering unsteadily round the place. The phone was in the hall on a long lead so my sister and I shut ourselves in the bathroom and called Tony, who was only just down the road in Primrose Hill.

'It's Derry,' I said. 'You've got to come and do something. He's appallingly drunk. Please just take him home. We can't get rid of him. He's marauding!' I didn't dare tell him about the precious wine.

Within five minutes Tony had arrived. Derry in the meantime was thankfully nearly comatose. Tony came in, clearly not really believing the situation was as bad as I had made out, but then stopped short when he caught sight of the corpulent form spreadeagled across the settee. What horrified him most, though, was when he saw the familiar bottle, a bottle he'd been salivating over for the best part of a year. He led Derry away like a farmer with a sated bull. If the same thing happened now, I wouldn't be so kind. As it was, I wanted to keep Derry sweet, not least because he was providing me with work.

The next day it was business as usual. Derry was a phenomenon. He was a big man and could drink a vast amount but after only a few hours' sleep he'd be up at six o'clock with his brain absolutely sharp.

Now that my mum was in Oxford, getting to see her was much easier. Realising it would take time for her to get to know people and build up her own circle of friends, Tony and I used to go up most weekends. She had bought a little terraced house just off the Iffley Road, but it had two bedrooms, so was perfect. It seems strange now, but the first friends my mum made in Oxford were Geoff and Beverley Gallop, and we would always meet up with them. They were living in a small flat in North Oxford and we became like a little family. Geoff was doing his Ph.D. at Nuffield College. His wife Beverley had been a teacher in Australia and later became a very successful potter. As Gale was only twenty years older than me, the age difference was never an issue. In spite of the David complication, my mum and Tony got on right from the start and in a way, from his point of view, she became a substitute mother. To her, Tony was still a boy.

I was finally beginning to realise how hard it must have been for her, living all those years under the same roof as her mother-in-law. There was a relative of Grandma's, a chauffeur whose employers lived in the north-west, and sometimes he would take us out in his car for long weekends. I remember a trip to Scotland when I was about nine and my sister was seven. Looking back there was obviously something going on between them, and he was a nice man, but Lyndsey and I were not terrifically encouraging, to put it mildly. Mum never complained, however, and, as a result, it was only much later I realised what a brake we had been on her love life.

Whenever Veena's parents came to London, Lyndsey would move out and stay with Charlie Falconer in the house he'd recently bought in Wandsworth. When he'd gone to view it, one of the things Charlie had liked was the little garden. 'This will be lovely for breakfast in the morning,' he said to the woman showing him round. He remembers that she looked at him strangely, but he didn't think any more of it. In fact, this house was just under the railway arches, directly beneath the main flight path to Heathrow and bang next to the underpass/roundabout/dual carriageway. You could never go out in that garden.

Once Charlie and Tony began sharing, I got to know the house quite well, and with it their domestic habits. When it came to basic housework, they were a disgrace. Slobs, the pair of them. I used to spend my entire time – as did Lyndsey when she was there – cleaning up, changing the sheets on the beds, not to mention the bathroom. I seemed always to be cleaning the toilet. You would arrive to find your feet sticking to the kitchen floor because it was so dirty. So the first thing I'd have to do was get down on my hands and knees and scrub.

That summer, Geoff, Bev, Tony and I went on holiday together to Brittany. Unlike me, Tony hated flying, and since Bev was newly pregnant, we went on the ferry. This venture required a car and Tony had this idea that he would like a Morris Minor, and he managed to find one through an ad in a local newspaper. Then after only two weeks, it just collapsed – completely packed up. Tony was absolutely furious. It was perfectly clear he'd been sold a dud, so he went back to the chap he'd bought it from and basically threatened him with legal action if he didn't give him his money back. He thought he was about to get into fisticuffs until he had the presence of mind to say, 'I'm a barrister', and the chap paid up. Luckily, one of my colleagues in Essex Court was selling his old Beetle, so Tony bought that instead.

As my mum had never learnt to drive, we'd always gone on package holidays to resorts, so this freewheeling was a totally new experience and I loved it. Only when it came to map-reading did the atmosphere deteriorate. Tony was quite used to this piling-everything-into-the-car kind of holiday. His mother had come from Ballyshannon in the Irish Republic so, when he was a boy, they'd gone every summer to his mother's family's place. Then, when the Troubles began, they switched to France.

All in all, we had a great time and that holiday consolidated a friendship with the Gallops that would continue on down the years, with Tony and me becoming Tom's (Bev's bump) surrogate godparents. Although it was Geoff who had introduced Tony to Peter Thomson, he and Bev were not religious themselves, so their children weren't actually christened.

That first summer we just followed the coast. Bev's pregnancy wasn't proving easy and my overriding memory is of inspecting the toilets at the various places we stayed at to ensure they were fit enough for her to be sick in. I also had my first experience of oysters.

We marvelled at the standing stones at Carnac: rows and rows of them – over 3,000 in all. And the swimming: from little coves to great sweeping Atlantic beaches of yellow sand. Not so different from Crosby, bar the temperature. At Nantes we turned the Beetle inland and headed down the Loire Valley.

Tony and I were now definitely an item. When he introduced me as his girlfriend, I no longer made a face and I would go to chambers' do's as a chambers 'spouse'. In spite of my fears that he would take umbrage, in the end Derry was fine about it.

The following September we drove to Italy. Tom Gallop had been born, so this time it was just the two of us. Love and marriage were definitely in the air. Marc and Bina had tied the knot with Tony as best man. Everyone said his speech was the best that summer. Like many other young barristers, we both worked in August: with everyone else away, it was a good time to pick up work. We started off in Calais and then made our way right down through France and Switzerland to Italy, to Chianti country, where we had rented the bottom half of a villa. The pale blue Beetle had survived the year but only just, and I can remember us trying to get up St Bernard's Pass, where it felt we were virtually pedalling, and just about making it to the top. In those days, the Michelin Guide had a category called 'Good Food at Reasonable Prices', marked on the map with a red R, and we would plan our route following the red Rs religiously.

Until he met me, Tony's debby girlfriends had all picked at their food. To go out with a girl who enjoyed her food was a real eye-opener.

'It's probably a class thing,' he said.

What did he expect? I mean, here was I, a working-class girl and we'd paid money for this food, so I was jolly well going to eat it. The idea of picking at a few leaves in a lady-like fashion verged on the criminal to me.

Derry, too, liked to see a girl enjoy herself, and when he was feeling expansive he would take us out to incredibly smart places, like Le Gavroche. He also introduced us to El Vino's, the celebrated drinking haunt of barristers and journalists on Fleet Street. It was incredibly expensive, so the only time I ever drank there was when Derry bought us drinks.

Enjoying eating is only a step away from enjoying cooking, and renting a villa meant I could buy food from the markets. Although I enjoyed cooking in London, in the seventies it was difficult even to get garlic, let alone the aubergines and peppers piled up in Siena. The pages of the notebook I kept that summer have as many descriptions of meals as they have of churches and architecture.

The two weeks ended all too soon, and the last morning I was up early, scrubbing the floors and generally leaving the villa as I would hope to find it. Naturally, Tony was nowhere to be seen. My last task, inevitably, was the toilet.

So there I am, on my knees, cleaning the toilet and Tony comes up behind me.

'You know, Cherie, I think maybe we should get married.'

Reader, I said yes.

CHAPTER 9

Marriage

Since early that summer I had no longer been living in Veena's flat. Her parents needed it back. Having lived in luxury for two years rent-free I could hardly complain.

The Bar is the ultimate non-linear networking web, with each set of chambers acting as its own mini hub. Whatever the requirement, chambers is always the best place to start, and so it proved in this case. A former pupil, I was told, had just bought a house in Hackney and was looking for someone to help pay the mortgage.

I already knew Maggie Rae in a professional capacity. Following her pupillage, she had gone off and become a barrister in Tony Gifford's chambers. This was an experiment in radical chic, one of the first chambers set up outside the Inns of Court, opposite the County Court in Lambeth. Once there she decided that the Bar wasn't for her and had retrained as a solicitor. The radical chambers experiment didn't quite work out either: Lambeth was just too far away from the clerks' network, so they moved to Covent Garden. Now qualified, she was a partner in the left-leaning firm of Hodge, Jones and Allan, who regularly sent family law work to Charles Howard in our chambers, which is how I'd started doing work for Maggie.

The house she had just bought was in Wilton Way, Hackney – one street north of London Fields, the only patch of green in the area. I had never been that far east before, and West Hampstead and St John's

Wood (even Blackheath and Wandsworth) were like Mayfair in comparison. The area hadn't always been so run down, as could be seen from the houses themselves, many of which were Georgian. Streets were both wide and wide apart giving generous gardens. Hackney's proximity to the City, however, had seen it heavily bombed in the Second World War and where the bomb sites had been filled in at all, it was with poor-quality housing and tower blocks.

Maggie's house was a complete wreck – in fact, the whole front wall was missing. It had previously been divided into bedsits and the only heating was a gas cooker on the top floor (my bedroom) in what had been a kitchenette. So there we'd be, up in my bedroom, the front wall covered with a tarpaulin and the door of the oven wide open with us huddled round it.

She was heavily into do-it-yourself and every free moment I was there with the sandpaper – from floors to doors to skirting boards. Tony got involved as little as possible; he has many fine qualities but DIY is not among them. Maggie had even constructed her own bed, admittedly from a kit, and persuaded me to do the same. This time I did enlist Tony's help; he would, after all, benefit personally. The result was totally hopeless. Not only was it wonky but it tended to collapse at just the wrong moment. Building that bed had one single advantage: we learnt very early on that DIY wasn't for us and when it came to looking for a house of our own, wrecks were out.

During the long drive back from Siena, my head had been full of plans for the future. Tony's proposal might have been a little unusual – definitely the wrong person on their knees – but I hadn't needed to think about my answer. We were best friends and lovers, surely the ultimate combination for a happy and successful marriage. And between us there was a constantly changing dynamic and I knew that life with Tony would never be boring. What more could a girl ask for?

Possibly a ring. But then I have always hated my fingers and Tony felt we should put everything we had into a house. There was just one thing he wanted to be sure of, he said, as we drove the Beetle off the ferry at Dover.

'What's that, my darling?' I asked, giving his knee a squeeze. Could he want me to tell him how much I loved him yet again . . .

'Promise me you won't say anything to anyone.'

I remember sitting there and thinking, What? Instead I said, 'I see.'

'Nothing to worry about. I just think we need to be sensible about how we handle it, that's all.'

As in, just-in-case-I-change-my-mind . . . My little balloon of happiness instantly deflated.

He did agree that we could tell my mother, and the first weekend we were back we drove up to Oxford to see her. Even then my husband-to-be pulled his punches, talking at some length around us buying a house. My mum, being very liberal-minded, thought he was saying, 'Cherie and I are going to move in together.' Only later, when Tony suggested buying a bottle of champagne, did the penny drop.

'You mean you're getting married?' she said. Up till then, the M word hadn't quite crossed his lips.

What really worried Tony was Derry. If he disapproved, it could have really negative consequences, he said. It was never a question of 'if', as far as I was concerned. Of course Derry would disapprove. He'd always had a *droit-de-seigneur* attitude towards me, though naturally he didn't put it like that.

'You're much too young to get married,' Derry said, to no one's surprise, when Tony eventually told him. 'Don't do it.'

Paradoxically it was Derry who made it possible, at least from a financial perspective. He brought Tony into a case to do with the Bank of Oman. For the next few months he was always popping back and forth to the Gulf. It was a nice earner, and it brought him in his first really big fee so we were able to start looking for a house.

My personal worry was closer to home. How would my mother react to my father giving me away? Unlike being called to the Bar, there were no precedents for one's mother walking up the aisle . . . For the time being it was an insoluble problem.

One morning early in November, I was at home, vaguely listening to Capital Radio, getting ready to leave for chambers, when I suddenly heard my father's name.

'Tony Booth, the *Till Death Us Do Part* actor, is in hospital after being severely burnt in a fire at his home. The other occupants of the building were unharmed.'

My first thought was to call Susie, though I hadn't seen her or my father in months. She was very angry. He'd been taken to Mount Vernon hospital, she said. Beyond that all I got was: 'drunk . . . locked him out . . . tried to burn the place down . . . may he rot in hell.'

I then called Mount Vernon. I should try to come in as soon as possible was all they would say.

I went on my own. I had nothing on that morning and Lyndsey had to go to work. In any event, her feelings towards the man who had betrayed her were still not good.

Northwood, the nearest underground to Mount Vernon, is four stops beyond Harrow on the Metropolitan Line. There are no tubes in Hackney, so I took a bus to Liverpool Street and from there it was direct but slow. At Northwood another bus to the hospital. The journey took over two hours.

My father tells a complicated story of what actually happened the previous night. It involves the SAS, counter-espionage, the IRA and a botched assassination attempt for good measure. Two SAS operatives, he claims (whom he met in a pub, naturally), helped him break into his own house by climbing on two paraffin drums to access a trapdoor to the loft. They then decided it would be easier to set fire to the front door, so they put a torch to the paraffin which subsequently exploded, and flames then engulfed him. I've never bought that version of events and, strange to relate, the two key witnesses have never materialised. Some facts are indisputable, however. He was certainly locked out of the flat; he was certainly burnt; and he was certainly very, very drunk.

I knew the layout of the house from babysitting. His flat was on the top floor of a pre-war mansion-house block. Opposite his front door was a box room where, among other things, he kept spare paraffin for the heater. He must have climbed up on the drum to access the trapdoor to the loft. Once there he could move about above the rafters and climb down through his own trapdoor. He had done it before. My dad was a heavy smoker and, on this occasion, insensible. Add paraffin into the mix and what happened is not surprising. In all likelihood, he had a cigarette in his hand. As he was hauling himself up into the trapdoor, it fell on to the paraffin drum – probably covered with spilt paraffin – and set it alight. It then exploded and he fell feet-first into a furnace of flame.

Apart from his feet and lower legs, the worst burns were on his hands. Even *in extremis* my dad knew what his most precious asset was, and his first instinct was to protect it. I know that's what he did, because over the months I subsequently visited him it became an obsession. When I first saw him he was in a terrible state. His hands were encased in what looked like plastic bags and he was rambling.

One of the nurses changed me a £1 note for some coins, and I called my grandma from the pay phone in reception. He wasn't as bad as I'd expected, I told her. It was a lie. I couldn't bear to tell her the truth. Just hearing her voice was enough to bring tears to my eyes, in a way that seeing my father hadn't. Then I had been in shock. Next I called Auntie Audrey. To her I told the truth. He was in a desperate state, I told her. Everything was desperate. The building was a prefab and there was a constant noise of people crying out in pain.

When there was nothing more to do, I kissed my dad's head and left. (Later, interestingly, when he was undergoing skin grafts, such ordinary human contact wouldn't be possible.) Meanwhile I had called and left a message for Tony. David, the chief clerk, said he was back from Oman but was with Derry reporting on the case. I said that my dad had had an accident, that I was going into chambers, and that I'd explain when I saw him, and could he please call me.

Back at Essex Court, I sat there waiting for Tony to ring. When he did it wasn't from chambers. I could hear the noise of a bar in the background.

'I'm having a drink with Derry in El Vino's. Why don't you join us?'

'Tony, my dad's in a really bad way. I need to talk to you.'

'So come over.'

'But you don't understand. He's ill, really ill.'

'Just come over!'

I went over. This was in the days when Fleet Street was still Fleet Street and El Vino's was packed with its usual crowd of journalists and a sprinkling of lawyers. It was still a very masculine world and women were not entirely welcome. I remember standing in the doorway looking across this mass of suits, and then I saw them sitting at a table with Richard Field, who had been Derry's pupil after me. All three had their heads back in laughter. I went over and Richard, now a tenant, pulled out a chair.

'Tony, I really need to speak to you,' I said. Neither Derry nor he took a blind bit of notice. I tugged at his sleeve and repeated what I'd said. The same words exactly. Nothing. Then I burst into tears.

'You know what, my dad is dying and you won't talk to me.' I got up and walked out.

Tony had no reason to like my father but once he realised that his life really was in danger, and – more importantly – saw how much he mattered to me, he felt terrible about how he'd behaved. He knew the moment I got up and left and then, of course, he came running after me. It was just bad timing: there he was, back from his first big job, full of stories of Oman and the rest of it – and my being in a state wasn't what he expected or wanted.

Whatever residual anger I might have felt about my dad evaporated over the next few weeks. Whatever bad things he'd done in his life, I decided, I would not wish this on my worst enemy. He had nobody now except me, so every Monday I took the tube out to Northwood. I felt I owed it to my grandma and to Auntie Audrey to be there. They had to know that there was someone from the family looking after him. He didn't want Susie, my grandma was too old to come down and his sister, Auntie Audrey, had her own growing family. Lyndsey came once but, as an articled clerk, she didn't have the flexibility I had as a self-employed barrister to make the long journey out to Mount Vernon.

My dad was now resident in the burns unit and making very slow progress: his lungs had been damaged through inhalation of smoke and he was having skin graft after skin graft. That was when he was in most pain: the thicker the graft taken the less the eventual deformity, but the greater the pain. Everyone there was in pain. You could hear them screaming, and people were dying all the time. When shifts changed I'd overhear the nurses saying, 'So and so won't survive the night.' One woman – a nurse like them – had 90 per cent burns. She'd been lighting the gas in the oven when it exploded. By the following Monday she was dead. The body can't survive that amount of damage. My dad nearly died twice from liver failure. He was, of course, an alcoholic.

Above all, they had to prevent infection. It was called barrier nursing. Before going in to see him, you had to dress yourself completely in plastic. While the grafting was continuing, in order to avoid the skin stretching he couldn't exercise. His legs and his arms were covered with what looked like stockings. We just sat and talked. His one great terror, to which he returned again and again, a question he kept asking me, was whether he would ever have an erection again. I mean, did I want to have this conversation with my dad?

My experiences over those months deeply affected me. My kids know that, when I die, I want to be buried. Whatever happens, I do not want to be cremated. Not only that, of course. My relationship with my dad changed. And he changed. But it also affected his relationship with Lyndsey. Her reaction was, 'Trust my dad always to go for the main chance.' Maybe. But he was very ill and it's only thanks to the wonderful nursing care he received at Mount Vernon that he's alive today.

My father's accident had one unforeseen advantage. No way, now, could he come to the wedding, so it was arranged that my uncle Bill, Audrey's husband, whom I'd known since I first arrived at Ferndale Road when he was just her boyfriend, would give me away.

As Tony and I were both members of Lincoln's Inn, we could easily have had the wedding in Lincoln's Inn chapel, but it was expensive to hire, and as my mum was now living in Oxford it made sense to have the wedding there. We were incredibly lucky that St John's gave us permission to marry in the college chapel, where Tony had been confirmed – in itself highly unusual – achieved through the intervention of a friend who had done his post-graduate thesis on the history of the chapel who persuaded the then-chaplain Graham Dow to do it.

The current chaplain was Anthony Phillips. We discussed the issue of my being a Catholic. The Church of England didn't have a problem. The question was whether I had a problem. In fact, since leaving home five years earlier, I had only been to Mass when I was in Liverpool. At the LSE no one even knew that I was a Catholic. I probably should have asked my father's second cousin, Father John Thompson, to be there alongside the Rev. Phillips, but I didn't want to push my luck. Anthony Phillips was doing us a big favour. I didn't want to say, 'Oh, and by the way, I'd rather you didn't officiate at the wedding.'

There was no stag night or anything like that. The two families had arranged to have a meal together and were meeting up at my mum's house. By six o'clock the bridegroom had still not turned up. He eventually arrived around eight and a jolly evening was had by all. But next morning, calamity! He'd forgotten to bring any underpants, so he had to scrounge a pair from the hotel. They were hideous, ill-fitting things with the most peculiar line round his crotch area, clearly visible in the wedding pictures.

Grandma was there, of course, and when she saw Tony her face lit up. 'I'm so glad she's marrying you. I like you,' she said. So that was a relief.

I had bought my dress in the Liberty sale. It was very pale ivory silk chiffon. It had the feel of a medieval dress, the sleeves split along the top and caught by little pearls. The bodice was satin, hand-painted and sewn with seed pearls. To go with it I had a skull cap with the same pale lilac binding as the dress and more pearls. As for the bridesmaids' dresses, Maggie had volunteered her services as seamstress as she had a sewing machine. We bought matching silk from Liberty's which she made to her own design. Unfortunately, like a lot of Maggie's DIY activities, it took longer than she antici-pated and we had barely finished hemming the dresses when the car arrived. The bridesmaids, Lyndsey, Tony's sister Sarah and Catherine, Auntie Audrey's daughter, went first with my mum. As the car was my mother's contribution, I'd decided we only needed one – then it could come back and collect me and Uncle Bill. Good idea, in principle, but Oxford on a Saturday afternoon is a night-mare, and my mum had miscalculated how long the journey would take. We waited and waited. The wedding was supposed to start at two o'clock but at two the car had only just arrived back.

'Tony will be so cross,' I twittered as we crawled through the traf-fic. 'He'll probably just go.' By the time we reached St Giles', I was convinced there would be no one waiting at the altar and a lot of strained faces. He always hates it when I'm late, and I often am. For once, though, it wasn't my fault, but he wouldn't have known that. I eventually arrived at the chapel at two thirty, by which time the poor trainee organist had been through his entire repertoire and had gone back to the beginning again.

The bridegroom hadn't left. I learnt later that he'd had his last cig-arette at five to two. I had never smoked, but I'd noticed that a lot of barristers smoked like chimneys as they tended to get nervy before going into court. I'd watched my grandfather dying and I wasn't interested in seeing Tony going the same way. It had been my one condition for us getting married.

At around three o'clock on 29 March 1980 Tony Blair and Cherie Booth were pronounced man and wife. Needless to say, I did not promise to obey. Otherwise it all passed in a blur. All I can remem-ber is that Anthony Phillips preached a really good sermon, about how in marriage you always had to keep moving, never stick, never be static: you have to move forward together. When he came to the bit about 'those whom God hath joined together let no man put asunder', he bound our wrists together with his stole, which I wasn't expecting, and had never seen done before, even though by then so many of our friends were married.

'Gosh,' Maggie said later. 'He really meant that, didn't he!'

The chapel was quite small. Apart from our families, most of the guests were from our chambers. The Master of St John's had offered us the use of his house for the reception, so we could literally walk from the chapel, which we did, as the mad March wind blew everyone's hats off.

Bill, Tony's brother, was best man. His ushers were Charlie Falconer, Chris Catto – a friend from Fettes – Geoff Gallop and Bruce Roe. Marc Palley and Bina were in Dubai.

In the absence of my father, I had asked Derry to make the speech on my behalf. This was a mistake: it was all about Tony. How marvellous he was and how lucky I was to have him. Naturally he cast himself in the role of Cupid. Afterwards, Freddie Reynold said he wished I'd asked him. I could have seconded that. Luckily my uncle Bill insisted on saying a few words about me, and very generous they were too.

As for my dad, his is the one telegram I can now remember.

'Congratulations', it went, 'from the proud father of the beautiful bride. Absent wounded.'

Late that night Tony sat down on the edge of the bed in our hotel bedroom in the Cotswolds.

'Well,' he said, sitting there in his striped trousers and braces, 'that was the worst day of my life.' Nothing to do with me. He was just overwhelmed with sadness that his mother hadn't been there.

CHAPTER 10

Politics

After months of fruitless searching, we had eventually found a house we liked in Mapledene Road, Hackney, due west of London Fields and a stone's throw from Maggie's. Although it was more than we could really afford, at least no DIY was involved, as developers were doing the renovation. It was still a building site when we bought it, so Tony moved into Maggie's with me – he had kept his room at Charlie Falconer's right up till the wedding.

We moved into our first real home shortly before Christmas 1980 when I persuaded my husband to carry me across the threshold. After the unconventional proposal, it was the least he could do, I decided. Number 59 was at the end of a row of four early Georgian houses. Then there was a gap before another row began, this time Victorian. The end one of these was empty when we moved in. The council was supposed to be doing it up, but in the meantime it was constantly attracting vagrants and thieves. During our first six months we were burgled three times. It didn't help that both Tony and I were out all day. The miscreants would climb over the garden wall then break the back door, which had glass panels. Once a family moved in next door the stealing stopped.

The first time it happened I lost all my jewellery – nothing that valuable, but it all meant something. David had always given me jewellery for my birthday and everything went, including a lovely silver and black enamel bracelet he had bought me for my twenty-first, and a gold sovereign on a chain that Grandad Jack had given me.

Neither the jewellery nor the culprits were ever found, but it was obvious where they came from. Across the road from us was one of the poorest estates in Britain – in those days as bleak a collection of tower blocks and low-rise maisonettes as you could get. Canvassing in the Holly Estate during the local elections was a salutary experience and a real eye-opener for Tony who, unlike me, had never come across social deprivation on this scale. People were so frightened, they would barricade themselves in their flats behind fortified doors. I had never seen him so angry. Night after night he would come back determined to do something about the crime and anti-social behaviour that plagued such places.

Yet just across the Queensbridge Road were some of the nicest houses in north London and – thanks to their insalubrious neighbours – still affordable. Like-minded people were moving in – Charles Clarke and his wife were near neighbours. Barry Cox, a producer with London Weekend Television, became a close friend.

Whenever I moved house, I also moved my Labour Party membership. I began in the West Hampstead Branch when I was at Weech Road. Once I moved into Abercorn Place, I transferred my membership to Marylebone, where meetings were held in the house of a woman called Audrey Millar and her husband. They had two children whom I saw there from time to time, both younger than me. Fiona was then at London University and her brother Gavin was still at school. He would later go on to read law himself, while Fiona would come to play a huge part in my life.

When I first moved into Maggie's in Wilton Way, I joined the Hackney Labour Party in which she was already involved. By the time Tony and I bought Mapledene Road, I was on the General Management Committee. I was also a school governor – because I'd been one before in Maida Vale and carried on. Not only was I chair of governors at Queensbridge Road Infant School, but I was also on the board of Haggerston Girls School.

Now that I was legally qualified there was more specialised help I could give. I advised and helped set up the Hackney branch of the Child Poverty Action Group and also provided legal advice for the

National Council of Civil Liberties. On Merseyside there was a huge tradition of doing things for charity when you could. There wasn't this southern connotation of Lady Bountiful dispensing her largesse. It was how communities survived. I remember my grandmother telling me about the tallyman club before there was any other form of health insurance. As a teenager, of course, I would stand on street corners rattling tins. The YCS was regularly involved in collecting money for specific causes. I remember a twenty-four-hour vigil we had in Liverpool City Centre for Biafra. We had to sleep overnight in the Catholic chaplaincy. Needless to say a lot of canoodling went on, but no actual complete terribleness. It was simply a combination of social action and socialising.

As I began to build up experience in family law I was asked if I would help out at a law centre in Tower Hamlets. The University House Legal Advice Centre was run by a marvellous woman called Ann Wartuk, one of those formidable and down-to-earth women who, in some respects, reminded me of my grandma. She would terrify everyone and could be quite a prickly character, but she certainly got things done.

We would go there every Wednesday evening: three of us – two lawyers and Ann. She would have seen people during the week and our job was to give advice to those who needed to take things a stage further or who needed more information than Ann could provide from her own experience. The place itself was a wreck. No money had been spent on it, and in the winter gas heaters would hiss in the background as we sat there with our coats on.

There were two major areas I was involved in. First were the horrendous housing problems. People would come in with bits of wall, or wallpaper with plaster attached, stuff that was just rotting away with damp, or infested with cockroaches. Some of it was old housing stock, Victorian or even earlier, but equally bad – and even more shameful in some respects – was the newer housing. It was quite hard in those days to get legal aid to take on the housing cases so I would do what I could in the way of writing letters to the council in an effort to get families rehoused.

Then there was the domestic violence. Most of that you could refer on to solicitors and, indeed, I would even see some of these people again as formal clients; they would often come through Maggie. This was when I saw housing conditions at first hand. The fact that these women were living in terrible physical circumstances was not helping their situation.

In the early eighties the Labour Party was going through troubled times. The Callaghan government of 1976–9 had failed to deal effectively with the unions, and the country had reeled under strike after strike, leaving the door wide open for Margaret Thatcher who swept into power in May 1979, the year before Tony and I were married. I remember sitting in the polling station at Abercorn Place just feeling the votes slip away, while at the same time being fascinated by the idea that Britain was about to get its first female Prime Minister, and it wasn't me!

In November 1980 Callaghan resigned. The leadership was now up for grabs, and with the election of Michael Foot over the former Chancellor Denis Healey, the left was clearly in the ascendant. The spectrum of people who considered themselves (and were) paid-up members of the Labour Party now ranged from hard-left neo-Trotskyists – known officially as Militant (after their magazine) or, rather more disparagingly, the Trots – to those on the right of the Party who, despairing of Foot's ability to deal with Militant, peeled off to form the SDP, in what was known as the Limehouse Declaration in early 1981. While not wanting to turn into proto-Liberals, people like Tony and me found ourselves somewhere in the middle of this arc. While we believed that the Trots represented a mad, extreme form of Labour that was never going to do anything for anybody, we felt strongly that nothing would be achieved by jumping ship and defecting to the SDP. If we wanted to get rid of the Trots we had to stay and fight. Political power was unattainable, we both believed, without the support of the unions and the working class, so the only viable option was to stand and fight within the Party. With that firmly in mind, we joined an organisation called the Labour Co-ordinating Committee, which was a left of centre but non-Trotskyist group.

Around the same time, Derry had been approached by his fellow-Scot and near contemporary John Smith – a rising star in the Labour firmament and member of the Shadow Cabinet – to advise on Militant. When Derry brought Tony in to act as his junior he couldn't have known what the repercussions would be. It was tantamount to being thrown in at the deep end. The more Tony saw what was happening from the inside, the more incensed he became. It was little short of a takeover, he believed. He would come home at night raging; tinkering around at the edges was useless, he said. The only way to achieve anything was through mainstream politics: in other words, becoming an MP. I can't remember a particular conversation, no Damascene conversion; it just became obvious that anything else was a waste of time and effort.

Westminster politics is very different from local politics and it needed a change of focus. On a practical level Tony began to do more trade union work, getting Derry to introduce him to his union solicitors. He also wrote an article against the need for a Bill of Rights, his thesis being that you would then be entrusting power to non-elected judges, who are basically white upper-middle class. He tried to get it placed in the *New Statesman* but it eventually ran in the *Spectator*.

Union membership was mandatory in those days if you wanted to be a candidate, so while Tony signed himself up with the T & G (the Transport and General Workers Union) in the north-east, I ended up in the central London branch of MATSU, the white-collar arm of the GMB (the General and Municipal Boilermakers Union). It was a complete farce. The only people who turned up to branch meetings were people like us, who basically joined the central London branch to get credibility and to get on to the candidates' list. We had been members of the Fabian Society for some time, but as CND was the big issue then, I signed us up for a family membership.

To get himself known, Tony put himself forward to give lectures at trade union conferences. Barristers were still viewed with suspicion by such audiences, and that was where I came in. I was his passport to working-class acceptability: 'I might be posh but this is my working-class wife whose father is Tony Booth, you know, the well-known left-winger.' At the end of these things, there would usually be some kind of sing-song and inevitably this would be my cue.

'Cherie will now sing you some Liverpool songs,' Tony would announce, to tentative applause. Then I would put my hands together, open my mouth and sing – 'The Leaving of Liverpool' or 'In My Liverpool Home', because Liverpudlians were always powerful in the trade union movement. Thus it was that Tony Blair and Cherie Booth got known within the regional Labour Party, and soon we were both actively looking for seats.

On 1 October 1981, Sir Graham Page died – not exactly a household name, but for residents of my home town he was a fixed planet. Since 1953 he had held Crosby for the Conservatives and his death turned it into front-page news, which it had never been while he lived. Shirley Williams, Secretary of State for Education in the Callaghan government, had lost her seat in the landslide Tory victory of 1979. This would be her comeback. But not for Labour. She was one of the 'Gang of Four', the founders of the Social Democratic Party. As a good Catholic girl, and the only woman in the Cabinet, her defection had struck me like a slap on the face. When it was announced that she was standing for my home town, I thought, For goodness' sake. I'll put my hat in the ring! My father was incredibly excited though I knew I wouldn't have a hope in hell.

There was no grand plan, but I have always believed that if an opportunity comes along you should grab it. Having been fascinated by politics for years, I felt I was at least as good as the other people I had seen put their names forward. If they could, why not me? I saw what was happening to Britain under Thatcher – unemployment figures rising inexorably, Right to Work marches that were just a visible sign of people's misery. It wasn't enough just to hope that somebody else would do something about it. That somebody could be me!

I didn't even make the shortlist, while Shirley Williams romped home to become the first SDP MP, in the process overturning a 19,272 Conservative majority, though the Tories regained the seat at the general election in 1983. However, it certainly got me thinking.

A few months later, at the end of February 1982, another Tory died: Sir Ronald Bell, MP for Beaconsfield. This time Tony put his hat into the ring. My father was partly responsible. Knowing Tony was interested in getting into mainstream politics, my dad arranged for him to meet a friend of his, an MP called Tom Pendry. They had lunch at the Gay Hussar in Soho and Tony came back that evening very excited. Tom Pendry had mentioned Beaconsfield. Why didn't Tony put himself forward for that? He wouldn't win, but it would be good practice and, more importantly, it was sure to be very high-profile, with the SDP bound to stand. He knew somebody quite senior in the local Labour Party there, he said, and he could put Tony in touch.

Beaconsfield had been Disraeli's constituency and basically it had remained Conservative ever since. The Beaconsfield Labour Party wasn't exactly thriving and it needed all the help it could get. Tony stayed with my mother in Oxford and drove into Beaconsfield every morning. He didn't come back to Mapledene Road until after the election on 27 May. I would join him there at weekends, otherwise I stayed in London, going up by train to help campaign whenever my commitments in court allowed.

The timing of the election couldn't have been worse for a party in opposition. We were right in the middle of the Falklands War; Argentina had invaded the island of South Georgia in March and at the end of April came the sinking of the *Belgrano*. The whole of England was in a state of war fever, with Mrs Thatcher cast in the role of Boadicea.

Everyone joined in the campaigning. Even our old friend Bruce Roe, a Conservative from birth, drove round the streets of Beaconsfield in a sports car, blasting out 'VOTE FOR BLAIR'. Tony's family was there en masse: Sarah and Bill and, of course, Tony's dad, and new stepmother Olwen. Leo and Olwen had married just four months after us, and I had kept the third tier of our wedding cake for them. They had met in Cardiff where Leo had been working on a tribunal. Olwen made all the difference to Leo's life, and – from my perspective – she was a dream mother-in-law. I grew very fond of her.

On the distaff side there was me, Lyndsey, Auntie Audrey and my mum. But the star turns in the Booth camp were my dad and Pat Phoenix. By this time they were courting, if not actually an item. After he was released from hospital in the summer of 1981, my father had returned to Ferndale Road, there being nowhere else for him to go, although my grandma was in no state to look after him. One evening they were watching *Coronation Street* and remembering that he had known Pat Phoenix in the old days – she played the Street's perennial sex symbol Elsie Tanner – my grandma suggested he go and look her up. The rest is history.

The presence of Tony Booth and Pat Phoenix could always guarantee publicity. I had met her once before on a Right to Work march with my dad in Manchester. Denis Healey was being booed by the crowd and Pat ran after him and, in the face of all the surrounding anger, talked to him very publicly, giving him her support. Beaconsfield was the first time I had seen her campaigning, however, and she was an inspiration. Always beautifully turned out, always with a ready smile, always gracious.

My dad didn't share Pat's innate sense of decorum, however. One afternoon, we were midway through a tour of the Chiltern villages with Pat and my father leading the way, and Tony and me in the car behind. It was rural England at its most beautiful – hedges overflowing with bluebells and cow parsley, and my dad decided to liven things up a bit by playing 'Give Peace a Chance' over the loudspeakers. This was immediately after the sinking of the *Belgrano*, so on many levels it was not a good idea.

Tony was having none of it. 'For God's sake, man, turn that racket off!' he yelled out of the window. It took some time for my father to comply, because he simply didn't hear: Tony Blair versus John Lennon at full volume was no competition. My husband failed to see the funny side of it. Fortunately, the message of peace and love and the subsequent altercation were heard only by the cows.

Most campaigning is not this glamorous: knocking on doors, smile at the ready and leaflet in hand, is not everyone's idea of fun but I have always loved it, not least because I love meeting people, which ultimately is what it is all about. Whether I have ever persuaded anyone to vote for someone they wouldn't otherwise have done is another question. But I could never be accused of being a shrinking violet. This was the first time I had campaigned on behalf of my husband. I don't think Beaconsfield Labour Party had any idea what energy and commitment they had got in Tony Blair. It is hard to imagine a group of people more fired with enthusiasm and the atmosphere was tremendous.

By no stretch of the imagination was Beaconsfield winnable, so the most important job was to identify who the Labour supporters were and to make sure they cast their votes on the day; important psychologically both to Tony and to the Party at large. I was happy to do anything required of me, particularly asking, in the nicest possible way, whether they were intending to support the young and vibrant Labour candidate who also happened to be my husband. Whenever we could we went together, working our way through the electoral roll of the town and its satellite villages, one street at a time. A long process – but we were so happy in our joint endeavour. Tony was in his element; everyone loved him, even die-hard Tory matrons who, once they saw it was the candidate himself coming down the drive, would personally open their front doors to shake him by the hand – though a couple did set their dogs on him.

Midway through the campaign Tony took time off to be best man for his brother. Bill was marrying Katy Tse from Hong Kong, also a Catholic. The wedding was behind Manchester Square, just north of Oxford Street, but the timing was very tight. I had brought Tony's morning suit with me, so he dashed in from Beaconsfield, changed, performed his duties, then dashed straight back again, not realising that he was still in his wedding kit. A prospective Labour candidate could hardly campaign dressed like that, so as soon as he realised, he had to dash straight back to the church again.

Tom Pendry was right. Just like Crosby, Beaconsfield was as high-profile as they come. Paul Tyler, the former Liberal MP for Bodmin, was standing as the SDP/Liberal Alliance candidate. Among those who turned up to show their support for the Labour candidate was Michael Foot, then Party leader, who came up and had lunch with Tony. Tony had discovered they were both fans of P. G. Wodehouse. The poor man was almost in tears, so happy to find this normal person among the otherwise slightly weird candidates, with whom he could talk about Lord Emsworth and the Empress of Blandings rather than be harangued about policies by the Labour left.

Vincent Hanna and the whole *Newsnight* team were covering the by-election for BBC TV and, following this lunch, the candidate and the Labour leader were doorstepped outside the restaurant.

'Whatever happens tomorrow,' the Leader of the Opposition said, 'in Tony Blair we have a man I know is going to go far in the Labour Party.' Not for the first time, P. G. Wodehouse had worked magic.

Tony's campaign had been based on local issues, joining forces with a local pop star's wife on an environmental issue. Indeed, towards the end of the campaign, a leaflet went out headed 'Why Tories are voting for Blair'. It turned out to be prophetic, but not in Beaconsfield.

Of course he lost. The Falklands War was at full throttle and it was inevitable. Beaconsfield was, in any case, a bastion of Torydom and still is. But Tony made his mark and this was the first time that he showed his skills at campaigning, and bringing people together. I remember the comments of one of the sketchwriters: 'In Tony Blair you have the candidate that every Tory mother would love their daughter to bring home as son-in-law.'

The night the results came in, the Labour-Party-appointed press officer added a final sentence to Tony's 'acceptance' speech: 'And that's why I pledge that I'll come back and fight this seat again in the eighty-three election,' he wrote at the bottom. When Tony saw this, he shook his head.

'I can't say this, Cherie,' he said. 'If I do, then I can wave goodbye to ever becoming an MP.'

'So take it out,' I said.

'Well – you know they've all been really great—'

'Don't be silly. Take it out!'

He did.

After the election, Michael Foot wrote Tony a very nice letter saying what a good candidate he'd been, and how he felt he had a lot to offer to the Labour Party and not to despair.

In fact, Tony showed no sign of despair. Quite the contrary. By now he really had the bug. He might be doing well at the Bar – and he was both incredibly hard-working and proving a skilled advocate – but he now knew that what he really wanted was to be at the Palace of Westminster. The problem was finding a winnable seat. Once they're elected, MPs tend to stay put, and de-selection is rare. Sometimes there are boundary changes, but even though everyone knew a general election was imminent, few seats were up for grabs. Winnable seats already had somebody's name on them. Which left resignation and death, mainly the latter. We became like vultures. In June Tony tried for Mitcham and Morden and got nowhere. In February he went for Bermondsey, which Peter Tatchell got. We both tried for Oxford East – not a by-election but everyone was now gearing up to the general election. I made it to the final selection but was trumped by Andrew Smith. (He didn't win it that time round, but did four years later.)

Following Peter Tatchell's defeat in Bermondsey, all the failed by-election candidates were called in by the National Executive Committee (NEC) to analyse what had happened. The view of everyone apart from Tony was that 'we haven't been left-wing enough'. It was then that Tony began to articulate what eventually became the political creed that led to New Labour.

What with all the excitement of Beaconsfield, we hadn't got round to fixing a holiday. Not for the first time my mum came to the rescue with a hotel in Portugal that she could book for us through the office. As neither Tony nor I had been there before, it sounded the perfect solution.

After Beaconsfield, Tony had decided to concentrate on the north-east. First, a seat in the Labour heartland was more likely to be winnable and, secondly, it was where his roots were. As usual, we worked through August, picking up bits and pieces, then one after-noon Tony called me in chambers.

'Good news and bad news,' he said. 'The good news is that a seat in Middlesbrough has come up and I've had a word with some of my mates in the T & G and they think I stand a good chance!'

'But that's fantastic! So what's the bad news?'

'One of the key selection meetings is when we're supposed to be in Portugal. So I'm afraid you'll have to ask your mum to cancel . . .'

My mum was furious. I was simply resigned. It was so late in the day we lost all the money.

In many ways, the constituency was exactly what Tony had been hoping for, which was how I came to spend the night of my twenty-seventh birthday in the Middlesbrough Travelodge while Tony went to the ruddy meeting. I can remember ringing my mum from this miserable hotel room on my rather miserable birthday and her saying, 'I don't know why you married that Tony Blair. It's just ridiculous.'

Around ten o'clock he was back at the hotel looking hang-dog and shamefaced. There was no point staying in Middlesbrough any longer, he said. Stuart Bell – who duly became the MP – had got it all sewn up long before. I have to say it came as a great relief. Middlesbrough had singularly failed to inspire me. Tony was determined not to be downhearted, displaying a character trait that would stand him in good stead – as the Astaire and Rogers song has it: 'Pick yourself up, dust yourself off, and start all over again.'

During Tony's Beaconsfield campaign, I had got to know the regional secretary of the Labour Party quite well. He had seen for himself that I was quite at home canvassing and generally holding forth, and one day in early spring he suggested I drop in and see him. He had some news, he said, that I might be interested in.

'There may be a seat going,' he said when I arrived. 'They're look-ing for a woman candidate, so I was wondering if you'd be interested?' I never found out why they wanted a woman particularly. It was a safe Tory seat, so perhaps they thought they needed to do something different to generate publicity. 'Thanet,' he continued. It rang a vague bell and for some reason I got it into my head that Thanet was near Southend. I knew from the courts that Southend wasn't that far from Hackney.

It had opportunity written all over it. 'Well, why not?' I said. 'After all, it's only round the corner.' He gave me a slightly puzzled look but then thought better of it. The more he told me, the more I liked the sound of it. The sitting MP was a chap called Billy Rees-Davies, QC, a notorious old criminal hack who'd got silk, it was thought, solely because he was an MP. He had only one arm, and used to claim that he'd lost the other during enemy action, making himself out to be some sort of war hero, but word had it that the circumstances were more dubious. But he was a well-known sort of rogue, one of those barristers who are more famous for the anecdotes about them than anything else. One story I remember was about a client of his waving a piece of paper from the dock.

'I'm sorry your honour,' Billy said to the judge. 'But I rather think my client wants to send me a billet-doux.'

To which the judge replied: 'I rather think it's a Billy Don't.'

He was a character with a capital C, so I thought, Well at least you can have a bit of fun with an opponent like that.

As I got into my car to go home, I had a thought. 'I suppose I had better go to some ward meetings and that kind of thing.'

'Oh no,' he said. 'Don't bother with any of that. Just go for the final selection. We'll get you a nomination and you can take it from there.'

Great!

It was only the night before the selection meeting, when I looked up my route on the map, that it dawned on me what a terrible mistake I had made.

Thanet was nowhere near Southend, except possibly as the seagull flies. It was the other side of the Thames, at the far end of Kent – very little of it on the motorway. During the long drive down, crawling through south-east London, I just prayed that I wouldn't be selected.

Fat chance. The constituency party consisted of about three men and a dog. I was the only woman and the moment I went in, I could tell by their smiles that, yes, they really do want a woman candidate and they're going to select me. Sure enough, they did.

I drove back feeling very odd. Marc and Bina had just had their first baby, so I met Tony at the hospital.

'Guess what?' I said. 'I've become a candidate.'

On one level it was quite a coup. Barristers were not flavour of the month in the Labour Party. At least I was a working-class barrister, which is slightly better than a public-school boy barrister, and for once being a girl had worked in my favour.

Tony smiled, a bit wanly, I thought. He obviously had mixed feelings. Yes, I had a seat to fight – and we'd had so many setbacks that we didn't actually think it would happen – but it wasn't that lucky because it was perfectly obvious that Billy Rees-Davies would get straight back in.

I'd rather been looking forward to sparring with him – it was the one bright spot on the horizon – but in the end, even that was denied me. The former Thanet West and Thanet East constituencies were changed to north and south to reflect the current demographic. The Tories took full advantage of this to chuck out Billy Rees-Davies, who everyone knew had been hopeless. My new opponent was Roger Gale. To take on someone of his background – a former pirate radio DJ and regional television presenter – could have been amusing, but wasn't.

Thanet's local organisation made Beaconsfield seem a powerhouse in comparison. It had no resources and very few members. As a constituency, it was a strange mixture. The main centre of population was Margate, and a lot of it was seaside land, full of old people who'd retired there, most of whom were too proud to be Labour. It was a sign of respectability to put a blue Tory sticker in their windows.

Even Frank Green, my agent, and the councillors were in their sixties and seventies. The few young people around were basically Trots who'd done their usual thing of infiltrating. Not that Thanet was exactly a prime target for the radical left.

The local Labour Party was not without ambition, however, and when my dad said he could probably get Tony Benn to come up and speak, the members were delighted and, of course, my dad came along too. The result was a very strange meeting. I was definitely the most conservative of the three.

For my little speech of introduction I raised a few smiles when I said how proud I was to be on the platform with these two Tonys who had been such a great influence on me and the Labour Party.

'I give you Tony Booth and Tony Benn!'

The third Tony – my Tony – was there as well, though very much behind the scenes. We had offered to drive Tony Benn down in our car, and on the way back he had really opened up. The three of us talked non-stop, both politics, and, more surprisingly, religion – about liberation theology and the influence of Christianity on socialism. We ended up at his house in Notting Hill still talking, where we met his wife Caroline, a lovely woman. We all got on very well and I had the feeling Tony Benn thought my Tony was an OK guy, although politically, of course, they were on different sides of the whole debate.

Thanet Labour Party was delighted with the meeting. It got more publicity than it had had in years, probably ever. Whether it won us any votes, however, is less certain. But there was a council election at the same time, so it was important.

My husband was supportive right from the beginning. On our way back from France the previous Easter, before the election had even been announced, we had stopped off in Margate to have lunch with my agent to talk about the forthcoming campaign. My feelings were a mixture of excitement and dread. The Conservatives were on a high, while the Labour Party was tearing itself apart.

Once we'd had lunch, it was time for business.

'Tony,' he said, 'Cherie and I need to talk things over, so perhaps you wouldn't mind helping my wife with the washing up?'

So Tony ambled off to the kitchen to do the washing up. She was a nice enough woman, I remember, but very much the supportive wife. The conversation drifted here and there. The pleasures of the seaside and her belief that seagulls were vermin.

'So tell me, Tony,' she asked, 'are you interested in politics or are you just doing this for Cherie's sake?'

For him this was the nadir.

CHAPTER 11

Sedgefield

Tony's thirtieth birthday was on 6 May, a Friday, and I'd decided to organise a surprise party. Then Mrs Thatcher called the election, so I had to start campaigning more or less immediately. I wasn't about to let her spoil the celebrations, however.

I arranged for Richard Field, our old friend from Crown Office Row, to keep the birthday boy busy until about eight o'clock. Maggie and I had spent the whole day cooking and I'd asked everyone to come at seven thirty.

Time passed. Eight o'clock came and went. Eight thirty. Just before nine the pair of them staggered in, having passed a pleasant few hours in El Vino's. I was furious. It wasn't Tony's fault, of course. The man I had relied upon to bring him home had himself had one drink too many. When everyone had gone I apologised to my husband for being less than gracious when they finally showed up.

He had stayed drinking, he said, because he was really depressed.

'The thing is,' he said, 'I don't really want to be a barrister any more. I just want to be an MP. And look at me. A general election looming and no seat.'

'You've done everything you could—'

'It wasn't enough. At least you've got Thanet.'

I laughed. 'I'll probably lose my deposit.'

'There's apparently one seat left in Durham. I haven't got a hope in hell, of course. But I've nothing to lose, so I may as well go up there anyway.'

So that's what he did.

He drove up the next day and stayed with friends of his dad's in Shincliffe. In fact they supported the SDP, but were delighted to help out. For some reason the constituency of Sedgefield had been abolished in 1974 and now they had decided to re-create it, hence the lack of candidates.

As a first step in the selection process, you needed a nomination from one of the wards. Tony was getting nowhere, until he called John Burton, secretary of Trimdon Village branch, a few miles to the north of Sedgefield itself, where they had yet to nominate a candidate.

'As it happens, we're having a meeting of the local lads on Wednesday,' he told him. 'We won all the seats on the council and we'll be having a bit of a drink to celebrate.'

Tony rang me every evening at my agent's house in Margate to tell me how he was getting on. The semi-enthusiasm he had set off with, however, was dissipating rapidly.

Although he liked the sound of John Burton's voice, he said, he wasn't convinced it would get him anywhere. It meant hanging around for another two days, and he felt bad about not helping the candidate for Thanet East, and, he confessed, he might even be missing me.

'You can't give up now,' I told him. 'What's two days in the greater scheme of things? From the sound of it, it's exactly the kind of seat you're looking for. And if it's right for you, there's a good chance you'll be right for them.'

When he arrived at John Burton's house, they were watching the final of the European Cup Winners' Cup between Aberdeen and Real Madrid. So the beers were handed round and at full time it was still a draw, then it went to extra time, then into penalties. Basically they were sitting round this television for two and a half hours without a word of politics being spoken.

When they finally got to talking about the election, Tony told them what a relief it was to find himself among normal people. In London, he said, meetings were erupting in violence, plate-glass windows were being smashed, people were being thrown off balconies. (That at least is John Burton's memory of the evening.)

'And now here I am sitting with you lot, watching football, which seems a great deal better than all that in-fighting.'

Indeed it was. Even though it was very late, Tony called me as soon as he got back to his dad's friends' house.

'I've got it!' he said. His voice sounded completely different. I could hardly keep my eyes open but I listened to him talking about these normal people and what a lovely bunch they were. He hadn't misrepresented his position. He told them he thought we should be in Europe – which flew in the face of Labour Party policy that said we should get out – and that the whole CND thing was a disaster, that he didn't believe in unilateral disarmament. They had agreed to support him, he said. The next few days were spent introducing him to everyone – from little old ladies to union people – who would have a vote at the selection meeting.

It wasn't enough. Tony had some nominations, but the left had organised against him and he'd failed to make it on to the final list. He was devastated, and John Burton was furious. The left was attempting to push through the former MP for Nuneaton, Les Huckfield, who had given up his seat when the boundaries were redrawn and who John Burton said he couldn't trust further than he could kick him.

'My last hope now', Tony explained when we spoke that night, 'is that the General Management Committee put me on.' Because John, it turned out, had one more card up his sleeve. The newly drawn-up constituency included part of Easington where he'd been to school, and the following night a group from there were at the General Management Committee meeting. John had recognised a couple of old friends and had a quiet word.

As the selection list was about to be closed, he stood up. 'I would like Tony Blair's name added to the shortlist,' he said. 'I'm not going to say anything about Tony Blair. I just want to tell you what the leader of our Party thinks about Tony Blair.' And he read out the letter that Michael Foot had sent Tony after Beaconsfield.

A vote was taken. John Burton was known as 'a canny lad'. He was a churchgoer. He played football. If he thought this Blair was worth it, then he probably was.

Tony got through 42 to 41. He was in with a chance.

As time was so short, the selection meeting itself at Spennymoor Town Hall was the following night and Tony won easily, by 73 votes to the runner-up's 46. The area was very run down. Coal mining was in decline and there were fewer and fewer pits. There were some small-scale factories in the industrial estate around Peterlee, and ICI on Teesside, but otherwise the main employer was the council. John Burton says that people knew something had to change. They had always voted for a Labour MP, but always suffered under a Conservative government. Although Tony didn't back down from his views on Europe and unilateral disarmament, they obviously thought that here was somebody who spoke sense and might eventually help get Labour into power.

When he called me that night, he was ecstatic but also rather terrified.

'Knowing my luck,' he said, 'I'll be the person to lose what is technically an unlosable seat.' Tony has always had the tendency to be pessimistic while I am incurably optimistic.

Tony moved into John and Lily Burton's house, sleeping in their daughter Caroline's room – she was away at college. When I joined him at the weekends, we took the two single mattresses off the beds and pushed them together on the floor. Lily laughed. It did her heart good, she said, to see two people so in love.

With John Burton's stalwart help, Tony ran a brilliant campaign. On the two weekends that were left before the election I took the train up to Durham on the Friday afternoon. The general consensus was that there was no point campaigning in Margate at weekends because there were just too many tourists around, so you couldn't tell what was what. We worked a five-day week. The local organisation was minimal. Once again the family came to the rescue. Tony's brother Bill and his new wife Katy came over, as did Lyndsey and my auntie Audrey, all knocking on doors and doing the tedious but crucial stuff of grass-roots canvassing and getting the vote out.

The big guns were in Sedgefield: my father and Pat Phoenix being the main attraction. It is difficult to over-estimate the effect that Pat had on people, not that they called her that. She was always 'Elsie Tanner'.

A number of the General Management Committee were Catholic and Tony soon learnt that John Caden, the parish priest of Sedgefield itself, was an independent county councillor and particularly influential. The word soon went out: 'Mrs Blair is a Catholic and of course is very holy and goes to church.'

Naturally, that Sunday found us among his congregation. He later became a very good friend and Tony's regular tennis partner. It may sound opportunistic but somehow, in a period of little over two weeks, the Labour candidate and his wife had to become visible and memorable. People had to know who Tony was. Everything was brought into play, even my voice. John Burton ran a folk group, called Skerne, named after the local river. Because of my folk-singing background, I knew all the words to their songs and, with the rest of the audience, would join in. Although John, and those close to him, knew Tony wasn't just a posh barrister drafted in by Westminster, such things did happen and it was important to show as quickly as possible that it wasn't the case.

Feeling very jittery, I took the train back to London from Darlington. Waving goodbye I watched Tony's receding figure standing on the platform, disappearing into the pearly June evening, and felt quite tearful.

The day before the election I sent him a card: 'From the candidate in Thanet to the candidate in Sedgefield, in the sure knowledge that one of us will be an MP tomorrow.'

The ninth of June 1983 was one of those perfect summer days that politicians pray for. Sunshine brings with it a general air of optimism and not having to chivvy or ferry people down to the polling booths in the cold or rain. Lyndsey was there to support me at the count and Bill and Katy sent me a bunch of red roses for luck. At Sedgefield, Tony had his dad and stepmother. It will always be a lasting regret that I couldn't be there with him, but Leo and Olwen could not have been prouder.

My result came in fairly early, and I can remember driving back to London with Lyndsey, listening to the results on the car radio, trying to work out when Sedgefield would come in. As for Thanet, we didn't do badly. I kept my deposit, which meant I got 12 per cent of the votes – one of the few Labour candidates to do so that year. Basically, Labour was decimated in the south-east, including Andrew Smith not getting Oxford. When we arrived back at Mapledene Road, I rang up Labour Party headquarters and asked them to call me when the Sedgefield result came in. We sat up with the television on, with the usual panels of experts and the famous Swingometer, but I was so tired I was afraid I'd fall asleep and miss it. They didn't have television cameras there. Sedgefield was a constituency of no importance. Except to us.

The next day Tony told me about the count, how the first boxes to come in were from the outlying villages around Darlington, which were Tory wards. They were all piled up on tables and he knew from Beaconsfield exactly what that meant. The Conservative candidate was in the lead. He hadn't known the reason, of course. He just thought, I've lost the seat.

'I was in such a panic', he later admitted, 'that I went outside and had a cigarette.' The first since our wedding day. He won, of course, with a majority of 8,281. I cried when I heard. Lyndsey and I just hugged and cried. I took the train up to Durham the next day.

Election postscript: As a comparative novice, when it came to writing my election address, I got Tony to go through it with me. Much later, when they compared his at Sedgefield with mine at Thanet, mine was more New Labour than his. Time being so short in Sedgefield, most of his had been written for him, so in fact he'd had more of an input into mine than he did in his own.

Tony might have been successful but the results for the Labour Party as a whole were disastrous. Any idea that going further to the left was the answer was dented. Tony Benn was defeated in Bristol. Michael Foot resigned and Neil Kinnock took over as leader.

Part of Tony's election promise was that, if returned as the member for Sedgefield, he would buy a house in the constituency. Thankfully, he didn't say we would move up there permanently, which was what he'd planned to do if he hadn't been selected: he had been determined not to be accused of being a London carpet-bagger.

While Tony might have been happy to move his practice to Newcastle, I knew that if I did, I could wave goodbye to specialising in employment law; it would be back to a diet of family, crime and accident cases. With Tony now safely elected, I could breathe again. We could have a home in the north-east but I could continue to work in London.

Immediately we began thinking about where to buy a house. Even though he had only been there three weeks, Tony had a good idea of the geography, it being so close to where he'd been brought up. Sedgefield is essentially a rural constituency made up of mining villages and farms. The small town of Sedgefield itself, he decided, was a bit posh and, as he'd had all this support from Trimdon, it made sense to base himself round there, and through John and Lily Burton we could tap into the community.

So while I went back to work, Tony stayed up in Durham, getting to know the people and looking for a house. It would need to be comparatively big, he had decided, as it would double as the constituency office. In the meantime, he continued to sleep on the Burtons' floor.

Tony first saw Myrobella in early July and I will never forget that phone call.

'Cherie, I've found the perfect house. It's fabulous! It's got seven fantastic Victorian fireplaces, an Aga and a hand pump in the kitchen!'

'Does it have anything else,' I asked, 'because we're expecting a baby . . .'

Throughout the campaign, I had been feeling a little peculiar, which I'd put down to anxiety. I still wonder whether it wasn't the night of his thirtieth birthday party, but we'll never be sure.

Before we got married I'd been on the pill, but as Tony had always worried about the long-term effects, after the wedding we practised other forms of contraception. Then, once I realised Thanet was a dead duck, I stopped taking precautions. My future, I decided, did not lie in politics, though I never imagined I would get pregnant immediately. Once Tony got selected, however, I saw that even thinking about starting a family was frankly not sensible, so I went back to using contraception again . . . a bit late. I *had* fallen pregnant immediately.

As for Myrobella, the answer to my question 'Anything else?' was no. The house was cleaned out. It had been owned by the colliery and had been lived in by the superintendent, hence the superior fireplaces. The last occupant had been the superintendent's widow. A friend of John Burton's had been planning to buy it, but luckily for us the reality of the renovation proved just too daunting. Everything needed to be done. Re-wiring, re-plumbing, the lot. Not that we had any intention of doing it ourselves.

The hamlet of Trimdon Colliery is about two miles from Trimdon Village. It's basically two streets of small terraced houses, at right angles to each other, with Myrobella roughly in the middle. The unusual name is not one of those unwieldy conjunctions of the owners' names as I had first supposed, but a variety of pear which grew in profusion in the garden. We bought it for about £30,000 and then spent about the same again doing what was absolutely necessary. We didn't move in till the following summer, by which time Euan had been born.

When I discovered I was pregnant, I was twenty-nine years old with seven years' call. My career was going pretty well. I had started to do much more employment law and less of the more general stuff. So far, so good.

I was only the second woman tenant that 5 Essex Court had ever had. The last one, when she found she was expecting, had left and never went back. That wasn't my intention at all. Nor could it be: although some barrister MPs continue to work, Tony had decided to give it all up and devote himself to politics. As simple as that.

Although on one level I was horrified, on another I knew he had no real choice, to the extent that it was not even worthy of discussion. If Tony had been a criminal barrister, he could have kept his hand in and the coffers reasonably full even if he had to turn down long fraud cases. That would have been different. But he wasn't. Crown Office Row was largely a commercial chambers and he had no experience of the criminal Bar. You can't carry on a career at the commercial Bar in the same pick-it-up, put-it-down way. The sheer mass of documents involved, the mass of legal research, the mass of client care make it impossible. He did one last case in the Court of Appeal and then bowed out for good. Financially, of course, this had implications. By 1983 he had been earning in the region of £80,000 per annum. This would now drop to an MP's salary of less than £20,000 – not a bad salary at all for the times but not enough to cover our outgoings, especially with a baby on the way. It's a situation most new parents find themselves in: thrilled on the one hand, anxious on the other. Financially it was going to be a real struggle. I was about to become the main breadwinner, a status that filled me with anxiety. Not that I had ever indulged in fantasies of being a stay-at-home housewife. Quite the reverse. The spectre of what had befallen my mother loomed large in my life. And it wasn't the fear of abandonment. I didn't think for a moment that Tony was about to abandon me – but then what new wife does? However, we are all mortal and accidents happen. Behind my mum was the example of my grandma. How often had she drummed into me the need for a woman to have financial independence as she recounted trudging the

streets of Crosby and Blundellsands in her desperate attempt to find
work after Grandad was hit by that crane. For two years he was
totally incapacitated, which led directly to my dad leaving school
long before he should have done, and it changed his whole life. That
was why my education meant so much to her. Nothing to do with
certificates; everything to do with never being dependent on a man
for money.

None of these practical considerations, however, took away from
the sheer excitement of realising that a baby was on its way. I have
always loved babies and the unexpectedness only added to the
thrill – like being given a surprise present which you have secretly
longed for. As for Tony, it only needed his precious Newcastle United
to come top of the First Division, and his cup would have been filled
to overflowing. Not only an MP, but a father too. We were on our
way to becoming a proper family.

Once the baby was born, I would be able to buy in childcare and
continue to work. Before a birth, however, comes pregnancy – something I couldn't delegate – and this was the first hurdle to be
negotiated. A barrister is self-employed. You receive fees for the
work you do and that's it in terms of income. In those days, a percentage of this would go straight to your clerk, while your rent was
gauged on a sliding scale depending on the size of your room and
how much you earned. Roughly this would translate to between a
quarter and a third of your income. This paid not only for the running of chambers – heating and lighting – but for the junior
administrative staff as well. The problem is that when you're not
working – that is, when pregnant – your rent still has to be paid. In
1983 there was no such thing as maternity leave, not even a mora-
torium on the rent.

The prospect of a pregnant barrister presented a challenge to
both me and chambers. My practice was far less lucrative than
Tony's and so I had to work as long as I possibly could. My stub-
born streak came to the fore. I would show everybody that I could
do it. Completely ridiculous, but there we are. It is certainly something I would not recommend now; fortunately, it's no longer
necessary. The Bar Council has made it a professional obligation for
chambers to enable women tenants to take a rent-free period. In
those days the view was, if you chose not to work for a few
months – whatever the reason – it was your decision. So I carried on

working, if only to pay the rent, which amounted to around
£15,000 a year.

Just because I was pregnant, I saw no reason to slow down, especially as the financial reality was beginning to dawn. Now that Tony
was MP for Sedgefield, he was up there every weekend and I'd go
with him, though usually on a later train. Then as now, on a Friday
night it would be standing room only. Young and healthy as I was,
this was a strain the bigger I became, not least because I had usually
been on my feet in court earlier in the day.

That autumn I got my first big break – a union dispute case called
Cheall and Apex which I did with Freddie Reynold – my first
reported House of Lords' case. It was about the Bridlington
Agreement – a concordat between trade unions not to poach each
other's members – and closed shops. It also involved European
human rights legislation which was not a big topic in the UK at the
time.

We spent Christmas at my mum's in Oxford then saw in the New
Year up in Trimdon. As Myrobella was a building site, we were still
staying at the Burtons', though we no longer slept on the floor as
once I was down I couldn't get up.

I was due on 29 January. At my first check-up after Christmas, I
was told that the baby was too small. 'The baby is not receiving sufficient nourishment,' the doctor said. 'You are doing too much. At
eight months this workload is completely unacceptable.'

I was taken in to Bart's hospital for bed rest, and went nearly mad
with boredom. After ten days, there being no improvement, they said
they wanted to induce me. I wasn't keen, I said.

'Mrs Blair. Your baby is not growing. It's not a question of not
being keen.'

Tony and I had gone to all the ante-natal classes at the National
Childbirth Trust and I had fully expected to have my baby naturally.
They broke my waters and put me on a drip and immediately I was
right into a very painful experience. My firstborn made his appearance at about eleven thirty, after an epidural and a high-forceps
delivery. So much for natural childbirth. As birth experiences go, it
was utterly ghastly, including a third-degree tear, because they
yanked him out. It was the human equivalent of going from 0–60 in
five seconds. Lyndsey and Tony's sister were now sharing a flat
together and when they arrived at the hospital I was still in trauma.

Blackpool, 1994. Tony's first Labour Party Conference as leader. After his triumphant speech doing away with Clause IV, I felt ridiculously proud.

The first photograph taken at Number 10.

After the euphoria, the trepidation. At this point we hadn't even seen inside our future home.

The third of May 1997. The ultimate bad-hair day.

Team photo: Princess Diana and Prince William after a game of football with Chequers staff. Alan the cook, in a white shirt, is behind Tony. Linda, the housekeeper, is far left.

Princess Diana with Kathryn at Chequers, taken by my mum.

April 1995. A proud day for the Booth family. Lyndsey, Mum and Dad joined Tony and the kids for the official photo when I took silk.

At least when I'm working I don't have to worry about what to wear.

May 2000. The Blair family, complete with new addition, taken by Mary McCartney.

The new grandparents: A proud Leo Blair holds his namesake. Tony's stepmother Olwyn and my mum were equally delighted.

A Leo, symbole du Royaume Uni de demain,
avec Tous mes vœux de bonheur!
Bravo Chérie! Bravo Tony!
Bien affectueusement,

J. CHIRAC
New-York
7-9-2000

Jacques Chirac sent us this photograph of Bill Clinton holding Leo at the United Nations.
Our new baby had everyone smiling.

Sitting on the steps outside the front door at Chequers. Although it looked very grand,
Chequers was where we had the most freedom to be ourselves.

June 1997. The Clintons' first visit to us in Downing Street. My mum and Lyndsey (left) were among Bill's staunchest fans.

Bill and Hillary Clinton were wonderful hosts and gave us photographs of particularly memorable occasions such as this, when opera singer Thomas Hampson sang at the White House.

Nicky and Kathryn play in the Downing Street garden, on the path leading to the door on to Horse Guards Parade.

Family life in the Great Hall at Chequers. Bill continued to drop in on us long after he left office.

There was blood all over the place and Sarah said it put her off having babies for ever. Luckily for the future of the planet, the pain is quickly forgotten by the new mother as she is overwhelmed by love for this perfect little person. This was certainly my experience, and from the first blink of those little unfocused eyes, the curl of those tiny fingers, I was hooked, and life would never be the same again. We called this precious creature Euan, after Euan Uglow and also a school friend of Tony's who had died far too young.

Tony had been there since the induction began. It would be nice to say that his presence had made all the difference. It would be wrong. He was completely useless. Like practically all stories of new fathers I have heard, he hadn't been expecting it to be quite so gory. My husband has always been good at empathising, but when it comes to childbirth empathy only goes so far. Once Euan was cleaned and wrapped and smelling delicious, however, Tony's pride and delight in his son was such that you'd think he had taken more than a queasy spectator's role. He made up for it later, becoming as adoring and hands-on a dad as anybody could wish for. The practicalities of the physical ordeal I had just endured took time to percolate through, however, as in the afternoon he told me I had a visitor. I was about to have my photograph taken, he informed me: the *Northern Echo* – Sedgefield MP, wife and newborn son being the theme. The caption I think was something like 'Euan brings Labour for Labour'.

I was given a rubber ring to sit on so that at least I could force a smile. As the guy went about his business, focusing and clicking, all I could think was, An appearance before the House of Lords is a doddle compared to this. I am never going to do it again.

My last thoughts as I went to sleep that night were of my husband: I hate this man.

Euan was comparatively small, so the numerous hats and coatees I had knitted came in useful, as he needed to be kept very warm, though they were far too big. He was both families' first grandchild and we were well looked after: my mum came down, then Auntie Audrey, then Olwen. But it couldn't last. I needed to get back to work; I needed a nanny.

Euan was christened by Father John at St John Fisher in Sedgefield and that same weekend I found Angela, who stayed with us for four years. I advertised in the *Northern Echo* because I wanted someone who wouldn't mind spending time in the north-east. Angela was a farmer's daughter from North Yorkshire with a strong Yorkshire accent and a passion for Man U. A down-to-earth girl, then in her mid-twenties, she had already worked for a couple of other families before us. She would speak her mind and was completely trustworthy and sensible and we just clicked.

No matter how confident I was that Angela would care for Euan as well, if not better, than I could have done, it was incredibly hard for me to leave him. Apart from the first few weeks I'd had sole care and to hand him over to somebody else – anybody else – was torture. We had our own little routine; everything was a pleasure and a game. For four months the centre of my world had resided in this small, helpless creature. I was still breast-feeding and my breasts had no scruples in showing exactly how they felt, so I'd be sitting in court, aware only of the intense pain of the swelling, and the knowledge that by the time I got out my bra would be soaked. I would sit in chambers and express milk with a breast pump during the day, put it in the fridge, then take it back home for the next day.

It was hard, but I knew I didn't dare slow down. I'd put in so much effort to build up my practice, that to let it all go – particularly at a time when Tony had effectively given up his – would have been mad. Tony's election had already drawn a line under any thoughts of standing for Parliament myself. There wasn't a pact between us, as has been speculated; it was simply impractical. Nor can I say I minded. I loved my job and, with Tony a committed MP – and I knew even then he was determined to go as far as he could – I would get all the political interest I wanted.

Our first summer at Myrobella, in 1984, was the year of the Miners' Strike. Although there were no longer any mines in the constituency itself, the Fishburn cokeworks were affected and a number of Tony's constituents were miners who worked in the Durham coalfields to the north of Trimdon. Herrington, one of the collieries marked for closure, was only eighteen miles away so it was all very close to home. Gary Kirby, one of the men who had been at Tony's first meeting at John Burton's house, was a miner, and he was arrested. It was a painful time, not only for the individuals and the families concerned but for the communities as a whole and, ultimately, the Labour Party.

Once we were a family, Nicky came along quite naturally. I didn't want Euan to be an only child and, given the system was now in place, we thought we might as well get on with it, especially as – in spite of working right up until the last moment with Euan – my practice had definitely flattened out.

I remember our second summer in Myrobella as a kind of idyll. Driving up the road from Sedgefield, through Fishburn, past the coke works, it was almost like going back to my roots. Perhaps it was to do with being pregnant, but retired miners were still entitled to concessionary coal, and the smell of coal fires – a smell that was always there, even in the summer – reminded me so much of my own childhood. Trimdon was, in some sense, going back into that community. Just as in Ferndale Road, we always had an open door, and there was a group of local kids – they must have been aged about ten – who would come in and play with Euan, by now a sturdy toddler, and I used to do cooking with them. I remember introducing them to garlic, showing them how to peel it. At that time garlic was incredibly exotic.

We went up to the constituency every weekend. Tony would usually have gone up on the Thursday, and I'd follow on the Friday. Looking back, I don't know how we did it. When Euan came along we became a two-car family. Tony had a Rover – Parliament had done a deal with Rover so MPs got them at a discount – and I had a beaten-up Mini Metro which got progressively more beaten up as I was such a terrible driver. I am someone who has no spatial awareness whatsoever. During my first driving test, I only lasted ten minutes before the examiner told me to stop.

'In the interests of public safety I'm terminating this test. Stay here. Do not touch the car. I'm going to go back and get your driving instructor to come and get you.'

On my second attempt I spent the entire time with my foot hovering over the brake, expecting the examiner to stop me at any second: failure number two. The third time, the test seemed to go on far longer than usual.

'I thought you needed settling down,' the young examiner explained. I put it down to it being the first test of the day and the lovely spring weather. On the way home I called Tony from a phone box.

'I passed!' I said.

'You can't have. It's a disgrace. He should never have passed you – you're a hopeless driver.'

The following day I volunteered to take Geoff and Beverley Gallop, who were staying with us, on a tour of junk shops round the backstreets of Hackney. At one point another car got a bit too close and there was the sound of a crunch. Paralysed with fear, I stopped the car where it was, found a phone box and rang Tony. 'You're going to have to come and get me.'

If anything, I found the open spaces of the north-east even more daunting than London, particularly the lack of lighting after dark. On at least three occasions over the years I landed up in a ditch with the kids screaming in the back, and many's the encounter I've had in Durham car parks with bollards that just spring out at you.

As far as people in chambers were concerned, my driving was a standing joke. To accept a lift from me was a rite of passage.

My second pregnancy was a doddle compared with the first. I was fit and well and had a support system with Angela and we had our own home in the constituency. I also had my friend Marianna. One Sunday in January when Euan was nearly one, Tony and I got off the train at King's Cross and bumped straight into Charlie Falconer.

'What on earth are you doing up here?' Tony said.

'Meeting someone,' came the red-faced reply. The someone turned out to be Marianna Hildyard, a barrister like me, and the love of Charlie's life, who until then had been a well-kept secret. Six months later they were married. Although her father was the British Ambassador to Chile in the seventies, she is totally down to earth and, whatever the crisis, Marianna – all wild Titian hair and sparkling personality – will be there with both love and practical support, and we have been close friends since practically the moment we met. As far as our pregnancies were concerned, we couldn't have arranged them better if we'd tried. Our due dates were less than ten days apart, and the months passed in fun and laughter.

On Thursday 5 December 1985 I woke up feeling unusually anxious. Tony was due to go up to Myrobella but I didn't want him to leave. I had a feeling the baby might be coming, I told him.

'But you've still got two weeks to go.'

'Euan was early.'

'Because Euan was induced!'

It wasn't that Tony was being difficult. It was a matter of diplomacy, he explained: Prince Andrew was going to be opening something in the constituency the next day, and he was due to have breakfast with him.

'If you can assure me that the baby's coming this weekend, then of course I won't go. And don't forget you've got your mum coming.'

Fridays being my mum's day off, most weeks she would take the bus down from Oxford to spend the day with her grandson. She didn't usually stay the night because she had to work on Saturdays. In fact, that weekend Auntie Audrey was also expected for her annual Christmas shopping expedition.

Tony left Mapledene Road around four p.m. and the contractions started in earnest around eight. At about nine I called Myrobella. No reply. I called the Burtons' house: Lily answered. The ancient Daimler that Tony had on loan for use in the constituency had packed up so John had gone to collect him from the station.

In the meantime my mum had begun to panic.

Finally the phone rang: Tony.

'There's no question about it now,' I said. 'I think you're going to have to come back!'

'How can I? The Daimler's dead and there are no more trains tonight.'

'Well, what am I going to do?' I knew I was in no state to drive myself.

'Get Lyndsey to drive,' he said. 'I'll borrow John's car and get there as soon as I can.' Lyndsey had only passed her test that week. She had never driven my car, never driven in the dark, never driven into central London and had no idea where Bart's was. Other than that it was fine . . .

The moment Lyndsey arrived I waddled out of the house in my dressing gown and eased myself across the back seat. Mum sat in the front with the A–Z and we set off. Between groans I gave directions, wincing at the crashing of gears and the regular stalling. 'Push your clutch down!' I yelled as the car bucked and whinnied through east London.

Somehow we got there. As Lyndsey lurched to a stop, I flung open the door and propelled myself towards the entrance. Once in a wheelchair, I was rushed straight to the delivery ward, my mum struggling to keep up. The moment we got there, I dashed to the loo, and they had to pull me off. Sure enough I was 10 cm dilated.

'How fascinating to see it from this angle,' I'd heard my mum say, as I was pushing him out.

I'm ashamed to confess that I wasn't very nice to her. 'I don't want you here!' I shouted. 'Where's my husband?'

Less than half an hour after we arrived, our second son came gliding into the world. He was born incredibly quickly. No drugs, no forceps. It was over in what seemed like minutes and my mum was the first one to hold him.

Tony arrived about four a.m., exactly twelve hours since he left, having borrowed John Burton's old banger and driven through the night on near-empty roads, which was a good thing as the brakes failed just as he came into London. On the way down, he'd been thinking about what to call him, he said, and had come up with Colin.

'Colin? You can't call a baby Colin!'

Fortunately my mum agreed and, as he was born on St Nicholas' Day, Nicholas he was.

The following week we took Nicky on his first plane journey when the entire family flew up to Sedgefield for Christmas, our second at Myrobella. To have a new baby at Christmas time was a joy, and we had a full house with my mum, Lyndsey and Grandma somehow all squashing in. Although she was becoming increasingly frail and forgetful, my grandma still loved babies and happily spent the entire holiday cooing with delight over her latest great-grandson.

This would be the pattern of our Christmases for the next twelve years. The family all assembled at Myrobella, me becoming an expert at cooking a huge turkey from our wonderful local butcher and next-door-neighbour Eddie Greaves. Not the conventional method certainly: it would go in the bottom oven of the Aga when we got back from Father Caden's midnight Mass and would be perfect by lunchtime the next day.

It was always over too quickly, and that year – like every other – by the beginning of January I was back at work.

CHAPTER 12

Departures

When Nicky was three months old we left Mapledene Road and moved to Highbury. With a baby, a toddler and a nanny, it was simply that we needed more space. Not only did the new house have four bedrooms and a conservatory – and two bathrooms – it was also better situated in terms of public transport, being midway between the Arsenal and Highbury & Islington underground stations. Ten Stavordale Road happened to be owned by Peter Stothard, then a senior editor at *The Times*. News International, the parent company, had built a massive printing plant for all its titles at Wapping, just east of Tower Bridge, and on 24 January, 6,000 newspaper workers came out on strike. 'Fortress Wapping' would become the battleground for the biggest industrial action that has ever affected the newspaper industry. From my employment law work I was only too familiar with the extraordinary Fleet Street practices where printers were kings. New technology would eventually do away with the worst of the corruption, but it would be a long, hard battle. Only in the person of Brenda Dean, a moderate leader of the printers' union SOGAT, was there a glimpse of a woman making her mark in a man's world. However, as loyal Party members we were, of necessity, on the side of the unions, and when viewing the house, and on subsequent visits, we were in the uncomfortable situation of hearing Peter on the phone trying to deal with the situation.

I was rapidly discovering that two children are very different from one. When we only had Euan, I had continued with the Labour Co-ordinating Committee – to the extent that I would even be breast-feeding at the meetings – but once Nicholas came along, it was just too much. For the same reason, I'd also had to stop the legal advice sessions at University House. Now that Tony was an MP, it wasn't appropriate for him to get involved in the local Labour Party, though I was, which was how I first came across the keen young man who used to collect subs in our area – Stephen Twigg. With two small boys, a more practical way of becoming involved in the community was through the Church and, almost immediately, we started going to St Joan of Arc, on the other side of Highbury Grove. Not only was it within walking distance but it had both a primary and a nursery school attached. We were learning that, as parents, you had to think ahead. I might not have minded being married in a Protestant church, but I was always insistent that the children be brought up as Catholics.

In July 1986 Pat Phoenix died and my dad was utterly distraught, not least because it came as such a shock. As for so many women of her generation, cancer was not something you admitted to – even if you were a heavy smoker as she was – and not until the end did she admit how ill she was. Although she and my father had been together for six years, and the subject of their marital status was regular tabloid fodder, they married only a day or so before she finally passed away in hospital. She had tried to persuade him to 'regularise' their relationship, but he had always resisted. He couldn't bear to think that she might be dying. It was her last great kindness: with their marriage my father would be financially secure. Pat's generosity was boundless, from looking after my dad, when he was physically and psychologically at rock bottom, to supporting Tony both at Beaconsfield and Sedgefield. She was an avid collector and Myrobella had been largely furnished with what she could no longer fit into her own house in Cheshire, including a number of risqué William Russell Flint paintings that adorn Myrobella's walls to this day and which still raise amused eyebrows. Her funeral was extraordinary and the streets of Manchester were lined with her fans.

The news hit me like a brick, not least because she had been having treatment in Clatterbridge, the same specialist cancer unit in the Wirral where I knew Auntie Audrey was then having radiotherapy. Auntie had been diagnosed during a visit to America three years earlier. She and Uncle Bill were there visiting old friends Gerry and Shirley Quilling. Gerry was a former USAAF pilot whom Bill had met when he was a pilot during the war. One afternoon, quite out of the blue, Auntie Audrey had called me at chambers. In those days phoning from the States was very expensive and she didn't waste time. It was breast cancer, she told me. She'd told Shirley that she had a lump, but hadn't wanted to go to the doctor about it. Shirley took charge at once. Told her not to be so ridiculous and arranged for her to see her own doctor.

As soon as he saw it he said, 'That's got to come off.' She went in and had the operation there and then. She was calling me because she wanted me to tell her mum, my mum and Lyndsey.

'But Cherie, whatever you do, don't say anything to my kids.' Catherine was then about twenty, Christopher a year younger, and Robert only fifteen. It seems incredible now that the taboo still had such power. You just didn't talk about it, as if you could deny its existence. When I eventually got involved with breast cancer, becoming a patron of Breast Cancer Care and other related charities, the importance of talking about it became very important to me, not least because I am convinced that had Audrey seen someone earlier the outcome might well have been different. As it was, she had the treatment and thought she was going to be OK.

Looking back, it's easy to see the signs, though I completely failed to do so at the time. She and Uncle Bill had stayed with us when they went to Buckingham Palace for a garden party. Auntie looked lovely, you could even say girl-like, although she was then in her late forties, and she was as slim as my earliest memories of her.

She was diagnosed shortly after she had campaigned so vigorously for Tony at Beaconsfield, and had been well enough to help me at Thanet too. When Euan and then Nicky were born, she took such pleasure in them, coming to stay with us whenever she could and boasting that she was the one who had fed Euan his first solid food. It was as if she knew she wouldn't live long enough to see her own grandchildren and they were the nearest she would ever get. Even though I was one of the only people who knew how ill she was, she never talked about it. Sometimes it was obvious that she was having the chemo and that things weren't all that great, which was why it was nice that she was there when Nicholas was born, but it was never clear how she was faring. She'd be ill and then she'd be well.

Once we had Myrobella, the family would always spend Christmas and Easter with us and Auntie and Uncle Bill would drive over for the day, bringing Grandma with them, while my mum would travel up with us. That Easter, 1987, Auntie came over on the Maundy Thursday, three days earlier than usual, in order to spend time with my boys, and it was obvious that she was very ill. She helped put Euan and Nicky to bed – as much as she could – and read them a story, but that night she was in a really bad way. By this time she had secondaries on her lungs, and they filled up with fluid and needed to be drained, so next morning Uncle Bill took her home. She couldn't breathe and she was in pain, and it was all very sad and distressing. As I held Nicky up to wave her off, I knew that this would be the last time I saw her. It was only then that I realised that whereas I thought she was coming to spend Easter with us, really she had come to say goodbye.

The following Tuesday they rang to say she had died at home. She was fifty-two. No age at all.

A week or so later, I was driving back to London from doing a case in Leicestershire, when the dam burst. I pulled over and, as cars swished past me in the rain, I just sobbed and sobbed. When I was a newborn baby it was Audrey who rushed home from her job as a telephonist to play with me. It was Audrey who had taken me in at lunchtimes when I was unhappy at Seafield. It was Audrey who showed me that politics wasn't just for men. It was Audrey and her husband and her children who showed me how a normal family life could be. She'd been a friend to my mum when my dad left us. She wasn't a saint but the world was a bleaker place without her. She was such a vibrant, outgoing person, who always had time for everyone. And now she had really gone.

Easter was late that year and her funeral was at the end of April coming up to May, and we sang the May Day procession hymn that is sung when Mary is crowned. It wasn't a funeral hymn – quite the opposite – but we chose it because we knew it was one of her favourites. Every year, with the rest of the good little Catholic girls, Lyndsey and I would dress up in white and parade round the grounds of the Park House nursing home singing hymns to honour Our Lady, whose statue would be crowned by the prettiest girl in the top juniors. In 1963 the May Day procession had coincided with my auntie Audrey's lying-in with her second child, my cousin

Christopher, and she came to the window and tilted the baby so that we could see him, and to wave at Lyndsey and me. I can't hear that hymn without thinking of her.

In 1987 we also said goodbye to Angela, who had become much more than a nanny. She and I had discovered a shared interest in athletics, and we would regularly go to Crystal Palace together and she is still a family friend. It was thanks to her that Nicky became a Man U fan while Euan remained firmly in the Liverpool camp. She was a very good cook and what she really wanted to do was run a sandwich business. That spring, a friend of hers heard that British Rail was starting a hospitality suite for first-class passengers, and suggested she contact them. The idea was that she could learn about running a catering business while being paid for it at the same time. So that was what she did.

Having had such success with Angela, once again I advertised in the *Northern Echo*. With no baby to look after, and Euan now at St Joan of Arc nursery every morning, I decided that a trained nursery nurse wasn't really necessary, and took an eighteen-year-old straight from school. She had never been to London, though she did drive. In retrospect, I realise it was asking too much. At the interview I had been pleased when she told me she was religious. It was only after she came down that I realised she was quite fundamentalist, and she was soon involved with a local sect in Highbury. One day I got home to find Euan in a terrible state. He was then just over four, and it seemed he had come out with a swear word and she had squirted Fairy Liquid into his mouth.

I was shocked, and it showed, but decided to do nothing before discussing it with Tony, beyond telling her that this was unacceptable behaviour. That weekend we went up to the constituency where we talked about sacking her, but by the time we got back on the Sunday she had already left. A note told us that her future lay with her new friends at church and she had decided to join them. So it was back to the *Northern Echo* for the second time in three months, but it taught me a lesson. A girl that young might be all right if you are in the house with them, but not otherwise.

Luckily we then found Gillian, who came from near Richmond in Yorkshire. She was another one of those fantastic young women who stayed for three years, until she left to get married, to the man who is still her husband and whom she met while living with us.

Kathryn was her bridesmaid and Euan, then aged seven, sang 'My God Loves Me' to the tune of 'Plaisir d'Amour' at their wedding.

I had never yearned for a large family. Once I had Euan and Nicholas, I decided that was quite enough. Yet in those weeks after Audrey died, I found myself thinking, I want another baby. What I really wanted – though I never voiced it, even to myself – was a daughter. I was able to tell my grandma that I was pregnant shortly before she died the following August.

Grandma never knew her own daughter, Audrey, had died. For some time she had become increasingly confused, so in many ways she had already left us. After my mum moved out of Ferndale Road, Uncle Bob had moved back in to keep an eye on her, but eventually he couldn't cope, so she went to a council retirement home in Seaforth. I wasn't very happy about this but as she could no longer look after herself, there was no real alternative. Realistically, I couldn't bring her down to London. She wasn't there long, perhaps a year, before she too passed away. Until I was two years old these two women had been everything to me, one a surrogate mother, one a surrogate sister, and losing both of them within six months marked a watershed in my life.

My father was utterly devastated. In less than twelve months he had lost his wife, his sister and finally his mother. It could have sent him back to the bottle – which he had totally forsworn after his brush with death – but, thank God, it didn't.

Our daughter Kathryn – blessed with the auburn hair of both her great-great-grandmother Tilly, and Tony's mother Hazel – was born on 2 March 1988, nine months to the day after the 1987 general election. That night we had been in celebratory mood: although the Labour Party in general fared barely any better than it had five years earlier, Tony had increased his majority.

For a newcomer to Parliament he had done well in the previous five years. In his maiden speech to the House of Commons, he had said: 'I am a socialist, not through reading a textbook that has caught my intellectual fancy, nor through unthinking tradition, but because I believe that, at its best, socialism corresponds most closely to an existence that is both rational and moral. It stands for co-operation, not confrontation; for fellowship, not fear. It stands for equality.'

However well this might have gone down in the reformist camp, it did nothing for the harmony of daily life at Westminster, where someone had clearly been playing tricks. When he arrived, Tony was allocated a room with Dave Nellist, the MP for Coventry South-East, one of three Labour MPs who belonged to the Militant tendency. This was a marriage made in hell. Not only was Tony a barrister – in itself a class crime – but he was a barrister who (when working with Derry) had tried to get Militant expelled from the Party. It wasn't long before Dave Nellist got himself transferred to share four walls with another, younger Militant tendency MP, while Tony was allocated a room with a Scottish MP called Gordon Brown. They found common ground immediately. Both were bright, both had been elected at the 1983 general election – and both had fought a previous election in an unwinnable Conservative seat, though Gordon's wasn't a by-election, so he was more established in Scottish politics. Gordon certainly considered himself the more senior, which I think Tony would have been the first to agree with, not least because Gordon was the older, though only by two years. Apart from what Tony used to relay to me, I barely knew him. As he didn't have a family, we tended not to socialise: our Labour milieu was in London while Gordon spent his time in Scotland and, in those days, he fell into the category of people who weren't used to the constant presence of small children.

It was inevitable that Labour would lose the 1987 election. No one really thought we had a chance except possibly those who would have 'no compromise with the electorate', which was one of Militant's slogans. However, the failure at the polls convinced Tony that something had to be done. He was determined to get into the Shadow Cabinet, and – together with Gordon – move the Labour Party from an unelectable force into an electable one, which was something that I fully agreed with.

At the 1987 Labour Party Conference that September, they both stood for the Shadow Cabinet. Gordon got in (becoming Shadow Secretary of State for Trade and Industry), while Tony was the highest runner-up. Their campaign manager had been Nick Brown, whom Tony had introduced to Gordon. He too had entered Parliament in 1983, when the previous incumbent of Newcastle East went over to the SDP. We had got to know him because, having a local constituency, he would regularly drop into Myrobella. He was basically a fixer, with fingers in all sorts of pies: he had been a legal officer for the GMB, and for a short time had been on Newcastle Council. He had future Chief Whip written on his forehead even then. He was unbelievably patronising, always calling me 'love', and clearly felt that women should be seen and not heard in the Labour Party. I always saw him as a bit of a political thug.

My career was also in a state of flux but, with things moving so fast in the Labour Party, Tony had other things on his mind. Along with many young barristers I believed that we needed to find another system of paying the clerks. While he was still at Crown Office Row, Tony had been pushing for just such a change, and he and Chris Carr had put their case to Derry. The old-fashioned way of the clerk getting 10 per cent when there were nine or ten tenants was one thing, they said. 'But now there are twenty-five of us, David is getting ridiculously well paid. We would be better off in a chambers of our own.' The split eventually happened, with Derry taking off his people and going on to form 11 King's Bench Walk. Tony had been very active in pushing for it but, ironically, almost as soon as it happened he left the Bar for good.

At around the same time tensions had begun to develop in 5 Essex Court. A split opened up between the silks in the north and the junior barristers down in London, who included me. Normally juniors would hope to build up their practice by picking up work that trickled down from the silks, but as the silks were on an entirely different circuit that wasn't happening. Then Freddie Reynold, who originally had taken me on, took silk, and he and Alastair Hill – another of the original London members who took silk at the same time – decided they too would do better to cut loose.

Word eventually got out that this was what was proposed. Those silks whose practice was entirely based in the north didn't really care, but those who had a mixed practice were not at all happy. It didn't help when George Carman, who by this time was famous, suddenly decided that he too wanted to join the renegades. We weren't that keen to have him because 'selfish' and 'George' were two terms that definitely went together. On the other hand, his income was useful.

I was for the split from the beginning, and once we moved into our new premises I became very much a player on the chambers' management committee. Also, although I wasn't the only woman, I became the mother hen, with everyone coming to my room and telling me their problems. My babies were at home, so perhaps because I couldn't channel all my mothering instincts into them, these grown-ups got it instead.

Everything was quite tense in the run-up. The northern silks refused to move out of the building, saying it was theirs, while we – who actually worked there – said it was ours. Today it is increasingly common for chambers to set up in premises outside the Inns, but it wasn't the case back then and space was at a premium. Eventually the Inn – in this case the *de facto* landlord – managed to find us space in New Court Chambers as they wanted to avoid a major fall-out on their doorstep.

For the first time in my joint career of mother and barrister, when I was expecting Kathryn I had some financial relief. Three months after I fell pregnant, Gail Carrodus, the other female tenant in New Court Chambers, also fell pregnant. Unlike me, she was horribly sick and unable to work. Feeling desperately sorry, they offered her a rent-free period, so I said, 'Hello! Do you think I should have a rent-free period too?' And they agreed. Three months. We were one of the first chambers to do that, and subsequently it was enshrined by the Bar Council – though it was a long haul and that didn't happen until the 1990s.

With Gillian my nanny's approval I had decided that this time I was going to have a home birth, not least because Bart's had closed down its maternity wing. Every few weeks I would visit my GP to check all was well and from time to time I'd have a scan. I should have had one at thirty weeks but work was picking up and I was just too busy. At thirty-four weeks, the doctor said I should leave it no longer. I couldn't see what all the fuss was about. Necessary for first-time mothers, perhaps, but not experienced hands like me. I was feeling fine and I thought the baby's head was engaged.

'I'm sorry, Mrs Blair,' the radiographer said, sweeping my swollen belly with the pick-up. 'That's not the baby's head that's engaged, it's the baby's bottom. This is a breech.'

The doctor's verdict was unequivocal: 'You cannot possibly have a home birth,' he said. 'Indeed, I rather think we're looking at a Caesarean.'

I was so adamant that I didn't want a Caesarean that they took an X-ray of my pelvis.

'Well,' the doctor said as I stared at X-ray, 'if you want to kill yourself, and your baby, then have a home birth, but otherwise you're going to have a Caesarean.'

I was booked in on 3 March. A few days earlier a computer had been delivered from chambers. We had just started to get computerised and I had resolved to teach myself to use it. Until then we had written everything by hand and a typist would type it up. It was an Olivetti, I remember, that used WordPerfect, and as soon as I began to get the hang of it I was hooked.

Tony had arranged to take me into the hospital later that evening, and I decided to use the time typing an advice on the new computer, though I was barely able to reach the keyboard over the bump. I was aware that contractions had started, but I carried on anyway while Gillian fussed in the background.

'Are you sure you're all right?' I would hear her say.

'Quite sure. I'm just going to finish this advice.'

'I'm really not happy about this.'

'I'm fine. Really.'

'You are not fine, and I'm going to ring Tony to come now.'

I was still typing away when Tony arrived. When we got to the hospital there was a queue for emergency Caesareans and it was then that I started to worry, because of my experience with Nicky.

'I'm warning you,' I said to Tony, 'if it's a boy I'm going to cry.' Then came the epidural, which they had agreed I could have, rather than a general anaesthetic. It took ten attempts to get the needle in, while I watched Tony turning whiter and whiter. Then, more quickly than seemed possible, the surgeon cut me open and scooped her up. A gorgeous baby girl. I cried anyway.

In fact I was soon screaming.

'In about two per cent of the population the epidural doesn't reach there,' the surgeon explained as he stitched me up. They had no alternative but to knock me out, just briefly, to do the stitches. And, far from being simple, I then had to stay in hospital for five whole days. When I got home I read the advice I'd been writing on the computer. Fortunately I had not had time to print out. It was complete and utter garbage.

My friend Francesca had also had a Caesarean a few months before. She had married John Higham, one of the barristers who had done their Bar Finals at the same time as Tony and me. Like us, they too had moved to Hackney and their first baby was born around the time I discovered I was pregnant with Euan. During those early days when I was an inexperienced mum at home on my own, she was very kind in showing me the ropes. A second baby followed a year before I had Nicholas. It was when she was feeding her that she noticed the lump in her breast. Her doctor, who was our doctor too, thought it was an engorged milk gland. It wasn't. By the time they realised it was cancer it had already taken hold. After her operation all seemed to go well, though the oncologist told her that she should not get pregnant again. But Francesca, who was half Italian, was a Catholic and she did fall pregnant and the cancer returned. As soon as the baby was viable, they gave her a Caesarean. It was a little boy, and – although tiny – he lived. His mother did not. I went to her funeral just three days before Kathryn was born, and wept for another good life lost, another family left devastated by breast cancer.

CHAPTER 13

Moving On

In 1989 I received the ultimate accolade for a junior barrister when I was given a red bag by Lionel Swift, QC, following a very difficult wardship case in which he was leading me. Blue bags are what all barristers carry their robes in, but a red one can only be given by a QC for what they deem to be exceptional work. Needless to say, there is a whole ritual surrounding their presentation, including the £10 tip that you are supposed to give the junior clerk who delivers it to your chambers.

Maggie Rae was the instructing solicitor in the case concerned, and everything about it had been difficult. The family of the children who had been taken into care were involved in prostitution. The grandmother was the madam of a brothel, and the mother was now putting her own children 'on the game'. The evidence was harrowing. At the end Lionel Swift showed his appreciation at how I'd handled the case by giving me the coveted red bag.

Now that I was the mother of a daughter myself, I was finding these family law cases increasingly hard to cope with. I remember a case involving a woman whose newborn baby had been taken into care. She was devoted to her child but the baby had had withdrawal symptoms when it was born. The mother was a heroin addict and the medical view was that she was going to die. She was devastated when the baby was placed for adoption.

In another case, a young woman was accused of injuring her baby, but she denied it. We argued her case and I convinced the magistrate that it hadn't happened. The baby was delivered back to the woman on the Friday. By the Monday she had called social services saying, 'I did do it, and I can't cope, and please take him back', otherwise, she said, she feared she'd hurt him again. The saddest thing about it was that now they were going to prosecute her for perjury on top of everything else and I thought, Please, don't do that.

It can be very difficult to protect yourself against emotional involvement. Unlike psychiatrists, we have no one to unburden ourselves to, although it was easier for me when Maggie was the instructing solicitor. I also did a lot of this work with Charles Howard and he and I would talk about our cases and give each other mutual support. I remember representing one client who was accused of sexually interfering with his children, which he denied, but I was deeply dubious about his denials. His defence was quite straightforward: 'I'm not a nonce; I didn't sexually abuse them. Yes, I did beat them, I did commit physical violence against them, but I didn't sexually abuse them.'

After the second day of the trial, things were looking bad, and we arrived at court the following morning to be told that he had committed suicide overnight. That wasn't to be the end of it, however. The judge said we had to continue with the case. The local authority wanted to make the findings a fact, and wanted to take the children into care. They didn't want them to be handed back to the mother, who they believed had been, at worst, complicit in the abuse or, at best, prepared to turn a blind eye. So that's what happened: the defendant had given his evidence, I had my instructions and the judge duly found against him.

There came a point where I could no longer face the hideous things that some people do to their children. It seemed rarely to be a matter of simple sexual intercourse. A lot of it involved horrible practices that these people forced their children to do, things that you then had to stand up and talk about in court as if it was the stuff of everyday life. Although the judges are all family law judges, and thus are familiar with most of it, nonetheless, you are obliged to go through the evidence point by point. I still think it's a really important job – so many women's issues throughout the world revolve around children and what happens when family relationships break down – but on a day-to-day basis, it was hard going and luckily I had another string to my bow.

It was through my work on employment law that I came to the notice of Michael Beloff, a brilliant man with impossible hand-writing – even worse than mine. When I joined 5 Essex Court back in 1977, I thought I was there for life. Then, during the eighties and cer-tainly by the end of the decade there was a movement for change at the Bar. It was no longer unheard of for people to move chambers. Individual sets were getting bigger, people were consolidating, Information technology was coming in. Specialisation became the hot topic and life in general common-law sets was becoming more pre-carious. Not only did commercial members of chambers earn much more money than criminal barristers, but, to add insult to injury, they would complain that their well-to-do clients had to sit in the waiting room with people who were quite likely to take their wallets.

Employment law was still a fairly unusual speciality. Like any other area of expertise, the more cases you do, the more people are likely to come to you again. If you can't do a case yourself you want to be able to pass it on – 'to return' it – to someone else in chambers, and solicitors prefer to return the case to someone who knows the area, so it was becoming increasingly difficult to be a lone specialist in chambers.

In addition to employment law, I had also done a bit of public law, which was Michael Beloff's field, and this too was starting to build up as an independent speciality.

Public law is about challenging decisions made by government or local government and education was one of the areas in which I had become involved early on, although it has now become a speciality in its own right. Foremost among the cases I was involved in were those challenging school closures, or cases brought by children with special education needs challenging the provision that local author-ities made for them.

Whatever your political views, as a barrister you work for whichever side approaches you, which, in the case of public law, could be either an individual or a local authority. Michael Beloff needed me, he explained, to service local authorities. Because 4–5 Gray's Inn Square was a set who dealt mainly with planning inquiries, they had a large local authority client base who would then come to them for other areas as well. In addition to public law, I had a background in family law so was thus in a good position to advise on local authorities' social service departments.

There are two kinds of law. The first kind is fact-based and that includes most of the criminal law, most family law and most personal injury: did he or did he not do it; did this or did this not happen? The law in these cases is generally clear. You cannot take someone's property, you cannot murder somebody, you cannot allow a piece of scaffolding to fall on someone's head without dealing with the consequences. Then there are other areas of law where the facts themselves may not be in dispute, but where the law itself is unclear. The argument between the opponents revolves around the legal consequences of these facts, and here public law is a good example.

In the late 1980s when grant-maintained schools were the first state schools to become independent of the local authorities, the question of ownership arose. While they remained state schools, the buildings and land belonged to the local authority. When the government passed legislation to make them independent, the buildings and land went with them. So what happened when a school that had shared a playing field or a swimming pool with another local school became independent? Once the school went grant-maintained, it could refuse to allow the other school access, or attempt to charge them to use it. When such a case got to court, it came down to arguing from the statute book about what Parliament had intended.

Planning law is very fact-intensive, and the planning barristers who largely made up Michael Beloff's chambers were great advocates who could cross-examine witnesses till they were screaming for mercy, but whose interests did not lie in analysing and debating the exact meaning of a word in a piece of government legislation. Although I believe I am a good trial lawyer, it was this type of intellectual argument that I enjoyed more. So, for me, moving to Michael Beloff's chambers would mean moving into that more stimulating arena, into areas of the law where cases I was involved in would set precedents.

In spite of my long attachment to New Court – who largely comprised the same set I had joined in 1977 at 5 Essex Court – I knew it would be a good career move, and yet I was still undecided as to what I should do. Tony has always been totally supportive of my having a career – he is not one of those men who is threatened by successful women – and by 'supportive' I mean real practical support. Without his help with childcare, both at weekends and on holiday, I would have found it much more difficult to cope. As he had a parking space at the House of Commons, we would usually travel into work together, and when he dropped me off that morning for my interview, he said I had to go for it.

'You would be completely and utterly mad to turn down Michael Beloff just because you feel loyal to Freddie and the others.'

As it turned out, I didn't turn them down because I wasn't offered the tenancy. Michael rang me later to say the chambers had been very divided, but that, in the end, they had decided against taking me on. He added, however, that he thought this would not be a long-term decision, and he would get back to me. Sure enough, in the following year he did, and I was offered the place.

Although my husband was only a backbencher, the politician Tony Blair was definitely starting to be seen above the radar. In 1988 he got into the Shadow Cabinet with the energy portfolio, where he demonstrated his ability by amending the privatisation legislation in Parliament and generally showing that Labour was competent in matters of government. Then he had the employment portfolio. At the time I was first approached by Michael Beloff, the big issue was how we would deal with Thatcherite labour reforms, in particular that of the closed shop, where workers had to belong to their union. Its original purpose had been to protect union members being discriminated against by employers bringing in cheap non-union labour. In 1989 Tony committed the Party to accepting the Thatcherite reforms, balloting and secondary picketing and the following year, all forms of closed shop were outlawed by the 1990 Employment Act. He might have outraged the left wing of the Party, but he made it far harder for the Tories to attack. These, of course, were all issues that I was familiar with because it was my field of law, but although there were areas of policy that we would disagree on, this wasn't one of them.

By this time computers had started to arrive at Westminster, which had even lagged behind the Inns of Court in its reluctance to embrace new technology. Unfortunately the secretary Tony shared with another MP hadn't really got to grips with IT, and the dedicated word processor she was working on was next to useless. Given I was then managing Tony's office expenses (as indeed I had done since he had become an MP), I inevitably became involved. I persuaded him not only to get a proper computer but also to get someone in the office who was more open to IT.

Tony originally came across Anji Hunter in Scotland when they were still at school. They subsequently saw each other in Oxford, as Anji was a friend of Tony's then-girlfriend Susie Parsons. Both girls had been at St Clare's, a private sixth-form college, but Anji had gone off to Ireland where she'd married and had two children. Anji reappeared in the mid-eighties as a mature student at Brighton Poly, where she was reading history and English. Tony said she could come and help out in his office during her summer holiday to see how politics worked. She graduated in 1989 and was looking for work. As they say nowadays, it was a no-brainer. Tony can't bring himself to be nasty, so Anji's first job was telling Tony's secretary that she was about to take early retirement.

Although being in the Shadow Cabinet did not affect Tony's salary, it gave him access to what is called Short money, named in honour of Edward Short, the Speaker of the House, who brought it in to support the funding of the Leader of the Opposition's office and the Shadow Cabinet. Short money is allocated on the basis of how many seats the opposition has, so in '87, when we didn't have that many MPs, you would have to get money from other sources, and in the Labour Party that was mainly the trade unions. The idea was for Tony and Gordon to pool whatever extra money they raised, but somehow Gordon always seemed to have more staff than Tony. We weren't the only ones who noticed that he put himself first. Mo Mowlam was another north-east MP we knew. Not only was her constituency just down the road in Redcar but she also lived close to us in Islington. Mo was strongly of the opinion that Tony was being taken for a ride by Gordon and should assert himself, as was Anji.

When 4–5 Gray's Inn Square duly offered me a place, I started worrying about what I was going to say to my old chambers. I had been with most of them for fourteen years, and it was just coming up to Christmas . . . I turned myself inside out with worry. 'How can I tell them? They will be so upset.'

And they were very upset. They had no inkling, and saw it as a kind of betrayal, as I would have done under the same circumstances. I had to give three months' notice, but I left just before Christmas and didn't go back. I was still working out my notice, in that I was still paying rent, but I ended the holiday with terrible back pain, and by the time I arrived at 4–5 Gray's Inn Square I was virtually horizontal; it was clearly the stress.

*

When I was at the LSE I had had a twenty-one-inch waist and was so skinny you could see my ribs. With each pregnancy I put on about one and half stone, then managed to lose two-thirds. So by the autumn of 1989 with Kathryn getting on for eighteen months old, I was about one and a half stone overweight and a size 14 instead of a 10. Intermittently I'd go on a diet, but basically I'd reached the stage where I was stuck. One day, sometime that autumn, I came across a handout in one of those free magazines that come through the door. It was directed at busy working women and/or young mothers who were feeling daunted by not getting back into shape. I qualified on both counts. It was a completely different approach to losing weight, 'freeing the body and feeding the mind'. I knew that I wasn't eating properly – with young children you tend to finish off what they're eating and then sit down for another meal with your husband. But with a full-time job and the constant feeling of guilt that I ought to be at home, eating sensibly was not something I was good at.

The course was called Holistix and it was run by a mother and daughter, Sylvia and Carole Caplin. Carole was a professional dancer, incredibly fit and with more energy than anyone I had ever met, and she made everything seem both easy and possible. I immediately signed up to do the course. When I started I was still in New Court Chambers and twice a week I'd get the District Line from the Temple to South Kensington station. They were basically exercise classes combined with workshops on healthy eating – a regime about as far away from my normal daily routine as could be imagined. 'Pamper yourself' was one of Carole's favourite phrases, and she introduced me to Bharti Vyas, who ran a beauty clinic in Chiltern Street. That was the first time I'd ever had a facial. I also had my first massage, and signed up for a course to learn how to do it myself, which I thought would be useful. In fact, over the next few years I was able to put my new skill into practice on Tony. I didn't take all Carole's advice, but I did begin to lose weight. At the end of 1991 Carole moved to New York, and once she was no longer around, I found I didn't keep up with the classes as much as I should.

Around the same time, Peter Mandelson came into our lives. Although he had been appointed the Labour Party's first Director of Communications in 1985, I didn't really get to know him until after the 1987 election. Peter was a politician to the ends of his fingernails. His grandfather was Herbert Morrison, who was Home Secretary in

Attlee's government and, so it was said, believed that he should have been Prime Minister instead of Attlee. Peter and I got on well from the start. He's charming, sympathetic, cultured, funny and clever, though I have to admit I never took to the moustache. He's also very open and completely belies the 'Prince of Darkness' public image he acquired in the mid-eighties thanks to *Private Eye*, which enjoys making mischief. Not being an MP, he necessarily worked in the shadow of elected politicians, namely – following the 1987 election defeat – Tony and Gordon, whose role was to give voice to whatever policy was currently being promoted. In fact, he was closer to Gordon but he wasn't partisan and would make use of whoever was around at the time. As Gordon's base was in Scotland – he was then going out with a Scottish advocate – he was often not around when needed, so inevitably Tony did more interviews. Wherever we've lived, we've had an open-door policy, and with Peter regularly dropping in, he gradually became introduced to our social circle. He certainly met Charlie Falconer at our house.

Peter made no secret of the fact that he wanted to become an MP. Neil Kinnock had always been very against it – his line was that he needed Peter to help fight the next election, which would be considerably more difficult if he was fighting a seat himself. Notwithstanding, Peter was selected for Hartlepool, a seat next door to Sedgefield, and Tony agreed to help him with his campaign. We were always finding a bed for him, both in Trimdon and Highbury, and, one way and another, as a family we got very close to him and my mum absolutely adored him.

What all of them were working towards was a more electable party. There were some things, however, that would not be jettisoned. At the end of the eighties, when Tony was Shadow Employment Secretary, he was responsible for developing the Party's policy on the minimum wage which the Tories were determined to fight.

After Tony had failed to get elected to the Shadow Cabinet in 1987, one of the old Labour Whips – an unreconstructed old right-wing Labourite – told him what his mistake had been. It was not being seen around enough in the bars at the House, he said. Unless Tony stopped going home between seven and ten he would never get anywhere in politics. Fortunately, Tony took no notice. Our children were far too important to him and, indeed, this so-called advice proved utterly wrongheaded. One of the things that the public liked about Tony was the fact that he was a family man. The House of Commons' timetable was not designed for fathers who wanted to spend a modicum of time at home with their wife and kids. By now, however, we had developed a routine. Every morning we would drive in together and Tony would drop me off at chambers and this would give us time to talk. Evenings were more complicated and revolved around the time of the vote. If there was a vote at seven o'clock, Tony would come straight home and be back at the House around seven thirty, by which time I would have returned under my own steam, put the kids to bed and would start the dinner. If the vote wasn't till later, he might pick me up at chambers around six o'clock and then put the kids to bed while I cooked dinner. Then we would spend some time together before he had to go back to Westminster to vote at ten o'clock.

Our time with the kids was obviously limited during the week, but we would always take over at the weekend, which the nanny would have off: good for her and good for us. Once Euan was at nursery, we no longer travelled up to Sedgefield every weekend; one week in two we'd spend at home in London. In our working lives we met barristers and politicians and that was about it. St Joan of Arc had given us a foothold in the local community. Through the Church we met people of all different types and sizes. There is always a shortage of those prepared to be school governors, so I was able to get myself selected as a Labour Party governor, and I was also a governor of Highbury Hill, the local girls' comprehensive. Governors have a very important role to play in the running of a school as it is they who appoint the teachers and the head teacher and, in my view, a school stands or falls on the quality of its teachers, so I wanted to make sure that we got it right.

We made life-long friends through St Joan of Arc, friends who would later be very important in all our lives, in particular Felicity Mostyn-Williams who, even with six children, manages to be a part-time academic in Oxford. Our children were friends and Orla, her youngest, is my god-daughter. When we eventually moved house again, we decided not to move the children to the neighbourhood school. Although it meant taking them by car – which Tony usually did – it kept us anchored in the community which had provided us with much-needed roots.

Inevitably there were times when Tony played the game, and there were some people whom he only ever met within the walls of the Palace of Westminster. John Smith was one. Derry, John and Donald Dewar had all been at Glasgow University together. The relationship between Derry and Donald ended when Derry went off with Donald's wife, Alison, and indeed married her. Derry and John, however, remained great friends and insofar as we were part of Derry's social circle we knew John Smith, but we didn't socialise and I never really got to know him.

He and Derry were both inveterate drinkers and I remember one occasion when Tony staggered in at six o'clock in the morning and then staggered back out again three hours later, heading for the House. When he arrived in the chamber, he found John Smith in full flow. He had got up, gone in and led a debate without a second's thought. Both he and Derry had this capacity to drink anyone else under the table, and yet still manage to perform the next day.

Around the time I moved to Gray's Inn Square, a new building became available for Shadow Cabinet offices. Gordon had assumed that he and Tony would go there together. Although they wouldn't share rooms, they would have offices next to each other, but Anji was of the view, and Mo and I agreed, that Tony should not move. Peter didn't express it quite as directly because of his relationship with Gordon. So when Gordon decamped to the new offices, Tony stayed exactly where he'd always been, with Mo Mowlam and the others down the corridor. It added a physical distance – there was no more just popping in and out – and it also sent a message that Tony was his own man. I don't think Gordon was very happy, but he had no real alternative but to accept it. As far as their ability to work together was concerned, however, nothing really changed.

CHAPTER 14

All Change

In the run-up to the 1992 election the mood in the Party was curiously subdued. Margaret Thatcher had resigned and her successor John Major was generally seen as a damp squib. The Conservatives were in disarray. The poll tax had alienated a huge proportion of the electorate. All in all, it should have been the perfect springboard for a Labour victory. Critics outside the Party, then and now, offered various reasons for Labour's failure at the ballot box: Neil Kinnock was not seen as a credible prime minister; the infamous rally at Sheffield was triumphalist. Within our group, however, nobody was surprised and, in spite of the traditional upbeat performance of politicians on the hustings, no one really believed we were preparing for government. While Tony was at the Sheffield rally, I watched it on TV but we both had the same feeling, which was, roughly speaking, 'This is not going to work.'

The press, meanwhile, had been hedging its bets and was on the look-out for Labour's rising stars. The Member for Sedgefield was definitely on the list, and Barbara Amiel, later better known as Mrs Conrad Black, came up to interview Tony for the *Sunday Times*. She had wanted to stay in Myrobella, but I put my foot down. While I was happy to be known as Tony's wife in the constituency, I didn't see I was relevant further afield, perhaps sensing even then that I would somehow fall short.

I hated the idea that I would be singled out and treated as some sort of celebrity. I wanted nothing to do with what I called showbiz life. Barbara Amiel herself was not like any working journalist I had previously come across, and I had always been suspicious of surface glamour, no doubt a view that I absorbed from my grandmother. But my grandmother was right: it was exactly that life – a superficial world filled with frivolous people – that had led my father astray, and turned him into a drinker and a womaniser. He had been completely seduced by it, with devastating consequences. It wasn't that I didn't relish the role of political wife. It was being treated as a celebrity that I objected to, as if politics was a strand of show business. It's part of the reason that I tended to come out with 'gaffes'. It didn't happen when I was in my own world, in chambers or in court. But when I felt uncomfortable and on edge, I would end up talking too much as a result of nervousness, and that's when it would happen.

Barbara Amiel duly came up and we took her out to dinner. I can't say I enjoyed the evening. She was very flirtatious around all the men, especially Tony. A few days later she phoned me, claiming she needed more from me. Reluctantly I agreed to see her at chambers. I remember little of our conversation, beyond her saying that she envied me having a career and children as she had never managed to do both. In the published profile, she wrote that I was prickly and recorded the fact that I hadn't wanted to answer her questions. And I hadn't.

The '92 election was the first time I saw how the kids might be affected by their father's being a politician. There was a huge anti-Labour poster by the school and I remember them getting very upset. God knows it was mild compared with what was to come. As for who should take over from Neil once he'd stepped down, John Smith was seen as his inevitable successor: he had been Shadow Chancellor and had gravitas. Tony, however, wasn't convinced he would put through the necessary reforms. John's line was 'steady as we go'; Labour was slowly clawing its way back, and eventually the electorate would see sense. Tony strongly disagreed. The electorate was not going to turn to us, he believed, until we had changed ourselves.

After the defeat, Tony was seriously of the view that Gordon should stand for the leadership against John Smith but, although it was discussed, Gordon said no.

'Well, if that's the case,' I said to Tony, 'why don't you stand as deputy?'

He toyed with it, the main question being not, 'Is this sensible in terms of my career?' but, 'Is this sensible in terms of the kids?' In the end we decided it wasn't. They were still very young and, basically, what was the point? Gordon himself was very against it. Only later did we discover that he'd done a deal with John Smith right from the outset. In return for Gordon's backing him for the leadership – with Margaret Beckett as deputy – Gordon would get Shadow Chancellor and, in the fullness of time, Chancellor of the Exchequer.

And so it came to pass. Neil resigned and John Smith was speedily elected leader unopposed, with Margaret Beckett as his deputy representing the left wing of the Party, while Gordon found himself Shadow Chancellor.

Change was definitely in the air. Tony decided he just couldn't cope with the to-ing and fro-ing from Highbury twice a day – getting across Holloway Road, the main artery from the north, was a nightmare. We needed to move further in, he said. Through Margaret Hodge we heard that a doctor and his wife, down the road from her in Islington, wanted to do a swap for a smaller house. There were a number of pluses: not only would travelling be easier, but we'd be within walking distance of my sister.

When Lyndsey finished her Articles back in 1980, I had suggested she talk through the options with Val Davies, a solicitor friend of mine from the LSE. She, in turn, suggested Lyndsey talk to the man she was then going out with, a partner in a large firm of solicitors. Lyndsey was very unsure of herself at the time but this chap – Garry Hart – was convinced that she would do well in the right place, and arranged for her to become an assistant solicitor at Herbert Smith, where she was allocated to a newly appointed partner, Chris Tavener. A few years later she and Chris married and, by 1992, had two children, Lucy – eighteen months younger than Kathryn – and James, who had just been born.

The drawback of the new house was that financially it stretched us right to the hilt, with nothing left over for improvements, a situation that was exacerbated when interest rates went to over 15 per cent following the financial meltdown of Black Wednesday.

Once we were settled in Richmond Crescent, we began to

participate in 'state-of-the-Party' meetings either at our house or at Margaret's. Peter and Mo would often be there, and also Sally Morgan, who was employed by the Labour Party in London.

Under the new regime, Tony became Shadow Home Secretary. At least in government, the Home Office is seen as a poisoned chalice, and indeed it was for Michael Howard. In opposition, however, it depends on what happens. What happened in 1993 was the horrific murder of James Bulger. The abduction of this small boy by two older boys, caught on CCTV cameras, was played and replayed on television – the first time I can remember such a thing happening. Law and order had previously been seen as an Achilles' heel for Labour, yet Tony's unequivocal and hard-line response was proof that this was no longer the case. He combined compassion with a streak of steel – that steel I had recognised so early in our relationship. For the most tragic of reasons, Tony became a familiar figure on TV.

He had already shown that he was at ease in front of the cameras – he was the only MP who had been prepared to go on television the day after the election defeat. He also happened to be young and good-looking, with a growing family, all of which resonated with the public, though if you had asked Peter, even then, he would have said that Gordon was the leader of the moderniser group. Unfortunately for him, however, the role of Shadow Chancellor is far less visible.

Tony was also an impressive debater, and in February 1994 two of the most contentious issues in British politics went before Parliament: capital punishment and lowering the age of consent for gays. These were both cross-party issues and Tony worked closely with Edwina Currie, who tabled the amendment to the Criminal Justice and Public Order Bill. He was showing in very practical terms how he could work effectively with people of opposing political views when he thought it necessary.

I hardly ever came in contact with Tory politicians, and probably a good thing too: the one time I did it was a diplomatic disaster. Within a year of Tony being elected, he had been appointed assistant Treasury spokesman, and Michael Howard, then Employment Secretary in Margaret Thatcher's Cabinet, asked us over to his house in Notting Hill for dinner. Around the table were Michael and his wife Sandra, Norman Lamont and his wife – Norman was at that time a Treasury spokesman for the Tories. Then there was Ann Mallalieu, QC, later a Labour peer, with her rather right-wing husband. It was the strangest dinner party I had ever been to, with people who, in the normal way of things, I would have nothing to do with at all.

In the normal way of things we socialised with people we generally agreed with. When we did have disagreements, Tony and I tended to be the ones who were the more moderate. It would have been unusual for me to be regarded as a raging Leftie, which was clearly the case on this occasion.

As for Tony, I had the distinct impression that they viewed him as rather a quaint specimen, trying to fathom how he could possibly be a Labour Party politician at all, as anyone with his talents and sense should surely be in the Tory Party.

Safe topics in such situations are hard to find and there is absolutely no mileage to be gained in having an ideological discussion with Michael Howard, a very able silk and member of the Tory Cabinet. Most alarming, as far as I was concerned, was that Ann Mallalieu seemed more right-wing than the others. In situations like these there is no point in being impolite. You make it clear that you disagree, which I obviously did, and get out as quickly as possible. As I didn't anticipate a long-term relationship, I wasn't that inclined to put myself out.

As we drove back to Islington I imagined them doing the washing up and saying: 'Tony was perfectly charming but Cherie was a bit, well . . .' Not one of us.

I wasn't completely unused to people expounding right-wing views. Certainly, 5 Essex Court had been a left-leaning set, but in general the Bar is a pretty conservative (and Conservative) place, and falling out with your colleagues is not something I would recommend, so the simple answer is to say nothing. I am not someone who seeks confrontation if I can avoid it – I get enough of that in my job.

Over the two years of John Smith's leadership Tony did what he was asked to do, gave policy speeches and so on, but felt increasingly frustrated because of the 'one member one vote' (OMOV) issue.

It may seem obvious that each paid-up member of the Labour Party should have a say in determining the selection of candidates, for example, but it wasn't then. In Hackney, Tony and I had been involved in the attempted de-selection of Ron Brown (brother of George Brown, the former Cabinet minister), then – after he defected to the SDP – in the selection of Brian Sedgemoor. Each ward would send one delegate to the constituency selection meeting. Tony was our ward delegate, but I was there as the delegate for the white-collar branch of the GMB. This had been another reason to join a union: once you were a union delegate the union would pay your dues to join the General Management Committee. Once you became a GMC member, you had a vote to decide constituency policy, which ordinary members did not. It was far from democratic. The practical reason for wanting OMOV was the hope that we'd get more sensible candidates, rather than the Leftie lunatics we'd been forced to put up with over the past few years.

OMOV was the great debate at the 1993 Labour Party Conference. Everyone knew it would be difficult: the unions wouldn't give up their leverage without a fight, and the unions were important, not only historically, but because most of the money that funded the Party came directly from them. Tony wasn't at all sure that John Smith was truly committed, or whether, if push came to shove, a deal would be made: 'I'll trade OMOV against your backing me in something else.' Unlike Tony, he didn't regard the issue as important, and to some degree they had a falling out. Tony was 'too impatient', he said. His view was that all we had to do was wait, and then we'd be in. OMOV did get through, though not without a struggle, and it was largely thanks to John Prescott's sway with the unions that this first plank in the modernists' platform was laid.

On 11 May the following year, Tony went to a Labour Party fund-raising dinner in one of the big London hotels. I didn't go. Late that night he came back saying he thought John Smith had looked very ill. The next morning we had to be up early, as he was flying to Aberdeen while I was due in Croydon at an employment tribunal.

Just as we settled the case, somebody came in and said, 'Have you heard?'

John Smith was dead.

I remember standing in the corridor not moving, with people bumping into me. I was in total shock. I went straight back into London. It was only when I was on the train, looking out at the gardens, filled with blossom, that I thought of his wife and daughters.

He was only fifty-five. It was a terrible warning about the pressures of public life.

I remembered a conversation we'd had barely a month before, when Tony and I took a rare weekend away from the kids. He'd been asked to speak at the European Business School in Fontainebleau, outside Paris. It was years since we'd been there, and we did all those things you do in Paris, including going to the cinema, something we never had time for in London. We went to see *Schindler's List*, a haunting film that left you feeling disjointed, and somehow suspended in time. Having dinner afterwards, Tony started talking about John Smith and how frustrated he felt under his leadership. He felt that the modernisers were grinding to a halt.

'It can't go on like this,' he said. Then added, 'But I've got this feeling that it won't anyway.'

'What do you mean?'

'I mean that something's going to happen. Got to happen.'

'Like what?'

'Some kind of bust-up. I don't know. But something. It can't go on like this.' Never could he have imagined anything so tragic or so decisive.

Tony called about two minutes after I got into chambers.

'You've got to stand,' I told him.

'It's difficult.'

'Listen to me. You have to go for this.'

He was about to board the plane. I said I'd meet him at arrivals. We'd pick up the car and talk about it then.

As I turned into High Holborn on my way to the tube, I bumped into our friend and former Hackney neighbour Barry Cox.

'Can't stop,' I said. 'I'm off to Heathrow to get Tony. When you talk to him, Barry, tell him that he's got to stand. I'm frightened he'll think that maybe he owes it to Gordon not to.'

When I got to Heathrow, I called Anji from a pay phone. Mo Mowlam had rung, and John Reid, all saying the same thing. 'He's got to go for it.'

As usual the arrivals hall was crowded, but it wasn't till I saw Tony come through on his own that I realised that many of those waiting were cameramen and reporters. They practically trampled me underfoot to get to him, shouting 'Tony! Tony!' For a moment it was mayhem, then he gave them a few words on the theme of 'it's a great shock', and of course it was. They may not have agreed on everything, but John Smith had been good to him, and Tony respected and liked him. Eventually I managed to get him down to the car park and into the car.

I am a barrister, an advocate, and my job is putting a case coherently. This time it seemed that all my skills had abandoned me. I just said: 'You're the best candidate for the job, and you can't let Gordon seize the moment through some misplaced sense of obligation.'

'He'll have all the Scottish MPs tied up.'

'No, he won't. John Reid's been on the phone already. Listen, Tony. This is your moment. You've got to take it. Who dares wins.'

He just sat slumped in the passenger seat with his eyes closed and said, 'I know.' But it was with no sense of triumph or eager anticipation. It was more resignation: 'I know.'

We both knew the arguments against it: the children and Gordon. Tony looked pale. It was a sign of how unnerved he was that he let me drive. 'John Smith was working too hard,' he said. 'Burning the candle at both ends.'

I knew that time was of the essence. My fear was that Gordon would just move in, and it would be a *fait accompli*, and I knew Tony was the right person for the job. By the next general election there would be people voting who had never known a time when the Tories weren't in power. The new leader had to be someone they could relate to. Tony had always been more appealing to the general public than Gordon, and more grounded in the realities of everyday life. What could be more grounding than bringing up a young family? Ironically, Tony was always saying, 'Gordon, if you really want to be leader, you need to get married.'

Yet he also felt it was a mark of how honourable Gordon was that he didn't marry just for appearances. On the other hand, if he had, in my view, he would inevitably have been a more rounded person, with another dimension to his life.

Nothing would happen until after the funeral, so to that extent discussions would be on-going, but we all had to know if Tony was going to stand. When we got to the office people were beginning to show their faces. Anji was there, and Mo and Peter Kilfoyle: the two of them would eventually head up his campaign. Also, to my great relief, I saw John Reid, one of Neil Kinnock's close advisers and an early advocate of reform of the Party. Although he and Gordon were both Scottish MPs, I knew he would support Tony. The voices were unanimous: Tony had to stand. And I think he knew in his heart that he was the better person to carry the moderniser message, if only because he embodied it better. It was about changing the perception of the Labour Party, making the Labour Party a party of government, and actually being a party relevant to people's lives. Having made my position clear, and knowing that I would see him later, I headed back to chambers.

The next day the BBC had Tony as the front-runner. And apparently Alastair Campbell – then a journalist with *Today* – had said on *Newsnight*, 'It obviously has to be Tony Blair.'

Over those next few days I had plenty of time to think things over. I knew this was a pivotal moment for Tony. I knew that he had what it takes. I knew it would make a huge difference to Tony himself, and I knew that he would have less time for the children, but I didn't think it would make much difference to us as a family. My practice was going in the right direction, we had just bought a big family house, and I assumed we would tick on.

My own belief is that he decided to go for it straight away. For him, the real question was not, would he stand, but how to reconcile Gordon, in order to preserve the modernisers' ticket. What he most feared was that if both of them stood, the modernisers would lose out through squabbling among themselves. Tony's main aim over those next few days was to persuade Gordon to give way to him. He wouldn't stand unopposed, the left would see to that, but even more reason not to risk splitting the moderate vote.

Getting Gordon to stand aside was no easy task. First, he was the more senior. Secondly, he obviously had his supporters just as Tony had. One of the key players, of course, was Peter Mandelson. That first night I remember sitting in our kitchen and asking Tony, 'And what about Peter? What does he think?' and Tony saying with a sigh, 'Peter is very conflicted.' I wish now that Peter's ambivalence had been better known at the time, because Gordon's conviction that Peter was instantly in our camp destroyed their relationship.

My job, as I saw it, was to make sure that all our friends were onside, which is why I said what I did when I bumped into Barry Cox. In fact, Barry then started to raise money for Tony's campaign informally. Then there were Charlie and Marianna. Charlie wasn't a political player at that point, he was just a personal friend who was interested in politics. There were Lyndsey and Chris Tavener, and Bill and Katy Blair. Our role – friends and family – was to support Tony in his decision, because we all knew he would come under tremendous pressure from Gordon.

John Smith's funeral was on 20 May, in Scotland. Gordon had gone back to his constituency fairly early on, while Tony just flew up for the funeral. The fact that Gordon hadn't been in London during the early stages was irrelevant to his campaign. We knew from day one that Nick Brown would be his campaign manager, and we knew Nick of old, and had a good idea of the tricks he would have up his sleeve. Nick is an old-style political campaigner and his people were basically going around saying, 'Gordon is more acceptable to the unions, he is more true Labour than Tony, Tony is a young upstart.' It didn't need Gordon in London to do that. In fact, it was more effective if he wasn't.

After the funeral Tony stayed with Nick Ryden, a friend from Fettes, and that night Gordon went round there to talk. Nick had only recently bought the house and not everything worked as it should. At one point, Gordon disappeared upstairs. He was gone for what seemed like a very long time and Tony was just wondering what on earth could have happened, when the phone rang. It was Gordon calling from the loo on his mobile. The handle had come off the door and he couldn't get out.

As the week went on Tony clearly had the momentum and I was coming to the view that if Gordon wanted to stand, he should just let him.

'You'll win anyway,' I said. 'So don't come to a deal. Just let him lose.' But Tony said no. The modernisers were a team, he said, and this was a team effort. He didn't want anything to break that up.

Back in London there was yet another meeting with Gordon. This time it was at Lyndsey's house in Richmond Avenue, just round the corner – one of the conditions of these meetings was that no one should see Gordon coming to our house. This was the meeting where essentially it was agreed that Tony would stand unopposed and Gordon would be Chancellor; that they would work together and that Gordon would support him, and the aim would be to reform the Labour Party and take power.

Part of Gordon obviously didn't want to accept that, but another part of him could see that Tony now had the momentum. There were plenty of ways he could have rationalised it to himself: that he had been unlucky in having the economic portfolio, which had failed to give him much exposure, while Tony, on the other hand, had had the law and order portfolio, which he made a lot of, and his response had struck a popular chord. It was always a given that they would work in tandem and that when Tony stood down, Gordon would take over. Tony also made it clear to Gordon that he had no intention of staying leader for ever and that when he did stand down he would support Gordon as his natural successor, assuming they worked well together as PM and Chancellor in the meantime.

As far as I know the timing was never discussed but when Tony left for Lyndsey's, I made my position perfectly clear, even if I framed it as a joke. 'If you agree with Gordon that you're going to do this for one term only, don't come back home. Because that's just ridiculous.'

But Tony was always very supportive of Gordon having his chance. He used to say in terms of ability that Gordon was way ahead of everyone and the irony is that if they'd only worked as closely together as originally agreed, his chance would have come sooner.

As for Granita, they did meet up there a day or two later. But by then it was all done and dusted. The Granita meeting was basically for them to talk about the announcement. It wasn't the forum for the kind of stormy discussions that had preceded it. No way would that have happened in public, in a restaurant.

My own reading of the myth – that is, that a 'deal' was done at Granita – was that Gordon didn't want to admit that he'd agreed anything without first discussing it with his people. At least, from Tony's perspective, it was already agreed.

Once that was out of the way, the next issue was the deputy leadership. How attractive was Tony to the unions? His membership of the T & G was not treated with any great seriousness. He was not seen as a union man. His dealings with the unions when he'd been Shadow Employment Secretary had not been easy. He'd got them to accept that the closed shop agreement would not be reinstated and he wouldn't be remembered fondly for that. On the other side, he had pushed through the minimum wage policy. John Prescott was very much a union person, though no one could be sure how the voting would go, not least because now, for the first time in the

Party's history, we had One Member One Vote, largely because of John Prescott's efforts.

Barry Cox raised about £70,000 from various people who came forward and gave money to support the campaign, and Anji was organising the hustings element.

Tony never takes anything for granted, but it was soon clear that he was the front-runner. I didn't by any means go to all his meetings because he was travelling round, and I had the children to look after and a career to pursue. I did go to some events in London and the south-east and went to a couple of the Question and Answer sessions where he was developing the relaxed style of campaigning that would soon become familiar, not just to Labour Party members, but to the whole British electorate: sitting down on the edge of the stage and rolling up his shirt-sleeves to his elbows. He did fantastically. I was so proud of him. We discovered friends in many quarters. I knew Harriet Harman through my work with the NCCL. Her husband, Jack Dromey, proved very helpful when we were looking at how to appeal to the more modernising element of the union movement. We already knew Charles Clarke from the days when he lived near us in Hackney. I knew Patricia Hewitt a little because her husband was a barrister with an employment law practice.

John Smith had died on 12 May and the announcement of the leadership election result was set for 21 July. But even though ten weeks felt long and drawn out, there was a real feeling throughout of a campaign and a goal and a 'let's do it!'

In all this Peter Mandelson stayed very much in the background, because he was such a controversial figure, not only in terms of trade unionists who continued to see him as the Prince of Darkness, but also because of his relationship with Gordon, who remained convinced that Peter had done the dirty on him. It was Kate Garvey, Tony's diary secretary, who came up with the idea that Peter should have a *nom de guerre*, and the name we used was Bobby, after Bobby Kennedy. The fact that Bobby was involved became the Big Secret.

Neil Kinnock also stayed out of the picture. He remained strictly neutral from start to finish, but the intimation we got from those who had been close to him – like Charles Clarke and Patricia Hewitt – was that Tony was Neil's chosen successor.

So much was going on, and I was so focused on the job in hand – which was getting Tony to stand, and then getting everyone to support him – it's perhaps not surprising that I forgot about my own role. The 'hang-on-a-minute,-if-all-this-is-going-to-happen,-I'm-going-to-be-a-bit-in-the-public-eye' moment was late in arriving. One evening, shortly after Tony had decided to stand, the phone went.

'Hi there, Cherie. Great to hear your voice after so long. So how are you doing?'

It was Carole Caplin.

CHAPTER 15

Nearly There

When Carole called I couldn't have been more delighted. The twin spindles of my life – politics and the Bar – were rather incestuous but Carole was completely separate. More to the point, I was still anxious to lose the extra stone.

She came round to the house the following Saturday.

'Well, this is all very exciting, isn't it?' she said, as she came in. Her call hadn't been entirely serendipitous. She'd just got back from New York, and knew all about what was happening and wondered if I needed some advice on hair and make-up. What were my thoughts? I didn't understand what she was talking about. I went to the same hairdresser I'd been going to for years, and as for make-up I just went to Boots. It would be useful, she said, if we could look through my wardrobe; it would help her determine my style.

I didn't really have a style. My clothes divided into two types: casual things to hang round the house with the kids, such as leggings, baggy tops, trainers, the occasional long skirt; then barrister suits, mainly black or blue, always with skirts as, in those days, trousers were not allowed. My work shoes had heels but they were reasonably chunky as I spent a lot of time on my feet, both in court and travelling. I also had the odd smart dress which I bought from someone called Ivona Ivons who ran a shop near Clerkenwell County Court. She would sort me out a couple of suits for work and perhaps a dress at the same time.

I wasn't uninterested in clothes, but on the other hand I didn't read fashion magazines or keep up with the latest styles. I'd just pop along to Ivona, and whatever was in that year I'd have. I was reasonably objective about my body. My strong points were my hair, which I had in abundance, and my skin. I had always had a neat bust and a small waist but my problem was big hips and thighs, so on the whole I avoided trousers as I thought my bottom was too big. Although I tried to look nice, we had three small children and two houses to keep up, so shopping for me was bottom of the list. The exception was work clothes as, operating in such a public arena, it was important to look smart. Shoes were not a priority. I had a black pair, a brown pair, a blue pair and a lightweight pair of beige sandals, and that was about it. It wasn't as if Tony and I went out to restaurants or clubs. Going out was about seeing friends and just sitting round a kitchen table talking. As most of our friends also had young kids like us, it was hardly a competitive environment.

Looking at the contents of my wardrobe through Carole's eyes, however, I could sense what was coming. 'I think you could do with some help,' she said. Of course she was right. I didn't have either the time or the knowledge even to think about changing my image. Everything was connected, she said. My weight, my clothes, my food. It would take time but she was convinced I could begin to see improvements more or less immediately, certainly in the couple of months we had before the results of the leadership election were announced. We started immediately. She spent the rest of the afternoon at the house.

The first thing that needed attention was what I ate, which soon extended to everyone in the family as she chucked out half the things in the kitchen. She opened the cupboards and went through everything saying, 'This is bad, this is good.' It was short-lived. The kids would have none of it. Within days the cupboards were restored to their former glory.

Once that was done, we went upstairs to the sitting room to go through an exercise plan with me. There was no time to lose. Since doing her workshops five years previously, I already had the basics, but this was specific. That's when she met Tony and suggested an exercise plan for him as well.

My wardrobe came in for the same treatment as the kitchen cupboards and most of what I had went straight into bin bags. Some things she made me put on before making a decision. Long jackets were more flattering, she said. I should go for low necks rather than high necks. Heels were good and I should wear more of them. On the one hand it was fairly horrifying to watch, but on the other hand I thought it was probably for the best. It was something that definitely needed to be done, but by nature I'm a hoarder. 'If you can't remember when you last wore it, chuck it' was one of her mantras.

To get my eye in, Carole took me shopping. Browns in South Molton Street was a revelation. It was the first time I had been anywhere so fashionable. But she was right about making an immediate improvement. I wore the dress I bought at Browns to a party midway through the leadership campaign and bumped into Fiona Millar, Alastair Campbell's partner and the daughter of Audrey Millar, at whose house I had attended meetings of the Marylebone Labour Party all those years before. She was feeling particularly frumpy, she said, as she'd only recently had Grace, her third child.

'But as for you, Cherie, you're looking great. Much more – how shall I put it – groomed!' How we laughed. Groomed is a word no one would have ever used to describe me, especially someone like Fiona, who always looked chic, which as the working mother of two small boys and a new baby was saying something.

The question of the deputy was still in the air. John Prescott and Margaret Beckett were standing both for the leadership and for deputy leader. The aim was to find the best balance. Myself, Peter and Anji were keener on John Prescott, who we felt would make for more of a contrast. Gordon was keener on Margaret Beckett. But it would depend entirely on who won the ballot, and as this was the first time we'd be using the electoral college (that we'd fought so hard for) no one had any real idea how it would work.

The twenty-first of July, when the results of the leadership election were to be announced, was a lovely English summer's day and, come what may, I knew it was important I look my best. We'd had a practice run for the party where I'd so impressed Fiona, and I had to admit that the results were a definite improvement on my own efforts. I had also discovered how much more confident I felt when I looked the part.

Downstairs at Richmond Crescent the combined Blair and Booth clans were gathering. My mum, my dad, Lyndsey and Chris, Tony's sister Sarah, Bill and Katy, who was involved with Chinese For Labour and had got its backing for Tony.

While I was getting ready upstairs the kids gave me a running commentary about the scruffy-looking types hanging round on the pavement opposite, men mostly, loaded down with cameras and camera bags.

About half an hour before we were due to leave, Tony had a word with them and agreed to do some pictures. He suggested the park behind the house where the kids and he often played football. So the photographers got us to sit on a bench while they snapped away: ones of us both looking at each other; Tony looking at the camera and me looking at Tony; and so on. It was the first time I had ever done anything like it at all. The nearest I'd got to experiencing any kind of press interest was at Pat Phoenix's funeral when I'd led my father into the church.

The oddest thing of all was being called Mrs Blair, as they shouted out instructions. Most people called me Cherie. My colleagues at the Bar certainly did, as did those involved with the Labour Party, where I was very much a person in my own right. Even at the children's school, where mothers might be expected to be called Mrs Whoever, I was known by my Christian name as both teachers and the head knew me primarily as a school governor. On a day-to-day level the only people who didn't call me Cherie were the clerks. To them I was Miss Booth.

Tony's union, the T & G, had provided a car to take us down to the Westminster Institute of Education where the results would be announced. The candidates all lined up on the stage, and when I saw Tony's face I knew he had won. He had won in all sections, including the union section which our people had speculated might prove more difficult. John Prescott was duly elected deputy leader, so it couldn't have been better. Then it was time to celebrate. Cars took us the short distance to Church House, just behind Westminster Abbey. It was a beautiful afternoon and both the building and the square outside were thronged with supporters. We were taken straight upstairs and out on to the balcony where Neil and Glenys Kinnock were already waiting.

Tony then made his leadership acceptance speech in which he thanked everybody who'd worked so hard for his campaign. Most of the names were generally known, but he couldn't resist thanking

'Bobby'. Soon that was the question on everyone's lips – especially among the press – 'Who's Bobby?' Eventually, of course, Peter's identity was revealed. Then it was 'Shock Horror, the Prince of Darkness has been helping Tony Blair'.

I didn't know Margaret Beckett very well in those days. I do now and have a great deal of admiration for her. Although she had just lost to both Tony and John Prescott, she came up with a warm and ready smile, with her husband Leo, to thank Tony for what he'd said and to wish him well. Just as she was leaving she added, 'I nearly forgot. Sylvie will be waiting for you outside.'

And I thought, Sylvie? Who is Sylvie?

Sylvie turned out to be the relief driver for the Leader of the Opposition. While Margaret had been standing in as leader, she had been driven around in the official car. No one had said anything to us about there being a car. From then on, whenever Tony was involved on official business, there would be either Terry – who became a true family friend – or the wonderful Sylvie to drive him around.

The next day Terry was waiting outside in the Rover to take Tony to the House. And this then became the pattern. If I was up early enough I'd get a lift and they'd drop me at Gray's Inn which was directly on their route. Similarly, when they were about to leave, I'd get a call and if I was ready to go too, I'd be there waiting on the pavement when the familiar red Rover drew up.

The office of the Leader of the Opposition was far grander than anything Tony had had before, certainly in size. It's at the heart of the Palace of Westminster itself, not far from where the Prime Minister has his office on the opposite side of the courtyard. There was in fact a suite of rooms that included the Shadow Cabinet room. Tony decided to use the one Neil Kinnock had used. Apart from anything else, John Smith's room was piled high with boxes of papers waiting to be dealt with. After all the excitement of Tony's election, it was a sober reminder. Tony asked me to take a look at the room he proposed using, and I was not impressed. It was in serious need of redecoration. The House of Commons offered to get it done, but Tony declined. 'I don't intend to stay here very long,' he said. 'I don't want to make these rooms too comfortable because I don't want to get too comfortable in opposition.' The aim was to get out and get into government as soon as possible.

With this in mind, Tony was pretty clear that he wanted Alastair

Campbell to join the team as press secretary. Alastair was a political journalist and Tony had got to know him in the House of Commons when he was the lobby correspondent for the *Daily Mirror*. Although a Labour man through and through, he was never interested in policy and he had never been part of our discussion groups. He and Fiona Millar were also great friends of Neil and Glenys. Fiona was a journalist, which was how the two had met. In fact, she had co-written a book with Glenys called *By Faith and Daring: Interviews with Remarkable Women*.

When Peter Mandelson first sounded him out for Tony, Alastair had said no. Then Tony talked to Alastair himself a few days after he moved into his new office. Alastair was equivocal, Tony told me, though he thought he could be persuaded. When Tony is determined, nothing will stop him, and on this he was determined. We were about to set off for our usual holiday in France, dropping in on friends. As Alastair and Fiona were spending the summer in a house in Provence, Tony proposed to go down there and talk him into it. He would convince Alastair, and I would convince Fiona. That, at any rate, was the idea. The parents of one of Tony's researchers – Tim Allan – had just bought a cottage in Tuscany and Tim suggested we go there for a week or so. Italy would be our last stop, and we could drop in on Alastair on our way.

Zigzagging across Europe was nothing unusual for us. Only my mum, who usually came with us, had a sense of where the places actually were. Originally we went to France because of Tony's fear of flying. By sheer will-power, however, he'd succeeded in overcoming it. Now we went because it had become the tradition. Our old Hackney neighbours Barry Cox and Katie Kay, and Maggie Rae and Alan Howarth, who were now married, had clubbed together to buy a house in a village called Miradoux, north of Toulouse in western France. This was another complete wreck – and, over the years, we had joined in cheerfully, helping to pull it into some sort of shape. But with three growing children, it had become a bit cramped. Then in 1992 David Keene, QC, came to the rescue. He and Michael Beloff were the *de facto* heads of chambers and David had recently bought a place in the Ariège, just south of Toulouse. We could go there whenever we liked, he said.

In the seventies David had stood as a Labour candidate, but in 1981 he had signed the Limehouse Declaration and gone over to the

SDP. David's 'place' turned out to be a château in a village called St Martin d'Oydes in the foothills of the Pyrenees. To the delight of the kids, it boasted a swimming pool, and as there was plenty of room Mum and the nanny could come too. In later years, Lyndsey and her family would sometimes join us.

Children like going back to familiar places, seeing familiar faces, and it gave Tony and me an opportunity to spend time with each other and with our friends. For years we visited these same two houses so it's hard to remember what happened when and where. There was the time, I remember, when we sang 'These Are a Few of My Favourite Things' for what seemed like hours, to drown out a storm that threatened to engulf Miradoux, with the fire-engine across the road clanging a merry accompaniment. Another year David's swimming pool turned bright green. That didn't stop the Blair family swimming in it. Swimming was a favourite activity. Our then-nanny Ros would devise complicated galas, 'the summer Olympics' as they were known, which involved convoluted races, biggest-splash competitions, even the funniest-wet-hairstyle competition, which Tony regularly won. For him, being in surroundings he felt so completely at home in, airing his French at the local shops and cafés, playing tennis, eating out in the local restaurants was the perfect antidote to life in England. Nobody to collar him on the street; no need to dress the part. He could slob around in shorts and T-shirts to his heart's content. A true holiday. Madcap lurches from place to place were part of the tradition. Barry Cox called us the House Bandits. The truth was that many of our closest friends had holiday homes and it was fun for us and the kids to join them.

Flassan, where Alastair and Fiona had their house, turned out to be as far away from the foothills of the Pyrenees as it's possible to be in France. Tony decided that the drive would be too daunting, so we dropped off the hired car and took the train from Toulouse to Avignon. It's not a journey I can recommend. We arrived at Avignon station late at night, the children understandably grumpy, to find an equally grumpy Alastair waiting for us. There was then a further drive of over an hour into the hills.

I didn't know Alastair that well in those days, though you always knew when he was around. He was tall and handsome, though not the kind of handsome that appealed to me. He had definite presence, and I knew from Tony that he had a powerful personality. What I didn't know was that he had a temper, and an ego you could build a house on.

On the way there, Tony had been through what he wanted me to do. Alastair was the best man for the job, he said, and he wanted him. It would mean him taking a big drop in salary, so both he and Fiona had to be persuaded that it was worth it. My job was to be nice to Fiona, to reassure her that Tony was a family man, that it would all be all right, that Tony had his priorities too and it wouldn't ruin her family life. So that's what I did, whether we were washing up, watching the children, or chopping vegetables together on the kitchen table:

'This is our chance to do something of real importance, Fiona. Tony feels Alastair has a real contribution to make. He says that Alastair is the best man for the job and I believe him. It won't be that bad as I'm not going to let Tony lose sight of the family thing.'

Of course it soon became apparent that both Fiona and I had been utterly bamboozled by our menfolk.

In the end, Alastair agreed. He didn't say so in so many words – at least not in my hearing – but we left for Tim's parents' place in Italy with Tony confident that he'd got what he came for.

Our onward journey was as chaotic as usual. We left Flassan at four in the morning, the children lying like sacks in the back of Alastair's car. Our train to Italy left Marseille around six thirty a.m. It was all a great rush and in the end we got on the wrong one – a stopping train – though at least we had a carriage all to ourselves, meaning we could sing songs – my usual way of keeping at bay their favourite question: 'Are we nearly there?'

CHAPTER 16

Hurdles

In 1993 Tony wrote a pamphlet for the Fabian Society, of which we had both long been members. In it he criticised the continued presence, unchanged since it was written in 1917, of Clause IV of the Labour Party constitution, which read:

> To secure for the workers by hand or by brain the full fruits of their industry and the most equitable distribution thereof that may be possible upon the basis of the common ownership of the means of production, distribution and exchange, and the best obtainable system of popular administration and control of each industry or service.

His position was, 'How can we be a party who are supposed to be of the modern world when we still have as part of our objective "the common ownership of the means of production and exchange"?' Everyone accepted that wholesale nationalisation was no longer part of our policy, but the fact that Clause IV was still there could be used as a stick to beat us with – either by the Tory press, who could pretend that we really did want to nationalise everything in sight, or by Militant, who could berate us for not getting on with what was supposed to be a key objective.

Only those closest to Tony knew what he was planning to do. The occasion, of course, would be the Labour Party Conference.

Scrapping Clause IV, he believed, would set the tone for all that would follow. On one level it was only a gesture – it was axing something that was already dead – but gestures are sometimes important and, if he could get the Party behind him on this, then the left would be out in the cold and the modernising process could begin in earnest. To be electable, we had to show that the Labour Party had changed, and it had to change, he said, if the electorate was to trust us to run the country. We needed to show that we had made a clean break with the past.

Paradoxically, the Labour Party as then constituted was a very conservative organisation. It didn't like change, and Clause IV was seen as part of the family furniture, handed down from generation to generation, a much-loved heirloom but now useless and out of date.

Although Tony's personal credit was running high, it was not enough to guarantee conference's acceptance. There were plenty of reactionary elements about, especially within union ranks, and he would need all the help he could get. Even his Shadow Chancellor was one of those he had to square. Gordon doesn't like rocking the boat, and his line was 'why bother given it doesn't really matter?' Tony's answer to that was 'public perception'. John Prescott would be the key, he decided, not least because he had been instrumental in getting OMOV through the previous year. Although Tony had always wanted him as his deputy, John had been elected by the electoral college, not chosen by Tony. He was independently mandated and would expect to be consulted in any event. It was also a way of reassuring him that he wasn't going to be side-lined. Tony and John came from entirely different wings of the Party, and had never been close, so the situation had to be finessed exceptionally carefully.

Meanwhile, I had my own agenda in relation to the 1994 Labour Party Conference. I was determined that the leader's wife would go out on that platform looking good enough to take on the world – or at least the massed ranks of the Tory Party – so I continued with my dietary regime and the exercising and found a new hairdresser. André worked at Michaeljohn, a smart London salon. He had no idea who I was when I first went in – just a new client with a haircut that needed disguising: a radical attempt by my former hairdresser to give me a more modern look had resulted in what can only be described as a mullet. André was then in his mid-twenties. Although his father was Italian, he had been brought up and trained in France and, as a result, had a wonderfully quirky accent.

The spiky fringe was not the look for a woman who wanted to be taken seriously, he decided, and short hair on top and the long bob looked doubly ridiculous after a hot day in court, crammed under a sweaty wig. Although I had a lot of hair, André explained, it was soft. The difficulty would be holding a style. As I wanted to have something I could handle myself, this became a major problem. Even after hours of blow-drying practice, I was incapable of making it look remotely 'done'. If I attempted any backcombing, it looked as if a mouse had crawled in to make its nest. It was the same with my make-up. Touching up what had once been done had never occurred to me. I had never renewed my lipstick in my life, nor worried about whether my nose or my forehead were shiny.

My new haircut had its first outing on 23 September 1994 – my fortieth birthday party – and I had booked Frederick's restaurant the previous March. For Tony's fortieth we had just had a party at home. Not a surprise party, but a surprise there certainly was. Among his things, I had found an old tape recording, with a label saying, BBC Radio Oxford: Ugly Rumours. Tony's student band! So I had taken it along to Barry Cox and basically said, 'You're in TV so could you get it put on a CD?' Halfway through the evening, I played it. The lyrics were deeply profound, sadly not matched by the reedy voice singing this plaintive dirge. Everybody thought it a great hoot. Everybody except one.

My mum had been warning me for some time that things would change, and not necessarily for the better, but even she was shocked when the *Evening Standard* took her photograph that evening. In fact, they photographed everybody, as if my guest list might provide a clue to who was out and who was in under the new leadership. But my party owed nothing to Labour or even Tony. I made a little speech about how much I owed my mum – not so different from the one I'd made twenty-two years earlier, the day before I left for the LSE.

Anji had already warned me to block off conference week. She showed me the stage set for the platform, because I'd need to be colour co-ordinated, she explained, or at least wear something that wouldn't clash. The previous year, at the OMOV Party Conference in Brighton, I'd heard that John Smith's wife had brought along a hairdresser who was being paid for by the Party. My thought then was, Why on earth would Elizabeth Smith need a hairdresser? Now I was thinking, I hope to goodness André will be available! He wasn't, so Carole volunteered to come to ensure that I didn't look a complete disaster. She had never been to a Labour Party Conference – she wasn't even a member of the Party – and when she asked if I thought I'd need an evening dress, I burst into laughter.

'This is a Labour Party Conference.' But I would need something for Scots Night and Welsh Night, not to mention the dozens of other receptions I'd have to attend with Tony. There would be media everywhere. It was all about photographs. I'd need something to arrive in, something for Tony's big conference speech, and possibly something to go home in. Obviously I couldn't call Elizabeth Smith for advice. I was beginning to realise the whole business was both expensive and a diplomatic minefield. If I went looking like a slob, it showed a lack of respect. If I wore the same thing all the time, that too showed a lack of respect. Yet, nor could I appear to be throwing money around. It was a question of 'damned if you did, damned if you didn't'. I remembered how Norma Major never seemed to get it right, at least as far as the press was concerned. A further constraint was that whatever designer I went for had to be home-grown and the look needed to be 'modern' to reflect the 'moderniser' label.

That year conference was in Blackpool and I hadn't been there since I was a little girl riding a donkey on the beach. For the first time, Tony had police security. The whole of one floor of the Imperial Hotel was sealed off. Access was by lift and there was a policeman standing outside our door, and Labour Party stewards patrolling the corridors. I'd had no idea it was run like this. Tony was permanently holed up with Alastair or Peter or Anji or Gordon or Robin or Sally or one of the others. I was feeling particularly unsettled as I had left Ros in sole charge of the kids. She hadn't even done a night on her own before, and this was for nearly a week. She was incredibly reliable and trustworthy and as mad on football as the boys were. All the same . . . Over the next few days, whatever else was happening, we would make sure we both spoke to them every evening, when you would hear them arguing about who was going to tell Mum or Dad this or that piece of 'news'.

Tony had been working on his speech for days, and it still wasn't finished. The slogan New Labour, New Britain had only been agreed the previous week, just in time to get the banners up for the conference. By the Monday the trickle of people around my husband had become a whirlpool. The debate about Tony's speech continued, every hour more frenetic and tense. I was the one person not involved. Anji had told me that on no account could I go down to the conference on my own. If I wanted to go, then somebody had to come with me. And suddenly I thought, This is utterly ridiculous. I've been coming to conference for years, what are they talking about? I'm hardly a novice. So I opened our door, sneaked down the backstairs to avoid the lift, and emerged into the hotel lobby, where I immediately caught sight of Glenys Thornton, my old friend from LSE days and, later, Hackney co-resident.

We were just having a chat, when suddenly there were lights and cameras all around and someone with a microphone asking Glenys who she was. I completely froze. The next moment, I felt a hand on my back and then on my arm, and Hilary Coffman was propelling me towards the lift saying, 'Thank you, Cherie', and it was back to my prison.

The pair of us stood in that lift not saying a word and I felt my blood pounding.

I had known Hilary for years. She had been head of press for John Smith and had also worked for Neil Kinnock. Alastair had brought her in to work for Tony. When the lift stopped at 'our' floor, she handed me over to Anji.

'I thought I told you not to go down there, Cherie,' Anji said as she walked me down the corridor. 'You really don't understand politics.'

'Thank you, Anji, but I do understand politics.' If looks could kill, she should have been dead. Our relationship was deteriorating rapidly. I couldn't believe it. I was being treated like a naughty schoolgirl. These people apparently considered themselves empowered to tell me what to do.

For years I had devoted myself to helping the Labour Party. Trodden freezing streets, given up weekends, evenings. I had even stood as a candidate, for goodness' sake, retaining my deposit against all the odds. As for my husband, he hadn't always been surrounded by acolytes tending his every need. I had been there from the beginning, encouraging him when he needed encouraging, listening when he needed someone to bounce ideas off, to talk things through. From first to last we were a team. Hopes, plans, dreams – ours was a true marriage, a joint endeavour. Yet this wasn't a negotiation with my husband: now it was ten other people saying Cherie Will Do This. Since I was a teenager I had been used to having my own political opinions, and not being allowed to voice them publicly any more was like having a limb cut off. I sensed that I was becoming a non-person. Someone to be wheeled out when appropriate, like an Edwardian child, to be seen but not heard.

My humiliation was made worse by the fact that part of me knew that I couldn't just go down and pretend that I was like any other delegate, because I wasn't. Not any more. I sat in our bedroom and felt highly unsettled, unable to concentrate on anything. I wanted to be involved, just as I always had been, but how could I? It had been made perfectly clear that I wasn't wanted.

It was then that Alastair started fretting about Carole.

'We can't have that glamorous-looking creature here,' he announced.

'Why on earth not?'

'Because I don't want people to know that you're having help with your hair and make-up.'

'Elizabeth Smith did last year.'

'That was different.'

'Don't be ridiculous, Alastair. How could it be different?'

'I'm telling you, Cherie, it's different and I don't want the press to know.'

'Because she's good-looking, you mean? Is that a crime?'

He stalked off. But Alastair had spoken and the rest had heard. From then on Carole was banned from going anywhere. She was stuck either with me or in her room and told not to go out under any circumstances.

The conference proceeded in the usual way: going to meetings, listening to debates on the platform, and in the evening attending the various functions, like Scots Night. I had done a bit of Scottish dancing at school – things like the Gay Gordons and the Eightsome Reel – but to hear it announced that 'the leader and his wife will now start the dancing' proved strangely paralysing, especially with BBC2 filming the whole thing for *Newsnight*.

You'd go in, shake a few hands, Tony would make a little speech, everyone would listen, then we'd move on to the next one. These were basically off-the-cuff remarks which reflected what he was thinking about, things that might end up in his speech. Wherever we went we were followed by film crews, on show the whole time. Meanwhile I tried to follow Pat Phoenix's example, trying always to be nice and to smile.

It was the first time I had found myself in this position of appendage, and it did not come easily. I am by nature a doer, not a stander and watcher. I had already decided that I would do something with the Labour MPs' wives. Not all wives were politically active. I already felt that wives generally had a raw deal in Parliament and the Labour Party in particular didn't look after them. The Tories were much better in their support for wives and children. The least I could do, I thought, was to invite them for tea. It was agreed that I would host a tea-party for the wives of the north-west regional MPs because few of the others would be there. In fact, this would prove the start of what became known as 'Spouse in the House', a support group set up by two wonderful women, Val Corbett and Sally Grocott, and Pauline Prescott and I became its honorary patrons.

Tony's speech wasn't until Tuesday. Purgatory, I decided, would be a doddle compared with this. The speech would go through between twenty-five and forty drafts, with everyone chipping in, including me, though the final tinkering was always done by Tony and Alastair.

On Sunday we went to church. Every year there was a non-denominational service organised by the Christian Socialist Movement. I remember how that first year I didn't have anything to wear and had to borrow a cream outfit of Carole's, which shows how effective the diet was and how disorganised I was. I had always enjoyed going to those conference services: a good crowd and a good preacher who would give us a thoughtful sermon, and there is nothing I like more than a rousing hymn. Tony and I are both believers, so the idea that there is an obligation to God about what we do is important to us, and the sermon frequently dealt with serious issues, such as Third World debt, or later asylum seekers, issues that the Church has a right to be concerned about but that maybe didn't entirely chime with Labour Party or, later, government policy. We always listened seriously to what was said.

The Labour Party conference is the biggest of the party conferences, not least because of the union involvement. That year I discovered for the first time how it's funded. Basically, interested parties rent stalls which act as a shop window for what they do, while some smaller stalls are given free to charities. One thing Labour

Party conferences are not short on is opinion formers, so this is a great opportunity for the organisations or businesses concerned to get themselves seen and talked about. One of the incentives given them to return year after year is the 'best stall' competition, judged by – yes! – the leader's wife. There are various categories: public sector, private sector, voluntary sectors and so on.

It took me at least two half-days to get round. I wasn't over-enamoured at the prospect. How would I judge? What were the criteria? That first year someone came along to show me the ropes and the funny thing was that I really enjoyed it. Apart from anything else, it was something to do. It was completely out of the limelight, a little bit nonsensical, but the stallholders genuinely seemed to value it. What they really wanted, of course, was a piece of their glamorous new leader, and if they couldn't have that, they'd settle for a piece of me, and I could spend far longer with them than Tony ever could. There were usually about 200-odd stalls and I made sure I went round all of them, having a general chat, having my picture taken with everybody. Over the years there were inevitably some hiccups, even though I was closely shepherded, usually by Fiona, sometimes by Roz Preston, who at one point had taken over running Tony's office from Anji. One year, a stand had Viagra on display, and my 'Oh we don't need that!' was duly trumpeted across the next day's newspapers. Every stall would press me to take its mug or its pencil, or (later) its mouse pad, so, naturally, I did, getting increasingly weighed down, not daring to refuse the kind offers, in case it showed favouritism. At the end of the week we'd divvy up this 'booty' among the staff who had been working so hard for Tony they'd had no time to find anything to take home for their own kids. My fairhandedness would later come back to haunt me when the *Daily Mail* claimed that 'Cherie used to go round the conference and Hoover up every freebie she could find'.

That Monday night, when the speech was into its nth draft, Tony was getting tenser and tenser. Gordon's speech had been that morning and apparently he had said something that Tony was going to say. While I was drifting off to sleep, the voices in the sitting room next door continued to rise and fall. Eventually I could stand it no longer. He has to get some sleep, I decided. He's going to collapse if he doesn't. So I got out of bed and went in. I am far from being a tidy person, but the state of that room was appalling. Papers all over the place, half-drunk cups of tea, and the odd beer glass, room-service trays with the remains of sandwiches, jackets here and there and some very grey faces.

'Tony,' I said, 'you have got to come to bed, because you must get some sleep. And as for you lot,' I said, pointing at Alastair, Anji and the rest of them, 'out. You've all got to go.' As it was he barely slept anyway and I spent a wakeful night with him tossing and turning in bed beside me.

That weekend was the first intimation I had of what was to come. Only the bathroom was sacrosanct, and then only if you remembered to lock the door. But to guarantee a bit of peace and quiet I had to go to Carole's room.

So finally on Tuesday it was Tony's big speech. The Clause IV moment had come. As he began to speak a hush descended, and I felt a shiver of anticipation. It was only at the end, however, that it became clear just how momentous it was. There was a brief moment of shock, and then the hall erupted. Around me I felt the excitement – the most brilliant speech a new leader has ever given. I have to admit I felt ridiculously proud. There was nothing fake or phoney about my clinging to my husband's arm. I didn't know it, however, but the pattern was then set, because it went down well with the press along the lines of: 'She's supposed to be this successful career woman yet she behaves like a love-sick teenager.' The press had me 'clinging to his hand like the adoring wife'. I was a breath of fresh air. My clothes were approved of, I was approved of. But the triumph, of course, was Tony's, and everyone was happy.

And then, within only a couple of hours, it all began to unravel.

'Where is she?' Alastair's voice boomed down the corridor. Then he came storming in.

What was he talking about? Who?

'Carole,' he bellowed. 'Where the fuck is she!'

Just then she emerged from the bathroom.

'I thought I told you to stay away from the limelight. But, oh no, you knew better. And now the press are on to you. Not only have they seen you, they know exactly what you are doing and who you are. And now our beautiful day has been ruined by this ridiculous woman.' He was literally spitting.

'What do you mean?' Carole said, looking aghast.

'What I mean is that you're a topless model!'

I just sat there and froze. 'I don't believe it,' I said, but nobody heard.

'I'm not a topless model,' Carole said.

'Yes, you are! And what's more the *Sun* has pictures of you, and tomorrow no doubt the whole world will have the benefit of seeing your tits. I want you out of here. Now,' he said.

Slowly the story emerged. Several years before, when she was in the pop video business, a boyfriend had taken pictures of her topless. She was eighteen. They were never published, but they would be now as he had just sold them to the *Sun*.

By this time Carole was in tears; then she left the room and said she was going to pack.

'How dare you,' I said to Alastair as he stood there, his arms by now folded. 'Don't think I don't know about you writing porn for whatever magazine it was. If we were all held accountable for what we did at eighteen then it's a wonder you didn't disqualify yourself from this job on several counts, frankly.'

'Cherie, listen to me, I'm a journalist. I've got a nose for these things. That woman is trouble. You can't possibly trust her. I don't want anything to do with her, do you hear? There's bound to be more coming out and if you want to know what I think, I think she's only here to sell her story.'

'So you're about to expel her from the Garden of Eden, is that it?'

'Your words not mine.'

Then Tony came in and suddenly I felt dreadful. He had been so happy, exultant. All those desperate hours working on the speech had paid off, and now here he was looking like thunder. He wanted to talk to me alone, he said. Alastair bowed out, and we went into the bedroom and he shut the door. I felt sick.

'I cannot believe this, Cherie. My God, this woman has been in our house! She's been in our bedroom sorting through your clothes. I mean who is this person? What do you know about her? Come on, think about it. What do you actually know about her?'

'You know who she is. She's an exercise teacher. I've been going to her classes for years. I was hardly going to cross-examine her about what she'd done when she was eighteen.'

'And to think I let you talk me into having a massage.' He sat down on the edge of the bed with his head in his hands.

'We have all done pretty stupid things when we were young. As for Alastair, he was an alcoholic, for God's sake. I don't condemn him for that, and I don't see why he should condemn Carole for being a bit careless.'

'Careless!'

The next day it got worse. Part of me was hoping that it wouldn't be her, or the pictures would be faked or something. But it was obviously Carole. Alastair continued his attack.

'You have to drop her, Cherie, it's as simple as that.'

'Well, sorry to disappoint you but I'm not going to. It wouldn't be fair. She has done nothing wrong and what's more she's done a good job and been incredibly helpful to me. You've even said yourself that I look great.

'And by what right do you tell me what company I should keep? It may surprise you to know that I have a life of my own, that I actually enjoy the company of people who couldn't give a stuff about politics, and I intend to hang on to it.'

Shortly after breakfast the phone rang. Carole. Her mother had just called, she said. The house was surrounded by photographers. Later it came out that she'd been involved with this Exegesis cult – though what this was, or is, I still have no idea. But by that time she had gone. It had been decided to get her into a safe house, because she couldn't go back to her mum's as the press was parked outside. Hilary Coffman and Tony's researcher Liz Lloyd had been deputed to take her out through the kitchens, and she stayed at Liz's for a few days in London. As far as the press impact was concerned, Alastair had managed to keep Tony distanced from it all. But I felt really bad about it, particularly since my role was to make things easier for him, not more difficult.

As for Carole, I was not about to give her up. She had promised me I'd have more energy, and I had and I knew I was going to need it. There was no mileage to be gained in rubbing anyone's face in it, but I continued going to the gym three times a week for an hour before work, and gradually the whole furore seemed to go away. Tony also recognised that he needed exercise and three times a week a personal trainer would arrive at the house shortly after six a.m. and put Tony through his paces. An old rowing machine belonging to Felicity's husband was put into service in Nicky's room. As the press interest showed no signs of letting up, increasingly I needed things to wear, so Carole would search things out and I would pay her to go. Who else could I realistically ask? Most of my friends were working mothers, like me. Like me, in terms of their clothes, their horizons were limited. Work suits, leggings, loose tops and not much in between. I didn't know ladies who lunched.

CHAPTER 17

Home Life

Back at 1 Richmond Crescent life continued much as usual, except that now Daddy didn't take the kids to school in the morning. All three were still at school in Highbury, though this would be Euan's last year.

The question then was where next? Children from St Joan of Arc went to four Catholic schools. The nearest was St Aloysius in Islington; then there was St Ignatius in Edmonton, some way to the north – this was the Jesuit school. Then there was Cardinal Vaughan in Notting Hill. Finally there was the London Oratory School in west London. Although all of them had reasonable journeys from Richmond Crescent, I was conscious that were we to move to Westminster, the only viable options were Cardinal Vaughan or the Oratory. Cardinal Vaughan had a very rigid catchment area, and boys from outside it stood a slim chance of being accepted – only one or two went from St Joan of Arc every year – whereas the London Oratory catchment area was the whole of London and six or seven would usually be taken. Both schools had a comprehensive intake and were entirely state-funded, although by a grant from central government rather than via the local authority. They didn't select on ability, but they were both good Catholic schools and there was stiff competition to get in.

Planning your children's education is always difficult; after factoring in all the Blair imponderables it became a nightmare.

Wherever he went, Euan would start in the autumn of 1995, and if the Major government decided to follow the normal pattern, the election could be in May 1996. I had to be practical. If the unimaginable did happen, in '96 or '97, if we did find ourselves in Downing Street, then that would be upheaval enough for our kids. Continuity would be crucial, so changing schools at that stage was not an option. Also with Nicky only two years behind Euan, we didn't want them going to different schools. In the end we opted for the Oratory. The journey from Islington was straightforward. Direct to Earls Court on the Piccadilly Line, and then one stop on the District. From Downing Street, Westminster tube was just round the corner, then it was straight there on the District Line. At the school's open day I had bumped into Helena Kennedy, whose own son was about to start. Any qualms I might have had about it being grant-maintained were settled then and there. If the 'right-on' Helena thought it was OK, then it was OK for me.

When Tony told Alastair he went ballistic. It would be disastrous for Tony's reputation, he said. He had a duty to send his children to the local comprehensive. Alastair famously 'doesn't do' religion, so he never understood why it mattered to me that my children received a Catholic education. And it does matter. Catholic schools continue to have religious assemblies and the children observe the feast days, things that no longer happen in non-religious schools. It wasn't only important to me, it was important to Tony. Although he wasn't a Catholic, he had been coming to Mass since the children were little. At St Joan of Arc, as in most Catholic churches up and down the country, the Sunday morning Mass was family Mass: a genuinely warm and friendly affair, if a little chaotic. It was a chance for the children and their parents to worship and socialise together. It was where I first met Felicity and all the other mums whose kids went to the school. In fact, Tony used to take communion on a regular basis, with them. He was a member of our church community. Few, if anyone, in the congregation knew he wasn't a Catholic. Euan and Nicky had by this time made their first Holy Communion. It would have been very odd for Euan to go to a non-Catholic school after being at a Catholic primary.

I don't know if Alastair thought this was me flexing my muscles because of the disagreement over Carole. Frankly, I think it unlikely. I might have been the official Catholic in our family, and Tony might have been dissuaded from brandishing his religious beliefs in public, but this was not politics, this was private and non-negotiable, and Tony told him so in no uncertain terms. Alastair gave him dire warnings, saying, 'You will live to regret this', but the truth is, we never did. It was the right thing for our family.

Of course the story leaked and, on 1 December 1994, it was front-page news in the *Daily Mail*, but Tony stuck to his guns. The London Oratory was not a fee-paying school. It was not selective. It was funded by the state. His children's education was not a political football.

Later, Harriet Harman sent her second son to a selective grammar school, St Olave's and St Saviour's in Orpington, while her eldest son was a year ahead of Euan at the Oratory. Yet again, there was a furore. Tony gave her his full support. What he wanted was to bring a good standard of education to everyone, whatever their religion or lack of religion. As it was, the Oratory was a grant-maintained school, essentially the forerunner of what are now Academies. And that was another of his goals: to show people that you could be aspirational, yet at the same time care about what happened to others. Above all, he wanted to jettison the idea that once people had done better in life, the Labour Party was no longer their natural home.

When John Smith took over as leader from Neil Kinnock in 1992, the Party paid £70,000 for his flat in the Barbican to be redecorated on the grounds that he needed somewhere suitable for official entertaining.

Now Tony was Leader of the Opposition someone from the Party came to look over our house in Richmond Crescent and, taking a dim view of the holes in the carpet, suggested we should use John Smith's flat for official entertaining, which we both felt was insensitive and inappropriate.

'If I'm having to entertain,' I said, 'I am not going to entertain in somebody else's house. It has to be done in ours.' As for bringing Richmond Crescent up to scratch, neither of us felt we could take any more money from the Party which, only two years previously, had spent so much doing up John Smith's flat. Under these circumstances I had no choice but to get a bigger overdraft to give the house a face lift. The moment we began to look beneath the surface, it was apparent that more radical work needed to be done. My dad was always complaining that he got ill every time he stayed in our spare room in the basement, that it was damp and unhealthy. It turned out he was right. The whole of the downstairs had to be damp-proofed and replastered, which involved borrowing £30,000 from the bank. Basically Tony's attitude to money has always been: 'I just want to do what's right, and somehow or other we'll sort it out.' Although I had long before accepted that I was the major breadwinner, it sometimes rankled that he would get the credit for maintaining the moral high ground while the responsibility of funding an increased mortgage, as in this case, would fall on me. It didn't strike me as odd, however. It was how things were when I was growing up. My grandma was always in charge of the family finances. Grandad would hand over most of his pay, and my mum would hand over half of hers.

When I moved to Gray's Inn Square, Leslie Page, the chief clerk, told me that chambers' 'game plan' would be that within the next five years, I would take silk. I moved in on 1 January 1991 and as we were now coming up for 1995, it was time to think seriously about what I should do.

Acceptance was far from automatic. At that time, the view of the senior judges was what ultimately decided the matter, so if you were thinking of applying it was a good idea to talk to a senior member of the bench to see what they thought.

Becoming a Queen's Counsel isn't guaranteed to give you a higher income. There is even a risk that you will see a drop. Someone with a good junior practice can earn well in excess of a silk whose practice is limited. As a silk you work with a junior and, unlike a pupil whom you can boss around, the relationship may not work out. It is often the case that the junior will bring you work, and if a junior doesn't like you, or finds you a pain to work with, then you're in trouble.

In those days silks couldn't work without a junior. Not only could you not appear in court without a junior supporting you, you could no longer do pleadings or draft court documents. By 1995, however, those rules were already bending because of murmurings concerning restrictive practices, and by the end of the nineties they had largely gone. Even so, I rarely do things on my own simply because the economics are better for the client: a junior is cheaper than I am and they can perfectly easily do the background stuff. Why pay my hourly rate when you can pay a lesser rate? What the silk is paid for – roughly speaking – is shaping the case and the eventual advocacy. Once in court, the junior is there to assist you, to make sure you cover all the points, make sure all your books are there, and generally act as your assistant. Where a trial involves examining witnesses, you might let the junior do some of the minor witness evidence. In fact, most of the cases I deal with don't involve witnesses at all, because they are about legal points so it's mainly about arguing the point of law. Whereas the junior would help you draft the written argument that you would file before the court, the oral argument would be done by you.

I went to 4–5 Gray's Inn Square in order to give my practice a boost, and it was certainly effective. I had stopped doing the more knockabout stuff, and was doing more High Court work, specifically judicial review cases, which are both interesting and – because they often involve challenging government decisions – also quite political and high-profile. As a consequence they bring you to the attention of High Court judges, the people who ultimately decide who gets silk and who doesn't.

The poll-tax cases were classic examples of public law, and guaranteed to make headlines. The cases would start in the magistrates' court where the magistrates would jail people who had refused to pay. If the defendant believed there was a legal error, then they could apply to the divisional court of the High Court to get themselves released. I would usually represent the local authorities to argue that the magistrates had got it right. One case I took on concerned a man who had been a member of the Militant tendency in the Thanet North Labour Party.

'I remember canvassing for you in nineteen eighty-three,' he said, 'before you sold out.'

People sometimes ask me how I deal with cases involving a law I don't particularly like. While I didn't think the poll tax was a good idea politically, I also believe that as Parliament passed that Bill, then that's the way it is: you have to pay. You can change the law, but you don't disobey the law. I think there is a real distinction between campaigning to change the law and blatantly disobeying it.

It's the old question that all the law students have to decide: do you have an obligation to obey the law? For example, Gandhi and his followers who flagrantly disobeyed the law – which they did – accepted that as a consequence they would be sent to prison – which they were.

A friendly solicitor in Manchester brought me a series of interesting cases against a body called ICSTIS, set up to monitor child chat-lines, to prevent huge phone bills being run up, which their parents would then have to pay. Some of these lines turned out to be sex lines, so I found myself defending the existence of sex lines that were being closed down by ICSTIS. It would start with a nice intellectual argument, but then the judge would say, 'Well, let's see some of these transcripts', and you'd have to read out what people were actually saying on the sex lines, and – standing there, reading out this stuff – you could see your case disappearing down the plughole. The judge, being only human, would think: I don't care how clever this legal argument is, those lines must stay closed. And that's what usually happened. Often in such instances, you know you are not going to win. Good as the intellectual case might be, I knew it was morally indefensible.

The reason I took these cases on – and others that I didn't necessarily approve of – was the cab-rank rule. It arose in the eighteenth century when John Wilkes and others like him were being tried for sedition and couldn't find lawyers to represent them as they were frightened of being punished by the government. If the legal system was to work properly, it was reckoned, they had a right to be represented. As a result, it is a matter of professional misconduct if you turn down a case if you are available and if you have been offered a reasonable fee.

There are some barristers – Michael Mansfield and Helena Kennedy are examples – who stand up and say 'I will not represent rapists' or 'I won't do this or that'. For me the advantage of accepting the cab-rank rule is that no one can claim that I pick a case because I espouse the cause. Sometimes I do espouse the cause, and it could be argued that I am likely to make a better of job of it. But it's completely and utterly irrelevant. Once Tony was Leader of the Opposition, it became even more important that I stick to this rule. I had to ensure I remained totally untainted by politics, especially when my field was so bound up with governmental decisions.

It was through doing public law cases that I started doing education law. With its high proportion of planning lawyers, 4–5 Gray's

Inn Square had very good contacts with local government. In the 1990s a whole system of special needs education was starting up, responding to children with physical, mental or behavioural diffi-culties. Because I was experienced in family law and was thought to be good with children, many of these cases began to come my way. I represented a little girl called Caris for whom I won a judicial review. Caris was a sweetie. We managed to get the court to overturn the local authority's decision to move her away from her special school. She had cerebral palsy; there was nothing wrong with this girl's brain, it was just her body that was damaged. Later her school, which was run by Scope, invited me to visit, and this was the start of my long relationship with the charity.

Although it has always existed, dyslexia was only formally recog-nised as a disability comparatively recently, and I did the first case concerning Pamela Phelps, a dyslexic girl who sued her local author-ity for failing to diagnose her condition, and we went right up to the House of Lords. The issue was whether the local authority was liable to a charge of negligence, and subsequently – in 2002 – I wrote a book on the subject; as the field was so new, there wasn't one that dealt with it.

These cases had been brought because education was a very new field in terms of the law. As a result, I had argued before the highest courts in the land, which meant that my profile and my visibility were becoming much greater among the judges.

When I joined 4–5 Gray's Inn Square, I was already a member of the IT committee of the Bar Council, and by 1992 I was chair. Thanks to this, I'd got to know several judges quite well. So when I had to take the decision about whether to apply for silk – four years of Leslie's five-year plan having gone by – I went to talk to some of them. Their response was encouraging. My practice, it was felt, would justify my taking silk and they suggested that it would be better to apply while there was still a Tory government. If I waited until Labour was in power, it would be harder to avoid allegations of favouritism. I also approached Michael Beloff and David Keene for their views. The advice from everyone was essentially to go for it. 'It's 1994 now, so if you don't get it the first time that still leaves 1995, whereas realistically the election would be 1996 or 1997.'

The form issued by the Lord Chancellor's office had to be in by early October. This was where you described your practice, said why you thought you should take silk, provided details of your last three years' earnings, and gave the names of your referees. I duly delivered it, but I didn't broadcast the fact that I'd applied in case my application didn't succeed.

As well as consulting the records they already hold, the Lord Chancellor's office takes soundings. The list of applicants will already have gone to all the High Court judges and above, and they will also take soundings from the circuit, from the Chairman of the Bar Council and the President of the Law Society about your reputation. They will go to the specialist Bar associations. In my case, as I was an employment lawyer, they would have gone to the Employment Law Bar Association and Administrative Law Bar Association (which covers public law).

The result is always announced on Maundy Thursday, the day before Good Friday, though you will usually know your fate the previous weekend when a letter comes through the letter box. If the envelope is thin, then it's a no. If it's thick, it's telling you what you have to do. So when a thick letter landed on the door mat and I ripped it open, it felt a bit like the moment I got my Eleven-plus results.

'The Lord Chancellor is pleased to recommend to her Majesty . . .'

I was lucky. I got it the first time. I was one of six women who took silk that year, the biggest number there had been for a long time.

I remember shouting up the stairs, 'Tony! I've got it!' He would have known exactly what I meant, and so in fact did the kids, because Tony's brother had got silk two years previously, so they knew it was a special thing.

By sheer chance, on the day it was announced, Tony and I had been invited to Windsor Castle. Traditionally the Leader of the Opposition stays the night, but that year – much to our relief – this was impossible because of ongoing repairs following the fire in 1992. It wasn't that we had anything against staying, but the following day, being Easter, we wanted to set off early for the constituency.

So on the day it was announced that 'Her Majesty is pleased to have appointed . . . Cherie Booth as her Counsel' I had dinner with the Queen in person! That a newly appointed QC should be able to thank the monarch personally on the very same day is probably unique. It wasn't the first time I had met the Queen. New MPs are always invited to Buckingham Palace with their spouses, and at that first meeting I remember being struck dumb, not knowing what to say and getting terribly confused as to how to curtsy. When I was little, I had been taught to curtsy at ballet class, but a ballet curtsy seemed a bit over-the-top for this particular occasion, so I managed a vague kind of bob. The idea that I refused to curtsy, either then or later, is a complete load of rubbish, though now I tend to bow. As a barrister I bow all the time – lady barristers are not expected to curtsy – out of respect to the court and respect to the Crown, so that comes completely naturally.

The ceremony where you actually take silk immediately follows the Easter bank holiday, and takes place at the Palace of Westminster. Once again this requires a trip to Ede & Ravenscroft: a new silk gown and a full-bottom wig. Lady barristers traditionally wore long skirts for the ceremony, but in 1991 Helena Kennedy had been allowed to wear the men's costume of knickerbockers, which were much jollier so I decided to go for them. When I tried them on, I was surprised at how ill-fitting they were at the front, with so much loose material . . . A red-faced assistant had to explain to me why. In the end they got a pair specially made.

It was a real family celebration: my dad came down, and my mum was there and Lyndsey and all three children. Being a Tuesday, it was one of the twice-weekly Prime Minister's Questions days, so Tony couldn't come with me, but at about eleven o'clock, when the ceremony was due to start, he came over to Westminster Hall to watch.

There were about seventy of us, and in order of seniority you swear an oath of allegiance and are presented with your certificate which states your precedent order. I was about seventh from the bottom, that is, seventh youngest.

After a little celebration in chambers, we went over to the Lord Chief Justice's court. There – again in precedent order – we were presented to the Lord Chief Justice.

My entire family had been sitting through everything, but by this time the kids were getting a bit restless and rather bemused at all this bowing and scraping and their mum in this ridiculous outfit looking like a pantomime Prince Charming. My dad meanwhile was getting himself photographed by the waiting press: no show without Punch. But I knew he was very pleased. I remember him saying, 'Your grandma would have been so thrilled that you matched Rose Heilbron.' And it's true. She would have been.

Finally it was party time. The car took us back to the house and everyone – friends and family – turned up to celebrate. Later that evening we ended up at Bill and Katy's and had a Chinese takeaway, Tony having now joined us. It was the end of a fantastic day, a very proud moment for me, a proud moment for my mum, and even the kids were marginally impressed. They were used to their dad being the Big Thing, but at least I got to dress up for mine. And they were able to participate in a way that they weren't really able to with Tony as we wanted to keep them in the background.

Around the time the London Oratory story first broke, I'd had a phone call from a very irate Fiona. Anji Hunter had told her that I thought Alastair had leaked the story. I had no idea where Anji had got that from, I said. Certainly not from me, because it wasn't the case. Fiona was clearly very upset and very stressed and it emerged that, despite what Tony had promised in August, life in the Campbell/Millar household had gone rapidly downhill.

'He goes off in the morning, then when I've just about given up on him ever coming back, he reappears. And when he is here, he's on the phone. Frankly, I could be an umbrella stand for all the notice he takes of me.' I thought, Join the club.

'Believe me, Fiona,' I said, 'I know exactly how you feel.'

After this conversation the idea emerged that if she was more involved, things might improve on the home front. Perhaps, Tony suggested, I could do with someone to help? Fiona was a freelance journalist. She had started on the *Daily Express* where her father had been a journalist. She sometimes did things for *The House*, the in-house magazine for the House of Commons; in fact, ever since the days of the Maida Vale Labour Party, she had always been political.

Fiona is very attractive with a shock of blonde hair, strong-minded and determined, but she can be very unforgiving. At that time it's fair to say I didn't know her very well, but we were friendly and I trusted her. The first thing she did was to get Philip Gould (the Labour Party's poll adviser) to slip a few questions into some of his focus groups to find out what people thought of me. As she was friendly with Lindsay Nicholson, then editor of *Prima*, a mid-range women's magazine, Fiona arranged for me to be a guest editor for their tenth-anniversary edition.

Lindsay's husband, John Merritt, had been a trainee reporter with

Alastair and they had become great friends. In 1993 John died of leukaemia, leaving Lindsay pregnant with their second daughter, as well as a three-year old – a terrible story. I took to Lindsay immediately – a really nice woman, a fantastically capable editor, and a good Catholic girl like me.

What had emerged from Philip's focus group was that I needed to project a softer image, to show that I was an ordinary mum, which I was fundamentally: though the idea that ordinary mums go round guest-editing glossy magazines was another matter. At first I thought 'guest-editing' meant that I had physically to edit the magazine, but Lindsay remained very firmly in the driving seat. 'My' issue of *Prima* would be built round my interests, she explained. On the lighter side, knitting emerged as the front-runner. I got my first knitting needles from my grandma when I was three. Tea cosies were my *pièces de resistance* and – I liked to think – were much sought after as collectors' items. However, for this exercise they wanted something that involved a pattern, so we went for a cable-knit jumper. I hadn't actually knitted it – I would have enjoyed the challenge – but there wasn't enough time. Instead it was my *Blue Peter* moment: here's one somebody else did earlier.

Then there were my more serious interests: the abuse of women and children. I had recently been approached by Refuge, the charity for battered wives set up by Erin Pizzey, and asked whether I would join its board. Until then, whatever charity things I had done since qualifying were directly related to my work as a lawyer: giving free advice to the Child Poverty Action Group and the NCCL, and of course my Wednesday evening sessions in Tower Hamlets.

In 1992 I had watched from the sidelines as two lawyers I knew well were groomed for office by John Smith. Derry was now Lord Irvine of Lairg, QC, the idea being that he would be a great reforming chancellor once Labour got in. Meanwhile Veena, whose parents' flat I had borrowed in Maida Vale, had divorced her first husband and had now married a charismatic barrister called Gareth Williams, and there was talk of him becoming Attorney General, or Solicitor General. It was Gareth who approached me about getting involved with the NSPCC's Justice for Children campaign. Its aim was to get lawyers to raise funds for the NSPCC's facility in Penge, which traced child-abuse rings and where they had specialist social workers who would support the kids through the court process. In those days we didn't have the video links we have now. For a child, giving evidence in a criminal trial is always difficult and sometimes traumatic, and part of what we were looking for – in addition to raising funds – was a change in the way defence counsel cross-examined, because many were still aggressive with even quite young children.

Although it might appear self-defeating to bully a child with a jury present, if the child then contradicts himself, the child is branded a liar and the abuser gets off. We wanted to change that climate. The Tories had already started exploring whether we could make things easier for children, and after Labour came in we did quite a lot to support victims in court, including battered women and rape victims, changing the rules so that they could give evidence behind a screen. All that began with the Justice for Children campaign.

By 1994 I was working primarily in the fields of employment and public law and hadn't been involved in family law in a professional capacity since shortly after Kathryn was born. It still interested me, however, so I accepted Refuge's invitation to go to the Chiswick Refuge. Erin Pizzey had now left and it was run by Sandra Horley, a dynamic communicator from Canada who has been battling for thirty years to raise Refuge's profile. I already knew of her as an expert witness in trials about battered woman syndrome – and why battered women kill. The first thing I had done for Refuge was to launch a new profile-raising campaign. So *Prima* allowed me to build on that. I wrote about how I had become involved as a young lawyer, and about how important it was for me and for women in general.

Tony's office was very dubious as to whether I should get involved. Why draw attention to myself? A woman brought in to look at the thorny issue of how I should present myself decided I was asking for trouble. 'People are going to assume that the reason you got involved is that your father beat your mother.'

'But he didn't,' I said. 'And that is not why I'm doing this.' In fact, in all these years nobody has once suggested that it was. Thanks to Fiona fighting on my side, the office finally agreed, but they remained decidedly apprehensive, muttering beneath their breath about not needing the extra hassle. They didn't get any hassle, and it started a relationship with Refuge that has gone on to this day.

In this, as in so much else, having Fiona there to fight my cause made all the difference. Over those early years she kept me sane: not only in the obvious way – keeping the post under control and running my diary once we got into Downing Street – but most importantly fighting for family life to be included in the thinking of Tony's office, something she and I had a common interest in. Later Roz Preston would play a similar role, but it was Fiona who set the standard.

In September 1995 Euan duly started at the London Oratory School. On the first day of term those mothers among us who could, went with their sons on the tube. They were only eleven, and most of them had never travelled on the underground on their own. We left home at ten to seven having arranged to meet up with Euan's friend at Arsenal station. At Earls Court we changed on to the District Line. By now the carriage was filled with boys dressed in the same uniform and they were chatting and joking to each other.

'Did you hear?' one boy said to his friend opposite.

'Hear what?'

'Tony Blair's son's going to be in our school today.'

Euan said nothing but he nudged me, and I gave him a little secret smile.

From West Brompton station it's about an eight-minute walk to the school, and that morning our route was lined with sixth-formers to mark out the way from the tube for the new pupils. As we walked down Seagrave Road the atmosphere was jocular and lively. A happy start, I thought, to this new chapter in my son's life. But as we approached the school there was a flurry of activity and other mothers walking in front of me pulled their children to one side. And then I saw them: three photographers – paparazzi – shouting out my name and running towards us. It was a horrible feeling. It was as if the Red Sea had parted and Euan and I had to walk up the middle, everyone turning to look and these guys running, their cameras held up against their faces. What could I do? If I tried to join the other mothers, it would end up with their children getting photographed as well, which would get me in even more trouble. I kept walking. By the time we got to the gate, Euan was close to tears and while everybody else waited until all the new pupils had arrived, we were bundled in, and then I was smuggled out of another entrance. I got back on the tube feeling upset and angry. Upset for my son, but furious with myself because I had failed to protect him.

Once back in chambers, I called Tony's office, told them what had happened and said that, in my view, it was a breach of the Press Complaints Code. It worked. No English newspaper printed the picture, although the 'story' was reported. I couldn't believe it. This was an eleven-year-old boy who was going to be travelling every day through central London on his own. Did I really want him to be recognised? Would any mother? Two years later when Nicky went to the Oratory, he refused point-blank to allow me to go with him on the first day, and who could blame him?

CHAPTER 18

Election Fever

When Euan started at the Oratory our early morning routine changed. Ros would take Nicky and Kathryn to St Joan of Arc, by which time Tony would already have taken Euan to the tube, first picking up a couple of other boys from outside their old school. They left before seven and on the way there would listen to the *Today* programme on the car radio, and talk about it together (later Euan would take to dropping intelligent comments into the conversation, getting astonished looks from whoever was around the house at the time). Once he had dropped Euan off, Tony would then drive back to the house where Terry would be waiting to take him (and me if I was ready) to the House of Commons.

Now that Tony was Leader of the Opposition, our visits to Sedgefield became less frequent. Looking back from the vantage point of a woman now in her fifties, I don't really know how I coped. Although we kept basic clothes in Myrobella, there was still a lot to take with us, not least the ruddy hamsters that, for some reason lost in the annals of the Blair family history, always came too. Live animals weren't the only thing to think about.

One Friday I was doing a tribunal in Cambridge against Charlie Falconer. As we had a dinner party in the constituency that evening, I'd done the shopping for it in London the night before. I thought the case was going to settle, but it didn't, and so we were fighting. So there I was fishing out my brief from my bulging briefcase, and

Charlie remembers watching in horror as a leg of lamb emerged, dripping blood all over the inside of my sleeve.

As the children grew older, Tony would increasingly go on to Sedgefield on his own: leaving on a Friday and returning early on Saturday evening. On weekends like those, when the nanny was having her well-deserved time off, I would finally have the time to be a normal mother. A favourite Saturday activity was the Sumix Centre, a children's choir based in Thornhill Square, where Bill and Katy Blair lived. After dropping the kids off at Sumix, I'd pop into them for a cup of coffee, then pick up the kids and go back home via Lyndsey's. Then it would be back to Richmond Crescent to help make supper for when Daddy got home.

I have always enjoyed cooking. Roasts were the Myrobella speciality – the Aga did them particularly well – and on a Sunday I would busy myself in the kitchen while Tony took the children for a walk, often to a place that we called 'Wind in the Willows', which was a house his parents had always hoped to buy, but never did. In London my repertoire revolved around spaghetti and lasagne. We always needed things that could stretch because you never knew who would drop in. It was Maggie Rae who had taught me how to cook with a reasonable amount of abandon. She is a great instinctive cook and will try anything, depending on what's available. I would often be experimenting, not always successfully it must be admitted. At weekends we would eat together as a family. During the week it was usually the nanny who would do the cooking for the kids, while I would make dinner for Tony and me.

By the end of 1995 election fever was mounting. John Major's government lurched from crisis to crisis and the general feeling was that it was hanging by a thread. Their majority was down to twenty-one and falling; rebels were declining the whip; dissent within the Cabinet over Europe was rife (Major called the Eurosceptics 'the bastards') and there was a tide of 'sleaze' culminating in a trail of brown envelopes in the 'cash for questions' scandal. And the repercussions of Black Wednesday continued to affect both business and individuals, including our family. Meanwhile, I continued to lose weight and Carole helped me build up my wardrobe. The days of thinking that Tony could go to a function on his own while I slobbed out in front of the television were long gone. I was part of the package.

Invitations arrived in every post from people I had never met but certainly heard of: David Frost invited us to his annual party in a garden square in Kensington. Suddenly we were on everybody's list. Tony's view was that if an event had political implications, then we had to go. So you do, and of course your picture gets taken. I can remember Ken Follett inviting us to his house in Cheyne Walk: a private dinner, or so we thought. The press had prior notice, however, and the moment we opened the car doors, cameras were clicking. Alastair was furious and gave Ken Follett a rollicking. No doubt he was rude in the way that only Alastair can be and I don't think Ken ever forgave him. Alastair took the view that they were doing it for their own publicity; the Folletts said they hadn't tipped off anyone, and were offended that he'd said they had.

The clothes-buying routine was slowly evolving into something less hit or miss. I was using Ronit Zilkha, Caroline Charles, Betty Jackson, Ally Capellino, Paddy Campbell and Paul Costelloe. All British designers. Clothes would usually have to be altered (that bottom, those hips) and soon they were suggesting a more organised approach. By the time I got to Number 10, we'd chosen from the collections which came out six months before they appeared in the shops. I'd go to the offices and warehouses once the particular designers had been ear-marked. In September it would be things for the following summer. In January or February we'd be buying for the following autumn–winter season. Whatever else was in the diary, there was always the Labour Party Conference.

Like every other woman, I basically like clothes, and it was fascinating to get a glimpse of how the fashion industry works. There I was in the thick of it, talking to buyers and models as well as designers. I saw just how thin the models really were and how they smoked non-stop and although I never saw them doing cocaine myself, I knew from what others told me that it was rife. I became very friendly with some of the designers. Paddy Campbell, for example, is a fascinating woman who started off life as an actress and we found we had a lot in common. I've watched her daughter Becky grow from a young woman into the successful mother of two, who is now possibly taking over the business from her mum.

I didn't specifically look for women designers, but apart from one or two it ended up that way. The lovely Paul Costelloe is an exception, a real Irish flirt, and I've bought things from Paul Smith. In

1995 Tony and I were invited to an event in the Indian community and they suggested that it might be nice if I could wear a sari, so I mentioned this to Bharti Vyas, and one of her staff – a cousin I think – was persuaded to lend me one of hers, and I loved it. A sari is incredibly flattering to my kind of shape. It really makes you stand properly and makes you feel a bit like a princess. A few weeks later, we went to a reception in the Sikh community and a young woman came up and introduced herself. She was a designer, she said, and would like to work with me.

'The thing is,' she said, 'you and I are the same shape, so if something works on me, then it would probably work well on you.' That was how I met Babs Mahil, who has designed all my Indian things ever since and who is just fantastic.

Early in 1997 Tony and I met Diana, Princess of Wales. Maggie Rae, by then a partner at Mishcon de Reya, had been involved in her divorce, and Diana had told her that she wanted to meet Tony. She was keen to show that she had something to offer this country, she'd said, and believed she could do a lot to help promote a more modern image of Britain. As the need for Britain to engage with the modern world was central to Tony's mission, he was quite taken by the idea.

It was all conducted in the utmost secrecy. Maggie Rae invited her to her place for dinner, and Tony and I were invited, as well as Alastair and Fiona. By this time Maggie had moved from her original wreck, but not very far. She was busy in the kitchen as she always is. Diana had already got there by the time Tony and I arrived and was down in the kitchen chatting to everybody. She seemed perfectly at home in ordinary surroundings, even making Alastair a cup of tea at one point. What most struck me, I remember, was how completely obsessed he was by the idea that she fancied him. She was certainly flirting with him, much to Fiona's irritation, but every time she moved out of earshot he kept saying to Tony, 'She really fancies me and she's only asked you so that she can see me.' Although he was doing it in a jokey way, such is his ego that part of him probably really wanted to believe it. She was certainly flirting with Alastair more than Tony.

There is no doubt that Diana was beautiful, more so in the flesh perhaps than came across in photographs. She was tall and slim and immaculately turned out. With me, I think, she was anxious to show her serious side. No doubt she'd worked out that this would go down better than the flirtatious eyelash-fluttering that had Alastair drooling. Although she said she was no great intellectual, she successfully projected the image of someone who had something to offer. And I believe she did have something to offer. If you have that kind of charisma it makes sense to use it. Tony could certainly see it, and no doubt in Tony she saw someone who also had charisma. I remember the one thing that came over strongly the first time I met her was how she felt about her boys, and how close to them she was, how much a part of her life they were.

She was concerned that William should be brought up in a more modern way than his father had been and she wanted to see a modern monarchy. She was keen to stress that she too was a modern person. By this time she was involved in the landmine issue and she put forward the idea that she could have a role in promoting Britain in the wider world as a sort of roving ambassador, and Tony was certainly considering whether there was a way we could use her talents for the benefit of the country. Although she didn't say she was actually a supporter of New Labour, she certainly implied that she was, though whether she really was is another question.

A few weeks later I met Norma Major at the *Daily Star* Gold Awards. We were both presenting awards – it was the first time I had been asked to do something like that on my own account. I hadn't met her before, but she came over and shook my hand – and the press took a picture which appeared everywhere the next day – which I thought was incredibly gracious of her. She didn't have to do it.

Over the eighteen months since he'd become leader, Tony's office had coalesced into a very strong team who over time became like an extended family. Anji Hunter – known, not entirely affectionately, as 'the gate-keeper' – ran his office, with Kate Garvey under her as diary secretary, while Liz Lloyd did research. Jonathan Powell had arrived a month or so after Alastair. Tony had wanted a chief of staff who knew about the Civil Service. He first went to meet someone in the British Secretariat at the European Parliament, but whoever it was decided they didn't want to come back to England. Then Jonathan's name came up. He was basically a diplomat, working in our embassy in Washington as First Secretary, which was where Tony had met him and liked him. What always struck people as particularly amusing, however, was that his brother Charles had been Margaret Thatcher's right-hand person.

There are four brothers in the family and Jonathan is the youngest. Another one – Chris – was in advertising and had been involved with the Labour Party at campaign level, so from him we knew that Jonathan was sympathetic.

As far as I am aware it wasn't an Alastair-type situation with Jonathan, in that he was interested in joining and did so. The difficulties this time were closer to home. Hearing them talk during those first few months, it was clear that Anji and Alastair were resentful of the newcomer. They were incredibly dismissive, saying that because he'd been in the Foreign Office, he didn't understand politics. But the point was that he knew how the Civil Service operated and that was why Tony needed him. For a while there was a definite jockeying for position, a 'we were here first' attitude and 'can you really be on our side because you've been working for the government all this time?' That was my perspective anyway. I was inclined to take Jonathan's part, first because I'm a bit perverse, but also because I thought they were giving him far too much of a hard time. He's a lovely person to have around, a Tigger-like character and charming in the way that Alastair is charming. The difference is that Alastair is a charming thug and Jonathan doesn't have an ounce of thuggery in him. I also like him because he's an eccentric – tall, gangly and always terribly untidy. Once we were in Number 10, Tony was always giving him his old shirts and ties. Jonathan doesn't really care about clothes.

Jonathan's role was to prepare our people for government, which he did brilliantly. He is a public-school boy, clever, fantastic on policy, and was Tony's right-hand man all the way through the Northern Ireland peace process. Tony couldn't have done it without a number of people, one of whom was definitely Jonathan.

After their initial shadow-boxing Jonathan and Alastair got on very well, not least because their areas of expertise were entirely different. Jonathan was in charge of the policy people; and the details of policy and the niceties of negotiating were the things he did well. Alastair hasn't the slightest interest in policy. He either loves you or he hates you. And people either love him or hate him. They did settle down, but at first I imagine there must have been times when Jonathan wondered, What on earth was I thinking of giving up my Foreign Office career to come here?

With all this going on it was perhaps not surprising that the office was intruding more into our family life than it had done before. If there was work to be done, Tony had a choice. He stayed in his office in Westminster, or he came home and the people he needed to see came with him. His visits to Trimdon became more infrequent and John Burton was left to keep constituency matters ticking over. Everyone was so focused on winning that it became all-consuming.

Almost the only person who didn't assume that Tony was going to win was Tony. His mantras were 'no complacency' and 'do not take anything for granted'. I had always believed in him and was absolutely sure he would win, but there were some things I had to plan for. I decided not to renew my car, for example. I didn't know what arrangements there might be for cars as and when and if we moved to Downing Street. I didn't want to buy a brand-new car and find that it wasn't suitable, so my old Metro limped on. At some point before the election ITV interviewed us both in Richmond Crescent and Michael Brunson asked me how I thought Downing Street would cope with having young children living there.

'Well,' I said, 'Downing Street will just have to get used to the idea of having noise and piano practice and friends round for tea.'

Alastair got very upset. I shouldn't have answered the question, he said, as it made the assumption that we were going to win. While we were doing the interview in the garden, Euan had been playing the piano inside, so Alastair negotiated that Brunson could have a shot of Euan practising in return for them not broadcasting the remark, but I was not happy. I considered my remark perfectly harmless and I would far rather not have had Euan involved in any way at all. Alastair just kept repeating, 'You can't take the electorate for granted.' Inevitably he won because he's a very forceful personality. Most of the time we got on perfectly well but I think he found me a bit of a dilemma. He once said that I had the brains of a man and the emotions of a woman and he found that very difficult. The truth is, he didn't like to think that women had equal capacity.

CHAPTER 19

End Game

From '96 onwards we were on an election footing, and when it wasn't called that October, we knew it would be May or June of 1997. The only piece of information lacking was the exact date. Then on 17 March John Major went to the Palace and Parliament was dissolved. He had hung on till the very last minute. Polling Day would be Thursday 1 May – a six-week campaign when it can be as little as three weeks. The view among Tony's staff was that the other side hoped we would run out of resources and steam. Not if Tony had anything to do with it.

After an hour in his make-shift gym in Nick's room, Tony would leave around eight o'clock for the daily press conference at Millbank Tower, the Labour Party campaign headquarters. Most mornings I would go straight to the Albany gym, a former chapel near Regent's Park. I'd exercise for an hour, shower, dress, sort out my hair and make-up, then go to meet Tony at Millbank .

In the months leading up to the election the routine had been pretty much the same. Once the campaign proper had begun, after my work-out I would leave the gym with another of the trainers who lived nearby and have a shower and change at her place, just to have a bit more privacy. Years later when this woman needed the money, she sold a story to the *News of the World*, claiming that Carole and I had had showers together, which is a complete load of rubbish. I knew the then editor Rebekah Wade and the next time I saw her I decided to have it out.

'You don't seriously think that I was taking showers with Carole Caplin, do you, Rebekah?' I asked.

She shrugged, then laughed. 'It's only a story,' she said.

That was much, much later, but even as early as 1994 negative stories had started to appear in the tabloid press, usually about my appearance. I didn't keep them – I'm not a masochist – but I did keep the letters that colleagues at the Bar sent me at the time, generally commiserating and expressing solidarity. One actually used the phrase, 'Don't let the bastards grind you down'. Little did I know that this would become grinding on an industrial scale once we were inside Number 10.

The campaign 'battle bus' was an old coach customised to the office's specifications and was cramped and uncomfortable. There were seats all the way round at the back and the windows were blacked out. This was where Tony and I sat. There was a table with a fax machine and a television and, at the front, there were tables and seats for the people who were with us, and the press would get on from time to time.

Alastair was always there, of course, and I'd have either Fiona or Roz Preston with me. Alastair and Fiona would usually sit together except when the press was there, when she would move.

'I don't want any Mr and Mrs pictures,' Alastair would say. He was always thinking from the perspective of the tabloid journalist he had once been, and he really hated that bus. It was pretty dreadful. It was constantly swaying from side to side and had an extremely unpleasant toilet somewhere in the middle.

For security reasons, Terry always followed in the Rover behind us, and at the end of the day – if we could – Tony and I would get out of the bus and Terry would drive us back to London, while the other poor souls had to lurch on a bit longer. Tony tried to arrange the itinerary so that we could be back at home every night for the sake of the kids, but it didn't always happen. With the help of St Joan of Arc and the Oratory, Ros continued to keep the daily routine going as best she could, with her mother and brother drafted in for ferrying duties, and my mum round the corner at Lyndsey's as non-driver back-up.

For six weeks we criss-crossed the country, seemingly non-stop. In the election campaigns that followed, I did much more on my own, but 1997 was the first, and Tony and I largely stayed together. It was

April and the weather was fantastic: the sun always seemed to be shining. When we went down to Bristol, I remember, we were scheduled to go on a little boat on the river and Carole found me a blue and white striped jumper: all very nautical. Manchester was the one place it rained, but I am very fond of Manchester so I didn't mind.

While we were in the area, I made a solo visit to Crosby. Crosby was not on our list of potentially winnable seats – all of which Tony did visit – so I just went with my dad. The welcome we got was tremendous. Claire Curtis-Thomas, the Labour candidate, was her usual dynamic self. 'Cherie,' she said, 'we can win this seat! I know we can!' She was a good candidate, but how could we possibly win Crosby? It had been Tory since the year dot.

Every evening Tony would give a set-piece speech to the Party faithful which he and Alastair would have worked on during the day. He always spoke so well, and so passionately, and each night there was this extraordinary feeling of moving forward, a momentum that was unstoppable.

The last burst was a five-day campaign covering the last weekend of April. Alastair had one final idea, which he considered a brilliant coup because nobody ever does it. We would go and visit night-workers, he said, starting with Smithfield meat market – somewhere my dad used to work when he was an out-of-work actor. This time I put my foot down.

'No, Alastair. Not unless you want to kill him. He needs to sleep.' No doubt it was a wonderful idea, but you cannot campaign all day and all night when you're on the final leg of a six-week marathon and still be breathing at the end of it.

Those last five days the crowds grew bigger and bigger. Every place we visited, there seemed to be more people on the streets and the pressure was building and building. The last day of campaigning found us in Scotland, a short hop from our roost in the north-east. In Stockton-on-Tees a platform had been erected in the market place. As we stood there, we were surrounded by a sea of faces, all shouting 'Tone-ee, Tone-ee' and 'we're on our way'. The sheer emotion, the good will, the intensity of it all was amazing and I will remember it for ever. It was as if everyone's hopes were pinned on Tony, as if he were a boxer or a long-distance runner. The feeling that everything depended on this one man. I must have realised it before, or sensed at least some of it, but standing in the market place in Stockton was when it really hit home. I too felt very emotional and so proud. But I also worried for him, because it was such a powerful thing that was happening. How could he possibly fulfil these people's dreams, their hopes?

And yet this was the hour when the Labour Party was really going to make good, and that's what I believed too. But there was also a huge sense of responsibility and I could sense Tony becoming more concentrated in himself. He was pulling back into himself, becoming almost quiet, realising that this wasn't just a vain hope. There was a real possibility that he was going to become leader of our country and the people expected him to make a difference.

The previous Christmas we had taken a long-promised trip to Australia and visited our old friends Geoff and Bev Gallop and their kids. Tony had lived there for some years as a boy, but had very little memory of it until he went back there again, and he loved it. He was struck by how young a country it felt, and that's what he wanted Britain to be. So many things were still stuck in the past and we weren't moving forward. In fact, under the current administration, we seemed to be moving backwards. John Major's most recent conference speech had conjured up a vision of ladies riding bicycles in English country lanes and cricket on the lawns, whereas Tony wanted Britain to embrace modern technology. Then there had been the Tories' nastiness over immigration and the gay vendetta inherent in the Clause 28 question. The idea that we should still be uncomfortable about homosexuality had to go, he believed. There was an atmosphere of negativity in Britain that Tony was keen to change.

As MP for Sedgefield, he knew only too well the feeling in the north that the south didn't really care what was going on in the rest of the country as long as it – as in the eighties – was doing OK. I knew too of the disparity of opportunity. I had brought up my own children, had been a school governor, and knew that often we literally had to make a choice between books and teachers, because there simply wasn't enough money, and that the only schools which did get any extra money were schools like the London Oratory that had gone grant-maintained. Travelling round the country, being shown the state of school buildings, I saw at first hand how close to collapse so much of the infrastructure was. And then there were the hospitals. In 1997 a number of health service authorities were in severe crisis with their funding. Old people were dying of hypothermia. We were told we couldn't afford a minimum wage, so there were people working as night-watchmen and caretakers, for example, and women working in shops, all for £1 or £2 an hour. Things had to change.

Tony was now being seen as the instrument for that change and there was a huge expectation that, with a change of government, we would have a change of culture: that the country would change practically overnight.

It was completely unrealistic. The one person who wasn't unrealistic about it was Tony. While those of us around him were caught up in the excitement, caught up in the feeling that history was being made, he was turning in on himself, concentrating on 'how am I going to take on this huge responsibility?'

Since he was first elected to Parliament in 1983, he had never had power, because the Party had never been in power. In the past year or so, various people had helped out: retired ambassadors, retired civil servants had come and given him seminars in the Shadow Cabinet room, about what it was like at Whitehall, about how things worked. Something similar had happened in Harold Wilson's time, but at least then there were some in the Shadow Cabinet who'd had experience of being in government. We had no former Cabinet ministers at all, and only a handful of people who had been junior ministers – all of them very junior ministers. Yet at the same time as making all these preparations, Tony was still thinking that it could be a chimera, that it could all go horribly wrong, as it had in 1992 when Neil Kinnock was convinced he was going to win. That last day Tony was the least buoyed up of any of us, I think.

After Stockton-on-Tees it was only a few miles back to Trimdon and Myrobella. The house was already full of Party people when we arrived: John Burton, of course, Jonathan Powell, Sally Morgan, Anji and Alastair, all talking about what they were going to do about the Cabinet. What were the first things to be done.

I could feel that Tony was still keeping himself back, but he knew plans had to be made, things had to be done – and quickly. The most immediate was making the Bank of England independent, which Tony was emphatic was the vital emblem of Labour becoming economically respectable. He'd wanted it to be announced during the election campaign but Gordon had thought it better to wait.

Around nine o'clock the kids arrived with Ros. They were amazed to see that Myrobella was now ringed by armed guards, sent by Durham police. The mobile incident trailer which served as their HQ was parked in the field next to the house, which in the summer was a mass of buttercups. We took the children over to see it, where we were shown an assortment of gas masks, bullet-proof vests and night-vision rifles. They let the kids look down the sights, but there was no great excitement. All three of them were rather subdued – as we all were, with reason. The whole experience freaked us out. Floodlights had been put up and we could see shadowy figures here and there, and there were police dogs sniffing round. From time to time a siren would sound when the motion detectors were inadvertently tripped. Myrobella had always been an open house, and suddenly it was being closed off. We weren't closing it, but it was being closed around us.

A few weeks earlier the security people had been to look over Richmond Crescent and they had produced horrendous plans, which included putting a police box in our front porch and one at the back, because, they said, there were potential sniper positions from a block of flats looking over the park. There would also need to be a provision for a 'siege containment' room, they said. And they would have to roof over our small back garden.

'But that's preposterous,' I said. 'What's the point of having a garden with a roof over it?'

I almost wasn't taking it seriously because I couldn't believe they really meant it and I didn't think that people could possibly live like that. At the start of the campaign our cars had both been equipped with IED (Improvised Explosive Device) detectors, as IRA car bombs were still a real threat. For the previous two weeks two policemen had been permanently on guard outside our house, and apparently there were also a couple in the park. Even so, when we arrived at Myrobella on that Wednesday I was still shocked. There had been no discussion that I was aware of; they had just done it. They were even arranging with John Burton to buy the house nearest us at the end of the terrace, as a police house. The owners were more than happy to sell, John said. And who could blame them? It might be the safest house in the north of England, but who would want to live next door to something ringed in steel, looking like a young offenders' institution rather than a quirky Victorian family home with seven fireplaces and a hand pump?

We had already sorted out the next day's outfits. Ronit Zilkha had been responsible for several things I had worn on the campaign, and she made the red outfit that I wore back in London, as I realised I'd need something pretty special. For the family walk to the polling station for the photographers, I wore a Betty Jackson outfit, and for the count that evening, a brown trouser suit with a long jacket by Ally Capellino – all in keeping with the British designers theme.

As the hours ticked by, our families began to turn up. Tony's dad and stepmother, and Bill and Katy, and his sister Sarah. My mum and dad, and Lyndsey and Chris. Myrobella was crammed. Alastair and Jonathan kept popping in, and Fiona would drift in and out. That afternoon, they all went away to have a rest. Tony was supposed to have a sleep too, but I don't think he managed to do more than lie down and close his eyes. The kids and I left him in peace. A guest house up the road had a small indoor swimming pool which the owners had said we could use. Meanwhile, first indications of the turn-out were beginning to come in: Philip Gould called to say that BBC exit polls were giving us a ten-point lead over the Tories. Everyone was in a state of suspended animation, because there was nothing more to be done. The people were going to the polls, the only outstanding question was, are we going to have a new government? The expectation, of course, was that we would.

Looking back, I don't know how I stood it. It felt almost as though you were in a bubble, as if instinctively you were trying to keep some sort of distance so that the whole thing wouldn't overwhelm you. The atmosphere was almost unnaturally calm.

We had to decide what to do with the kids. They were too young to stay up all night, so we put them to bed and promised them that we'd get them up for the count, which wouldn't be until nearly midnight. Euan barely slept, but Nicky certainly did because I can remember the trouble we had waking him and how Tony had to carry him downstairs. He was only eleven then, and still half asleep. Euan was already thirteen and so had taken a lot more of an interest, while Kathryn was still a little girl at nine, and just very excited, largely because she loved the new outfit I'd got her from Marks & Spencer, the blue check that she wore for the picture.

There was never any question that they shouldn't be involved. It wouldn't be like it had been with my father: once he became famous, we were completely cut off from anything to do with his life. We were superfluous to requirements and, from my own experience, I knew what that did to you. I was determined that history would not repeat itself, that our kids would not be incidental extras to what was happening to their father. This was something that we were doing together as a family. Later I would be accused of double standards, of wanting to maintain their privacy while parading them before the cameras. To have kept them out of those pictures would have been to deny them their place in what would affect them all their lives. This was a journey we were going on together and they had to know they were as important to us now as they were before. Leaving them out was not an option.

I felt very shaky. While everyone around was focused on Tony, the Party and the country, I thought increasingly of what lay before me, of those three little people who hadn't asked for any of this, who hadn't been canvassed for their opinion and who had no concept of what the future held. It was now my job, as never before, to make family life work. However much he wanted to, realistically Tony would not be there in the way he had been before.

I thought it might be a bit difficult for my mum and my dad to be there together, but in the end it was fine. One thing my mum has always known is that the old rogue was completely devoted to the Party, so for him this was a Big Thing.

At ten p.m. the polls closed and we all gathered round the television. Tony was upstairs in our bedroom, just lying on the bed staring at the ceiling. He didn't want to come down. When *News at Ten* came on, somebody went up to get him. He shambled in and stood at the door and Michael Brunson began to speak.

'The predictions are that it's going to be a Labour landslide.'

'Don't be ridiculous,' he said. 'I accept that we're going to win, but a landslide, no. It's ridiculous.'

At about eleven thirty John Burton arrived with Tony's protection and said we should go to the count. During the last two weeks of the campaign, he had been provided with five protection officers who would be on duty, two at a time. There was Bob Pugh the inspector; a DC called Simon Gill; Ian Webb, who was then the DS; and John Blum, another DC. Cathy Spalding was the only woman on the team. At the time I wasn't aware of the implications. They had been on the bus, but as we were constantly surrounded by people we didn't take much notice. What were five more among so many? It wasn't as if this was going to be our life. It was, of course, but I didn't realise it then.

We went down to Newton Aycliffe Leisure Centre where the count for Sedgefield and the neighbouring constituency was being held. Outside there was a feeling of Mardi Gras. Inside it was even more the case. Everyone was ecstatic. Meanwhile Tony was pacing about, talking to people about what they had to do tomorrow and what the first things on the agenda would be. By now he had accepted that we had won, but he barely managed a smile. I was sitting with the family in a room at the back watching television, when there was a news flash.

'Labour gains Crosby.' My sister and I sat there open-mouthed and then clasped each other in near hysterics and jumped up and down. We just couldn't believe it; the whole Booth family was just amazed, delighted and astonished in equal measure.

And then it dawned on me: if we've won Crosby, anything is possible! A few minutes later Michael Portillo went down, beaten by young Stephen Twigg, who used to collect my sub when we lived in Stavordale Road.

Sedgefield was a foregone conclusion, but Tony won it with an increased majority of 25,000. His only regret, he said when the crowd had quietened enough to let him speak, was that his mother was not there to see it. But his father was. As soon as we could, I got the children into the waiting car and, with my mum and Ros in charge, waved them off to the airport. They were going home, I told them. But I would see them in the morning. From there it was back to Trimdon, to the Labour club, just to say thank you to our supporters, and then to Myrobella.

The phone rang at about two in the morning.

'This is Downing Street,' the voice said. 'We have the Prime Minister for you.' It was John Major conceding defeat and he wished Tony well. I was in the room, but I didn't hear what he said, just Tony's muted response.

He and I were there alone, and I clasped both his hands in mine. 'I know this is a huge responsibility,' I said, 'but you'll be fantastic.' And he was very calm, very much in awe of what was happening, just because the vote of confidence was so big. I believe he'd always secretly thought he would win, but never imagined he would win by such a huge margin.

A private plane was waiting at Teesside airport to fly us to London. The party at the Royal Festival Hall was already in full swing, but there was no risk that it would be over by the time we got there. As we flew down, results were still coming in, and Alastair was keeping everyone up to date with the score. Gradually the scale of the victory became impossible to ignore, and at one point Tony put his head in his hands and said, 'What have we done?'

There's a picture of the two of us, taken by the photographer Tom Stoddart who'd been with us throughout the campaign, of Tony and me on the plane, with Tony scribbling a few notes for what he was going to say, and he was in another place. All I could do was put my arms round him and say, 'It'll be all right. We're all coming too.' That was how it was going to be, whatever else happened: we would be there with him, and indeed we were. We went in together, and we came out together. And we're still all together, and that's really important. There was a kind of weird calm, complete calm.

As we crossed Westminster Bridge, dawn was glinting along the river. The streets round the South Bank were packed with people and I thought that it must have been like this in 1945 when the war ended. Terry was driving and, either from the excitement or because of barriers blocking off streets, we went the wrong way and had to turn round and back up.

We were both very subdued. Tony says that he never really got to enjoy that night. He made his speech about the new dawn rising over London, and a new dawn for Britain. It was six o'clock in the morning by the time we left, and we emerged from the smoky, raucous atmosphere inside the Festival Hall into the clean light of the early morning and someone gave us a glass of champagne, the first either of us had had.

None of what was happening seemed real. I remember looking into the crowd and seeing Barry Cox and Katie, Maggie Rae and Alan Howarth. David Keene was there. Val Davies and Garry Hart. Then Peter Mandelson and Neil and Glenys Kinnock. They were all there, lots of Party people I'd known for ever, all in absolute ecstasy. But Tony and I felt none of it. We just went home and tried to grab a couple of hours' sleep, but we only slept fitfully, even though we were exhausted.

Jonathan was the first to arrive later that morning, then came Alastair. In the meantime Ros had got the kids up and dressed. Then it was time to go.

'See you next at Number 10!' I said, and kissed the kids goodbye. Ros was going to take them there later.

First Tony had an appointment with the Queen, the ceremony known as 'kissing hands', the formal invitation to the new Prime Minister to form a government.

As we walked out of our old front door, shouts rang out and I realised what all the banging had been about while we'd been trying to get some sleep. Across the road a scaffolding platform had been erected for scores of photographers. All our neighbours were out in the street to cheer us off, and when we walked up to shake their hands I suddenly had the feeling that we were saying goodbye – and we were really. That's what it was. I looked up at the sound of Kathryn's voice shouting 'Hey, Mum! Up here!', and saw her waving down to us, her red hair glinting in the sun. Then Tony and I got into the Rover, a police car behind us, with Jonathan and Alastair bringing up the rear. And as we drove down through King's Cross, a motorbike escort with us all the way, cars stopped to let us through and drivers beeped their horns and the people on the streets waved. And all the time, above our heads, the sound of a helicopter. I thought it must be the police, but now I realise it was Sky News filming us, the rotors pounding the air. But I'll never forget that journey, through all those bits of London that are normally in gridlock. We didn't stop, just drove straight down past Euston heading towards the Palace.

I had been to Buckingham Palace a couple of times before, but not to this part, the Queen's audience rooms overlooking the garden at the back. As the car swung in past the Victoria Memorial, I couldn't get over the crowds and Tony and I didn't dare speak, we just held hands.

Once inside the Palace, we were taken up to the first floor, where I was introduced to the Queen's lady-in-waiting, Lady Susan Hussey. The Queen's private secretary and press secretary then explained to Tony what would happen while the lady-in-waiting told me what I had to do, which was basically to wait outside until the Queen rang the bell – the sign that I should go in. The Queen would receive me briefly and that would be it.

Tony was in there on his own for about twenty minutes. Then the bell rang, and I went in, the door being opened by a footman. I can't remember not curtsying, so I probably did. It was a big room and the sun was shining through the large windows, and this iconic figure was standing there next to Tony, looking tiny beside him.

'Well, Mrs Blair,' she said. 'I have just been congratulating your husband. With all this excitement you must be tired.'

'Tired but happy, Ma'am.'

'And tell me, have you decided yet where you are going to live?'

'Well, I think we'll probably move into Number 10, but we won't make up our minds until we've actually seen what it's like.'

'You mean you haven't seen inside Downing Street? That does surprise me.'

She smiled again, picked up the bell and the audience was over. We were escorted back downstairs and I fully expected to see Terry and the Rover waiting for us. But there was no sign of the Rover, just a Jaguar, the Prime Minister's Jaguar. Then I saw it was Terry in the driving seat looking as pleased as Punch. They had tried to persuade Tony to change and take John Major's driver, but he'd said no. He wanted to keep Terry and Sylvie.

As we pulled out of the Palace a great roar went up – around the Victoria Memorial the crowds were going mad. Up the Mall, then turning into Whitehall, the noise was deafening. The car stopped at the bottom of Downing Street. For once people had been allowed in past the big gates and the pavements on either side were packed, everybody shouting 'Tone-ee, Tone-ee', and 'Labour's Coming Home'. As we made our slow way up that street, clasping the hands that were thrust out to us, I realised that these were staff and members of the Labour Party, as I recognised many of the faces. Above their heads, the windows of the Foreign Office were full of more hands waving. I looked up the street to see if the kids had got here safely, and there they were, standing next to Fiona's three, and the Mostyn-Williams children, all waiting for us to come up, little flags in their hands, their bright faces grinning, shining with excitement.

I stood with the children and Tony walked a pace in front of us while he waited for the hubbub to calm down. Then he spoke.

'For eighteen years – for eighteen long years – my Party has been in opposition. It could only say, it could not "do". Today we are charged with the deep responsibility of government. Today, enough of talking – it is time now to do.' He turned round and walked over to us. We posed for a press shot together, then somebody banged on that great heavy knocker and the door opened.

CHAPTER 20

New Dawn

Over the last few days of the campaign, Tony had been getting memos from the Cabinet office at Number 10, setting out how things actually worked. From the most basic (there was no direct dialling, for example, all calls went through the switchboard, which we were told was always known as 'switch'), through to the 'cast list': who people were, what they did, who they answered to, from messengers and 'garden room girls' – as, to my horror, the women who provided the secretarial help were known – to the Cabinet secretary, the head of the Civil Service, who was then Sir Robin Butler, and Alex Allan, the principal private secretary to the Prime Minister, and the most senior civil servant inside Number 10. Ultimately, of course, they all answered to the Prime Minister, and now that person was Tony.

Nothing can describe my mixture of emotions as the door closed behind us. Not only awe in the historical sense – the knowledge that everyone from William Pitt to Churchill and Attlee had been there – but anxiety: that their baton, heavy with responsibility, had now been passed to Tony. There was also an undercurrent of unease: I felt like the unnamed narrator of Daphne du Maurier's *Rebecca* must have felt when she arrived at Manderley for the first time as a bride. As the new Mrs de Winter, she might have been the mistress of the house on paper, but in reality she was utterly powerless, because she had no idea what she was up against.

As we walked down the corridor lined with staff, I was reminded of the scene from the Hitchcock film – the old house, the servants lined up to greet their gawky, unsophisticated new mistress. And just as at Manderley, where the staff had all previously worked for Rebecca, these people now clapping us in were civil servants who'd been working for a Tory government for years and years, and there must certainly have been some among them who were hoping that our tenure would be a short one. None of our own people were there. It really felt like walking into the lions' den. These people, smiling and clapping as we made our way along the long corridor towards the Cabinet room, were all strangers at this point. Later, I realised that it was just as unsettling for them having to deal with us.

While Sir Robin Butler and Alex Allan talked to Tony privately, the kids and I hung round in the corridor outside making faces at each other. After only a few minutes Tony emerged, raised his eyebrows and took my hand in his. We were off to inspect the accommodation.

As we'd been sent the ground plans several months before as part of the standard pre-election contact between the Civil Service and the opposition, to some degree I knew what to expect, though I have always found architects' plans hard to visualise. Then, a few weeks previously, Jonathan had been allowed in to take a look. From what he'd seen, he said Number 10 would be too small for us, and although Number 11 was definitely in need of a lick of paint, it was a much better place for a family. Our first stop, because it was nearer, was the Number 10 flat, so recently vacated by the Majors. Jonathan was right. Two bedrooms were a reasonable size, but the other two were very small. The five of us might just have squeezed in, but what about when my mum came to stay? Or Ros, come to that, without whom I literally could not function? Norma Major had redone the kitchen, and knocked two rooms into one, but it was still a bit cramped, not helped by having such low ceilings. Originally these had been the servants' quarters. It hadn't been lived in by a prime minister until the Douglas-Homes, and for them it was little more than a pied à terre. The Churchills, the Edens and the Macmillans had actually lived downstairs, not up in the attic. The nicest thing about the flat was the bottle of champagne left there for us by the Majors, with a note saying, 'Good Luck. It's a great job. Enjoy it.' A generous gesture and one I wouldn't forget.

Number 11 was the only real option, we decided. It was on three floors, with rooms set round a central staircase. It turned out to be a whole house minus the ground floor and, although the shell was original, it had been gutted and totally rebuilt in the sixties.

From the outside, Downing Street looks like a sedate Georgian terrace. The frontage, certainly, dates from the seventeenth century, but behind it everything opens out in a way you would never expect. Once inside, the only sign that these were originally individual residences are the multiple staircases. The most famous, however, the one lined with portraits of previous prime ministers, was actually designed to link the much grander mansion that lay behind and which faced the other way. It wasn't until 1735 that the various individual buildings were connected – by long corridors – by the then Prime Minister Sir Robert Walpole. Directly beneath the grand reception rooms on the first floor, overlooking the garden and Horse Guards Parade, are the equally grand Cabinet room and the PM's private office. Directly above the grand reception rooms are the distinctly ungrand rooms that make up the Number 10 flat.

The black and white marble-floored entrance hall that lies immediately behind the front door is the domain of the custodians, as the doorkeepers are known – and all visitors to Downing Street enter this way before being escorted to their eventual destination. Go straight ahead and, at the end of a long corridor, you arrive at the Cabinet room and the offices of the Prime Minister and his staff. Turn left, and you are in fact in Number 11, the offices of the Chancellor of the Exchequer, and – beyond this – the Press office – originally the Chief Whip's office – in Number 12. What is known as the Number 11 flat actually extends above Number 12.

We were introduced to this labyrinth of staircases and passages by Carol Allan, then the house manager, and John Holroyd, in charge of protocol. They had both been at Downing Street a long time and knew the building well. I told them that I hadn't made up my mind about what we were going to do. Above all, I said, we didn't want to disrupt the children too much, and certainly didn't want to move their school. Nicky was in his last term at St Joan of Arc, so in the back of my mind I was thinking that we would possibly stay at least till the end of term and maybe we'd move in over the summer.

Apart from the hall, Number 11 had plenty of light and the rooms were all high-ceilinged and generally spacious. As we walked round I realised that it was a good deal bigger than Richmond Crescent.

Yes, it was very old-fashioned – it had last been done up many years before with an unattractive mustard-coloured carpet and flock wallpaper – but we'd already been told it could be redecorated. The worst thing was the haze of cigar smoke that clung to everything. It was like going into a jazz club on a Sunday morning before the cleaners arrived, Kenneth Clarke's last, all-too-enduring legacy.

The children, however, were entranced. They'd discovered a secret spiral staircase that led directly down to the garden. And what a garden! 'It's as big as the park,' I overheard an excited Kathryn telling a friend later. The bedrooms had already been divvied up. Shrieks of 'bags I have this one!' rang out from upstairs. Euan had gone for one with an enormous desk only to discover later that once the desk had been removed, the room itself was smaller than his younger brother's. The problem with the bedrooms was the lack of storage beyond a series of heavy mahogany wardrobes that smelt of mothballs and cedar. My heart sank at the sight of the kitchen. It might have been state-of-the-art in the sixties, but that was then. The sink had ancient taps you could barely get a kettle under, and everything was incredibly utilitarian and bleak, with a beaten-up pine table in the middle.

Then every so often it would hit me: what was I thinking of, complaining about taps, when our little family was about to embark on an extraordinary voyage? In some ways I was too overwhelmed to take it all in, and needed the children's excitement to bring home what had really happened and where we were. Tony was Prime Minister! This was Downing Street! Who cared about taps!

'You've given me food for thought,' I told Carol as we made our way down the staircase outside the front door of the flat on the first floor.

'When you know what you want to do, just give me a call,' she said. The trouble was that I had no idea what I wanted to do. Tony was anxious to keep everything the same as it was, both for him and the kids. It was barely two years since we'd got Richmond Crescent as we wanted it. Now, even the idea of going through all that again made my heart sink. And yet I knew that the most important thing was for us all to be together as a family as we had always been. And although it would involve a lot of work, the flat at Number 11 had an amazing amount of space. But it had to be a family decision and that meant the opinion of the kids was vitally important.

We had both been concerned that they should not feel excluded in all that was happening, so we'd decided that the only people present would be people that they knew and, above all, lots of children. Among those we'd invited were my friend Felicity Mostyn-Williams, from St Joan of Arc, and her brood of six. Then there were Alastair and Fiona's three, and finally my sister Lyndsey's two, so there was a great deal of high-spirited rushing about and general merriment.

By the time we got down from our tour, friends and family were all milling around the state dining room, already making inroads into the buffet lunch that had been laid on. The kids, faced with this huge table of food, had gone completely wild. The hubbub was tremendous – adults, children, everyone buzzing – admonishments to calm down being totally disregarded. The whole building seemed to be ringing with shrieks and laughter and I remember wondering if it had ever seen such a day in its entire history.

Outside the sun continued to shine and, while the children careered around, the bemused and slightly shell-shocked grown-ups sat in the garden, took photographs and generally marvelled at where we were and what had happened. I'd be chatting normally, then suddenly catch someone's eye, and we would both burst into fits of spontaneous laughter. I felt like punching the sky! He had done it! My husband had done it!

Then around five it was time to go. After all the pumping of adrenalin and excitement, we had run out of steam and we simply went home. It was surreal. One moment we were sitting on the terrace outside the Cabinet room at Number 10, the next moment I was in the kitchen at Richmond Crescent, poking around in the fridge, wondering what to do about supper.

Lying in bed later that night, trying to get to sleep, I thought back over our day. So many extraordinary moments I was determined not to forget. As we came out of the audience with the Queen, I'd asked Tony what had happened. 'I mean, did you really have to kiss hands?'

'Not exactly,' he said. Before he went in, the Lord Chamberlain had explained that actual kissing wasn't required. It was more like 'a brushing of lips over her hand'. Next thing, Tony was ushered into her presence and, seeing the outstretched hand, was just moving forward to 'brush his lips over her hand' when somehow – feeling both bemused and nervous – he managed to trip over the edge of the carpet and ended up falling on top of the hand with an ardour that neither he nor Her Majesty were quite anticipating.

Her composure was quite unruffled, he said, and with a reassuring smile she told him that he was her tenth prime minister and that her first, Winston Churchill, was in office before Tony had even been born.

'Don't worry,' I told him, as we settled into the car on our way to Downing Street. 'I know that her tenth prime minister is going to be as good as the first, even if his hand-kissing technique could do with brushing up.'

Although exhausted, we slept not much better than we had the night before. Our bedroom was on the first floor, the bed between the two front windows, and the non-stop racket in the street – police needing to chat and talk every two hours when they changed shift – made sleep practically impossible. They might as well have been in the bedroom with us, frankly. As I lay there, staring at the ceiling, it became obvious, as it hadn't been before, that staying in our old house just wasn't viable if we were to have any privacy at all. Tony couldn't possibly run the country from here, and as we didn't want to be separated that meant we would all have to move into Downing Street. The security people had made it clear that if we stayed in Richmond Crescent it would be turned into something resembling a detention centre. The glass in all the windows had already been changed and net curtains had been put up. The road itself was cordoned off with bollards at both ends. It was unfair to expect our neighbours to put up with this. They hadn't asked for any of it. At around six o'clock a lorry came and began to dismantle the scaffolding erected for the press. As I lay there, listening to the clanging and banging outside, I thought about the logistics of it all. The best time to do the move, I decided, would be half-term, which was in about three weeks' time.

I can't remember now exactly what time the bell went, sometime around eight thirty. Ros was two floors up, still asleep – officially she was off-duty at weekends – and as nobody else was getting it, I pressed the intercom.

'Flower delivery for you, Mrs Blair.' It was one of the policemen.

'Can't you just put them inside the door?'

''Fraid not. I'm here on my own.'

I padded down to the front door and opened it, yawning, hair like a bird's nest, and bleary-eyed.

Everyone now knows what awaited me outside. Every tabloid editor in the world knew exactly what picture would go on their front page that Sunday and the photographer no doubt made a fortune.

The flowers turned out to be from the governing body of St Joan of Arc. It was really sweet of them, but I'm sure they wish it hadn't happened the way it did. I can laugh at it now. If the marketing people wanted me to be like the woman in the street, they couldn't have planned it better. So perhaps in the end it didn't matter, but as I shut the door I remember leaning my forehead against the back of it, my eyes closed, thinking, Oh my God, Tony will kill me. I could just hear him saying, 'How could you be so stupid as to go down in your nightdress without even putting on a dressing gown.' In fact, he didn't. He had more pressing matters to attend to.

All that effort over the past weeks to turn me into a suitable con-sort for the Prime Minister, and I ended up looking like the mad woman from the attic. I did object to how my nightdress was mocked, however. It was a perfectly respectable grey cotton nightie from the Next catalogue. All natural fibres, not remotely cheap and nasty as the press claimed.

Over breakfast I told the kids what I felt. The business with the flowers put the final nail in the coffin of any idea I'd clung on to of staying where we were. We couldn't. The press would be there the whole time, the entire neighbourhood would be disrupted. I told them that I thought we should probably all move to Downing Street, and I was wondering about half-term.

'Why wait till then?' they chorused. 'We've chosen our bedrooms, so why don't we just move in now?' They were very firm. If we did it on Monday, the May bank holiday, they'd be back at school by Tuesday.

I called Carol Allan. She would meet me at Number 10 in an hour, she said. With Nicky and Kathryn safely off to their music lessons, Ros and I left for Downing Street to play musical chairs and other furniture. The Civil Service consider Number 10 and Number 11 as government property and didn't want us bringing our own furniture into the building. This presented problems. The two sofas in the Clarkes' sitting room were very down-at-heel and nothing had been touched for years. Knowing Gordon wasn't going to be using the Majors' flat, I felt quite comfortable about taking what we needed from there and arranged for a sideboard and some lamps and two sofas to be brought over, though as the Number 11 sitting room was bigger they were a bit too small. Kathryn inherited the twin beds from their spare room, complete with Laura Ashley sprigged bed-covers. I wanted each of the kids to have two beds so that friends could stay, and it turned out there were a couple in storage which we could have. The same with desks and wardrobes.

The kitchen cupboards had less to offer in the way of equipment than a holiday cottage. In the short term Ros and I could bring things over from Richmond Crescent. I had not even begun to think about what was going to happen to everything there.

Tony spent the rest of the weekend closeted with Jonathan and Alastair working out his Cabinet appointments. On our way out I spotted Harriet Harman and our own local MP Chris Smith waiting outside the Cabinet room where Tony was seeing people, distribut-ing portfolios. I'd already been informed that, whereas a back door did exist, we should always use the Number 10 door whatever the circumstance, even if coming in laden with groceries.

Meanwhile, I tried to make sense of how I was going to move the whole caboodle in on the Monday. Carol Allan agreed that they would open the windows and fumigate the rooms before we came in, so that was a start. There was no time to organise a removal van, not that we really needed one anyway. All we were taking were our per-sonal possessions, clothes, the kids' toys and general bits and pieces which all went in one of the Number 10 vans – what they call a comms wagon, which is used to transport secure telecoms equipment for the Prime Minister when he's travelling. With the help of Ros, her mum and her brother, we managed to accomplish all that on the Monday morning. As house moves go it was fairly unglamorous, so I was amazed to discover that, thanks to the fabric shoe-holder that Carole had bought to organise my shoes – photographed being car-ried in by Ros – I had become Britain's answer to Imelda Marcos. John Holroyd came in with a hammer and helped the kids put up some of their posters and pictures on the wall, so it was quite sweet, but it was not set up at all for a family; that would take several years.

There was one near-disaster. Kathryn and her friend Bella Mostyn-Williams, having decided that her wardrobe was exactly like

the one in *The Lion, the Witch and the Wardrobe*, climbed in looking for adventure Narnia-style. The first we knew about it was an
almighty shudder that echoed through the entire building as the
whole vast edifice crashed to the ground with them in it. Fortunately,
neither of them was injured, but if it hadn't been clear before, it was
now: this was no way to furnish a room for kids.

That Monday evening Bill and Katy Blair came round bearing
their usual gift of a Chinese takeaway. Over the following ten years,
they never appeared without one. The next day being Tony's forty-
fourth birthday, we squashed round that pine table, and raised our
glasses, both to him and to the first night in our new home. And,
incredibly, it was already beginning to feel like ours. The Party had
given us a framed poster and the kids had stuck it up in pride of
place beside the sink: 'New Labour. Britain just got better'. And it
was true – you felt it in the streets, in the smiles of the people, in the
air of jauntiness. It was as if a great weight had suddenly been lifted
from everyone's shoulders.

The following morning, a huge birthday cake arrived courtesy of
the *Mirror*, and somebody sent an even more enormous bouquet of
red roses, about 350 of them, one for every Labour MP.

I didn't see them delivered, as for me it was business as usual, this
time in the Court of Appeal. It was a big case about the TUPE, the
Transfer of Undertakings Protection of Employment Regulations – a
European Union measure which protects employees when their companies are bought out, in order that their terms and conditions are
preserved. The reporters' bench was unusually full. When I stood up
to open the case, I remarked how gratifying it was to see so much
press interest in the technicalities of the Transfer of Undertaking
Regulations. Some of them were there for the right reasons, in that
it was an important case in terms of industrial relations, but most
were political reporters, all wanting to see what I would do. They
lasted about fifteen minutes. Little did I know as I stood there, discussing the finer points of employment law, that a bombshell would
await me when I got back to Downing Street.

At the end of 1996, when the move to Number 10 became a
probability rather than a possibility, the accountant suggested I
undertake an income and expenditure exercise, such as you might do
when applying for a mortgage. The results weren't exactly encouraging. I have the page in front of me now. There are question marks

everywhere, but the general picture shows that, whereas Tony's income would go up, mine would go down – I didn't know how being the PM's wife would affect the number of cases I could take, but it would certainly be fewer. And with the official duties I'd have to carry out, I knew I'd have less time to devote to my career.

We'd been told that living in Downing Street would be treated as payment-in-kind, and would therefore be taxed, yet we still had a big mortgage to pay on Richmond Crescent, plus the overdraft I'd taken out for the refurbishment. I didn't want to give up our home. I didn't know how long Tony would be Prime Minister, so I needed to make sure that we had a home to go to once we left, if Labour lost the next election. On the plus side, I knew that MPs and ministers were about to get a 26 per cent salary rise, which Parliament had approved a few months earlier and which was due to take effect following the 1997 election. After years of enforced restraint, the Senior Salaries Review Body had recommended the increase to bring politicians into line with the Civil Service. With that increase, I decided, we could probably manage. Then Gordon threw a spanner in the works.

At the first Cabinet meeting of the new Labour government, the new Chancellor announced he was not going to take the salary increase and he put pressure on the others not to accept it either. Tony told me as soon as he got back to the flat and I couldn't believe it. All my calculations were based on the increase. This wasn't an optional perk: the SSRB had recommended it and Parliament had endorsed it. Ministers were specifically mentioned. 'We believe that additional recognition of the job weight of the Prime Minister and Cabinet ministers is long overdue.' As the Leader of the Opposition *did* take his increase, this meant that Tony was now earning less than William Hague.

I remember sitting at the table at the kitchen at Number 10, putting my head in my hands and staring at the now completely redundant financial breakdown, as Tony tried to calm me down. I wouldn't be calmed down. How dare Gordon do that? What did he know about financial commitments? He was a bachelor living on his own in a flat with a small mortgage. Tony admitted it was a problem, but every problem, he said, has a solution. I just had to find it. He wanted to get on with the business of governing.

Despite my reluctance, the obvious solution was to rent out the house in Richmond Crescent to cover the mortgage. But it wasn't that simple. First, the advice was that this should be done through the Foreign Office. As I would later discover when we needed a new nanny, we could no longer go through the *Northern Echo* or the *Lady*. From now on it was Civil Service-vetted agencies only. It was a security issue.

'Your problem', the Foreign Office official explained, 'is that the people we deal with don't want to live in Islington. They want to live in Kensington or Knightsbridge.' Surely, I thought, there might be a junior official who wouldn't mind slumming it in N1. They came to have a look.

'If you're going to rent out this house, it'll have to be completely redecorated, because it's not suitable for the sort of families it would be suitable for.' I was entering the world of doublespeak.

OK, so despite the Foreign Office advice, we'd do it privately. 'Forget it,' said Alastair. When Norman Lamont rented out his house, the tenant was revealed as some sort of Miss Whiplash – manna from heaven for the tabloids.

'So what do we do?' I asked him. 'We can't afford to go on paying the mortgage. It's as simple as that.'

'Why don't you have a word with Michael,' he suggested.

Michael Levy was the Labour Party's fundraiser-in-chief, and was also a friend and a successful businessman; if anyone knew what to do, he would, Alastair said.

Michael had been very good to us during the run-up to the election, letting the kids go to his house in north London and use his swimming pool, just to give them a break from Richmond Crescent; and he also played tennis with Tony.

'Sell,' he said. No other options? 'No. Sell.'

We put it on the market, got an offer in fairly quickly and accepted it. I didn't want to leave our home and I worried about losing our footing on the property ladder. I had seen what had happened to my mum when she was trying to buy somewhere in Oxford. If you haven't got another house to sell, you very quickly get priced out of the housing market. After the sale of the house we had £200,000 left. I suggested putting the money into another smaller property. At least that would keep us on the ladder. No. As Prime Minister, Tony was not allowed to have any investments, and if we bought a house without intending to live in it, this would be classed as an investment. I gave up. We were obliged to put the money into a blind trust with me as the sole beneficiary.

The one bright spot on the housing front was Chequers. When Tony first became Leader of the Opposition, I remember Jill Craigie, Michael Foot's wife, coming up to me at some do and saying, 'I don't envy you much, but I do envy you Chequers.' As the wife of a Cabinet minister in Callaghan's government, she had been there, and with that kind of recommendation I couldn't wait to see it.

The Friday of our first visit, the auguries did not look good. The curator, whom Mrs Thatcher had chosen to run Chequers, had been a career naval officer – officially Chequers is a ship and is staffed by naval and airforce personnel – and we'd heard she had no experience of children. Sadly, she had taken over from her predecessor just as Mrs Thatcher was ousted, and her successors – the Majors – preferred to go back to their house in Huntingdon at weekends, so hardly ever went there. When they did, they found things rather more regimented than they were used to. Meals had to be at regular times, and the curator believed in staying up until the Majors went to bed, which it seemed they found less than relaxing. It didn't sound to me like the kind of regime that would go down too well with our kids, and I wondered how she would cope with having children running round the place, let alone going a bit wild.

John Holroyd did his best to allay my fears. 'We very much want you to use Chequers,' he said. 'It hasn't been used recently as much as one would hope, so staff morale has gone down as a result, and I do assure you they're all looking forward enormously to your coming. While it's true that the curator isn't used to having children around, there is no reason to think they won't charm her as they are already charming everyone here. Unfortunately,' he continued, 'she won't be able to welcome you herself this weekend, as she's injured her back.'

The moment we arrived, driving up through the Victory Gate, with this historic Tudor pile standing four-square ahead of us, I couldn't believe it. We left the children outside kicking a football, relishing the acres and acres of space, while Linda the housekeeper showed us round. All ancient panelling, gorgeous oil paintings, ornate carvings, mullioned windows and rooms big enough to run races in.

As we went back to the children, Tony began shaking his head.

'We can't possibly bring the kids into this place,' he said. 'They'll wreck it.' From outside we heard the sounds of squabbling and decided they needed to walk off the excess adrenalin. Grass led away from all sides of the house, apart from the front, into woodland – wonderful and unsettling at the same time. By now the kids were really playing up, and Tony began to raise his voice, shouting at them to 'just behave!' Suddenly he looked round and saw that we were being followed by the protection officers. And he went stiff with frustration and bewilderment.

'I don't believe it,' he said through clenched teeth. 'I can't even yell at my own kids, because the police will hear.' Never again would Tony be able to walk anywhere without being followed, albeit at a discreet distance.

By the end of the weekend, however, it was obvious to us that Chequers was a good place to be. There was an indoor swimming pool. Did we want to use it? Under Mrs Thatcher it had been drained, because she didn't swim. The Majors had used it, and in fact Norma had learnt to swim there, but because they hardly ever went, the heating had been turned off. Our answer was a resounding yes.

It had been presented to Chequers by Walter Annenberg, the then American Ambassador to Britain, in memory of Richard Nixon's visit. It's built like an orangery, with a glass roof and glass sides that open completely in the summer, but because it's basically an indoor pool we could swim here all year round. As far as the kids were concerned, it was complete heaven.

For ten years Chequers became our bolt-hole. Although from the outside it might look like a stately home, the atmosphere was far more comfortable and domesticated than that would suggest. I will never forget the huge sigh of relief when on a Friday evening the Jaguar turned through the gate into the east courtyard and Linda or Ann, her successor, would come out to greet us, and the children would run in, throw off their coats and rush off to their bedrooms, or to see the rabbits, or to find Alan in the kitchen to see what treats they could scrounge. Alan was still there when we left, but Linda had moved to California with her husband. She was always smiling, not the bossy warrant-officer type at all.

The curator's back trouble turned out to be serious. She never returned, and the Trustees proposed putting Linda in charge officially. She and Alan had both been at Chequers since the mid-1980s, so they knew exactly how everything worked.

Chequers was the one place in the world where Tony could be just a dad, and kick a ball around with his children like any other father. It was an illusion, of course. As we were quickly learning, police and security people were always around, but at least at Chequers we didn't see them. At least there we had the space to lead a normal life.

CHAPTER 21

Special Relationship

The first official visit we hosted at Downing Street was – appropriately enough – the Clintons'. It was barely a month since Tony took office, and I remember everyone being very excited, because they all wanted to meet Bill: the kids, the nanny, my sister and my mother. For the benefit of the press, we greeted the most powerful political couple in the world outside on the front steps. I had a special outfit made by Ronit Zilkha: non-threatening was the brief from the office. Heaven forbid that I should look like a career woman. The office was terrified I might turn into Hillary Clinton.

The Downing Street administration also had concerns about Hillary, albeit on a more pragmatic level. She would need somewhere to 'park' herself, they said. The Number 11 downstairs loo was deemed unsuitable for the wife of the American President. Only the bathroom off our nanny Ros's room met the standard: the Clarkes' former guest room being the sole part of the flat that had been decorated in the last ten years.

At least by the time Hillary took her look around, Number 11 had noticeably improved in terms of the jazz-club haze. When I recounted to Hillary my run-ins with Downing Street over the most modest improvements (such as built-in wardrobes for the kids and a new kitchen) she was amazed. In America, she told me, the incoming President's wife had the choice of keeping the White House the way it was, or redecorating. There was a charitable fund entirely devoted to its refurbishment, for which the First Lady would actively seek donations – and get them. When I suggested to the Cabinet secretary that we might do something similar to refurbish the state rooms in Downing Street or indeed Chequers and save the taxpayers' money, the answer was no.

Rather than some over-formal dinner in Downing Street, we decided to take the golden couple out to a restaurant – a far more personal way, Tony felt, of getting to know them. The Pont de la Tour has a fantastic position on the river, overlooking Tower Bridge, part of a refurbished warehouse complex, and as we arrived people were hanging from flat windows and packing the open walkways to cheer both Tony and Bill, who was of course a huge international superstar.

Bill is an incredibly sociable person who loves ideas and loves talking, but who only really gets going after ten. If the evening takes off you are guaranteed a fantastically interesting discussion, though possibly regretting it the next day. That evening did take off, the first of many we would enjoy together and, like so many others, it went on far longer than anyone expected. Although by nature Hillary Clinton is not a touchy-feely type of person, I found her to be much warmer than her public persona might suggest. She has tremendous dignity and cares passionately about her and Bill's joint project which was to make the US the land of opportunity, not just for the advantaged but for everyone.

Part of the restaurant had been sectioned off for us that evening, though it had been agreed that we would order from the ordinary menu. What we ate, however, would not be revealed. Or that was the intention. The next morning, however, 'Cherie Eats Foie Gras' was front-page news. Apart from the usual eye-rolling from Alastair, the result was a torrent of abusive letters from animal lovers. The venom they unleashed shook me to the core.

There were so many of them, we decided to set up a standard reply. Until this incident I had replied to every letter personally. Before moving into Number 10, Fiona and Roz Preston shared the job of looking after me, paid for by the Labour Party, and one of the first things we'd done on arrival was to see what Downing Street could offer in terms of secretarial support. After a great struggle Norma Major had persuaded them to fund a secretary for four days a week. Like so much in Downing Street, you were never told what might be available: it was up to you to find out.

Nor were you told what things cost. Chequers came with a full complement of staff, yet there were charges that would arrive out of the blue, like the cost of laundering napkins. It all depended on who had used the napkins. If it was family or official visitors, then they were paid for. If the napkin was used by somebody not on the list, then we were billed. The system was confusing to say the least. As for Downing Street, this didn't arise as we were self-supporting.

We had a nanny for the children – Ros first and later Jackie, the nanny who succeeded her in 1998 – and a cleaner for three hours every day. That was how the wonderful Maureen came into our life. She was soon indispensable, especially as it became clear that the flat was as much a public space as Tony's office. I remember laughing when Hillary told me that the White House had four chefs. At Number 11, just as in Richmond Crescent, the nanny would usually shop and she and I would share the cooking between us, though on Sunday nights I would get back from Chequers like a teenager returning to college after a weekend at home, piled high with dishes – for which we paid – prepared by Alan to help me over our busy Monday and Tuesday nights when we had receptions.

Unfortunately the precedents I was setting were all proving negative. No previous prime minister's wife had had a full-time career. No previous prime minister's wife had had school-age children living at home. Since Euan was born I'd had two demanding jobs: mother and barrister. Now I had three, and juggling with three balls is not the same as juggling with two. My role might not have been official – as I was never allowed to forget – but it was time-consuming and important and I had no intention of letting Tony down. We were in this together.

When the animal rights letters arrived I asked if we might get help from the garden girls, so-called because their office on the lower ground floor overlooks the garden. My request was turned down. I was reminded that their role was to service the Prime Minister's office. Then I asked about ordering some Downing Street notepaper. They agreed to a heading reading, 'from the office of Mrs Cherie Blair, QC', but wouldn't sanction 'from the office of Cherie Booth, QC'. In Downing Street terms I was Mrs Blair, the head garden girl explained.

'Agreed,' I said, 'but I am not Cherie Blair, QC. You could search with a magnifying glass but no such person exists in the annals of the

English Bar.' A compromise was eventually reached. I could use the address, but not the crest. If I wanted to use the crest, then I would have to be Mrs Blair. The Foreign Office has a similar culture, in spite of the fact that more than half of the wives of leaders I have come across over the years use a name different from that of their husband.

Over ten years on, I no longer feel I need to make the point. But in 1997 I felt I was hanging on to my identify by the thinnest of threads. I was entering a system which seemed to proclaim: 'You are a non-person except in so far as you are an appendage to the PM.' I don't feel like that any more.

No sooner did some of these replies with the Downing Street letterhead (minus the crest) begin going out, than the *Daily Mail* ran a diary piece by Lady Olga Maitland, saying how ridiculous it was that I was calling myself Cherie Booth, QC, and not Cherie Blair.

'But isn't she married to somebody else?' asked Fiona.

Indeed she was. It transpired that Lady Olga Maitland was the daughter of the 17th Earl of Lauderdale, hence the 'Lady'. She was actually married to a barrister called Robin Hay and between '92 and '97 had been the Tory MP for Sutton and Cheam until she had been ousted by one of the so-called Blair's Babes. This was clearly a matter of sour grapes.

Feeling reasonably gleeful, Fiona then wrote a private letter to the *Daily Mail*, not for publication, pointing out that it was a bit rich to object to my using my maiden name when Olga Maitland was doing exactly the same.

The garden girls were not allowed to help, and even if they had been it would have been impossible. Nor could the horribly over-worked correspondence unit lend a hand. When John Major was in Downing Street, letters to the Prime Minister had been running at around 5,000 a year. Once Tony came in, the trickle became a spate and they simply couldn't cope. Not surprisingly, given the pressure they were under, the occasional mistake crept in. One example was a letter from a school for the deaf asking if Tony could visit them. It was written by the children themselves, yet they had been sent a two-line 'thank you for your letter but the PM doesn't send out autographs' standard reply. As by then I was known to have an interest in special-needs schools, the head had written to me, enclos-ing copies of the original request and Downing Street's reply. While accepting that the PM was busy, she said, the children had made such an effort, that maybe they should have got a better response. I couldn't have agreed more.

I realised that this was one thing I could do to help. From then on it was established that any letters from children would be passed on to my office, so that even if Tony didn't give them his personal reply, they would get one from me. We ended up with a vast correspondence; as I soon discovered, the more you answer people, the more they tend to write back.

Within a matter of weeks we attended our first international summit, the G7. These annual meetings were hosted by the seven most powerful industrial nations in the world: Canada, France, Germany, Italy, Japan, the UK and the US – and in 1997 it was the turn of America. Denver, Colorado, was thus the setting for Tony's first major appearance on the world stage. For me, flying over on Concorde was a dream come true, and I still find it incredible that some way hasn't been found to keep this masterpiece of engineering in the air. The pilot and his crew were clearly the best of the best, and invited me to go into the cockpit as it landed – a real privilege and something I will never forget.

It was all very American. The welcoming event was a country and western concert. In the presence of assembled Denver worthies, the ceremony began with the various leaders and their wives being trundled on to the stage, in order of protocol. Heads of state came first in order of time in office, followed by the heads of government. Tony, being the newest, was the last.

'The Prime Minister of Great Britain and Northern Ireland, the Right Honourable Tony Blair MP, and Mrs Cherie Blair', the unseen voice announced. As the spotlight picked us out, we walked on to the stage to thunderous applause. It was a totally surreal experience, just as a few hours earlier, as we walked down the steps from Concorde, the welcoming band had struck up 'God Save the Queen'.

The G7 (or G8 as it is now that Russia has joined the group) is unusual among summits in that the wives (or husbands) are an intrinsic part of the event, and a separate, parallel programme is organised by the host wife. As the G7 the following year would be the turn of Britain (Birmingham), we were making the most of this opportunity to see how it worked. Tony had his team, and I had

Fiona, although she hated flying and hated even more leaving Grace, who was still a toddler. André was also with me, though Alastair made it clear that his presence was to be kept strictly under wraps. He hadn't even been allowed to come on the same flight. It was André who vetoed the cowgirl outfit that greeted me on arrival, complete with tasselled boots and cowhide hat.

'You are *not* wearing that, Cherie,' he said as soon as he saw it. And he was right. It was pure fancy dress, with what André described as a tablecloth for a skirt. Tony's outfit was equally over the top. However, the shirt, he decided, was bearable, so he wore that with a pair of his own jeans. Unfortunately mine was an all-or-nothing situation, and to go out representing my country looking like Doris Day cracking her whip on the Deadwood stage just wasn't appropriate. The Denver stage would have to make do with smart casual. In fact, the only people who seemed to mind my not joining in were the British press. The truth is that, had I worn the tablecloth, it would surely have taken its place in the gallery of Cherie's sartorial disasters.

In spite of Alastair's warnings that André should maintain a low profile, somebody saw him. Alastair's response was to say that Mrs Blair's hairdresser was a private matter and that I was paying André myself, as indeed I was. Then the story became spendthrift Cherie, chucking money away like nobody's business. It was a steep learning curve: whatever I did, I couldn't win. It was the twentieth-century equivalent of the stocks, I decided: anything could be thrown at me with impunity. I was even accused of doing away with Humphrey, the Downing Street cat. While it is true that I am allergic to cats, God knows that the labyrinth known as Downing Street had plenty of places for the poor boy to go. The prosaic truth is that he was old. It was not me who decided it was time for him to retire, but the domestic staff who had to keep cleaning up after him. In the end Humphrey was taken in by a newly retired Cabinet office messenger and went on to enjoy a happy retirement in Bromley.

The spouses' programme started on day two. With the other wives – there were no husbands at this time – we set off on one of those trains that you see in Westerns, complete with viewing platform at the back. As we chugged up into the Rockies to gaze at the magnificent scenery, I was struck by how Hillary worked the watching crowds, lined up along the embankments. Suddenly, something caught my eye, and at the same time Hillary said, 'I think we should go back in now.' As we all trooped back inside, I mouthed, 'Did you see what I saw?' She laughed and nodded. A man had 'mooned' at the passing train, but fortunately none of the other ladies' sensibilities had been affronted, as they clearly hadn't noticed. A display of line-dancing by a local pensioners' group awaited us at our destination, and once again I saw how Hillary took the initiative, introducing us with an off-the-cuff speech, all utterly spontaneous. Even then I realised I was watching a master class.

What I would have done without André on that trip I do not know. No time was built in for anything as mundane as packing. Although, for a visit of this length, the PM always travelled with an entourage of policy advisers, press officers, duty clerks, garden girls, protection and 'comms' (communication) people, they were simply there to help him conduct his business. Their sole contribution to the domestic side of things was a note saying what time the luggage had to be ready for collection. That last morning in Denver, André found me in a state of panic, and began to help, folding Tony's shirts, collecting the little piles of things he would take out of his pockets at night, sorting out his suits, while I scrabbled round trying to retrieve odd shoes and socks from under the bed.

Next stop was Washington, where Tony and Bill were having bilateral talks, but by the time I unpacked, I realised there was nothing he could wear; it all needed to be professionally pressed or re-ironed. This time André wasn't there to help: Alastair had forbidden him to travel on the same plane, and he'd had to fly via Chicago. It was ridiculous because when he wasn't with us it all fell apart.

Hillary asked if I'd be interested in seeing how she did things. By this time she had been First Lady for five years, so she and her staff had a huge amount of experience. Although there were obviously big differences – Tony wasn't head of state for a start – nonetheless I thought we could still learn from the way the White House handled the workload.

Her office was situated in the East Wing where an entire department was devoted to invitations and menus. Being invited to the White House, she explained, was seen as an honour: invitations became like family heirlooms, lasting long after the dinner was forgotten. This hive of activity was known as the calligraphy department: everything was printed from copper plates, and names and envelopes written in the most beautiful italic handwriting.

'But it must be so labour-intensive,' I said, looking round at the mass of heads bent over their work. She explained that most of them were volunteers, old and young, who worked in the White House for the love of it. Some of them stayed for years, serving each president faithfully, doing the invitations and certain correspondence, like the person I met whose role was to answer the mail to Socks, the Clintons' cat. Others were 'interns', young graduates who would spend around six months working in the White House solely for the experience. This system, pre-Monica Lewinsky, seemed an entirely good idea, and on my return to Downing Street I put forward a proposal to the Cabinet office about the possibility of using interns as a way of coping with the rising tide of correspondence and associated work that we were struggling to deal with. This proposal was adopted and interns were brought into a number of departments. They were graduates of Peter Hennessy's government administration course at Queen Mary's College. They worked in a number of places, including my office, and were invaluable, but after a few years it became apparent that it wasn't really saving the government that much money. Although they weren't being paid, there had to be people to supervise them and plan everything, so in 1999 the intern programme was stopped. By this time Fiona was working the four-day week alone, as Roz Preston had left London. Because of the sheer volume of work we had been allocated a full-time secretary to help us, Pauline, a civil servant who came from the Ministry of Defence.

My tour round the First Lady's office was incredibly useful. Hillary showed me the White House gifts they would take with them when travelling. Not the gifts that would be exchanged on official visits – but smaller things, like White House key-rings for example, for people who had generally been helpful. Nothing very costly, but a token that was much appreciated. She told me also how, with the millennium coming up, she was planning a series of lectures in the White House, that would start in 1998. I later did the same.

Her final piece of advice would resonate the longest.

'You've got to recognise', she said, 'that you're not going to please everyone the whole time, and you're certainly not going to please the press, and therefore you should just do what feels right for you, and so long as you feel it's right for you then don't get too upset about what other people say.'

The furore over André had been so intense that Alastair banned him from coming on the next overseas visit. I would have to make do with local hairdressers like everybody else, he said. At the end of July 1997, after a hundred and fifty years, Hong Kong was being handed back to China. It was both a political and a royal occasion, and involved a mass exodus of senior personnel from Britain, including the Prince of Wales. As a result there was a problem of transport. The Queen had the Royal Yacht *Britannia*, and she also had an aircraft. As the plane was nearing the end of its life, there had been talk of getting a new one, to be shared by the Prime Minister. In the end this was shelved for PR reasons, and from then on planes had to be chartered from British Airways. The Prince was returning on the Royal Yacht which was already moored in Hong Kong, so it was decided that the Prime Minister would use the royal plane, while Prince Charles travelled out with the Foreign Secretary on a chartered BA plane. This was the occasion when famously Prince Charles was obliged to travel business class, Robin Cook, his wife Margaret and Foreign Office officials having commandeered the first-class cabin. In a highly amusing, if ill-advised, epistle to friends, the Prince complained about how poky he found it.

Our method of transport – the royal plane – was old and slow. The good news was that the front cabin transformed itself into a bedroom with two separate beds. The bad news was that it took nearly twice as long to get there, as we had to refuel in Vladivostok. When we got out to stretch our legs we were instructed not to move beyond a small area round the plane. Not that we would have wanted to, it being ringed by Russian soldiers toting machine guns and looking distinctly menacing.

As always in these circumstances, as we came in to land in Hong Kong, there was a queue for the loo. By now I knew that the red carpet would be waiting, that photographers would be there and I needed to look the part. Carole had worked out all my outfits meticulously, including the arrival one that had been brought on board in a suit-carrier. Suddenly it was 'Cabin crew, seats for landing', and I was still in the loo making myself look respectable. The plane was old and there was no question that we were dropping rapidly down on to Hong Kong's terrifying runway. There was nothing to do but just get on with it, I decided. At the moment of touchdown I was standing on one leg, my bum hard up against the folding door, the other leg on the loo seat, desperately trying to pull on my tights before emerging in the official outfit for the walk down the steps.

On the way back from that trip Alastair said, 'We can't do that again.' André's presence, he belatedly realised, had certain advantages. By the time the plane landed, I would be appropriately dressed and immaculately coiffed, no matter how long the flight or befuddled my head. No hairdryers are allowed on board, but André became a dab hand with gas-heated curling tongs. The chances of managing those myself are nil.

As the handover ceremony began, just before midnight, the heavens opened and I watched in admiration as Prince Charles began reading out a message from the Queen which, thanks to the tropical downpour, was disintegrating in his hands. He was standing directly in front of me, his white tropical suit becoming increasingly diaphanous, which afforded me an interesting perspective on the future monarch. At midnight the flag of the People's Republic of China and the regional flag of Hong Kong were raised simultaneously to the unfamiliar strains of the Chinese National Anthem, and as the People's Liberation Army goose-stepped their way into the hall, I felt a shiver run up my spine.

CHAPTER 22

Journeys

Princess Diana had been determined not to lose touch with Tony. Shortly after we moved into Number 10, Maggie Rae let us know that the Princess was keen to see him again and she wanted to bring William and Harry to Chequers. Alex Allan, the principal private secretary, nearly had apoplexy when he found out.

It would be quite wrong, he said, for Tony to see Diana before he'd seen Prince Charles. So sometime in those few weeks, Tony did in fact see the Prince, and Diana and William duly turned up at Chequers one Sunday in early July.

Over lunch she talked again about wanting to play a more prominent role in public life. She was determined that William be given a normal, modern upbringing, to make him, as she put it, 'fit to be king'.

Again she was very relaxed, this time chatting with my mum, and being lovely with Kathryn. She talked about how she would like to have more children and how she longed for a little girl. We sat there on the grass, with Kathryn tucked between Diana's knees, watching the three boys and Tony playing football on the north lawn. Later, when she and Tony went for a walk, William came with us to the swimming pool, where my lot all had a great time showing off, while William was really sweet to Kathryn. She was totally in awe, not because he was a prince, but because he was a handsome fifteen-year-old and she was only nine.

The afternoon was deemed a success, relaxed and normal, and in the Blair household Princess Diana was regarded as a good thing.

That summer we went to Tuscany for our holiday, staying at a house belonging to Geoffrey Robinson, and had the usual jolly, relaxing time. Nothing had really changed, we told ourselves, as Ros's swimming gala got under way. Yes, we had to pose for the press at the beginning of the holidays – for which it agreed to leave us in peace for the rest of the time – and yes, the garden girls were somewhere in the village and the 'tecs were somewhere in the shadows, but we could forget about them. Or at least try to.

Towards the end of the holiday we were invited to the house of Prince Strozzi and his wife, because the Mayor of Moscow – Putin's mentor – was staying as their guest and had asked to meet the new star on the Western political horizon. Although our backgrounds couldn't have been more different, Irina and Girolamo were soon firm friends, and over the succeeding years the Strozzis became a regular stop on the Blair summer itinerary

Arriving back in England at the end of August, we went straight to Myrobella. The following weekend was the annual prime ministerial visit to Balmoral, so we had a few days to flop. The Prime Minister is never really on holiday, however. The *Mail on Sunday* was apparently threatening to publish the name of a British spy in some far-flung part of the world, and Tony became convinced that, if his name was revealed, the guy would be killed.

That Saturday night we went to bed in the hope that Alastair had managed to sort it out, then at around three in the morning the phone went. I have a vague memory of it ringing somewhere out of reach, before I drifted back down into a deep sleep. The next thing was the intercom buzzing outside our bedroom.

As Tony rushed to the landing I thought, Oh God. The *Mail* has done it. It's printed the spy's name and he's been killed.

A minute later he was back, as white as a sheet. It was the police, he said. There had been an accident. 'It's Diana.' The bell on our bedside phone hadn't been working, which was why we hadn't heard it. He picked up the receiver and called the duty clerk in Downing Street.

I watched him as he listened, saying nothing.

'A car crash in Paris,' he said eventually. 'She's in a coma. They don't think she'll pull through.'

It was awful. I saw her sitting there on the grass hugging her knees, only a few weeks back, and thought how full of life she'd been, talking about wanting to have more kids . . .

Finally the call nobody wanted. All I heard was Tony repeating, 'I can't believe this. I can't believe this.' We were to say nothing to anyone. It would be announced to the press shortly.

He was shocked and upset. What remained of the night, Tony was on the phone, or watching the television, or both. There were so many things to think about. There was the issue of the paparazzi, but he didn't want to make a knee-jerk response. He didn't know whether he should speak to the Queen or to Prince Charles.

When the kids woke up, we told them what had happened. And they were upset because they felt they knew her and they liked her.

Tony had agreed with Alastair that he should make a statement before morning service. Alastair was usually anti anything that involved the Church or God, but on this occasion even he agreed it might be appropriate. It was obvious that it had sent a shudder through the nation and Tony needed to say something to embody what it was the people were feeling.

The Catholic church, St John Fisher in Sedgefield, was deemed inappropriate as there was nowhere for the press to stand, so we went to St Mary Magdalene in Trimdon, where Lily Burton, John's wife, played the organ. By the time we arrived the television cameras were in position, and Tony said what he did, and, it's fair to say, caught the mood of the nation with his 'She was the people's princess'.

We returned to London that night and got Terry to drive us past Buckingham Palace to see the flowers that were already piling up round the base of the gates. Back in Downing Street we opened a book of condolences which everyone signed.

Now, of course, the success of the film *The Queen* has somehow resulted in it becoming the official record of that extraordinary week, but it wasn't quite like that. For example, from a pedantic perspective, the way that Number 10 was portrayed was completely wrong, not to mention me and Tony: I never swear and Tony is a good deal taller than Michael Sheen. But there are more serious points to be made.

For a start, I never felt there was the opposition from the Palace to what Tony was suggesting; in fact he had been asked to become involved by the Lord Chamberlain. Things were complicated because Robert Fellowes, whom I had met the day we first went to the Palace, was Diana's brother-in-law, married to her sister Jane. The family's main concern over those first few days was simply to protect the boys, because they were so young and so distressed, and they really didn't want them exposed to anything more. They weren't thinking beyond that. They just wanted to pull together as a family, and didn't see why they should share their grief with the rest of the world and, in a sense, why should they? I think they hoped that they could just get on with it. Accept what had happened, do what had to be done.

I think that's what Tony really wanted too, but as the days went by it became apparent that this wouldn't be enough.

When we first arrived in Number 10, we were told of detailed plans that existed in the event of the death of the Queen Mother. The protocol people had it all set out, exactly what was to happen, and when, that you were to wear black-tie mourning and so on. Both Tony and I even had to take suitable black outfits with us on holiday every year in case she died. And now, with the death of Princess Diana, they were treating this as another such event. Their main concern was that it should be carried out with all due deference to precedent and protocol, including the business about how she wasn't Her Royal Highness. Even in death that had to be observed. When the body was flown back, came the question of who was going to meet it. Tony suggested he go and the Queen agreed. But then Prince Charles decided that he wanted to go, while the protocol people clearly would rather he didn't.

The last remaining question was the flag. Protocol decreed that it should only be flown at half-mast when the sovereign dies. Princess Diana was not the sovereign, QED.

The business of who should be invited to the funeral was another protocol issue, yet it seemed important to Tony that Diana's charities should be given priority over foreign dignitaries – and indeed members of the government – who had had no involvement with her. I don't believe the family themselves had much to do with this scrabbling and squabbling. They were really too upset to do anything except hold themselves and the children together. Of course, Tony did talk to the Queen, and from my understanding, it was less her personally than the system that was creating the difficulties.

Throughout it all, Tony believed that, as Prime Minister, his priority was to make sure that all this didn't damage the monarchy; that they got through unscathed, and he succeeded.

For obvious reasons the traditional Balmoral weekend didn't happen that year. Instead we were invited for lunch. It was very low-key, just the Queen and Prince Philip and some old family friends, with the conversation revolving around agriculture, stag-hunting and fishing. Sitting there, I thought this is really weird: yesterday, at the lunch in Number 10 following the funeral, there I was sitting next to Hillary Clinton and Queen Noor of Jordan talking about current affairs, and here I am today with our head of state talking about the price of sheep.

No mention was made of Princess Diana or of the previous day's events. The Queen and Prince Philip were very kind, however. The Queen loves driving, and that afternoon they took us in the Range Rover on a tour round the Balmoral estate with the Queen providing a running commentary, talking about the landscape which she had known from a girl. At heart she's a countrywoman.

At one point I made a real *faux pas*, butting in when the Queen was talking to somebody else. We had been given a list of instructions of what to do and how to behave but, what with one thing and another, the rule that you only talk to the Queen when the Queen talks to you had slipped my mind. It never would again: I was given a look by one of the courtiers that I will never forget.

That winter I learnt that Tony's driver, Sylvie, had breast cancer. Not that it stopped her living. Motorbikes had always been her thing – there was always a specialist magazine in the glove compartment of the Jaguar – and, shortly after the diagnosis, she went out and bought a Ducati, the ultimate Italian bike. Then, on 3 December, came news of a tragic accident. Sylvie was in collision with a lorry and didn't survive. We went to her funeral a week later and Tony spoke for everyone who knew her.

For both of us, the people we work with are central to our lives. This is nothing to do with politics – although it should be. I never forget that my grandma worked as a cleaner and I never want anybody to be treated as she was treated in Blundellsands. What is important is not what people do for a living, but that they are treated with respect.

1997 was our first Christmas at Chequers. Everybody still came to us, as they had at Myrobella, and in some ways it was just the same, although on a much bigger scale, starting with the tree. At about twenty feet tall, it took several people just to get it inside the front door. Its home was the corner of the Great Hall, and by the time Christmas Eve arrived it was decorated and surrounded by the usual array of colourful presents; and with the kids' stockings hanging up beside the great fireplace, it's hard to believe there could be anywhere more perfect to spend Christmas. Rituals developed as rituals do over the ten years we were there. We still went to midnight Mass, and there was still the usual early morning chaos as in any family with young children. There was the visit to the police bothy, beside the entrance, before lunch to hand over our presents. Then it was more presents and champagne for the staff on duty including, at my insistence, a few carols to get us in the mood. Finally would come Alan's wonderful lunch. This was one definite change in the proceedings. My overnight-turkey routine was no longer needed. As for Alan's Christmas puddings, they were in a class of their own. As early as October, the children would help him prepare both the puddings and the cake, everyone taking their turn in stirring the huge bowl of sticky mixture.

That first December, Alan came to see me very perturbed.

'Whatever is the matter, Alan? Why so down in the mouth?'

'Number 10 has said I can't have the usual Christmas turkey.' Every year, he told me, the British Turkey Federation would turn up at Downing Street with a huge bird to be given to charity and a photograph would be taken of them presenting it to the Prime Minister. They would also present a smaller bird for use by the family and staff on Christmas Day; this was the one that was sent down to Alan. It turned out that Alastair had seen this in the diary and vetoed it. His worst nightmare, he said, was having a photograph of Tony and a turkey on the front cover of *Private Eye* looking foolish. As I was quite used to looking foolish by then, I offered myself up as an alternative. Luckily the Turkey Federation agreed, so that became a regular fixture on my Advent calendar for the next ten years, and Alan got his turkey.

The plan had been for Tony and me to go away on our own – a week in the Seychelles just after Boxing Day. Everything was organised. My mum would look after the kids, and then Ros would take over for the last few days. It didn't happen. In the end I couldn't bear the thought of being without them so we all went: Tony and me, my mum and three extremely lucky kids. We had a wonderful time despite the fact that the press had a field day when it discovered that, twenty years earlier, the villa we were staying in had been used as a location for the infamous soft-porn movie *Emmanuelle*.

In January 1998 the Monica Lewinsky scandal finally broke and my heart bled for Hillary, coming on top, as it did, of the Paula Jones sexual harassment suit. Inevitably I thought back to all those young interns, and our guided tour of the West Wing by the President himself, of the Oval Office and the little room off it with the photo-copier. My reaction was basically, Oh Bill, how could you?

From the young woman's point of view, I can quite see how it happened. Bill Clinton is a tremendously charismatic man who is able to mesmerise anybody he meets and give them the feeling that he is totally interested in them and what they are saying, which is clearly not always the case. As for him, I thought he was bloody stupid.

Just a few weeks later we were due in Washington for Tony's first formal visit as head of government. If I had been impressed by Hillary before, I was doubly impressed by her now. Dignity is not the word.

Yet I could see for myself how angry she was with him. Not just for humiliating her, but for jeopardising their joint project, and I could also see how desperately he was trying to win back her approval. The shining light in all this was Chelsea. She is a fantastic young woman, incredibly sensible, intelligent, talented, and very much her own person with her feet firmly on the ground, and I think that says something about the parenting they've both given her. In many ways she reminds me of Tony's brother Bill, one of those people who was always grown up, even when he was a boy. Chelsea is just terribly reliable and you know exactly where you are with her. In all this time she was a very important link between her two par-ents. I think that the fact that she was both supportive of her mum and understood how her mum was feeling, yet at the same time was able to forgive her dad, was a very important part of why they stayed together.

People have wondered whether Tony or I felt ourselves placed in a difficult situation, given our Christian beliefs. The same thing had been asked a few months earlier when Robin Cook, Tony's foreign secretary, was outed by the press as being involved in an extra-marital affair. The answer in both cases is no. Obviously we both believe in marriage. Once that ring is on your finger and the promises are made before God, then fidelity should be a given. But how people conduct their lives is ultimately their own business and, as far as Bill Clinton is concerned, a British prime minister is never going to undermine an American president. As for me, I was never even tempted to raise the subject with him – nothing to do with him being President of the United States. It wasn't me he betrayed, and with my father's back catalogue I am not unused to men's infidelity.

I did, however, discuss it with Hillary.

In her view, the way the right wing relentlessly pursued it was all part of a wider attempt by their enemies to discredit Bill. The most important aspect, she said, was not to let it undermine the presidency. So on a political, strategic level that was the line they took, that this had been politically motivated and stirred up by those who wanted to undermine the Democratic presidency. On a personal level, however, there is no doubt that she was furious and hurt – and rightly.

The idea, however, that men just can't help behaving like that is nonsense. It's a myth which actually leads to a lot of mischief in the world; it's why women are stuck behind burkhas. As for the idea that men are inflamed by the slightest glimpse of an available body, I don't believe it for a second. Uncontrollable sexual urges are nothing of the sort. Of course men can control them, just as women can. What I find particularly worrying is that so often these situations involve the powerful boss and the vulnerable young woman.

When Tony was still Leader of the Opposition, I had been approached in chambers for help by Catherine Laylle. Her children, aged seven and nine, had been abducted by their German father and, in breach of all the conventions, the German courts had done nothing to help her get them back. Sadly, I could do little for her at the time, but later she sent me a book she had written about her experiences. Imagine my surprise when, in 1998, I met the newly appointed British Ambassador, Christopher Meyer, and his wife.

'You probably don't remember me,' she said. It was Catherine.

She was determined to ensure that other parents did not suffer as she had, and asked me and Hillary to be among the first patrons of PACT, the charity she was setting up to deal with the tragedy of abducted children, and that first afternoon in Washington we both spoke at the inaugural reception. For a woman under extraordinary emotional pressure, Hillary coped magnificently. I could only thank her for being such a wonderful role model, both to career women in general, but to me in particular. Thanks to her example, I was getting better at making off-the-cuff speeches. In America this was expected, while Number 10 was still coming to grips with the fact that I could walk and talk. The system was simply not geared to a prime minister's spouse who wanted to be involved. As for Catherine Meyer, her story eventually had a happy ending, although it would be nearly ten years before she saw her boys again.

That night an official banquet was held in our honour. It was one of those evenings where you are skin-tinglingly aware that 'this is extraordinary' even as it is happening. There we were, lined up beside the President and First Lady of America, shaking hands with America's finest, including Barbra Streisand, Robert Redford, Harrison Ford and Steven Spielberg. The dinner was followed by a proper, full-length concert at which both Elton John and Stevie Wonder performed, although clearly his version of 'My Cherie Amour' couldn't match the classic Tony Blair rendition. Sitting there, with the Union Jack and the Stars and Stripes both very much in evidence, I can still remember the feeling of awe.

Washington 1998 was the first time André was acknowledged as a semi-official member of the party, in that his name appeared on movement lists as A. Suard, Personal Assistant to Mrs Blair. I still paid for him, but he was always treated differently from the rest of the group. This still makes me angry, not for me, but for him.

The NATO summits and other bilateral visits Tony had made without me in the previous six months had been chaotic. He was travelling more than any prime minister had ever done before. Everyone wanted to meet Britain's new, dynamic young leader and his schedule was ridiculous, yet he was operating in a twentieth-century world with nineteenth-century back-up.

When the bags weren't outside his door at the appropriate time, the garden girls would end up throwing whatever they could find into his suitcases. It wasn't their fault – it wasn't their job – but things were disappearing at an alarming rate: watches, cufflinks, not to mention socks, the odd shoe, shirt and trousers. At the next stop on the itinerary, it would all need pressing and crucial things couldn't be found. Gradually it dawned on them that having André around wasn't such a bad idea after all . . .

What had triggered the change in attitude vis-à-vis André was our first trip to Japan a few days into the new year. I had insisted on his coming along. Alastair could stamp his foot as much as he wanted, I was blowed if I was going to turn up looking anything less than my best. And it wasn't only that. There was the constant packing and unpacking, not to mention the sheer organisation required to keep us looking up to the mark; we were representing the country after all. André was more than happy to do it, and God knows we needed him.

After years of being reasonably laid-back when it came to travel, these visits were unbelievably concentrated. You might leave Heathrow in the winter then land in glaring sunshine with temperatures in the nineties, yet be forbidden to wear sunglasses or even blink. The clothes you left in (smart) had to be stashed away in suit-carriers before you landed, while those you arrived in had previously been brought on, also smart and crease-free, for both the temperature and the welcoming committee.

There were so many things that needed to be thought of. Jet-lag; getting up in the middle of the night; preparing in advance what you were going to wear coming down the steps on to the tarmac, when all you can think of is throwing off the previous night's outfit and crashing into bed before a dawn flight on to the next destination. André took care of everything. In the morning he would come in and wake us up and run the bath.

'Just five minutes more, André—'

'No. Get up. If you don't, I'll open the curtains.' The ultimate cruelty. Somehow he'd always manage to find a fresh lemon for my morning hot water – I don't drink tea. Ordering such a basic thing from room service was more or less impossible and I rarely succeeded. Frankly, getting a plate of black pudding would have been easier.

Also Tony was used to André; after all, he'd been part of our lives since 1994. Tony could write his speeches – as he often did on those trips – sitting in his underpants, and if André was around it didn't matter, but if an unknown chambermaid or hairdresser walked in, he'd freeze. In those early days it was so disorganised. You couldn't guarantee we'd get a separate sitting room, so Tony would be having a meeting while I'd need to get dressed and, much as I love my country, I draw the line at displaying my fleshier parts to senior members of the Foreign Office. I'd end up grabbing my clothes and going along to André's room.

He was also good company. The second night in Tokyo, as Tony was at a men-only function, André and I joined some of the other non-participants from the office, and went to a noodle bar. I loved it, particularly the warm drink that came in a small bottle, which I didn't realise you were supposed to share. Tony's staff were far better travelled than I was and later admitted that they didn't know how to tell me that sake wasn't just a Japanese version of tea, even though it did come in little cups . . .

By the time I got back to our room, I was feeling very happy indeed, having laughed and sung my way through the latter half of the evening. My poor husband was not impressed, largely I suspect because he'd had an extremely dull dinner himself. The evening had a positive outcome in that André got the thumbs-up from the office. They decided he was a 'good egg' and saw how smoothly the Blair machine operated when he was around compared with the mayhem when he wasn't. And not just on the practical side. Alone of all the people around me, he saw how stressed I was and would help me relax. As the years went by that would become increasingly important, because there was never enough time for what was crammed into the schedule, let alone breathing space between appointments. We would have one hour before, as André would say, 'Bang they are gone again.'

I was beginning to realise too that I didn't simply have to be an appendage on these trips. I was starting to see how I could create a role that would be of real benefit.

It didn't happen overnight. It's fair to say, however, that the Foreign Office proved much more open to my having a public role than did Whitehall, largely I suspect because ambassadors' wives have always had a public role, whereas wives of UK-based civil servants remain largely anonymous. While our embassies abroad would find that I was useful, once back in Blighty I was surplus to requirements.

*

From the moment Tony arrived in Downing Street, Northern Ireland had always been a priority. Within six months of Mo Mowlam beginning talks with Sinn Féin, Gerry Adams and Martin McGuinness were in and out of Number 10.

The children made full use of the 'secret staircase' that led directly from the Number 11 flat to the Downing Street garden. I had brought back Euan and Nicholas a skateboard each from the trip to Washington and they were trying out their skills after school when I had an irate phone call from Alastair.

'Get those kids out of the garden.'

'Whatever for? They're just having a bit of fun.'

'Well, take a look out of the window, then get them out before the press gets wind of it.'

So I did. And there, to my astonishment, were Gerry and Martin on the skateboards showing the boys a few tricks.

A few weeks later I happened to be taking Ralph Lauren around, and as we came into the White Room there were Gerry and Martin. Naturally, I introduced them to my visitor and was intrigued when Gerry began talking rather knowledgeably about clothes. Nothing daunted, I carried on with my tour patter.

'This room has a very famous ceiling,' I continued. 'Each corner has an emblem representing part of the United Kingdom,' and one by one I pointed them out. 'The rose is for England, the daffodil for Wales, the thistle for Scotland—'

'And I think the last one', Gerry butted in, 'is about to fall off!' – this being flax, the emblem of Northern Ireland.

'No, no,' I said, smiling. 'It's the symbol of friendship between our people,' and I whisked Ralph away before I did permanent damage to the peace process.

Easter 1998 would be crunch time. Tony was still in Belfast when the children and I set off on our planned Easter break to Spain. First an official visit with the Spanish premier, José María Aznar, and his wife, then on to Cordoba to stay with our friend Paco Peña, the Spanish flamenco guitarist, and his wife Karin, whom we had got to know through Derry many years before.

We arrived at the Aznars' official country residence outside Seville on the Wednesday. The national nature reserve of the Doñana was a World Heritage site right by the Mediterranean – utterly wild with fabulous dunes – and the whole area was closed to the public, so the kids and I were able to spend time there feeling unfettered and free. We were supposed to be staying only one night, but the talks at Hillsborough Castle were still going on, and Tony was determined not to let this chance slip through his fingers. If he were to leave, he felt, then the whole thing could fall apart. Thursday came and went. Then Friday. The whole world seemed to be teetering on a knife-edge. The Aznars were very understanding; there was no question of our having to move on, they said. Children are a wonderful bridge at times like this, and as the Aznars' were similar in age to ours, everyone was getting on fine, including my mother, who – as so often when the children were along – came with us. Then, with a huge sense of relief all round, came Friday and what became known as the Good Friday Agreement. On the Saturday, Tony finally arrived and it's fair to say that, by then, the Aznars and the Blairs knew each other pretty well. It helped perhaps that we were all lawyers. José María's wife, Ana Botella, was also a TV journalist, very independent and popular in her own right. On Maundy Thursday she took us to watch the traditional Easter parade, and everywhere we went she was greeted warmly by the crowds. She had achieved a lot with her role and I was not surprised when, a few years later, she was elected to Madrid City Council. Over those few days we had some useful discussions and I became even more determined not to sit on the sidelines and do nothing.

People often wonder how a left-of-centre politician deals with politicians from the other side of the political spectrum – something that happens all the time at head-of-government level. The answer is, pretty well. Foreign policy is largely concerned with mutual interests. With America, for example, whether the President or the administration is right or left, the chances are that the mutual interests with outside powers remain the same. Obviously there can be areas of dissent and, in the case of Spain, Gibraltar comes to mind.

That Easter, Euan had just turned fourteen and, although the *Today* programme was no longer required listening in the Blair household, he was comparatively well informed politically. With the insouciance of youth, he decided to bring up the issue of Gibraltar with José María. After the first shocked gulp from both sides – the hosts and an embarrassed mum – there was much laughter, and we went on to have an interesting discussion, something that would never have happened in ordinary diplomatic circumstances.

When Alastair heard the story, he decided it was too good to waste, but as we had long since agreed that our kids would always stay beneath the parapet, my mum agreed to take the 'blame' on this occasion.

Longer foreign visits are limited to when Parliament is not sitting: October, usually during the Tory Party conference, the New Year and Easter. That year, immediately after our return from Spain, Tony and I set off for the Middle East, first Egypt and then on to Israel. The embassy there had asked if there was anything I particularly wanted to do. Following the various special education cases I'd been involved in, I'd heard of a diagnostic process called the Feuerstein method, named after a professor practising in Jerusalem. It was a fascinating encounter: it turned out he ran a centre that helped both Israeli and Arab children with disabilities, particularly Down's syndrome. Expectations for these children, he believed, were too low; they could do far more, he told me, than people imagined and had a particular empathy with the elderly. The centre had developed a scheme whereby these young people would visit old people in their homes. He told me how one old man had collapsed when he was being visited by a boy with quite severe Down's syndrome, and that this young man had been able to ring the emergency services and get him aid in time. Through my charity work I had met a lot of Down's children, and it was a joy to see how happy they appeared.

The contrast with what I saw the following day couldn't have been starker. Gaza is essentially just one big refugee camp. I was later taken by Mrs Arafat to a school for special needs children in Ramallah, on the West Bank, which she herself had set up. Here they were provided with loving care, but little else, and were desperately in need of equipment and toys. As a result of the constant shelling, she explained, the proportion of premature babies is high and many babies are damaged at birth. It was all very upsetting, particularly when I thought of the facilities I had just seen only a few miles away.

The entire visit kept switching from one extreme to another. That evening we landed in Saudi Arabia. As a special sign of honour to Tony, not only was I allowed to walk by his side but the Foreign Minister also shook my hand. That night, however, it was Saudi business as usual. While Tony went off to a male-only dinner, I had a female dinner where even the servers were women.

When in the male world, women are completely covered up, but underneath, I discovered, they were far better dressed than I was. One woman recounted how her small son would pay great attention to what shoes she was wearing before they went out, as he was terrified he would lose her. Once she was covered up, the shoes were the only way he had of telling her apart. We were talking in English and it was clear that many of these women were well educated, and were familiar with London and Paris.

'Don't you find it restricting not being able to drive or to go out?'

Not at all, they answered, with a laugh. 'We live such easy lives, it's fine.' Yet over the following years, when I met these same educated women again – and others like them – it was clear it was increasingly *not* so fine. They were in a gilded cage, and once you have been shown a broader horizon it's hard to put up with a cage for ever, which is why I think change will come as people realise there are other things they can do. The next day, back in London, when I was donning my own black robe, before going into court, I couldn't help but think of both the parallels and the differences between us.

CHAPTER 23

Changing Gear

Involvement with a particular charity often stems from personal tragedy, and in this I am no exception. My auntie Audrey was only the first of many wonderful women whose lives, having touched mine in one way or another, were cut short by breast cancer. I can't remember now the first time I talked about her in public, but in 1997, shortly after we moved into Downing Street, I became a patron of Breast Cancer Care. I am also a patron of RAFT (Restoration of Appearance and Function Trust), devoted to helping patients in need of reconstructive plastic surgery, based at Mount Vernon hospital where my dad had such fantastic treatment following his horrific accident. Money is only part of what enables a charity to achieve its objectives. Equally important – sometimes more so – is raising public consciousness and, eventually, changing perception. In my early years, spare cash was never much in evidence but I had been able to help in other ways: as a schoolgirl through practical help, working with Down's syndrome children – and later through my legal expertise. Now the man I had married had opened up another avenue. Well-known names, from royals to media personalities to someone like me who is less easily pigeonholed, can focus press attention in a way that, sadly, individual case histories cannot. Even in the nineties, breast cancer was not really talked about beyond the medical pages of serious newspapers and, as I saw it, my job was to get women to talk openly about it. Only by removing the taboo, by making the vocabulary of self-examination and mammograms, of lumpectomies and prosthetics, part of the language of every woman, whatever her age, nationality or background, could progress in early detection be made. Thanks to Alastair's decision that where Cherie was concerned, less was more, I had become a bit of an enigma. As a result, when I did speak or write, it was published and noticed.

The death of David Attwood's brother Michael at such a young age had never left me and, in the spring of 1998, I heard from Fiona that her friend Lindsay Nicholson's daughter Ellie, whom I'd got to know when I'd 'edited' *Prima*, was suffering from the same kind of leukaemia as her father had died of. When I went to visit her in Great Ormond Street hospital, I had been hugely impressed by the work of Sargent Cancer Care and asked if I could be of help. I have been involved with them ever since. As a sad footnote, Ellie died in early June 1998 and I went with Alastair and Fiona to the Requiem Mass.

That summer of 1998, I was able to extend my charitable networking in an unexpected quarter. Walking round the grounds at Highgrove – our first visit – Prince Charles was telling me how they would sometimes allow groups in to look at the gardens. My cousin Paul Thompson, one of the family priests, had been working for many years for a drug-prevention charity based at Liverpool Cathedral called SHADO. He had recently died, still only in his forties, from an embolism following an accident to his knee, and I'd been asked if I would like to get involved. Each year, one of SHADO's main fundraising events was a sponsored walk ending up at a stately home. In 1997 I'd been able to welcome them for tea at Chequers. Plucking up courage, I asked the Prince whether he would consider allowing SHADO to look round his garden. Drug-related charities find it extremely difficult to attract funds and I was quite prepared for the Prince to say no. He didn't, and in 1999 SHADO's sponsored walk ended with tea and cakes at Highgrove.

It was now time, I decided, to unlock the potential of Downing Street itself. Although Number 10 had been used to host charitable receptions, by both Margaret Thatcher and Norma Major, I felt we could do a good deal more. The great state rooms on the first floor were empty for so much of the time. Why not put them to greater use?

In particular, both Tony and I were keen to extend the range of people who saw behind the famous façade beyond the 'great and the good'. Gradually a system evolved whereby on Monday nights Tony and I would host a large reception for over 200 people who came from a particular sector of work – such as the police or social workers. Then every Tuesday I would host a reception for a charity. Initially they were 'mine', that is, those charities I was patron of or otherwise officially involved with. But that was purely practical: I offered and they accepted. As word spread of these Tuesday evenings, however, so requests from other charities began to come in, and between 1998 and 2007 I hosted one every week, apart from August and the holiday periods. Regulations governing the use of public buildings prevented these evenings being direct fundraising events, but they could be used by the charity to raise its profile or as a thank you to major donors. The charity would pay for whatever food or drink was involved. Guests were limited to a maximum of forty so that I could talk to each of them personally. We would give them the use of the rooms, and I myself would address the guests about the charity, its aims, its successes and how they could help, and would have my photograph taken with each one. It was never advertised, never mentioned in the press, but somehow it got around, and over the following years I was able to learn so much about the fantastic unsung work that goes on up and down our country and overseas. As I'd learnt from the incident involving the letter from the school for the deaf, once it becomes known that you are not someone who shuts the door, the requests grow and grow. From the contacts I was making during Tony's official visits abroad, I became increasingly aware of the potential of what is loosely – and often disparagingly – called networking. On my return to England following my trip to Gaza, for example, I was able to arrange for equipment and supplies to be sent out to a girls' school run by Mrs Arafat and the centre for disabled children. Britain's expertise is something I am very aware of in these fields and it does not necessarily need expensive equipment to change people's lives. The approach to disability in the Middle East, for example, is a cultural rather than a financial problem, and by bringing people together much can be achieved.

I was also aware of how the average constituent had no chance of visiting Downing Street, so every month I invited ten MPs from across the parties to each bring three children, with a parent, to tea. It was a way of ensuring that kids from all over the country had that opportunity. I always said to the children that I hoped that one of them would one day come back as prime minister and that, if they did, I wanted them to promise to invite me back.

That summer we did our usual lurch across Europe, made less spontaneous by the constant presence of protection officers – nice though they were – and garden girls. By mid-August, our increasingly unwieldy cavalcade was back in France, at David Keene's château. Security concerns meant that we could no longer stay with Maggie and Alan in Miradoux but we managed a day trip, which is why we were there when the news came through of the Omagh car bomb.

Omagh continues to appal. Twenty-nine people died and well over 300 were injured in the blast. Responsibility was later claimed by a nationalist splinter group calling themselves the Real IRA, as opposed to the Provisional IRA whose political arm, Sinn Féin, had been party to the Good Friday Agreement. As Tony's clothes were all back at the château, he had to borrow a suit and black tie for the immediate television response. He then flew straight to Belfast from Toulouse airport.

Although not physically present at Hillsborough during the talks, Bill Clinton had played a key part in the negotiations, and two weeks after the atrocity, on 3 September, Bill, Hillary, Tony and I flew into Omagh to see for ourselves the devastation that had been achieved by just one bomb attached to an old Vauxhall, callously parked in the main shopping street on a Saturday afternoon. Hillary is not as spontaneously charming as her husband and this was the first time I had seen her compassionate side. She was moved beyond words by what we heard and saw. It brought tears to your eyes to talk to these people who had lost loved ones.

But this was not tragedy tourism: Tony knew that it was imperative to get Sinn Féin to condemn the bombers and at the same time persuade the Protestants not to react, and he also knew that Bill's physical presence, his unequivocal condemnation of the atrocity, and his renewed commitment to the peace talks would be crucial, if the terrorists were not to achieve their aim.

Until we arrived at Number 10, I had considered chambers as archaic a set-up as was possible to imagine at the end of the twentieth century. I was wrong. Downing Street was positively feudal.

On the technical side, computers featured hardly at all. That obviously had to change as, by 1997, everyone in Tony's office was using computers. Then there were the garden girls. They were the *crème de la crème* of the Civil Service PAs, but until we moved in they were obliged to wear skirts; trousers were even forbidden at Chequers.

'This is just nonsense,' I told the Cabinet secretary. 'There are Tony and I in our jeans – it's ridiculous to expect the garden girls to be wearing twin set and pearls.' So grudgingly that was allowed.

Then there was the question of rooms. The best and largest in Number 10 was the domain of the two principal private secretaries: one from the Foreign Office and one from the Treasury. As John Major had worked in the Cabinet room itself, this had a certain logic, as there were big double doors connecting the two rooms. Tony, however, preferred something less grandiose. All that was available was a former waiting room on the left of the Cabinet room, so that was where he was put. When I found out where he was spending his day, I couldn't believe it.

'Why are those two civil servants having the big room while the Prime Minister is in this little cubbyhole?'

The problem was simply lack of space. Downing Street was cracking at the seams and no amount of shuffling people around would solve it. The staff worked ridiculously hard and always under pressure. How they maintained their extraordinary good humour, given the cramped and uncomfortable conditions, remains a mystery.

The solution required a bit of lateral thinking. The appointments department – several rooms as well as several people, of whom John Holroyd was the visible tip – was moved along the corridor into the Cabinet office, which had plenty of space. There was actually no real need for them to be in Number 10 at all.

It was around this time that I had a brainwave. What about the Number 10 flat? That was completely vacant. Although officially Gordon's, as we'd done the swap, he didn't use it. Also I had noticed that a room opposite the entrance to our flat seemed to be used by the Treasury for storing chairs. Meanwhile, personnel had a room the size of a large cupboard off a corridor next to the main entrance of Number 10 and visitors were having to hang around the entrance hall because there was no waiting room. I just thought, This is completely ludicrous. So I put all these ideas to Tony and said he should talk to Gordon about it. 'You've got to do something,' I said. 'It's simply not fair to your staff.'

'Cherie, please listen to me. I'm sure you mean well but don't get involved. At some point we'll get round to it but, frankly, there are more important things on the agenda.'

I wasn't surprised. I'd had plenty of experience of my ideas being discounted. This time, however, I decided to take the law into my own hands. So I picked up the phone and spoke to Sue Nye, Gordon's long-time aide, and said, 'I want to come and see Gordon.'

Consternation in the Treasury! They immediately rang Tony to find out was what going on. He then called me and asked me to explain myself.

'I simply want to make the case that it's in everyone's interest, including his as Chancellor, to husband public resources. You won't go and see him, so I will.'

By now, I had my appointment, so it was too late to do anything to stop me. Off I trotted to the Treasury and was duly ushered in.

'Look, Gordon,' I said. 'We've got a real problem at Number Ten. It's overcrowded. The personnel department has nowhere they can talk to people alone. Yet there's a perfectly good room outside our flat which is currently unused.' And if that wasn't acceptable, then what about the Number 10 flat? Surely part of that could be used, I suggested, if only as meeting rooms.

'I've got no objections personally,' he explained. 'But I owe it to future Chancellors of the Exchequer to preserve the integrity of the Chancellor of the Exchequer's rooms.'

'Are you telling me you can't ease this terrible overcrowding because of some hypothetical situation in the future? Come on, Gordon. If only as a personal favour to me . . .'

I began to think that Tony had been right. I should never have got involved in the first place. No doubt Gordon had a thousand more pressing matters to worry about than an empty room at Number 11. No doubt it wasn't my place to push. But the pressure on the staff at Number 10 was becoming unbearable. However, as I sat there, getting nowhere, I started to feel I'd overstepped the mark. He said he would think about it, and I left.

Later I was informed that he'd decided that we could have the room opposite the flat entrance. Unbelievably Number 10 then spent

£10,000 redecorating it, but at least it released more space down-stairs, so it was worth the embarrassment.

As for Tony, he did eventually move to the principal private sec-retaries' room, but this time no thanks to me. That room became known as 'the den'.

By chance, Tony's first visit to China, in October 1998, coincided with an initiative organised by the Bar Council's international com-mittee, relating to a conference in Beijing concerning the rights of the accused. Practising barristers came out from the UK and presented a mock trial to demonstrate how the British (common-law) system worked: how the accused is deemed innocent until proven guilty; how we cross-examine, and so forth. I wasn't able to stay for the performance barristering; my job was simply to introduce the session and generally explain what delegates were going to see. I then went off to see a group of women lawyers for a round-table discussion about discrimination law. We looked at what they thought the issues were in China, and I talked about how we dealt with those same issues in the UK. It all went very well and marked the moment when programmes began to open up for me.

I had taken the decision fairly early on that there was not much point in swanning round the world as some sort of glorified tourist. If you're going to do it, you might as well do something useful. Increasingly, whenever Tony and I went away together on official visits, it became standard for me to have my own programme.

It was clearly important that I did nothing overtly political, but gradually the Foreign Office began to see how I might be useful. From its perspective, the great plus was my profession. As a barris-ter I had the credentials to talk to other lawyers anywhere in the world. As our embassies would always have some sort of pro-gramme in hand involving the law, my ability to talk to judges and senior lawyers proved useful: I could take soundings, test the water at an informal (though informed) level. The promotion of women's human rights, for example, is not always an easy subject to address, particularly in non-Christian countries, yet not only would this fulfil the embassy's human rights objectives, but anything that encouraged people to use the common-law model was obviously good for our legal services, which play such a large part in our invisible exports.

The Bar's China initiative was vitally important, because of the need to protect Hong Kong's legal system, which is based on the English system. With China poised to become a major player on the world's stage, a key Foreign Office objective was to encourage the Chinese, both in Shanghai and Beijing, to adopt the Hong Kong way of doing business.

China was then still a country of bicycles and blue Mao-suited workers – male and female, everyone looked the same. Just six years later, on my next visit, the consumer revolution was in full swing. Men and women could be clearly identified, and cars had transformed the look of the streets while still being driven as if they were bicycles. Colour was everywhere, except in the sky, which remained an opaque grey whatever the weather – the result of the appalling pollution.

Before that first visit, Hillary Clinton had warned me about bugging. When she and Bill had been to Beijing, she told me, their security team had rigged up a sound-proof tent in their bedroom, the only place, they were told, where they could talk in safety. After a good night's sleep at the official guest house attached to the Forbidden City, Tony and I awoke to find André in a state of near-hysteria. He'd woken in the small hours to find somebody in his room going through his things. Most of our delegation, we later heard, had had the same experience. If that wasn't enough, André said, he'd been having a shower when he saw that, instead of the mirror misting up, as it does everywhere in the universe, a large rectangle remained unnervingly clear . . .

Early the following year, Tony and I paid our second visit to South Africa. We had first gone in the autumn of 1996, during his pre-election tour of world leaders, and I was able to visit Albie Sachs, who'd been appointed by Mandela two years earlier to lead the team writing the new South African Constitution. As a human rights lawyer it was both a fascinating experience and a real privilege to be able to discuss the way the Constitutional Committee was drafting the human rights elements of the Constitution. I also visited the Truth and Reconciliation Commission, the brainchild of Archbishop Desmond Tutu.

Nelson Mandela defies all preconceptions. In person he is tall and incredibly wiry with that shock of white hair above a calm, near-beatific face, but what strikes you most forcibly is his old-world courtesy, and not only to the great and the good. The first time he came to see us in Downing Street, Euan was off school with a cold but very anxious to meet the great man. When it came to it, our son was completely overawed, and managed to stammer out, 'It's so wonderful to meet you.' And Nelson Mandela, with this gentle voice, replied, 'And it's really nice to meet you, Euan.' And you felt that he really meant it. On another occasion, Euan introduced him to his friend from the London Oratory, James Dove, whose father was from South Africa and who had been involved with the ANC during the apartheid years. Again, Mandela was incredibly courteous to this young man whom he didn't know, but it was clear that this was something he did all the time and which was very meaningful, especially to young people.

Tony's last official visit, in 2007, just before he stepped down, was also to South Africa. It was a great joy to find Mandela still alert though incredibly frail and the people around him were very protective. No one can use flash photography near him, for example. All those years spent breaking up stones in the glaring light of Robben Island affected his eyes. He still has the most incredible presence, partly because of who he is. But also, despite that, he's gentle and unassuming; so unassuming, in fact, that you start thinking that perhaps it isn't genuine, but it is.

During our visit in 1996, we had been taken to an Aids orphanage called Nazareth House in Cape Town – part of the same order that ran the orphanage just down from Seafield School in Crosby. Nuns, I have found, fall into two distinct categories: old battle-axes or really sweet. These were the sweet ones and they were thrilled to see Tony. There was a little girl called Ntombi, who for some reason attached herself to Tony. Then aged about three or four, she lifted up her arms and demanded to be carried, which he duly did. When we asked about sponsorship, we were warned that she was HIV-positive, and, with sad smiles, the nuns reminded us of the graveyard which we had already seen, with names and dates recording tragically short lives. Tony and I looked at each other and the decision was made. Thus Ntombi was the first child we sponsored from Nazareth House. Over the years we developed a real relationship: she wrote to us and we wrote to her.

We have since sponsored other children from Nazareth House. All the children were HIV-positive, but many had other disabilities as well. One little girl we met that first time, for example, had been abandoned in the road and ants had eaten out her eyes. As for Ntombi, she is still very much alive. She did really well at school and at fifteen was able to return home to live with her grandmother and other members of her family. Now children like her no longer live in the orphanage but are looked after by foster mothers, in a 'family' of around seven children in a nearby township. These foster mothers are themselves set up and funded by the nuns, while Nazareth House houses only the most severely disabled children.

In her gap year, our daughter Kathryn went over to work at Nazareth House. I had told her the story of the little blind girl, and the first time we spoke on the telephone she was able to tell me she was still there. Sadly, however, she died shortly afterwards of meningitis. Her death was a big blow as they'd hardly lost a child for years, the treatment of Aids having improved so dramatically in the meantime.

This is not the place to go into the vastly problematic question of Kosovo, its history as an ethnically Albanian province within Tito's Yugoslavia. Although predominantly Muslim, Albanian Kosovo is considered by the Serbs to be central to its identity as a Christian front-line state, with a number of historically important – and beautiful – medieval monasteries. Under Slobodan Milosevic, Serbian forces had increased ethnic repression in Kosovo, but as the nineties drew to a close, with Serbia busy on its home front, Kosovo freedom fighters (the KLA) were fighting back. By the end of 1998 the situation was acute. Demands that Serbia solve the problem fell on deaf ears and the fighting intensified. Atrocities were happening on both sides and, as a result, refugees were pouring out of the country into Macedonia, to the south. The hope was that, threatened with air strikes, Serbia would withdraw. Tony was convinced – along with the British military – that only the threat of ground troops would shift Milosevic. America, however, did not relish the idea of 'body bags' and, during the spring of 1999, Tony was putting all his energy into trying to persuade the Americans, via Bill Clinton, that the threat of ground troops was the only language that Milosevic understood. In opposition the Labour Party had been highly critical of the then Conservative government's weakness over Bosnia when Milosevic had been in charge.

Throughout that time, Tony would be constantly on the phone to

America. Because of the timing, these calls would often come late in the evening, when he was in the flat. If he made the call, he would do so from our living room where the special secure line to Washington was installed. When the calls originated from America, and came late at night or in the small hours of the morning, I would answer them as the phone was always on my side of the bed. The disruption never bothered me as I have always been more of a night person than Tony.

Although I never heard both sides of the conversation, I was very aware of how Tony was constantly saying to Bill: 'This cannot go on, we must do something. If we face Milosevic down, not only will he back down but the Russians will make him back down. But they have to understand that we really mean it.' On 24 March, bombing of the Serbian capital Belgrade began. After that, the only further threat was a land invasion, increasingly the option preferred by NATO military on the ground. Four NATO countries, Britain, France, Germany and Italy, had troops on the Macedonian border ready to intervene, but America continued to stay out.

'I feel I'm out on a limb here,' Tony used to say. 'As if I'm on this big tree, at the end of a branch, and at any minute it's going to give. They'll saw through and that will be me done for.' 'They' being the more cautious among Clinton's advisers, busy sawing away at the branch with Tony right at the end.

On 24 April 1999 he went to Chicago to deliver a speech to the Economic Club of Chicago. The world, he said, is such that now you cannot just let these appalling things happen. You have to intervene and, in terms of Kosovo, success was the only exit strategy NATO was prepared to consider. 'We will not have succeeded until an international force has entered Kosovo and allowed the refugees to return to their homes.'

A week later both he and I were in Macedonia. This was the first time since Tony took office that British troops were poised for action and, by speaking to our soldiers on the front line – part of the Allied Rapid Reaction Corps led by General Mike Jackson – and seeing the refugee disaster for himself, he believed he would be in a stronger position to argue the case for American involvement on the ground.

As with all such visits, Tony's itinerary was not broadcast in advance and at the end of the previous week I had spent two days in the House of Lords arguing an equal pay case on behalf of part-time

Leo endears himself to the corgis at Balmoral.

Like father, like son. A moment of relaxation in the sitting room of the Number 11 flat.

The launch of Matrix Chambers. As specialists in human rights, we were determined to be non-hierarchical.

My study in the Number 11 flat. With the heightened security following September 2001, I increasingly found myself working at home rather than going to chambers.

The Bushes arrive by helicopter on the lawn at Chequers. We only came by helicopter once – with the Aznars – flying from the barracks between Downing Street and Buckingham Palace.

Bromley-by-Bow, London. While I no longer practise family law, the welfare of women and children continues to be very important to me.

Horseplay with Leo and Kathryn in the hall of the flat. Tony has always been a hands-on dad.

André and unidentifiable alien in the kitchen at Downing Street.

Leo stands guard over his daddy's red boxes in the Number 11 flat. Sometimes four or five would arrive at the same time, all equally beaten up.

On an independent visit to Russia, in 2003, at the invitation of Lyudmila Putina. Although from very different backgrounds we got on extremely well.

Greeting the Putins in front of Number 10.

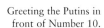

Laura Bush and I were always happy to have a chance to catch up.

A quartet of Downing Street wives: Lady Wilson, Norma Major, the Countess of Avon (Clarissa Eden) with me, in Lincoln's Inn for the launch of *The Goldfish Bowl*.

July 2006. The G8 Summit in St Petersburg and the traditional photo of spouses, though Angela Merkel's husband is missing. From left: Laura Bush, Bernadette Chirac, Maria Barroso, Flavia Prodi, Lyudmila Putina and Laureen Harper.

May 1999. With Yasser Arafat and his wife Suha. This was my first visit to Palestine and it made a deep impression.

I try to meet children wherever I go. These school children in Kuala Lumpur show why: you can't help but be buoyed up in their company.

There was no disguising the presence of children in the Number 11 flat.

workers at Barclays Bank. The following Monday found us in Skopje, the capital of the former Yugoslav Republic of Macedonia, as we had to be careful to call it, because of the sensitivity of the Greeks who believe they have rights to the name. The capital was little more than a provincial outpost and our embassy little more than a consulate. Just talking to the staff, some of whom were Muslim, you realised that it had been quite difficult for the two groups – Muslim and Christian – to work together with such terrible things going on just a few miles away.

A helicopter took us to a large refugee camp on the border with Kosovo. Everywhere you looked, there were white tents, rows of them stretching far away in the distance. The moment they realised who it was, the shouts rang out: 'Tone-ee! Tone-ee! Tone-ee!' They already saw him as the man who was going to get them out of this horror. We moved from tent to tent with an interpreter, listening to stories of how they'd lived for years perfectly peaceably within their community and how their neighbours – previously friends – had turned on them and threatened them with violence. We heard how they'd managed to get out, leaving everything behind. Although from the outside these tents were identical, inside they were all different. Each woman had done what she could to make her tent welcoming and comfortable. Not for us, but for what remained of her family. It was humbling.

From there we were taken up to the crossing point itself, looking out across no man's land to the queue of refugees waiting to cross over into Macedonia, into the sanctuary of the camp. The queue snaked back as far as I could see. Everyone was laden with suitcases and bundles of what were probably clothes and linen. We were then taken up to the head of the queue where people just wanted to shake our hands. The interpreter went with Tony, while I talked to people who spoke English, by definition educated. I remember a lawyer and a professor at Pristina University, both of whom had led completely uneventful lives until now. Life under communism may not have been particularly comfortable but they had never really known hardship. Now this had happened. They would live, but they had no idea what awaited them – not a job in a university, that's for sure.

As someone who was born in the fifties, I had no personal experience of the war, but in our playground, games of Germans versus

English were still commonplace, and I remembered, too, the stories that Mr Smerdon used to tell us of concentration camps. As I walked down this unending queue, faces marked by exhaustion and fear, I was deeply shocked. These people were being picked on because of their religion, because they were Muslim. What did Europe think it was doing? It had been there and done that. We didn't need to go back.

Three months later, at the end of July 1999, Tony returned, this time to Pristina in Kosovo itself, and this time as a true hero. His plan had worked. America had agreed to commit ground troops, and the moment it had done so, Milosevic backed down. There are, apparently, hundreds of small boys called Tony running around the newly independent Kosovo.

CHAPTER 24

New Horizons

My post-1997 career at the Bar was progressing as well as could be expected given the difficulties of reconciling the Downing Street diary with the Gray's Inn Square diary. That wasn't my only problem. Shortly after we moved in, Number 10 decided to 'take a view' on a case that I had been approached to do. I resisted. As a professional woman, I told them, I had to be allowed to get on with my profession. I invoked the cab-rank principle, my line being that as soon as I started making choices, then I was in trouble. It was a case of 'Sorry if you feel uncomfortable about that, but believe me it's better this way'. Even though they knew this was my position, over the next ten years the office would sometimes indicate that they would rather I did not do a particular case. I never knew exactly who it was 'taking a view'. Tony would simply deliver the message. As for who was standing behind Tony, it was 'the office', 'Number 10'. It was as if these anonymous people would all participate in a discussion – including my husband but excluding me – and come to 'a view'. The rationale was always the same: the press would write stories along the lines of 'Cherie is suing the government', and how embarrassing was that for the PM? My voice was never heard in these discussions, although only I knew the answers. Sometimes Fiona and subsequently Hilary Coffman would fight that battle for me, though after a while they too were excluded. I always argued that to pursue the cab-rank rule was the only way to deal with it, otherwise it would be opening up a can of worms, and that argument was always accepted until the next difficult case came along and we went through the whole thing again.

My fears that my career would suffer were already being justified. It wasn't so much the money – I loved my work. Not only were my official duties taking their toll, but while a few people wanted Cherie Booth, QC, because they wanted the attendant publicity, others wouldn't touch me with a bargepole as publicity was the last thing they wanted. It was rarely overt, but word got round.

Shortly after we moved into Downing Street I remember sitting as a judge in a case concerning an old lady who had been evicted from her retirement home as she was being disruptive, going around complaining that the other old ladies were stupid. Before I passed judgement she told me, 'I want you to know that I have always voted Labour, and I voted for your husband in the general election.' On the basis of the evidence I imposed a suspended possession order on her, in effect delaying the eviction provided she behaved herself in the future, at which news her attitude towards me suddenly changed. 'I will never vote Labour again!'

For the first four months of 1999 I had been involved in a complicated case concerning the Bank of Credit and Commerce International (BCCI). At its peak, this bank, which started life in Pakistan, operated in seventy-eight countries, had over four hundred branches, and claimed assets of $US 25 billion. Then, in 1991, it went down in a huge scandal having been found to be involved in money-laundering, bribery and various other sins. The legal implications of the fall continued for the next fifteen years and I was involved in just a small part of it – a group action taken by the former employees, most of whom were Muslims living in the UK but who came originally from Bangladesh or Pakistan. After the fall of the bank they were finding it next to impossible to get work: as this was a dodgy bank, they were regarded as dodgy people. It was all a bit of a nightmare. Both sides agreed on four people whose cases would serve as test cases, but there were another three hundred clients behind them whose cases could be settled on the basis of what we achieved for these four, so not only was there tension between the four individuals but also between them and the wider group. Nor did the problems end with the clients. Although I was overseeing the case, four juniors and three different sets of solicitors were involved. In addition the Legal Aid Board was using it as a test case for a new kind of financing in these long cases. And long it was. We went into court at the beginning of February and it wasn't over until the middle of May. In the end, although we won on the law, we actually lost on the facts. Whereas it was accepted that, in principle, the employees should get compensation, the four individuals selected as test cases were not able to convince the court that they had in fact suffered loss.

The following year I became involved in another group action, this time for ICI. On this occasion, my client was a large company rather than the employees, and having the resources of ICI behind me proved a good deal less of a headache. Even so, once it was over, I regretfully came to the conclusion that, given what I was doing at Number 10, long witness actions like these were just not feasible. When I have a court commitment, there is no flexibility.

Arguing the same point of law but from the opposite point of view happens all the time, and it certainly keeps you intellectually focused. In 1997 I had done a case where a lesbian rail worker had wanted to claim free rail travel for her partner. Heterosexual partners, even if they weren't married, were entitled to this perk, but Lisa Grant couldn't get it for her same-sex partner and claimed sex discrimination. I argued the case for her in the European Court in Luxembourg but we eventually lost. Six years later – after the Human Rights Act was implemented in Britain – I again found myself arguing a sex discrimination case relating to a lesbian, but this time from the other side. A lesbian teacher had been forced to resign because of bullying by pupils due to her sexuality. This time I was arguing for the school, exactly the opposite of the position I had taken for Lisa. The case went right up to the House of Lords and we won at every level, not least because of the earlier decision on the Lisa Grant case. They accepted my argument that sexual orientation discrimination is not the same as sex discrimination, and so we won.

Under the British legal system, judges start life as barristers and you learn the ropes by sitting on the Bench part-time as a 'recorder'. In 1996 I had been appointed as an assistant recorder and in July 1999 I was made a full recorder. Both recorders and judges are kept up to date by a body called the Judicial Studies Board and towards the end of September I went, together with Marianna Falconer, on one of these three-yearly up-date courses. On the night of the twenty-third Marianna and I plus a couple of old barrister friends went out for a birthday supper: my forty-fifth. I was feeling very positive. That summer we had had a good break at the Strozzis' in Italy and Tony was feeling relaxed. All the energy he had expended over Kosovo had been worth it. Sitting there, raising a glass of champagne, there was only one little shadow on my immediate horizon: my period. Where was it?

'It's a bit odd,' I told Tony when he rang me that night from Chequers. 'I'm usually so regular.'

'So what does that mean?'

'Probably nothing,' I said. 'Probably just my age. Don't worry.'

He wasn't about to. He was working on his conference speech and so paid little attention to anything else. But there was a small niggle at the back of my mind.

A few weeks before, we had been on the usual prime ministerial weekend to Balmoral. The first year we had actually stayed – in 1998 – I had been extremely disconcerted to discover that everything of mine had been unpacked. Not only my clothes, but the entire contents of my distinctly ancient toilet bag with its range of unmentionables. This year I had been a little more circumspect, and had not packed my contraceptive equipment, out of sheer embarrassment. As usual up there, it had been bitterly cold, and what with one thing and another . . . But then, I thought, I can't be. I'm too old. It must be the menopause.

Once back from the course, I met up with Carole at the gym.

'I know it sounds odd,' I said, 'but do you think you could get me a pregnancy testing kit?' It was hardly something I could pop into the local chemist's for. She brought it round on the Thursday and on the Friday morning, Lo and Behold. I just couldn't believe it.

I rang Tony immediately.

'The test,' I said. 'It's come up positive.'

'So what does that mean?'

'It means I think I'm pregnant.'

'Oh my God.'

That evening he came back from Chequers and as soon as there was an opportunity, I showed him the little dipper and explained the significance of the blue line.

'How reliable is it?' he asked. I said I didn't know but that Carole

had got me another one, though I'd have to wait to do that the following morning.

'We'll have to tell Alastair.'

Alastair and Fiona came up the next morning before we set off for
Bournemouth and the conference. The second test had shown the
same little blue line.

'So how pregnant are you, exactly?' Alastair asked.

'I don't know.'

'Are we talking weeks or months?'

'Weeks.'

Frankly, he was more amused than anything else. They took the
view that, given it was still very early days, the best thing was to
keep completely quiet. By chance, I had already agreed to come back
to London on the Monday for a Breast Cancer Care event. I'd leave
a little earlier than planned to see my GP.

Tony insisted we tell Sally Morgan, who was travelling with us on
the train. We couldn't just sit there and not tell her, he said.

'Weird to think that when we go up to Conference this time next
year, we'll be struggling with a pram,' she said. We ended up giggling
like school kids.

As arranged, Fiona and I took the train back to London on the
Monday. Rather than risk making a big deal of it, I went along to the
general surgery at the Westminster Health Centre. It turned out that
my usual doctor, Susan Rankin, wasn't there, so I saw another partner.

'So, Mrs Blair,' he said. 'What can I do for you?'

'I think I'm pregnant,' I replied with a smile. The poor man fell to
pieces.

I had to calm him down. He didn't want to do an internal examination, he said. Feeling obliged to have at least a bit of a prod of my
tummy, he kept saying, 'Susan should be doing this.'

'What about one of your tests?' I suggested. 'Presumably they
would be reliable?'

Relief flooded over him.

'Well?' Fiona said, when I went out.

'End of May.'

The next day it was very hard not to mention it. Traditionally we
had a lunch for family and friends while Tony made the final adjust-
ments to his speech. My half-sister Sarah, who now worked as a

journalist under the name of Lauren Booth, had just had a miscarriage – she had written about it in a newspaper – so the last thing
I wanted was to upset her further. I didn't tell my father for the same
reason – that is, that he might have let it slip.

Only those in the know would have spotted the twinkle in Tony's
eye at a particular point in his speech that afternoon. By pure coincidence, Peter Hyman, one of Tony's speech writers, had drafted a
passage about children.

'To our children, we are irreplaceable. If anything happened to
me, you'd soon find a new leader. But my kids wouldn't find a new
dad. There is no more powerful symbol of our politics than the experience of being on a maternity ward. Seeing two babies side by
side. Delivered by the same doctors and midwives. Yet two totally
different lives ahead of them.'

As Tony spoke those lines he glanced at me because we both knew
that very soon we would be in that hospital ward ourselves.

The plan was to keep the number of people in the loop very
small. Now that it was confirmed, I decided I wanted a bit of private time with the idea of this baby. Also I was conscious that,
particularly at forty-five, things could go wrong, although I was personally convinced that everything was going to be all right. I had
decided I wanted to get past the twelve–thirteen-week mark before
extending it beyond the tight-knit group. Also we were due to go to
Florence for a Third Way seminar that Tony and Bill had set up, and
the last thing I wanted was for the focus to shift on to me. We'd
wait till we came back from Florence, by which time it would probably begin to be obvious, but at least we would be in control of the
announcement.

I told my mother and my sister and Jackie, our nanny. In July
1998, Ros Mark had left us to do a teacher training course – a long-
held ambition. Jackie was thrilled. For any nanny worth the name,
school-age children are all very well, but a baby is heaven.

I was a bit worried about telling the kids. I wanted them to know,
but I can remember feeling, They are going to think this is disgusting. I mean, parents! But they were fantastic about it and really
excited. Kathryn came with me to an early scan and as we walked
along to the ultrasound department I realised with a start that, with
me being so obviously middle-aged, people might think my pre-
pubescent daughter was the one who was pregnant.

Once the Labour Party Conference was over, Susan Rankin gave me a proper examination. 'You do realise', she said, 'that the statistics for Down's and other abnormalities shoot up at your age.'

I did, but having got this far I didn't want to risk any damage to the baby, so I decided an amniocentesis was out. I had a blood test and a scan, however, and – within the parameters of my age – all appeared well.

Over the next few days, the tight-knit group appeared to be stretching. Tony told Anji because, he said, she would be upset if he didn't. Then he told me he'd told Gordon.

'What business can it possibly be of Gordon's?' I remonstrated.

'You have to understand, Cherie. It's a very sensitive topic for him. The whole issue of my being a family man is very sensitive to him.' He was only thinking of Gordon's feelings, he said.

Pregnant or not, we trundled on. As nobody knew, there were no concessions to my delicate condition. A few days later I took the train from Liverpool Street station to Norwich to celebrate the opening of new offices for a big firm of Legal Aid solicitors. Halfway there, overcome with nausea, I was sick all over everything. It was in the middle of the afternoon and fortunately the carriage was empty, so I was able to go into the toilet and clean myself up. Then I went back to the carriage to scrub away at the seat and the floor, all the time thinking, This is hard, hard, hard.

Another time we were up in the constituency and it was just me and Dave, a Number 10 driver. Suddenly I knew I had to be sick. Dave stopped the car, retrieved a bucket out of the back and held it while I vomited my guts out. He was so kind that day that I swore then I would love him for ever.

I was finding out the hard way that I wasn't thirty any more. At one point I went up to Liverpool to do something for Jospice. Now a worldwide hospice movement, it was started by Father Francis O'Leary, a Crosby boy born and bred. As always, I stayed with my old friend Cathy, who now had six kids, her youngest being then about four, while her oldest was older than Euan. Exhausted from the journey, I went upstairs to one of the girls' bedrooms where I'd be sleeping. The six-year-old had just got back from school and the four-year-old was generally rushing about. I was sitting on the bed, trying to catch my breath, when Cathy came in with a cup of tea and I burst into tears.

'What on earth is the matter?' she said.

'I'm pregnant. And I'm just remembering what it's like. The chaos, the noise. How can I possibly do all this in Downing Street?' It wasn't the first time I'd had such negative thoughts. It had taken over two years, but we had just got everything organised in Number 11 – the kitchen, our bathroom, the children's rooms – and now we were going to have nappies and we were going to have sleepless nights. Sitting there, I was overwhelmed by the enormity of it all. And at the same time, I thought, How dare I? Here was Cathy struggling to make ends meet. Her husband had just lost his job, she was doing part-time teaching and there she was, a good Catholic mother, bringing up these lovely, happy children.

One afternoon in mid-November, I had a call from Fiona. I was due to give a speech at the AGM of the Mary Ward Legal Centre, of which I was patron.

'Just to warn you, there may be a slight problem,' she said. Piers Morgan, editor of the *Daily Mirror*, had just spoken to Alastair and implied he knew I was pregnant. 'He needs him to confirm or deny it, and Alastair can't lie.'

'I don't see why not,' I said. 'It's not his baby. Why doesn't he just say he doesn't know?'

'Because he does know.'

'But who could have told the *Mirror*?'

'Lauren?'

'No. She doesn't know. I didn't tell her.' And anyway, I knew my half-sister would never betray me, not over a thing like that. I went through everybody in my head. Sally Morgan wouldn't do it, nor Anji, even though I hadn't wanted her to know. I was sure it couldn't have come from the hospital. The scan had been registered under a different name and they hadn't put me on the computer. There was always Gordon, but what could he possibly have to gain by telling the *Daily Mirror*?

I called Alastair: 'Why can't you just say that it's early days and we don't want to announce it yet?'

'Don't be ridiculous, Cherie. This is his big scoop.'

'I don't want Piers Morgan to have a big scoop over my body, thank you very much.'

'OK, then we'll put it out over PA [Press Association]. The only way to handle it now is to make it a non-*Mirror* exclusive.' This suited Alastair because, if Piers Morgan did get a scoop, the other papers would be furious. For Alastair, dealing with the tabloids was like juggling with raw eggs.

'We'll have a quote from Tony and a quote from you,' he said and put the phone down.

On the way to the meeting, Fiona's mobile rang. It was Rebekah Wade, deputy editor of the *Sun*. 'The announcement must be out – you might as well talk to her,' Fiona mouthed.

I took the phone. I'd known Rebekah for some time and had a certain amount of respect for her: a woman making her way in the male world of Fleet Street.

We had a girly chat, along the usual girly, just-pregnant lines, and that was that. The next morning, this intimate girly conversation was plastered all over the *Sun*. From being a *Mirror* exclusive, it had become a *Sun* exclusive and Piers Morgan was furious. To this day he remains convinced that I spoke to the *Sun* deliberately to thwart him. What I certainly didn't know when I talked to Rebekah was that, at the time Fiona handed me the phone, the news had not gone out on PA. It did go out eventually that night, but not till later. Though I have my suspicions about how the *Sun* found out, they have never been confirmed.

The truth is that Piers still had his coup. He made sure everyone knew that he had got the story, and that it was he who forced Number 10 to go public. But Rebekah was the only person who actually spoke to me. And Piers never forgave me for spoiling his party and, over the years, his resentment turned into outright hatred.

From then on Cherie and the pregnancy were everywhere. The coverage was so positive that we heard there were some in the Brown camp who thought we'd done it deliberately, in order to undermine Gordon. However there was something rather unnerving about reading Dr Thomas Stuttaford in *The Times* going on about ancient mothers and the risks of brain damage and the rest of it. 'Of course she'll have a Caesarean,' the press said, and they had all the diagrams. And I thought, Actually, wait a minute, guys, this is my body and my decision!

My obstetrician, Zoë Penn, said that as Kathryn had been a Caesar, normal practice would be to have another one, but I was adamant that, because the aftermath had been so grim, unless it was dangerous to the baby I wanted a normal birth. The concern was that the stress of labour would open up the scar, which would be damaging to me. But it was irritating to find that the entire world, including Professor Robert Winston, opined that Zoë Penn would be doing my Caesarean. I had met Robert Winston a couple of times but had never talked to him about my pregnancy. Why do these people, who don't know anything about it, presume to talk about my pregnancy with such conviction and knowledge?

The timing was exactly what I wanted to avoid. That weekend we went to Florence and the Italian press was convinced the baby had been conceived when we were on holiday with the Strozzis – not helped by the Strozzis' own conviction that this was indeed the case. Of course Hillary and Bill were there, so they were very nice, and the Schroeders, whom we were friendly with as well. In fact, everyone made a great fuss of me, but it was as if everybody wanted a slice while I wanted to keep this tiny thing inside me safe and secret.

We were always very clear that if the baby was a boy we would name him for Tony's dad. He was going to be all the things that Grandpa Leo could have been but for the fact that he'd had a stroke in his forties. He loved politics and it's well known that he had ambitions to stand for Parliament himself – as a Tory! Now he was finding life even more frustrating as he'd recently had another stroke and lost the ability to speak. I was so convinced the baby was a boy that we didn't really think of a girl's name. Bookmakers were by then taking bets and I remember Euan coming to me and saying, 'Why don't I just put a bet down?'

'Don't you dare!' I said. 'The press would have a field day, and rightly so.'

Among those who did put a bet on was one of the Protestant negotiating team in the Northern Ireland talks.

After the announcement he had sidled up to Tony to congratulate him.

'Great news, Tony. And what might you be thinking of calling the new arrival?'

And Tony told him.

A few months after Leo was born, Tony was again in Northern Ireland and saw this same fellow sporting an impressive tan.

'You're looking well,' he said. 'Been on holiday?'

'Yes, indeed,' he said. 'And all thanks to you. I got very good odds on Leo if the Blair baby turned out to be a boy, and the whole family got to go away on the proceeds.'

The other question that every parent is faced with is, where will the new baby go? The obvious place, in our set-up, was Euan's room, next door to ours. As Euan had just turned sixteen, the sensible thing was to put him on the attic floor above. It was currently being used as offices and a bedroom for the duty officer, but it would make a nice little flat, with a small bathroom already there. The duty officer would still need somewhere to sleep, and as the Number 10 flat was still unused that appeared to offer a solution. This time no way was Cherie going to see Gordon, so it was all done through the office. While Gordon agreed to release the rooms, there were conditions attached. He wanted to make clear that this was a short-term arrangement and that when Euan went to university – at this stage over two years away – he wanted those rooms back. Tony agreed.

'What do you mean, you agreed? Where's Euan going to live when he comes home in the holidays?' I demanded.

'Don't worry,' he said. 'It'll never happen. Once we've got the rooms, it'll never happen.'

And indeed it never did, and Euan moved upstairs and felt very grown up and not ousted by the new arrival at all.

During those first few years as the Prime Minister's wife, I was driving myself into chambers every day. I had become increasingly frustrated at the way things continued to operate there as if we were in the nineteenth century. I tried to persuade Leslie to use the computer accounts system we'd had installed, but he would hear nothing of it. He still did everything in his ledger. Leslie Page was a legend among clerks: a boy from a modest background made very good indeed who, by this time, lived in a huge house in Surrey. I had suggested getting management consultants in to do a review, which was also greeted with a distinct lack of enthusiasm, this time by senior members of chambers. We didn't need outsiders to show us how to run the business properly. I was then approached by a student from the London Business School looking for a project. This time it was agreed: not least because it wouldn't cost anything. One of the things we were asked to do was to describe our strengths, and analyse what we thought we provided. Leading edge of the law and brilliant advocacy were the qualities most cited. When asked about service, however, the end-user – the client – was never mentioned. All very amusing, but also worrying, as though we deemed it their privilege to be able to brief us rather than our privilege to serve them.

Attitudes have changed enormously over the past ten years, however, and we are now much more conscious of needing to reach out and make ourselves attractive to clients. Once upon a time your silk would come into the room and pronounce, and the client would say, 'How kind of you to see us' and 'Thank you so much'. Now it's more about teamwork. What I find interesting is how much of this change in attitude has been driven by the freeing up of restrictive practices: by the fact that we are now allowed to advertise, and that barristers no longer have exclusive rights to speak in the courts.

My first big push to modernise chambers had happened before I took silk. My pupil at the time was David Wolfe. I'd always kept an open door in my big room at 4–5 Gray's Inn Square and people would regularly come in and eat their lunch there, and we'd chat. In every chambers I'd been connected with, tensions had always existed between commercial lawyers and the others. It was a difference of philosophy.

After the election of the Labour government in 1997, the first Queen's Speech sought to apply the European Convention on Human Rights in our own courts, rather than having to take those cases to Strasbourg. It was due to be implemented in October 2000, and from 1998 onwards like-minded people began to talk about the possibility of setting up an interdisciplinary set of chambers which had human rights at its heart. At the same time it would be modern, with modern systems and where the clerks wouldn't have to call us Sir or Miss. The plan was to take a more international approach, taking human rights cases in courts outside the UK. There were lawyers in London who did international law, but they were mainly commercial sets. There was the odd barrister who did individual cases in Strasbourg, but they were spread out across several sets of chambers and were all juniors. If this was to take off, they needed a silk. Many of the people interested in the idea had either been pupils of mine, or people I had brought on in Gray's Inn Square. In all, there were about five or six of us.

Things began to firm up in October 1999, when David Wolfe

came to see me. The first official meeting was at the Russell Hotel in Russell Square. About ten people were present. I was the only silk, and we talked about who else we might approach.

While discussions continued, we heard that the old police station at the end of Gray's Inn, used by traffic wardens for the last few years, was being converted into offices by the Inn. One of the problems in setting up a new chambers with an entirely new ethos was finding a building that we wouldn't need to share. We had imagined we'd have to move outside the Inn and take on a commercial lease. Now this rare opportunity had presented itself we had to grab it, even though we weren't entirely ready. We all told our various chambers, and the die was cast.

As part of the belated modernisation of 4–5 Gray's Inn Square, we had recruited Amanda Illing. She had worked as private secretary to the Director of Public Prosecutions, Barbara Mills, and by the spring of 2000 had learnt the skills of clerking under Leslie Page and Michael Kaplan, who had clerked me. So Amanda became our first clerk, although she was never called that, except by me through a slip of the tongue. Now she was our practice manager, later practice director, and has been a source of strength throughout.

Inevitably people fell by the wayside. While some wanted a niche practice, I was among those who favoured something more encompassing. In the end there were twenty-six practitioners and those among us who were silks personally had to guarantee the bank debt that would be needed to start up a new set.

Usually chambers are called after their physical address or, occasionally, male lawyers a long time dead. 'The old police station' hardly sent out the right signals and it was Clare Montgomery, QC, a successful criminal fraud practitioner, who came up with Matrix, a definition of which she had found in a dictionary: the intersection of ideas. By this time the Bar was increasingly split into criminal and civil sets. We were doing the opposite, bringing together the disciplines but focusing on human rights and civil liberties. A sub-meaning of Matrix turned out to be fertility. As I was pregnant, and four other members' wives were also pregnant, this seemed a good omen. However Matrix on its own, we decided, sounded a bit too radical. Thus Matrix Chambers was born.

Every aspect was subject to scrutiny. To start with, we were non-hierarchical. Instead of listing our members by seniority of call, we were listed alphabetically. Allocation of rooms was done by drawing lots. All very well in theory, although I had my doubts when I came bottom of the ballot. By then, anyway, thanks to my familiarity with IT, I was increasingly working from home. The old police station was ready for occupation on 1 May. I finished my last case on 17 May. To the delight of the press, it concerned parental leave. I was acting on behalf of the TUC against the government which, as we saw it, was taking too long to phase in parental leave under the EU directive. Cartoonists went to town on the theme of Blair *v*. Blair. We were in the Lord Chief Justice's court, and as I stood up, the Lord Chief Justice said, 'In the circumstances, Ms Booth, would you like to sit down?' and I replied, 'Thank you, but I'm better on my feet.'

And I was. I was vast. I had been expecting the baby to come early – none of my other three having made forty weeks – and towards the end I was sleeping badly. I would get up, leaving Tony in bed, and go next door into what would become the nursery, and sit in a rocking chair we had just bought. There, with the lights off, I would rock gently, looking out of the window where, clearly, at the back of the building I could see a photographer from the *Daily Mail*, outside the back gate, waiting. They came in shifts. Day in, day out, for three weeks. I had this horror that I would go into labour and this photographer would burst in and take pictures. And I thought, I don't want to bring this baby into the world with the *Mail* peering into my room. Why can't I have my baby in private?

Since the beginning, the *Mail* had been at the forefront of every negative story going. If an unflattering photograph came their way, they would print it. It was like a vendetta. That March they had been approached by somebody notorious in the publishing world offering to sell the manuscript of a memoir written by our former nanny, Ros Mark. They must have known that I would fight this tooth and nail, and the result was Blair against Associated Newspapers, which they lost.

Ros was naive, but the *Daily Mail* didn't have that excuse.

The first we knew about it was when she rang us in a panic. The *Mail* was outside the house in Lancaster where she was a student. They were trying to get an interview, she said. At this point we knew nothing about a book. We simply thought she was being harassed by the press who'd found out about her connection with the Blairs. She didn't know what to do, so I suggested she ring Alastair. He in turn rang the *Mail* and asked what the hell they thought they were doing, harassing the nanny. They told him that she had written a memoir, and was trying to sell it. They had been sent extracts, they said.

We were astonished. Everybody, including Tony, including Alastair. We all knew her so well. Ros was a sweet, sporty girl, who had a lot of love in her which she had given freely to the children. She had been with us for four years, and how we would have coped with the transition from Richmond Crescent to Downing Street without her is hard to imagine. By now Alastair was in touch with the agent who implied, Alastair said, that Ros herself wasn't the only person responsible, but that her mother and brother were involved. Ros, it would seem, had simply provided the anecdotes and the detail: the day-to-day life of a nanny in a chaotic, but otherwise totally ordinary family who found themselves in extraordinary circumstances.

In many ways it was a very warm depiction, but quite unpublishable as a book. From Tony's and my point of view, it risked being at worst embarrassing, but in terms of our kids it was impossible. No matter who you are, you cannot write about children in that way, their personal habits, tantrums, foibles, illnesses, their quirky ways, no matter how lovingly recounted. It was a total invasion of their privacy.

As an employment lawyer, I had always had proper contracts with my nannies, and as part of that they would sign a confidentiality agreement. In fact, when Tony became Leader of the Opposition, I even got Ros to sign another one, just to tie things up.

I spoke to the government's legal department but they said it was a private matter. I then got on to my old friend Val Davies, by now a partner in a big City firm, and asked her to take out an injunction, which she did.

That Sunday the *Mail* ran a couple of paragraphs. Nothing about the children – and I'm not surprised, as it was all very domestic stuff – but an unguarded comment by Bill Clinton that Ros had overheard, and another couple of comments about different people who had come to stay in Downing Street.

We weren't able to stop the press reports – the fact that the Blairs' nanny had written a book – but everything concerning the manuscript had to be handed over to us, and the *Mail* was ordered to pay my initial legal costs. We were also awarded costs against Ros, but I chose not to enforce them. It should really have ended there, but by this time Ros had become involved with a woman, whom the papers would later describe as a fantasist, who was working on the manuscript, in spite of the terms of the injunction which gave all copies to me. Extraordinary allegations started coming out. I then had to start taking gagging orders out against this woman as well. The judge granted the injunction, saying she had in effect 'blackmailed Mrs Blair'. It was a complete nightmare.

The baby was due on 23 May, but on the morning of the nineteenth, I knew that labour had started. Always one for putting off that trip to hospital until the last possible minute, there was just one more thing I decided to do. Euan was taking his GCSEs and his headmaster had suggested I went in to discuss how best to ensure the press didn't get hold of his grades. Needless to say, we were followed, but Robbie, one of Tony's drivers, did a quick U-turn in Victoria Street and managed to lose them. Jackie came with me as she was intimately involved with anything to do with the children's schools. Fiona came too as this was connected to the press.

My contractions were getting stronger. Little does he realise, I thought as I listened to Mr McIntosh, that as we sit here discussing how to keep my son's GCSEs out of the tabloids, I'm about to give birth in his office.

I was so terrified about the press finding out, I'd refused to tell Chelsea and Westminster we were on our way, so Robbie just drove round the back and we snuck in. I was taken straight into one of the delivery suites. Then there was the question of Tony. Obviously the moment he arrived, the press would know what was happening. In fact they had got wind of it anyway and they were all gathering outside. My contractions stopped immediately. Even the thought of that phalanx of photographers was enough to freeze me.

Sally Benatar, the only woman on Tony's protection team, had by now arrived, and she and Fiona waited outside as labour got well and truly under way. My other children were all fairly quiet births, but, my goodness, I made up for that with Leo! I remember the nursing staff saying how I didn't have to worry about how much noise I made because the room was soundproofed. 'No one will hear anything,' they claimed. Only later did I realise that the room wasn't that soundproof at all, and poor Sally, who was in the early stages of her first pregnancy, was deeply regretting having volunteered. At around eight Tony said he couldn't wait any longer and came over. The detectives all put their heads round the door to say hello, and every one of them looked as if they were going to be sick. Leo was born just after midnight. His was by far the longest of my four births and I think part of me was holding on because I was still terrified of being photographed. It was stupid really, but when you're pregnant you do get these fixations and I just thought, I do not want to be photographed looking like that. Giving birth is very private. You think you're very ugly and that the whole thing is horrendous. You think, I don't want my husband to see me like this, let alone the entire world. In the end, of course, you don't give a damn.

From Tony's point of view, it was the best birth, because it was entirely natural. Euan's was scary as they had to use forceps. Kathryn's was scary because I was being cut open and Nicholas – the only one that had been calm and natural – he'd missed completely. I had kept fit, and had refused all drugs because my aim was to get out with the baby in complete privacy, and that meant as soon as possible.

A few minutes after two a.m. I walked to the waiting car, the baby in my arms, Tony by my side. That was that. No one expected us to be back that night. The boys were waiting up for us – Kathryn was staying with a friend – and my mum was there to help, and all was well with the world. As I fed my new baby for the first time, I felt totally safe. I was in my own bed, in my own home, and no one was going to come running through the door and snatch a picture.

We knew that there was a hunger for photographs, so I had asked Mary McCartney if she would come and take them. I had got to know her through Breast Cancer Care, her mother Linda having died of breast cancer. We decided they would be charged for, and the proceeds given to the charity. So literally the next day – shades of when Euan was born – André came in to make me look presentable. Mary duly took the photographs: one for the press, and one with all the kids for us. Unfortunately they'd been up so late the night before that they were horribly badly behaved, and Nicholas ended up with a bruised eye, thanks to Euan, while my mother was in tears.

CHAPTER 25

Future Imperfect

Leo's timing was impeccable. He arrived on the Friday before the bank holiday weekend. For ages I'd been pushing Tony to take some paternity leave, but he'd refused, saying, 'I can't. I'm the Prime Minister.' But from the moment he clapped eyes on his son, he was so besotted he really wanted to spend time with him and, as Parliament wasn't sitting, it wasn't that difficult to cancel all his outside engagements. Of course he was still on the phone and read his papers, but basically he was based in the flat enjoying being a new dad.

When Leo was about six weeks old I decided I needed a break, and to start getting back into shape. Cliff Richard, whom I had met at a charity event a year or so before, had said that if ever we wanted to get away, we could borrow his villa on the Algarve. Tony and I had dropped in on him there the previous Christmas while we were staying with John Holmes, who as Tony's foreign affairs principal private secretary, had gone through all the Northern Ireland negotiations with him, and who had just been made ambassador to Portugal.

So while Tony stayed at home to keep an eye on the kids, Leo and I – together with Carole and my mum – flew off to Portugal for a week's holiday. It was exactly what the doctor ordered. Sunshine, good food and gentle exercise. Everything went well until the phone call from my husband on 6 July, telling me he had just come back from the police station with Euan after he'd been found sprawled across the pavement in Leicester Square.

'But he's home now and he's safe,' Tony said, when he called to give me the glad tidings. 'I won't suggest you try to speak to him because he's incoherent. But you don't have to worry because I'm in charge.'

'If you were really in charge, this wouldn't have happened.'

It was a short conversation. When I put down the receiver I turned on the television. The news had even reached Portugal.

The false name Euan had given was one he used regularly, as he'd been advised to. Having a name like Euan Blair was guaranteed to give him trouble, particularly on the rugby field. Once they knew which one he was, opponents would regularly try to foul him.

Fortunately I was going back to England the following day and it was a very shamefaced sixteen-year-old who greeted me. His father wasn't much better. I wasn't really cross. The press was making a meal of it, but the reality is that had he been the son of anybody else they'd have just said, 'OK, don't do it again.' As it was, because of press pressure, he had to be given a formal caution.

The local police station was obviously out, so Euan and I were told to take the emergency escape route, a gloomy old tunnel that ran under Whitehall itself, right into the Ministry of Defence. In the event of a terrorist attack or a bomb scare, it would take us straight to the nuclear bunker.

A car was waiting on the far side of the MoD and we were taken to a police station in south London where Euan made a statement, and was given the caution.

'If you don't get into trouble again,' the kindly police officer said, 'when you're eighteen this will be wiped off and there'll be no record at all.'

Euan looked decidedly cheered: 'You mean once I've turned eighteen, no one need ever know?'

My heart sank. My sweet, innocent boy, I thought. You don't realise that they'll never let you forget that at the age of sixteen you were drunk and were cautioned.

Because of giving birth to Leo, I had missed that summer's G8 summit in Okinawa, which is why André wasn't there to prevent my husband wearing a hideous multi-coloured Japanese shirt which the

British press delighted in. When he got home, Tony explained that they were all given a choice of shirts and he had chosen the least offensive. To his amazement when Bill Clinton appeared he saw he'd picked the most hideous of all.

'Why on earth did you choose that?' Tony asked.

'Take it from an old-timer,' Bill had said. 'Sometimes when you go to these summits you're in a rock or a hard place situation. If you don't wear it, you offend your host. If you do, you're made a mockery of at home. Now you, Tony, wearing that particular shirt, people at home might conceivably think that you actually chose to wear it. Me, wearing this shirt, everybody at home is going to think, "Boy, is that Clinton diplomatic, being so nice to those foreigners – there's no way he would have chosen to wear that. What a good man he is!"'

The UN doesn't go in for funny outfits and as that September's Millennium General Assembly was a one-off, I was determined to go. I was still breast-feeding, however, so I would need to take Leo. The first question was, can I take Jackie? The answer from the Cabinet office was absolutely no. Fortunately Leo has known André since the day (literally) he was born, and so André agreed to be his stand-in nanny. During the entire trip, whenever I had to be somewhere else, André looked after him: changed his nappies, gave him his bottle of expressed milk, everything. André has had a lot to put up with from me over the years, but he never expected to have to introduce the British Prime Minister's son to the American President, yet that is exactly what happened.

We were staying in the UN Plaza Hotel, which because of its position doesn't have to try very hard. I was late returning to the room, a circumstance with which André was all too familiar. The baby bag was packed and Leo was strapped to his front in the sling when two FBI men arrived at the door. They told him to bring the baby; Mrs Blair would meet him at the destination. More than a little unnerved, he was ushered into a limousine – one of five, four of which were empty – and off they set. Then, disaster. Leo filled his nappy. Worst of all, it was of the explosive variety and André had forgotten to pack an extra set of clothes. As André always points out, he is not a professional nanny and he panicked.

'Excuse me,' he said to the secret service man beside the driver. 'I have a problem.'

This bodyguard was totally unfazed and seconds later, André says, they screeched to a halt. The door opened and he was ushered out, Leo still strapped to his front, to find himself being escorted into Ralph Lauren.

'My!' said the greeter – the place had been completely cleared of customers – 'You must be important!' Then the penny dropped. 'Oh my God, it's Baby Blair!'

They were whisked into the back of the shop and once André had cleaned Leo up and put on a new nappy, he was presented with a brand-new outfit, dungarees and a jumper resplendent with the American flag. Next stop the Waldorf Hotel, where he was assured I would be waiting. He was taken up through the kitchen entrance – the route of choice for American presidents and their wives – then up to the presidential suite on the top floor, which was bristling, he says, with bodyguards, earpieces and mobile phones. Finally he arrived at a pair of double doors.

'The President will see you now,' he was told, and the door was held open.

'What about Mrs Blair?'

'She's not here yet. You're to go on in.'

He was petrified. Making his way down the empty corridor he began calling out, 'Hello? Hello? Anybody there?'

'In here,' came the reply, and André pushed open the door from where the voice was coming, to see Bill and Hillary at the far end of a room the size of a tennis court.

I arrived about five minutes later, to find Bill holding Leo and generally cooing, although my son's red face showed that he had clearly been exercising his lungs until very recently. André gave me one of his looks.

'Cherie,' he hissed. 'Don't you ever do that to me again.'

We all then proceeded to the UN to meet up with Tony. They were just coming out. The first group to emerge were the Chinese. They are usually very stiff and unforthcoming, but seeing Leo in his little American jumper was too much, even for them. They stopped and talked and had their pictures taken with Baby Blair. Then Chirac came out, and it was the same thing. Tony couldn't believe it. 'Why on earth', he said, 'is the British Prime Minister's son wearing an American jumper?'

'It's a long story,' I said.

*

The general election in 2001 was set for 2 May, to coincide with local elections, but following a severe outbreak of foot and mouth disease, it was postponed until 7 June. This was a major disaster for farmers and the government was entirely right to wait until the situation was under control before going to the country, but it was singularly bad timing for me, as I was about to start the ICI case on 8 May. When I took it on, I had assumed the election would be done and dusted by the time it began. Fortunately, as it was a very long case, the judge agreed we could have a 'reading day' every Friday. In addition there were a couple of public holidays: May bank holiday, and the second spring bank holiday in the old Whit week.

As a result, although my campaigning with Tony was confined to the weekends, I was able to do some on my own with Angela Goodchild who, for the weeks of the campaign, took over my diary. As Fiona and Roz were 'special advisers' paid for by the government, they were forbidden to do anything that might be deemed party political. Angela had been a volunteer at Labour Party headquarters in the '97 election and had then come in as a part-timer, a Labour Party employee in the political office, to help with Tony's more personal mail. With the publicity surrounding the founding of Matrix, members of the public increasingly saw me as a first port of call for legal advice and I was flooded with queries. As Downing Street understandably couldn't help – anything to do with the law was clearly my professional domain – I negotiated to pay for Angela's services one day a week. We got on very well and, from then on, whenever I went on political visits, Angela would accompany me.

For those four weeks in the run-up to the election, every Friday I'd visit marginals close to London. On the final week I was able to be at Tony's side. The Monday was a bank holiday, my junior did the Tuesday and Wednesday, and the election was on the Thursday. Friday was the last 'reading day'. The following week it was back to work with ICI.

It was another landslide, Labour losing only one seat to the Conservatives. The press, however, didn't look at the huge majority, but claimed instead that it was a victory for apathy because of the low turn-out. Tony – rightly in my view – took it as a sign that the public were happy with the way he was going, and hadn't thought there was much need to register their vote. There were ministerial changes. Robin Cook was removed from the Foreign Office, and there was talk of Gordon Brown taking his place, but it didn't happen. Gordon, who had married Sarah Macaulay in August 2000, had recently been upping his demands that Tony commit to going. But Tony knew he still had a lot to do, particularly in the area of public service reforms – namely health and education – and he was determined to see them through.

There were not only changes at Cabinet level, the office also was given a shake-up, Tony moving Alastair out of day-to-day press management, while Anji was given a new post as head of government relations. Fiona too was promoted, to head of events and visits. As a result, Angela began to take on more for me, and, when Pauline left, Sue Geddes joined to assist with my official diary, although the then Cabinet secretary, Richard Wilson, insisted she take the title of assistant to Fiona Millar . . .

Everybody knows where they were on 11 September 2001. I was in chambers: I had two separate case conferences, one in the morning and one in the afternoon, and had just finished the morning conference when the news started to come through. My first instinct was to go back to Number 10. Whenever something important is happening, Downing Street is the place to be. Tony was in Brighton, where he had been due to address the TUC conference. As it was, his speech was simply handed out to delegates. He came straight back to London. His overriding feeling was that everything needed dampening down and confidence maintained, particularly in the financial sector. He was convinced that America would feel beleaguered and we had to let them know they weren't alone.

Tony remained very visible. From the start his was the opposite of a bunker mentality. In his first television address, less than an hour after the news of the attacks came through, he said: 'I hope you will join with me in sending our condolences to the people of America and to President Bush from the British people. This mass terrorism is the new evil in our world perpetrated by fanatics who are utterly indifferent to the sanctity of human life. All democratic countries must unite to eradicate this evil from our world.'

Three days later, at a special session of the House of Commons, Tony made a fantastic speech, sending out a message, not only to Britain, but to the world:

One thing should be very clear. By their acts, these terrorists and those behind them have made themselves the enemies of the civilised world. The objective will be to bring to account those who have organised, aided, abetted and incited this act of infamy; and those that harbour or help them have a choice: either to cease their protection of our enemies; or be treated as an enemy themselves . . . We do not yet know the exact origin of this evil. But, if, as appears likely, it is so-called Islamic funda-mentalists, we know they do not speak or act for the vast majority of decent law-abiding Muslims throughout the world. I say to our Arab and Muslim friends: neither you nor Islam is responsible for this; on the contrary, we know you share our shock at this terrorism; and we ask you as friends to make common cause with us in defeating this barbarism that is totally foreign to the true spirit and teachings of Islam.

Even before Tony was elected Prime Minister, he thought it important to learn about Islam – Britain has a sizeable and import-ant Muslim population and, as far back as January 1997, Khawar Qureshi – a lawyer friend of mine, now a QC – took us to visit the Regent's Park mosque. He knew we were interested and knew Tony wanted to meet and talk to other Muslims. The summer of 2001, while we were on holiday, Tony had in fact been reading the Koran.

The *Washington Post* was soon rating him alongside New York's Mayor Rudolf Giuliani as 'the only other political figure who broke through the world's stunned disbelief'. Among the victims were 67 from the UK, a small number compared to the eventual toll of 3,000, but it remains the largest terrorist attack on British citizens. That Friday we both attended a memorial service at St Paul's Cathedral. It was a powerful occasion: not only were we all in a state of shock, but it was so moving to see the relatives – wives, chil-dren – because so many of the missing and the dead were reasonably young. As Tony was anxious to have a face-to-face meet-ing with the new American President, George Bush, the following week we flew to America. In the intervening days he had already had meetings with all the key European leaders. He believed the response to the attacks should be international rather than America just going it alone.

On that long flight across the Atlantic I remembered the conversation I'd had with George, when he and Laura had stayed at Chequers the previous spring. We were all having dinner together, and the conversation had been extraordinarily open and frank, thanks in no small part to the presence of the children. George had been talking about the Star Wars missile defence system, initiated by Reagan, and how he saw that as the ultimate shield.

But I had grown up under the shadow of IRA terrorism. 'Surely,' I'd said, 'the real danger is not from Russia or any other country sending bombs, but from individual people in a terrorist attack?'

George looked bemused at the suggestion. America had no sense that such a thing could ever happen to them, and that's what made September 11th so shocking – because it was a terrorist attack, and no amount of missile defence systems would have made an ounce of difference.

On arrival in New York we went first to a processing centre near the river. Everywhere you looked people were putting up pictures of their loved ones on the walls, with messages and contact phone numbers, in the hope that they would still be found alive. It was only nine days since the attack and it was all very upsetting. Knots of people talked in hushed voices. There was a section run by the British Consulate, and we talked to those who were counselling the bereaved, who had themselves barely slept in days. We had meant to go on to a fire station, but with downtown Manhattan still in a state of paralysis, even with a police escort and motor-cycle outriders, we were too short of time, so we went direct to St Thomas's Church to a memorial service for the British dead.

We knew they wanted Tony to do a reading, but the question, coming over in the plane was, what? It was very difficult to get the right tone. Magi Cleaver suggested an extract from a novel by the American writer Thornton Wilder called *The Bridge of San Luis Rey*. Magi had been seconded from the Foreign Office to manage the Civil Service side of the events and visits office. (The arcane regulations decreed that as a special adviser herself, Fiona could only manage other special advisers.) She was a tiny little bossy-boots of a person and everybody seemed petrified of her, but she was charming and lovely to us. She took me completely under her wing, and I loved her. Having started her Foreign Office career in Chile during the time of Allende, she was interested in all things South American, which was why she happened to have the book with her. The reading ended: 'There is a land of the living and a land of the dead, and the bridge is love, the only survival, the only meaning.'

After the service I was able to talk to some of the victims' families, including wives who were pregnant, and with whom, I am happy to say, I have been able to keep in touch as they rebuilt their lives. At the time, they were still living in hope that their husbands would be found alive. Following the service, Tony went straight to Washington for talks with the President, while Bill Clinton agreed to come to the fire station in Tony's place, New York fire-fighters, of course, having become the heroes of the tragedy. This particular fire station had been chosen because it had been so badly affected by losing people in the rescue operation, and in those kind of circumstances Bill is at his best. The men we met were just fantastic, brave and strong. One I talked to I recognised from one of those iconic photographs. At the end they presented me with an American flag – for Tony – folded up in a triangle, with a plaque signalling their appreciation of his support, a thank you from the fire-fighters of New York. For years it was on display in Downing Street, but now we have it at home. I was insistent that we took it when we left: a powerful memory of a haunting visit.

By the time we got back to London, a whole new security regime was being put in place. It had been decided that from now on I would have permanent police protection. What this meant in practical terms was that I stopped going into chambers every day. Like Tony, I could no longer drive; wherever I went I had to have a Number 10 driver and a close protection officer. Once I got back into Number 10, I had to stay there. No picking the children up from friends' houses, no dropping them off at sports activities, no popping out to the shops, or going for a run in St James's Park. Or rather I could, but a detective had to come with me. Everything had to be planned in advance and marked on the appropriate schedule. The children were no longer permitted to travel by public transport. One of my main concerns in keeping their faces out of the newspapers was wanting them to lead lives as normal as possible, which meant tubes and buses. In fact, we had managed surprisingly well. The nannies too were unknown, and could take the children for a hamburger without any fear of them being recognised. Euan was far from pleased. He had been taking the tube to school since 1996 and the idea of being driven by the police did not go down well. Nicholas wasn't much happier. Kathryn, on the other hand, was still only twelve and hadn't fully understood what freedom felt like.

Security at this level takes some adjusting to. If you have police protection you have police protection: it is not some sort of optional perk. You literally cannot go anywhere without having somebody else with you, and they have to know where you are and what you are doing all the time. One evening that autumn, on the spur of the moment, Kathryn and I decided to go to the theatre, to see *Blood Brothers*. It has memories for me – it was written by Willy Russell, whom I knew when he was running a folk club in Liverpool, and starred Barbara Dickson who, long before she was famous, did a gig at Trimdon folk club. We were about to set off, when I suddenly remembered. The 'tecs had left for the day and I hadn't made any provision for late-night duties. I felt bad, but rang them up and said perhaps they could meet us at the theatre. 'I'll just get a taxi there,' I said.

'Sorry, Mrs B. You can't do that. You'll have to wait till I get there.'

'But we'll be late.'

'Well, then you'll just have to be late.'

Another issue was the nuclear bunker. When we first moved in I had inspected it, to see if it was suitable for children. There were army-style bunks, and I couldn't see how I could ever take them down there. Downing Street staff were divided into groups: Red, Blue, Green and Orange. In the event of an emergency, Red group had to come down with us, the Blues were to muster on the lawn, the Greens were sent home but on call, and so on. Alastair was in the Red group, but Fiona was in the Green group, and I thought, No way is Alastair going to come in with us and leave Fiona and his kids at home if there's nuclear Armageddon. I told the powers-that-be as much. 'Just how realistic is this as a plan?' They asked if I wanted to bring the children to show them, and I said no. It was totally underground and really spooky. Now I had to address it seriously, so Jackie and I went down, as instructed, taking clothes and games and books for the children. Apart from the hum of the air-conditioning it was as quiet as the grave. Jackie agreed with me that, if it ever came to it, this place would completely freak them out. With the new increase in security levels, the burden on Jackie became ever greater.

In early December the *Daily Mail* ratcheted up its attacks on me. This time it was in relation to Leo. They demanded to know whether he had had the MMR vaccine. 'Come Clean, Cherie,' was the headline. The great issue of the day was whether the MMR vaccine caused autism. A report – since wholly discredited – had said that it did. Then the *Mirror* joined in. I had innocently responded to a letter sent me by the mother of an autistic child, saying I was 'keeping an eye on things'. It had seemed fairly innocuous at the time. I saw no reason to parade my family's vaccination records to anybody.

A number of people around me, whose views I respected, were vociferously against all forms of vaccination. Over the years I had listened to their side of the argument and, it's fair to say, I was in two minds. I did get Leo vaccinated, not least because it's irresponsible not to – there's absolutely no doubt that the incidence of disease goes up if vaccinations go down – and he was given his MMR jab within the recommended time frame. I was adamant, however, that I would not give the press chapter and verse. They had no right and it would set a bad precedent, and everyone – by which I mean Alastair and Fiona – agreed.

CHAPTER 26

Frontiers

The invasion of Afghanistan began less than a month after 9/11. The destruction of the Twin Towers was generally acknowledged to have been the work of al-Qaeda, the terrorist organisation run by Osama bin Laden. Their training camps were known to be in Afghanistan, funded in part at least by the Taliban who provided support and safe haven. In 1998 Bill Clinton had launched cruise missile attacks on these camps in retaliation for the al-Qaeda attack on two US embassies in East Africa, but with little effect. On 7 October 2001 the aerial bombing campaign began and Kabul fell a little over a month later.

At the beginning of the New Year, Tony and I set off on an official trip to Bangladesh, India and Pakistan. By now the Foreign Office had taken on board my usefulness, and while Tony talked with the various officials I was able to visit a number of projects related to women.

In spite of the many pluses – the colour and the vibrancy – poverty in the sub-continent always comes as a shock, and yet huge efforts were being made to harness the entrepreneurial skills of the women. Near Dhaka, I visited a micro-credit scheme run by an NGO called BRAC, which not only set up the co-operative where women learnt to manage the micro-finance loans they were given, but also delivered elementary health care. One woman would be trained in basic principles and techniques and have access to malaria tablets and contraception. Another would be trained in women's basic human rights in Islamic law: simple books to teach women that their husbands didn't own all their property; that their husband's family couldn't just take their property away from them; and that they had rights under Sharia law.

The British High Commission continue to be very involved in dealing with forced marriages and related issues and I was taken to a refuge for women whose husbands' families were in some way dissatisfied – either by their physical appearance or their dowries. In order to substantiate their claims that these women were in some way sub-standard, the husbands' families would pour acid from car batteries over the new brides' heads. According to Human Rights Watch, 280 women were killed and 750 injured in Pakistan in 2002 alone. In Bangladesh there were 485 attacks that year. With the ever-increasing availability of car batteries, these horrific attacks multiplied. Their injuries defied description. They had no faces left, or at least no distinguishing features. It was as if they had melted. Hugging these women was, for me, a way of defying their aggressors. I know how much it means to have human contact, and luckily I have never felt any physical repugnance towards any human being, though that is the purpose of these cruel and cowardly attacks.

Having recently spent so much time with people from both Bangladesh and Pakistan in the BCCI case, I was particularly interested to see where they had come from and the lives they had left behind. At that time in Bangladesh both the Prime Minister and the Leader of the Opposition were women, yet they both hated each other with a passion, which did no good for their political relationship either. Khaleda Zia was the first woman in the country to hold the position of prime minister. She was the widow of the assassinated President of Bangladesh, Zia ur-Rahman. Her rival Sheikha Hasina Wazed was the daughter of the first President of Bangladesh. It still seems extraordinary to me that in a country where being a woman is no barrier to high office, women themselves are treated as being of less value than animals.

Wanting both to be comfortable and to show due respect, my clothes for this trip had all been made by Babs Mahil. She also wanted to make something for Tony – the result was a Nehru-style suit that he wore to the state banquet in India. Personally I thought he looked very handsome. Not so the British press who, true to form, had a real go. Sadly he never wore it again. Although Alastair claimed to approve, he was generally of the opinion that Tony could wear anything as long as it was an ordinary suit. He was to be the final arbiter of taste.

When we arrived in Bangladesh, it wasn't even his own suit that Tony was wearing. That was deemed too crumpled by Alastair, and so Magi Cleaver was dispatched to the terminal to find one. Some bemused young man, who turned out to be from the Department of International Development, was persuaded to give up his suit for an hour so that the British Prime Minister looked sufficiently smart. For the rest of the trip, of course, André was in charge, but it just goes to show that if André wasn't there, things fell apart.

Our next destination was not on the official itinerary. We were under a complete press embargo. 'You don't have to go,' they had said, but I was determined. 'I'm going with Tony.'

It was nearly two months since Kabul had been taken, but it was still far from safe, which was why we were flying in the middle of the night, and I knew we were going no further than Bagram airbase.

Unsurprisingly, this was the first time I had travelled in an army plane. It was designed for carrying troops and I'd been warned in advance that it was lacking in the most basic creature comforts. There were no normal seats and the loo was literally a bucket. Not that I saw it. I decided I would rather die than climb over the press to go to the bucket in the back. In fact, there weren't that many of us. But Tony and I were lucky enough to be taken into the cockpit and we were there from take-off till landing.

The crew were basically special services people who had been flying in and out of Afghanistan on various missions since the war began, and made it seem as easy as the school run. These were the kind of dare-devil pilots beloved of writers, not faint hearts in any way. Tony and I sat in the back of the cockpit where the engineer would normally sit, and above us was a sort of see-through dome where the gunner would stand and direct the fire. As we took off, Tony asked if he could stand up and watch. So there he was, looking like an illustration from the *Eagle,* peering out into the night and asking them about this and that. One of the pilots took on the mantle of tour guide, pointing out different peaks, and telling us when we were crossing the Khyber Pass – an area that is lawless to this day. As we flew into Afghanistan air space over the mountains of northern Pakistan, all the lights went off. Yet even though we might not be seen, we could always be hit by a heat-seeking missile, the pilot helpfully explained. An indication on the radar that we might have been spotted resulted in immediate avoidance tactics, and the plane began to swerve and sway, the idea being that any missile already deployed would be misled, aiming for where we had been rather than where we were now. So Tony's standing up there watching all of this, while I'm strapped in thinking, Why did I come? I've got four children at home, one of whom is less than two years old. It was barmy of me to think this was a good idea. It sounds like bad fiction, but as I was sitting there, my entire life really did flash through my head. All I could think about was that, if I hadn't come along at least one of us would have been alive for the kids. Then, at one thirty a.m. we landed in Bagram airport.

It's only when you land in a military plane that you realise that a commercial landing is basically done for the benefit of the passengers. There was no question that we had touched ground.

Make no mistake, January in Afghanistan is cold. I had my big heavy coat on, but it wasn't enough. The red carpet was out. I hadn't expected this kind of welcome. I was soon disabused of its purpose.

'Whatever you do,' they said as we walked down the steps, 'stay on the carpet.' Bagram airport had been mined by the government forces and while some of the mines had been cleared, there was still a way to go. 'We can guarantee that as long as you stay on the red carpet you'll be OK.' For ever after, when I find myself walking on a red carpet, I remember that arrival at Bagram.

Even though it was the middle of the night, we were greeted with due ceremony by President Karzai and his Cabinet. I was so grateful to have landed safely I could have kissed them all.

The SAS had played a very important part in the invasion, and I sat there, totally enthralled at the stories of how they'd stormed the Taliban hideouts, real tales of derring-do, impossible to imagine how close they'd been to death and how, against all the odds, they'd managed to pull it off. The Department of International Development gave an impressive presentation on what we were going to do to help Afghanistan build itself up again. The Afghanis themselves repeated over and over how grateful they were and how fantastic our people were at doing these things. If you want someone to help rebuild your country, they said, the British had what it took.

While Tony had a meeting with the President, I was introduced to the Minister for Women, Sima Samar, and together we spoke to a group of women soldiers helping with peace-keeping, asking them what their impressions were. Each day more and more women, they told us, were visible on the streets, although fewer were uncovering their faces. The minister told them that, for the people of Kabul, the very presence of these young women doing responsible peace-keeping work was an important step towards the recognition of women's right to see and be seen. When I asked her what I could do to help, what the women of Afghanistan wanted, her message was simple: Please make sure you keep the pressure on the men. Please don't forget the women of Afghanistan.

It was while we were talking with troops based at the airport that Tony took a call from Gordon Brown's office. I knew from his face what it was. Gordon and his wife Sarah's newborn baby, Jennifer, had died. We had been on our way to Hyderabad when the news had come through that she was dangerously ill. She had been born prematurely in hospital and although she was a fighter, things were not looking good, and throughout the trip I had found it very hard to smile for the cameras knowing what they were facing back home.

As a comparatively new father himself, Tony was all too aware of the emotional strain they were under.

We arrived back in England on the Tuesday and on the Friday we were in Scotland. We went first of all to their house. Sarah was so calm, and it was very brave of her to let us come. It was the first and only time I ever went there. Whereas in the old days Gordon's flat had always been a bit of a mess, Sarah had made their house into a welcoming home. There is something terrible about a baby's funeral, and for that to happen with your first baby is utterly devastating. My heart went out to both of them.

I first met George Bush at Camp David at the end of February the previous year, shortly after he took over as President. From our visits to Washington, we had got to know Al Gore, the Democratic candidate, and his wife Tipper, reasonably well, so I think it's fair to say that our hearts sank when the result was finally ratified. Bush was, after all, a Republican. In fact, Tony felt very strongly that Gore was playing it wrong and that he should have used Bill more – not distanced himself from him. He seemed not to realise how much good will Bill still commanded, and he is one of the great communicators. Like the rest of the world, we followed the whole drama of the election and for me, as a lawyer, it was fascinating to see the Supreme Court splitting on political lines. It would never happen like that in the UK because the appointment of our judges is not so politicised.

We had watched George W on television and felt that he didn't seem comfortable with foreign affairs, yet Tony was determined they should have a good relationship. Others of our Party – notably Alastair and Sally – had a more mixed view.

'Let's face it,' I said. 'He's probably not looking forward to it much either. He knows we're friends of the Clintons, and he also knows you're a Labour prime minister and all the rest of it, so everybody's going to be a bit nervous, everybody's going to want to try and get along.'

The fact that the encounter was in the semi-rustic setting of Camp David was indicative, in a way, of the difference between the two men. With Bill Clinton we'd been entertained lavishly with a formal banquet at the White House, with Stevie Wonder and Elton John. The Clintons never really got going till late, whereas the Bushes were tucked up in bed by ten. We had come from Ottawa, where I had been half frozen, having not thought how heart-stoppingly cold it would be. From Washington we were flown out in the presidential helicopter, *Marine One*, which is less like a helicopter and more like a small plane.

I had been to Camp David once before with the Clintons and it was not what I expected. I thought it would be a country home rather like Chequers, but Camp David is literally a US Army base, or rather a Marine base. You all stay in wooden 'cabins' named after trees. There is a lounge, a bathroom and two bedrooms, all decorated to a luxurious standard. When the Clintons were there, I remember that the hand lotion and soap came from a supplier in Arkansas. The cabins are all spread apart, and whenever you venture outside, you're followed by military personnel.

That first night with the Bushes, we had an early dinner. The meal over, the President said, 'Why don't we all watch a movie?' So we did. He got all the new releases on DVD, he explained, and that night we watched *Meet the Parents* with Robert de Niro. There were armchairs ranged around, and I sat next to George, and he was soon laughing away. It was a perfectly friendly evening, very low-key. It wasn't just us four; we had been joined by our ambassador, Christopher Meyer, and Catherine, and of course Jonathan, Alastair and the others.

This was the famous occasion that George made the remark about him and Tony having Colgate toothpaste in common. In fact, they got on remarkably well. George is actually a very funny, charming man with a quirky sense of humour. The reason he gets a bad press, he says, is 'because I talk Texan'. Bill Clinton was also from the South, but while Clinton may talk Southern, he doesn't think Southern, whereas Bush thinks Texan.

There had certainly been a slight sense of anxiety before the meeting, but by the time we left, the general consensus was that 'he's a guy we can easily get on with'. We may not agree in terms of domestic politics but in terms of international diplomacy that is largely irrelevant. And the special relationship is precisely why, when the Republicans took over, there was never any question that we wouldn't do everything we could to get on well with them too.

As we were escorted to *Marine One* after breakfast, I realised that we hadn't been back to our cabin to get André or our luggage.

'Don't worry,' I was told. 'He'll be on the helicopter.' He wasn't, but by the time I found out it was too late.

André wasn't the only one who'd been left behind. There was a garden girl as well, not to mention our luggage. Apparently they had both been waiting patiently for us to get back from breakfast. Obviously somebody had to arrange for another helicopter to bring them back to Washington, and Christopher Meyer was not amused, claiming that it was somehow my fault. Yet as any teacher knows, counting your charges in and out is the first thing you do on a group trip. And whatever my role may or may not have been, it certainly didn't include that. My own view is that André arranged it on purpose just so that he could spend a bit more time surrounded by all those gorgeous Marines . . .

The next time we saw the Bushes was at Chequers a month or so later. By then we knew that George didn't really like formal entertaining, and if they'd come to Number 10 we'd have to have had some kind of formal dinner. They were much happier in an informal domestic situation than anything that involved pomp or staying up late. We were very clear that we wanted it to be just *en famille*, and when told that Condoleezza Rice wanted to stay the night, we said no. Everyone could come for the meetings, I said, but there were to be no sleepovers apart from the family. The day they were arriving, Linda, who was then running Chequers, came to see me.

'I've managed to accommodate Mr Bush's doctor,' she said. 'I've put him in my room.'

'What doctor?' I asked.

'Dr Rice.'

'Dr Rice?' And then the penny dropped. Condi, as she is always known, had conned Linda into thinking the President needed to have his medical doctor close at hand. It made me raise my eyebrows a little. Having said that, she is actually a brilliant woman and I admire her very much.

Like us, the Bushes are very family-orientated. Laura was an only child brought up by her mother, and she married into this big family, with everyone having loads of children. But she and George only had the twins, one named for her mother and one for his: Jenna and Barbara. That evening at Chequers was very much a family affair and, as well as our children, James Dove, Euan's schoolfriend, was there. He had always been interested in politics and, perhaps because he was present, the conversation was more wide-ranging than it might have been if it had just been us. Certainly I couldn't see me or Tony raising the question of capital punishment, but that's exactly what one of the kids did. So there we were discussing the death penalty: in one corner an American president who believed in it; in the other, a human rights lawyer who very definitely did not. I stated my view: said that it was inherently wrong and that if you make a mistake you can't put it right.

George just said, 'Well, that's not the way it is in America. We take the eye-for-an-eye view.'

But it was completely and utterly good-hearted. The way George handled those kids and their questions, I thought all credit to him. And I know that both James and Euan were pleasantly surprised that he could actually string an argument together and didn't turn into some sort of raging bigot. I often say that I must be the only person on the left that George Bush gets to socialise with. But no one can say – at least not me – that he doesn't have a sense of humour.

One of the last things Clinton did when he stepped down from office was to sign the Rome Treaty which set up the International

Criminal Court (ICC). After the Balkans War and the Rwanda genocide, the UN decided to set up the International Tribunal for the
Former Yugoslavia and the International Tribunal for Rwanda. The
success of these tribunals led to the setting up of the ICC as a permanent court based in The Hague, which would try people charged
with crimes against humanity and genocide either when their own
country had no infrastructure or where the country asked the international community to conduct the trial. Yet, in signing this statute,
Clinton knew full well that Congress would never ratify it.

In recent years America has signed very few international charters,
a pattern described as American Exceptionalism. This is essentially
an attitude of moral superiority, a belief that America is qualitatively
different from other nations, so does not need to be told what to do
by international treaties. An example is the International Covenant
on the Rights of the Child (CRC). This has been signed by every
country in the world bar two: Somalia, which has barely got a government, and the United States. One of the reasons America didn't
sign the CRC was that, at the time, it was still executing juveniles.
The Supreme Court has subsequently abolished this horror, but whoever the president is, it will be difficult for him, or her, to get
Congress to change its attitude. Once a country has signed a treaty
it then has to ratify it. In the US this needs to be done with the
approval of Congress. Congress, it should be remembered, is full of
people who don't have passports. So when Clinton signed the Rome
Treaty for the International Criminal Court to be set up, he knew it
wouldn't be ratified. It was simply his way of singeing Congress's
beard.

Once an international treaty is agreed, it is then opened for signing and will usually only come into force when an agreed minimum
number of countries has signed. By 2002 it was becoming clear that
the Rome Treaty would soon reach the magic number. It was the first
international treaty to provide that the Court should have a minimum number of women judges and I had become involved in the
campaign to make sure we had enough women nominated to exceed
the minimum figure. As very few international courts have women at
all, this became a particular hobby horse of mine.

Everyone in the international legal community was resigned to the
fact that the US would not ratify the Rome Treaty, and would thus be
unable to nominate any judges. But then came rumours of something

worse. George Bush, it was said, was going to formally un-sign the treaty. To take America's signature off. One of Tony's advisers suggested he approach George directly, on a personal level, saying, 'This is just silly. Nothing is going to change. It just gives the wrong message to the international community; it makes them think you simply don't care.'

I agreed. 'You must raise it, Tony,' I said, over and over, until the opportunity came for me to take matters into my own hands.

George and Laura had invited us to visit them after Easter 2002 at Crawford, their ranch in Texas. As Euan and Nicholas were both busy revising – Euan for his A levels, Nicholas for his GCSEs – I decided to take Kathryn and Leo on a trip to Disneyland while Tony stayed with the boys in England and met me later in Texas. We went with my friend Val Davies and her twins. After four days of full-on fun, we spent Easter with Bob Dudiak, an old friend of mine from the LSE, who had a holiday home in Florida. While Jackie stayed another day at Bob's with the children, I set off for a breast cancer charity event in Dallas which I was doing jointly with Laura.

Laura is a very warm, genuine person whom I liked the moment I met her, and someone I immediately felt completely comfortable talking with. It was clear that we had common ground; like me, she was interested in other women and women's issues generally. When we met we would talk about our families and about literature, because we share a love of books. We had more of a women friends' relationship than I had had with Hillary. With Hillary our conversations were more ideas-based, and of course we had our politics in common. To a degree, when she and I first met I was a little in awe. As Bill's wife, she had already been the First Lady for a number of years and experienced in the job. But when Laura and I met, we were much more on an equal footing, and have remained so. Our children, too, are more of an age.

Laura trained as a teacher and, in an exchange between colleges, had done part of her training in Oxfordshire, so was surprisingly well informed about life in England. I knew that Laura was involved in a breast cancer charity, but it was the American ambassador to Hungary who suggested this joint event when she heard I was going to Texas anyway. It was my first experience of the sheer professionalism of American fundraising and it was extraordinary: people paid at different levels to get different levels of access. At the reception, Laura and I stood beside each other and people made their way up the line. So far, so normal. Just like one of my Downing Street receptions, I decided, and began chatting to those at the head of the queue. Next moment I heard a voice breathing in my ear. 'Mrs Blair, you're to stop talking to these people. Just stand here, shake their hands and let the photographer take the picture. That's all they've paid for. We've two hundred and twenty people to get through, so please understand. All they want is their picture with you and the First Lady. Please don't talk to them. That's not the point.' So that's exactly what we did. It was a conveyor belt.

Then came dinner. Again, because this was Texas, everyone was basically Republican, and these were Texas Republicans. I found myself in a near-intolerable situation. These women would start by saying how lovely Laura was, and I would concur, and then they'd start comparing her to 'that terrible Clinton woman', going on and on about Hillary in the most disparaging way, and I couldn't believe anyone could be so rude. I didn't say anything. There was absolutely no point and I didn't want to make a scene but I had to keep reminding myself that half the proceeds of that night were going to Breast Cancer Care. And as I watched Laura being her usual charming self, I saw her in an entirely new light. She lived in a different world. At least the people from the UK's Breast Cancer Care who had come out were not disappointed. Like me, they were knocked out at just how professional everything was. It was fantastically successful and we raised vast sums of money for a very good cause.

It was a big honour to be invited to Crawford. This was the Bushes' private home. I travelled from Dallas by car, but it soon became clear that they all hopped around from helicopter to helicopter. These are rich oil people. The road was just like one of those in an American movie where you drive at a steady pace through miles and miles of emptiness. Eventually you come to Crawford, the 'town', where there's a café, a petrol pump and little else. The press who had come out with Tony were furious because there was nowhere decent to stay. I remember thinking on the long drive out, If I were the American President and could live anywhere, I don't think this is the place I would choose. The house, however, was delightful. Clean lines and modern, with paintings everywhere and no clutter. A really warm place.

There was still one thing that needed to be done, however. Just before meeting for lunch on our last day I had one final go at Tony.

'Have you mentioned the thing about the International Criminal Court?'

'Don't fuss, woman. I've got important things to do.'

Well, so had I.

'Look, George,' I began. I was, as usual, sitting next to him. 'I just wanted to talk to you about the International Criminal Court. People are saying that you're going to un-sign. While everybody understands Congress is not going to ratify the treaty, do you really want to stick two fingers up to the international community? I know Clinton put you in this position, but it's not going to affect anyone in America, so why not leave it as it is? Then at least you'll seem to be part of it. But, particularly now, when you've got all this good will from the international community, why rock the boat?' And he looked over to where Condi was – she was never far away – and beckoned her over.

'Condi,' he said, 'remind me to get you to tell me something about this.'

Tony had been sitting at another table with Laura, and had heard nothing. As we finally said our goodbyes, George put his hand on Tony's arm.

'Tell you what, Tony. That wife of yours,' he said. 'She's very persistent on this International Court thing.'

Tony's smile faded as he hurried me towards the waiting car. 'Cherie, what can you have been thinking of?'

Just as the car was about to pull away, George came running out after us and the driver wound down the window.

'And now,' he said. 'I understand why Clinton signed that bloody thing in the first place. It's all your fault, Cherie!' It wasn't true, of course. I had never raised it with Clinton, but we all laughed and he took it in good spirit.

Sadly, my little intervention made no difference. In the end the President did un-sign it. But I think it's also the nature of the man that he didn't take it as a personal insult either. It was a point of view; it happened not to be the point of view of his adviser.

As for the campaign to get more women judges, we were very successful. In fact, we exceeded the quota number.

CHAPTER 27

Collision Course

The Queen Mother died while Kathryn, Leo and I were in Florida. We were back in Downing Street on 8 April, and Kathryn and I walked to Westminster Abbey to the lying-in-state to pay our respects. The Queen Mum was always at Balmoral when we went there and, even in her late nineties, she was a formidable woman; there was a lot of steel in her. After Leo was born I would take him with me, and that first year, when I asked the Queen if I could introduce him, she was more than happy. To my astonishment she said, 'Mummy would allow Leo to have a picture taken with her.' So we have a photograph of a queen born in 1900 holding a baby born in 2000.

The year 2002 must have been a difficult one for the Queen. Those great celebrations – fifty years on the throne – and yet only weeks before the razzmatazz began she had lost both her mother and her sister, who had died in the February.

The Queen Mother's funeral had been planned for years and was very different from that of Diana but, inevitably, sitting there, in the same seat, in the same coat, brought back memories. By chance the following day also focused on the past when we gave a reception for Jim Callaghan's ninetieth birthday. All the key figures of my political youth were assembled in the Pillared room: Michael Foot, Tony Benn and Denis Healey. One important person missing was Audrey Callaghan, Jim's wife. By then she was suffering from Alzheimer's and the way Jim talked about her in his speech was so touching. Sadly, she died shortly afterwards and Jim died just ten days later. They had been partners for so long that he simply didn't want to carry on without her.

At the end of the month, Number 10 saw another celebration in a similarly nostalgic vein, when Tony hosted a Golden Jubilee dinner for all the Queen's former prime ministers, Tony being her tenth. I wanted each of them to be represented, those who were still with us obviously, but also representatives of those who had passed on: their widows or other family members. I hadn't realised how delicate this would prove to be. To represent Alec Douglas-Home, we invited his eldest son, the 15th Earl. Then a message came through from other members of the family who thought they should have been invited. The seating plan was also problematical, the key question being which prime minister should sit next to the Queen, and then, who would flank Prince Philip. No way was Ted Heath about to sit next to Margaret Thatcher, and I imagined John Major had little desire to be near her either.

In the end Edward Heath sat next to the Queen. Although Jim Callaghan was fractionally older, Heath had been PM before him. Tony was on her other side, as host. Margaret Thatcher was placed next to Prince Philip, and I was his other bookend. The Prince and I have always got on very well. Although I'm not good on horses – animals generally in fact – we share an interest in IT.

By this time the redecoration of the state rooms at Number 10 was finished. It's done on a ten-year cycle and a social anthropologist would have fun looking back through the various colours. What in Mrs Thatcher's time was the Blue room, the Majors had turned into the Green room. It was now a rich terracotta, which the committee had been advised was 'period appropriate'. The adviser was intent on turning it back into a 'pure Kent' building and had wanted to remove the gilding that Mrs Thatcher had put in, but this had been so expensive and so elaborately done, it would have cost a fortune to remove. Norma Major took one look at the new colour and said she really liked it. Mrs Thatcher was not so impressed.

'This is disgusting,' she said. Another room that displeased her was her former study on the first floor, which hadn't in fact been involved in the recent refurbishment. 'What have you done to my lovely room?' she barked. 'It is just appalling.' In this case she was right. It had been horribly brutalised in the intervening years and I was determined to do something about it.

Her choice of colour may have disappeared in the (now) Terracotta room, but over the door, within the plaster frieze, is the figure of a little man going up a ladder with straw on his back – a nod to 'Thatcher'. I, too, have left my mark. Just before we left Number 10, my plans to return Mrs Thatcher's study to its former glory were finally completed, and the official opening was a very tearful one, as this was one of the last things I ever did in Downing Street. I was known universally as Mrs B and if you look carefully, you can see a group of six bees carved into the wood of the book-case: five big ones and a little one.

That evening I had never seen the Queen more relaxed. She seemed always to be smiling. 'What a relief,' she said with a laugh as she came in. 'No need for any introductions.' Everyone was soon sharing reminiscences and I found it fascinating to hear about different families' experiences of living in Number 10.

A few days later Tony and I had dinner with Roy and Jennifer Jenkins. Jennifer had been reading a history of the American First Ladies, called *Hidden Power*. 'Somebody should do a version for this country,' she said. Coming so soon after that fascinating dinner with all the prime ministers and their families, it got me thinking. I had all the contacts and, most importantly, I was about to have plenty of time on my hands: very disconcertingly, I had just discovered I was pregnant again.

Needless to say, I was astonished. Leo's birth had seemed like a miracle, and here I was nearly three years older. Although the idea was daunting, to say the least, I realised that it would be nice for Leo not to be what amounted to an only child. As before, I went to see Susan Rankin, who arranged for me to have a scan in-house.

The radiographer was in raptures. 'I have never seen a baby in a mother of your age that wasn't conceived by IVF,' she said.

Tony was less enthralled. 'I'm not sure I want to be a father at fifty,' he said.

This time we decided to say nothing to anyone about the pregnancy. Not Alastair, not Fiona, certainly not Gordon. Not even my mum and dad. Only Jackie and the children knew. Unusually for me, I wasn't feeling at all well. It was going to be a hard pregnancy, I realised, and I was feeling grim most of the time. In fact the *Mirror* published a picture of me sitting down after an official photo with the Queen during a lunch at the Guildhall, part of the Jubilee celebrations. I'd been standing up for the picture, but then had felt incredibly weak. Needless to say, this was taken as proof of how rude I was, and how anti-monarchist, the caption being something like 'Cherie Snubs Queen'.

That year it was as if the past, the present and the future were on a collision course. In May Tony came back from an EU meeting in Madrid where he'd been talking to José María Aznar. Aznar had first been elected Prime Minister of Spain exactly one year before Tony; he was now two years into his second term and told him he was planning to announce that he wouldn't be standing for a third term and that he'd be designating his successor. It had got Tony thinking. Even when we first arrived in Downing Street, he had always said there would come a point when you would grow stale, and that after two terms – or a maximum of ten years – it would be time to move on, and on a practical level it would mean I'd have got most of the kids through school and some even through university. Of course this was before Leo turned up.

Even during his first term, there had been tensions between Tony and Gordon. Many of these were provoked by the behaviour of Charlie Whelan, Gordon Brown's equivalent to Alastair, who, it was claimed, would spend half his time 'briefing against' Tony – setting up the story that Gordon was the power behind the throne, and the man taking all the decisions. Few believed it, but it was irritating nonetheless. More damaging was the claim that Tony had done a deal with Gordon – the so-called Granita pact – a deal that he was now reneging on. Though Tony had always said that he felt that two terms were probably enough, to my knowledge he never gave a guarantee on timing. Yet Gordon was always trying to pin Tony down, with his 'When are you going to go?'

So when Tony had this conversation with José María Aznar, he got very taken with the idea. It was not that he would be capitulating to Gordon's demands, he explained, it was rather that by making a public announcement it might encourage Gordon to play ball. 'It would reassure him that I am willing to go, and therefore he might start co-operating, and we could get the health and school reforms through.'

'You must be mad,' I said. 'It might work for José María and his successor, but Gordon would only take advantage and you'd be severely weakened in the eyes of the other people who count.'

Fortunately, Sally, Jonathan and Alastair all thought the same, and by June Tony had accepted that if he wanted to get his reforms through he needed to stay at Number 10, not announce he was planning on packing his bags.

The shadow over Iraq became increasingly thunderous, and Tony was increasingly concerned. That spring America had renewed bombing in the no-fly zone in an attempt to disrupt Saddam Hussein's military command structure. In early June, when Bill Clinton came to Chequers for the weekend, I found them both crawling round the floor of the study, which was covered with maps. Bill was saying how he had always felt that Iraq was unfinished business, that Saddam Hussein was a dangerous person and a serious threat to world peace. From the intelligence he had seen, he was convinced that they had weapons of mass destruction. He certainly wasn't advising caution – after all, he had initiated the bombing – but he was advising Tony that the UN was bound into the whole process. I could sense his frustration at no longer being in a position to take these decisions.

Carole was around that weekend. She was there to do some training with Tony and I'll never forget her coming into the Great Hall, and within seconds engaging the former president in conversation.

'You need to remember the importance of stretching your back,' she was saying, while arching her own, right in front of him, all white leggings and leotard at full stretch, her long hair sweeping the ground. I could see Bill's eyes widen and I quickly moved her on.

The more I thought about it, the more I liked the idea of a book on the wives of Downing Street. I even had a title for it: *The Goldfish Bowl*, because that was what it felt like. I mentioned it to Fiona but she was dead against it, thought it was a really bad idea. What I needed, she said, was to lower my profile, not raise it. But I remained excited by the prospect. As we planned to go up to the Lake District for a few days before going on holiday to France, I decided to run it past Cate Haste, Melvyn Bragg's wife, who was a social historian, to see what she thought.

*

First there was the Commonwealth Games in Manchester. I have always loved athletics. Although I am no athlete myself, I utterly identify with this desire to be the best at what you do. It's all about the potential of the individual, about testing yourself against your limits, and I love the way it's either triumph or disaster – the strength of character you need to pick yourself up after disaster, or even after triumph, to know that next year you have to do the same thing all over again. What keeps all athletes going, I believe, is the need to excel in their chosen field, however narrow that field might appear from the outside. Once the charities I was involved with got to know of my interest in athletics, I would meet the runners at the end of the London Marathon. Or bring them to Downing Street a week or so before. When the pictures were published in their local papers, the money raised could be considerable.

By the summer of 2002 there was talk that I might become involved with the Olympic bid for 2012, so I was invited to the opening ceremony. Kathryn, Leo and Jackie came with me. Kathryn was then fourteen, and the best bit for her was meeting the Beckhams. For me it was fascinating to watch Leo with Brooklyn. Even at that first encounter, here was this three-year-old, terrifically co-ordinated, already a sportsman, and obviously his father's son. Whereas mine very much took after his mother, still staggering round, but already talking the hind legs off a donkey.

Police protection isn't an optional extra and, even staying with old friends in Manchester, a special hotline had to be put in as there was no room for the 'tecs to sleep in the house. Instead I had a huge red panic button and two uniformed police kept guard outside all night.

Tony came up for the closing ceremony, and that evening the heavens opened. All the dignitaries were sitting at the front, so it was the Queen, Prince Philip, Tony and me. Plastic macs had been provided and I put mine on, not least because I was pregnant and feeling so grim. The Queen, on the other hand, sat there stoically in the rain, as did my husband. The rest of the games had been brilliantly organised, but it was felt that they really ought to have got Her Majesty out before the storm erupted.

As the terrible foot and mouth epidemic had been causing so much damage to the British tourist industry, we'd arranged to spend a few days in the Lakes, though being on holiday in Britain is never so relaxing, particularly for Tony, as the media would never leave

May 2005. It was my good luck to be in my home town when Liverpool won the Champions League in a nail-biting penalty shoot-out against AC Milan.

July 2005. David Beckham may have caught more eyes as an ambassador in Singapore, but Tony was tireless in persuading IOC delegates to give London their vote.

Nelson Mandela with Leo in the Pillared room at Number 10 in July 2003. Mandela is old-fashioned courtesy personified.

Kofi Annan with Raj and Veena Loomba at the launch of the campaign for International Widows Day at the UN, spearheaded by the Loomba Trust of which I am honoured to be president.

January 2002. One for the shredder: Tony a dead ringer for Jim Hacker in *Yes Minister*, while I am my usual photogenic self.

Bagram airport, January 2002, with Sima Samar, Afghanistan's Minister for Women, and two impressive young service women.

July 2003. Visiting Antony Gormley's installation of terracotta
figures in Beijing. I had never seen Tony so distressed.

Sharing a happy moment with Zara Willis. My work in education
law first brought me into contact with children with disability
and I continue to be involved through specialist charities, in this
case The Children's Trust.

A school for street children in South India. The Foreign Office
eventually took on board that I could be useful.

My fiftieth birthday party, with my dad and half-sisters Bronwen and Jenia, over from America. My old mentor Freddie Reynold can just be seen behind them.

My fiftieth birthday party. Chequers had never seen (or heard) anything like it.

With Tony celebrating my sister-in-law Katy Blair's fiftieth birthday.

Left: Farewell to all that: Alastair, Sally Morgan and Philip Gould take tea in the rose garden at Chequers – Tony's favourite place for working.

Below: May 2005. Outside the back door at Myrobella. This was the last time I would cast a vote for my husband. Note the camera behind us. We were under constant surveillance.

With the Queen outside Number 10 after the Golden Jubilee dinner in 2002 to which all her former prime ministers were invited.

Meeting Pope John Paul II was for me the ultimate benediction.

The photograph that caused the uproar. I went straight from giving my lecture to meet Pope Benedict as requested.

It was with mixed feelings that we left Downing Street for the last time.

Chinese takeaway: the favourite Blair stand-by.

him alone. But we took Leo to the Beatrix Potter museum and the weather on the last day was glorious and reminded me of when I used to hitch my way on the M6 from Crosby all those years ago. In the end we had a good time.

On 5 August we were back at Chequers. As I had a conference at Matrix on the morning we were due to leave for France, I had taken advantage of being in London and booked myself in for my next scan. It was the same radiographer as before and, again, she was really excited, going on about how rare it was for someone my age to have a naturally conceived baby. She was just moving the sensor across my oiled stomach when suddenly she stopped.

'There's no heartbeat,' she said, still staring at the screen. For a moment I didn't understand.

'What did you say?'

'There's no heartbeat, Mrs Blair. I'm afraid the baby's dead.'

'Ah,' I said. 'So that's why I'm feeling better.' Because I was. Ever since the storm that night at the Commonwealth Games, the constant nausea had disappeared. I told her I needed to go to the loo. She pointed me to one immediately off the room and the moment I sat down the bleeding started. Later I thought it was almost as if, now that I knew, my body could let go.

By the time I emerged from the cubicle Dr Rankin had appeared. They were going to have to do a scrape – a D&C – she said. She would call Zoë Penn. 'We'll try to get you in and out as soon as possible.' Nobody need know. For the time being, I should go back to Downing Street and rest.

I stood numbly by the door in the waiting room and the 'tec came over.

'Come on now, Mrs B, no dawdling. You've got that holiday to think of. Can't have you missing that flight.'

'I don't think I'll be going on holiday,' I said. I felt embarrassed. He didn't even know I was pregnant, and I didn't know what to do or say. 'I need to speak to the PM.'

'Are you all right, Mrs B?'

'Just get me the PM, and take me back to Number 10.'

The flat was empty and silent. Leo's toys were stashed away in hampers. We weren't meant to be coming back for several weeks. There was usually so much noise, music coming from the kids' bedrooms, piano practice, the kettle, the washing machine, a TV on in the background somewhere. Ordinary sounds of family life. I walked upstairs suddenly feeling very, very old, and crawled between the sheets and just lay there, strange sounds ringing in my ears. Only when Tony got through did I let go.

He said he'd come up to London straight away, after explaining things to my mum and the kids. Twenty minutes later he called back. The kids were OK, and he hoped I understood, but he had to tell Alastair. Ah, yes. Alastair. I lay there just waiting. Then the phone again: this time the two of them on the line. There were implications in not going on holiday, they said. It was known we were going to France. It was all to do with Iraq. There had been talk that we might be sending troops in. If we didn't go on holiday, the concern was that it would send out the wrong messages. They had decided that the best thing was to tell the press that I'd had a miscarriage.

I couldn't believe it. There I was, bleeding, and they were talking about what was going to be the line to the press. I put down the receiver and lay there staring at the ceiling, as pain began to grip.

Finally Susan Rankin rang. I should get to the hospital as soon as possible, Chelsea and Westminster, where I'd had Leo. Zoë Penn would meet me there.

When I began to come round from the anaesthetic, and was being wheeled out of the operating theatre, who should I see but Gary, one of the 'tecs. He was looking so distressed that I burst into tears, sobbing and sobbing, and saying, 'But I really want my husband.' In fact Tony was there, but because of the security issues it was Gary whom I saw first.

As for Tony, his main emotion appeared to be relief. 'You know you felt there was something not quite right, Cherie,' he said. 'So it's probably all for the best.' I realise now he was simply trying to make me feel better; it just came out a bit oddly. Of course, he was right, but I was surprised at just how badly it hit me. It wasn't as if I was childless. I had four lovely, healthy children. But I was overwhelmed by this great sense of loss. To me, more than anyone else, this baby was real. I had seen it. I still have the scan.

I decided to go ahead with the book. It seemed appropriate. While in the Lakes I had talked to Cate Haste and, unlike Fiona, she'd thought it a good idea. It would be based on interviews with the former wives. I had met them all, and sensed they had strong, idiosyncratic views and real stories to tell. Fiona was still against the idea. She thought I'd be accused of taking advantage of my position. I pointed out that there was a precedent: Norma Major had written a book about Chequers and no one had criticised her. After that wonderful Golden Jubilee dinner, I really wanted to share the history of these fascinating people. I found them inspiring. Perhaps Fiona didn't see it that way. Perhaps she felt I should have suggested doing it with her.

But I believe her unhappiness was less to do with me than with Alastair. She was getting progressively resentful of the time that Alastair was spending with Tony and this in turn was affecting her and my relationship, which was rapidly deteriorating. Fiona was firmly in the camp of those who believed Britain should not get involved in Iraq. It was a non-stop tirade. 'Why don't you just tell Tony to stop it? He'll listen to you.' And it wasn't only me she harangued, but Alastair too. If it was bad for me, it must have been terrible for him. No let-up at work or at home. My response to her was always the same. 'Listen, Fiona. I don't see the papers. I don't see what he and Alastair see, and if Tony tells me, as he does, that if we don't stop Saddam Hussein the world will be a more dangerous place, then I believe him. And in my view you and I should be supporting our men in these difficult decisions, not making it worse by nagging them.'

The discussions over the possibility of Tony not standing for a third term had certainly made me aware of just how vulnerable we were. The bald truth was that however comfortable and 'ours' we had made the Number 11 flat, it was only a grand version of a tied cottage. We had no tenure. Once we were out, we were out with nowhere to live. Certainly there was Myrobella, but no way could I carry on my career from County Durham, and with three children at school in central London we had to stay in the area. Other prime ministers hadn't been faced with either of these problems. Thanks to Denis, the Thatchers were wealthy long before they took up residence in Downing Street, and the Majors had kept their house in Huntingdon.

Over the last year the talk at every dinner party was house prices. Between 1997 and 2002, particularly in London, they had risen dramatically and our old house in Richmond Crescent was now worth over £1 million. Our friends would tease us about our lack of a house. But it was no joke. To make matters worse, the stock market had taken a tumble after 9/11. As a result the money in the blind trust had gone down. The blunt truth was that we were substantially worse off than we had been when Tony became Prime Minister five years earlier. At the time I was pondering on all this, of course, I was pregnant with my fifth child, which further tends to concentrate the mind. How would we ever get back on the housing ladder?

That August we returned to our favourite corner of France for our summer holiday, this time to a rented house. But renting a house on the open market with the security features the protection guys required was difficult. We eventually found one, but it wasn't ideal and as I was feeling generally very low, I can't say it was the best holiday of our lives. We had friends in the area however, and as my miscarriage was now public knowledge people were very sympathetic.

Jackie was taking some well-earned rest with her family, so Maureen, our household help and babysitter, came along, and that surprisingly bluesy Scottish voice, coming from her pint-sized person, enlivened many an evening's singing and playing from the local guitar wannabes, who naturally included Tony.

Among the mix of familiar faces was an English girl called Caroline, married to a Frenchman who ran a foie gras business. Euan's A level results had just come through. He had decided on Bristol University, and while Caroline and I were chatting she asked if I'd thought about buying somewhere there for Euan, rather than renting. The short answer was no, I hadn't. Well, you should think about it, she said. Why throw money away on rent, if you have the potential to buy? At least that way you could have capital growth. She had a friend in Bristol, called Sheila Murison, who taught at the university and who, as a business sideline, bought places and then let them out to students. I decided it was certainly worth investigating, and asked her to ask her friend to keep her eyes open. That night I mentioned it to Tony. I wasn't supposed to talk about investments at all, but I thought a general question was reasonable. Did he think it was a good idea in principle? No, he didn't. He thought it was ridiculous.

Well, it wasn't his decision. The main reason for the blind trust was that I was the sole beneficiary and the more I thought about it, the more do-able it seemed.

I wasn't much more cheery when the time came for Euan to go to Bristol. Within two months I had lost my last baby, and now I was losing my first. It may sound stupid and sentimental, but that was how it felt. It was thirty years exactly since I had pushed my poor old mum out of the door of Passfield Hall, her face streaming with tears, and I remembered how embarrassed I had felt and how I just wanted her to go so that I could get on with my new life. Now here I was at another hall of residence. I didn't cry when I said goodbye to Euan, although he clearly knew that tears weren't far away, saying, 'Mum, I think it's time you left now.' Tony wasn't able to come. Euan and I had a pub lunch together and that was fine.

Tony wasn't exactly sympathetic to any of this. Iraq was looming ever larger and the tension both in the flat and in Number 10 was palpable. Leo, delightful though he was, didn't make life any easier. The phone would go in the night and Leo would wake and then he would cry. I'd get up, and go to his room to comfort him and, as often as not, end up lying beside him, and falling asleep, squashed uncomfortably into the wooden bed designed as a racing car, waking a few hours later with numb limbs.

Shortly after I got back from France, Caroline's friend, Sheila, got in touch and we had an exchange of emails about what I was looking for in terms of a flat, that is, two bedrooms, between £225,000 and £275,000. Then at the beginning of October she emailed me to say she'd found a development called The Panoramic which I might be interested in, and she forwarded me the catalogue. Although the list price – £295,000 – was more than my maximum budget, she was thinking of buying one herself and the builder had already quoted her a discounted price. As there were only five left of an original fifty-five, she was sure she could get this for me. And she did so. On 6 October, she said she'd negotiated a price of £269,000, a reduction of £26,000. She added that as a garage was included, the price could probably be structured to pay separately for that and thus get the flat itself below the £250,000 threshold at which point stamp duty kicked in. Of course any such manipulation would be viewed as tax evasion, and I couldn't do that. Later it was claimed that I got a special discount: it just wasn't the case.

I then discovered that the web price was only £275,000, and emailed Sheila to say that the reduction was therefore only £6,000 and presumably we could do better than that. I left it in her hands as

I was about to accompany Tony on a trip to Moscow where he would be meeting Vladimir Putin for talks about Iraq following the publication two weeks previously of a dossier based on various intelligence agencies' assessment of Saddam Hussein's arsenal of weapons of mass destruction.

In the meantime, the protection people had to look at the security implications of the flat and Bristol Special Branch duly did. From their point of view it was fine. They did say, however, that – if possible – it should be bought in another name, preferably that of a company. I told them it would be bought in the name of the Trust. I had already spoken, in principle, to the Trustees and they were happy to release £100,000. I would fund the rest with a mortgage. I hadn't intended to buy so quickly, but the money was sitting there. As I couldn't speak to Tony about it, I asked Fiona what she thought.

'It's a risk going to see it yourself,' she said. 'Someone is bound to spot you.'

'I could always ask Carole to go for me.'

She shrugged and said, 'Up to you.' Things between us were becoming really tense.

It worked out perfectly. Carole told me she was going to Bath the following weekend with a friend and Bristol was just down the road, so I contacted the developers and made an appointment for her to see it with Euan. After all, he was the one who was going to be living there. As it happened, I couldn't have gone anyway, as I was in Bermuda for a week on a commercial case, leaving on the nineteenth. When I called Carole to confirm the time, she said she might take her friend along – her new man, she confessed, an Australian called Peter Foster. I said fine. I had guessed there was someone around – I'd recognised the signs – though she had been unusually coy.

She called me in Bermuda. She'd had a look at a couple of the flats, she said, and thought they were OK. Euan hadn't gone with her in the end. 'But,' she said, 'I took my friend along – he's a businessman and knows about these things, so I thought that could be useful. He thinks it's a good deal. In fact, he's thinking of getting one himself. Here, he can tell you.'

The new man came on the phone, confirmed what Carole said and added he thought I could get the price down. I knew that already, of course, but I didn't say so. He also told me, just as Sheila had, how with a bit of manipulation with the garage I could avoid stamp duty. Again I made it quite clear that I wasn't interested. By this time I thought he sounded a bit pushy, but I thanked him for his help and that was that. Or so I thought.

CHAPTER 28

Mea Culpa

A week later, on 28 October, the day after I got back from Bermuda, I had an email from Peter Foster, the new man in Carole's life, attaching copies of floor plans of The Panoramic. He appeared to have been talking to the developers on my behalf, which was ridiculous – Sheila Murison was handling all that. I supposed he had been talking to them anyway about his own possible purchase, and talking about mine as well strengthened his hand. In another email, he put his mortgage broker in touch with me and I passed the details on to my own accountant, who I'd been with since 1982. Again there seemed little harm in it.

The business of the blind trust was very difficult. I couldn't discuss it with Tony, yet I couldn't spend a quarter of a million pounds on a stranger's say-so, however much Carole might sing his praises – which she did non-stop. So I made an appointment the following Saturday to view the property myself. I also contacted a couple of estate agents and arranged to see another place the same morning.

So I went. Two of the available flats were next door to each other, and it occurred to me that if I got both I might trigger a discount; then Euan could be in one and I could let out the other. Mortgage rates were low and I needed somehow to build up capital so we could eventually buy a new house. I discussed the possibility there and then with the person showing me around, and offered an overall figure of £430,000, which in the end was what I paid.

The next day a further email arrived from Peter Foster. Carole was obviously relaying everything that was going on, but given that she had just told me she was pregnant, this wasn't the time to be prickly. I knew how much she longed for a baby and my heart went out to her. This was probably her last chance. Her boyfriend was obviously pitching for a job, but the truth was that I didn't have any need of him. In one of his emails he said he knew some letting agents, so to keep Carole happy and him out of my hair, I said he could forward me their details. I was puzzled by his wanting to get involved, and started feeling distinctly uneasy.

The Manchester Trust agreed to allow £100,000 to be invested and the rest I raised by mortgage in the normal way through my bank. We exchanged contracts on 22 November, and completed a week after.

On Sunday 24 November, Downing Street special protection officers received a report from colleagues in Cheshire. They'd had a tip-off: a convicted conman called Peter Foster was claiming he was involved with the Blairs through Carole Caplin. He planned to involve her in a scam concerning a diet tea, which had already landed him in prison. There was also some talk of involvement in a property deal and he'd boasted that he'd met the Blairs' son Euan. Then Alastair rang. He'd just had a call from a former newspaper colleague, Ian Monk, now working in PR. He was advising Carole and Peter Foster, he said. Foster had just lost a deportation case and, as Carole was now expecting his child, he was looking for 'advice'. He also claimed he was being blackmailed – by the man who had tipped off the police – and having contacted the *News of the World*, via Max Clifford, they were planning to set up a 'sting', that is to record a meeting between me and Carole and Peter Foster.

I felt sick, Tony was beside himself, Alastair was merely grim. Sooner or later, probably sooner, he said, it would come out. For him this was the ultimate I Told You So. Carole would now have to go. We saw Carole at Chequers that Sunday and faced her with it. She admitted she knew all about Foster's past, but he was completely innocent: he'd been stitched up by the security services.

'Please, Carole,' Tony said, clearly exasperated. 'This is ridiculous, the man is a fantasist. You've got to understand; we cannot be connected with a criminal.'

She then presented Tony with an extraordinary letter from a

lawyer in Fiji, 'putting into context' his shady past. This was hardly reassuring to anybody who had ever spent time around villains and criminals, as both Tony and I had done as barristers. It was classic stuff. To say he was dodgy was putting it mildly, and we told her so.

'You're talking about the father of my unborn child,' she said, and burst into tears. It was horrible. It was as if it had just occurred to her that, if he went, she'd be left literally holding the baby. Frankly, neither of us could spare the emotional energy. Tony had Iraq to contend with. Politically things were very hot, with anti-war groups becoming increasingly vociferous; the last thing he needed was this, and I knew it. I was supposed to be his support, not his undoing. As for me, in addition to my official engagements, for two weeks from 25 November to 5 December, I was sitting as a recorder in Isleworth Crown Court. I also had late-afternoon appointments with some former prime ministers' wives for the book: Lady Wilson, the Countess of Avon (Lady Eden), and Jim Callaghan's daughter, Margaret Jay.

We told Carole that, while it was her life, that man was never coming near any of us. It was all we could do. She agreed that she would keep away from Downing Street. Indeed, for the time being I kept away from her entirely. This was a shock to both our systems: we had worked out together at the gym most days when I was in London for as long as I could remember.

On Saturday 28 November the headline in the *Daily Mail* ran: 'Cherie's Style Guru Has Fallen For A Fraudster'. That afternoon, the *Mail on Sunday* sent through a list of twenty-two questions to the Downing Street press office, all Foster-related. It was horrendous and Tony was fuming.

'I told you not to buy any bloody flats.'

'He had nothing to do with the bloody flats. I have never met the guy. He has never been here, he has never been to Downing Street. What more can I say? I can't believe you'd believe a convicted conman rather than your own wife! Telling lies is what the man does for a living!'

'So you categorically deny you have had any contact?'

'Apart from a few emails, no. I'll show them to you if you like.' Technology and Tony are like oil and water and, waving that offer aside, he dashed off the form, filling in yes's and no's – mostly no's – then faxed it back. Unfortunately I think he told Alastair in very firm terms that I'd had no contact with him whatsoever. I, on the other hand, didn't talk to Alastair at all.

For the next few days a stream of denials issued from Downing Street. Then, on Thursday 5 December, the *Daily Mail* published the exchange of emails between Peter Foster and me. Alastair's look of superior satisfaction changed completely. I had never seen him so angry before. As he saw it, he had lied to save my face and he was determined that if anyone went down for this, it wasn't going to be Alastair Campbell.

That morning Hilary Coffman came to my bedroom while André was doing my hair. She knew time was short: I had to be in court at Isleworth, at nine thirty a.m. Within seconds she was giving me the third degree, clearly on instructions. I have known her a long time as a faithful servant of the Party, and she was clearly uncomfortable about doing it, not least because she was a friend of mine professing not to accept what I was saying.

'But, Hilary, don't you see, there isn't a scandal. It's you lot who are making it into a scandal. Look, I've used my own money to buy two flats. I've paid the going rate for them. Nobody paid £295,000. OK, so I got a discount on the published price, but that's standard – it's a marketing ploy to make you feel you've got a bargain. No, I didn't know him. No, I have never met him – I once said hello to him on passing at the gym. No, he has never met Euan. No, he has never been to Chequers. No, I did not ask him to help me avoid paying stamp duty. No, he was not my financial adviser. No, I did not find him a barrister. No, I did not intervene with immigration or any government official or legal representative on his behalf. No, No, No, No, NO, NO.

There came a point where André could stand it no longer.

'How can you do this to her? Just look at what you are doing to her! I'm going to tell someone. You cannot do this to her,' and he stormed off.

In the mirror was a face I barely recognised. My chin was wobbling. My reflection was blurred as I blinked to try and control the tears. On my dressing table were photographs of all the children. If things had gone differently in two months' time there would have been another one . . . I was forced to issue a statement saying Peter Foster was involved. Damage limitation is the term, I think.

When I got back from court, Magi Cleaver phoned. André had

been to see her, she said, clearly very worried. Was there anything she could do? I said I thought not, beyond not giving up on me. She told me that there'd been a change of plan: it was felt that I should have someone with me on the trip to Warsaw and she had volunteered to come. I felt a huge sense of relief. I was patron of the Lord Slynn Foundation, educating lawyers in Eastern Europe about the EU, and was due to speak at a conference for them in Warsaw and then visit a centre for abused children as president of Barnardo's. It would all be all right, she said. 'Chin up. You've been through worse.' But I wasn't sure that I had.

Fiona's take was slightly different. 'Everyone in the press office hates you,' she told me. 'They've told lies on your behalf and none of them ever wants to work for you again. They want nothing more to do with you.'

I bumped into one of the press officers in the corridor beneath the flat at the entrance to the press office. 'I'm so sorry all this is going on, Cherie,' he said.

I had other support too. On the home front, Jackie and Maureen kept me going, and my office team – Angela and Sue – were being amazingly loyal, though they told me they'd been warned not to come near me.

The next day I called my accountant, Martin Kaye. He got his forensic team in to do a full search of my computer, the one in Downing Street, and at Matrix, and presented a full report of all the email exchanges to Number 10. The next two days I was again sitting as a judge. What a relief to put on the gown and wig. Never had I so appreciated my cloak of anonymity and safety. During all this time I had tremendous support from my colleagues and that gave me such heart.

We passed a frosty weekend at Chequers. Tony was on the phone most of the time, in his study, the door closed. Iraq. Alan was making his usual Christmas puddings and I went with the children to have a stir and make a wish, while Jackie was keeping everybody cheerful. I found it all very, very hard. It was about to get worse. On the Sunday the *News of the World* got in on the act. We later discovered that they had offered Peter Foster £100,000 to tell his story. For now they were questioning the discounts on my clothes. That night Bill Clinton dropped in at Downing Street and gave me a big hug.

On Monday the 9th, Peter Foster's solicitors issued a statement saying that I had contacted them about his deportation case but that I hadn't intervened in any way, that it had only been to reassure Ms Caplin. This, of course, did more harm than good. But it was true. I had phoned them, but all I was doing was checking that everything that should have been done had been done. I knew perfectly well that he hadn't a chance of winning his appeal. His record – prison terms in three continents, including Britain – spoke for itself, but I wasn't going to say that to my girlfriend. And she was still my friend. I had just heard that she had lost the baby.

André arrived at eight o'clock to do my hair. That night I had a reception for the Loomba Trust, whose aim is to educate the children of widows in India. In the afternoon, I had my annual children's Christmas party. Every year children from one charity are invited for tea. Father Christmas comes and there's an entertainer, and at the end we turn on the lights on the tree outside the front door. I tried to enjoy myself but I felt like a pariah. André was just getting up steam on my behalf when Alastair came storming into the bedroom. Until now he had refused to talk to me, either sending in Hilary to do his dirty work, or using Tony as a go-between. I think even Tony didn't want him to talk to me. My husband put himself between us as a shield because he knew Alastair was so angry.

'That's it,' Alastair said, his arms folded, looking at me via the mirror. 'It's now political. The Tories are asking questions and your husband is going to have answer them. One more time, Cherie, did you at any point have anything whatever to do with the immigration case?'

'I've told you, no. You're determined to humiliate me, aren't you? I know you've been briefing against me.'

'I don't need to. You do it all on your own.'

'Don't you dare talk to Cherie like that!' André exploded.

'You mind your own business,' Alastair retorted. 'Remember you're just a fucking hairdresser.'

'Apologise,' I said.

'I don't think so,' Alastair snorted. 'For the last time, I want that woman out of your life.'

'She has just lost a baby, her boyfriend is threatened with deportation. I'm not going to abandon her. I've said I won't talk to her, isn't that enough?'

'Don't forget you brought all of this on yourself.'

I felt terrible for Carole and very weepy. The news about the miscarriage had taken me straight back to that dreadful afternoon only a few months before, when I'd been lying upstairs bleeding. Even with four children already, I had felt utterly bereft. How Carole would be feeling, I could only imagine. Banned as I was from any contact, I couldn't even comfort her. The whole situation was ridiculous. Tony could talk to her, but I couldn't.

That morning I spent an hour with Lady Wilson, talking about her life in Number 10 in the sixties. Listening to her, I realised that, in forty years, little had changed. She had often been lonely and unhappy. She was the first of the Downing Street wives who came from a background that wasn't 'establishment'. Her son Giles had been a teenager when they'd moved into the Number 10 flat, and, even after all these years, it pained her to remember the impossibility of him simply getting in and out without a great song and dance being made of it. She remembered how she would wake in the middle of the night to find a garden girl at the end of the bed taking dictation. To retain her sanity, she told me, she would take the bus to north London, where they used to live, and cry on the shoulders of friends. The lack of privacy, the loss of identity – I heard the same stories over and over again. Different women, different backgrounds, different generations, but all bound together with a strong sense of public service, seeing their role as that of support and comfort to the prime minister.

Just before lunch André called me from the salon. 'How are you feeling?'

'Not great, André.'

'You know I'm not her greatest fan, but I think you need to see Carole.'

'She's banned.'

'That's my idea. You meet at my flat!'

'But when?'

'This afternoon. I have it all worked out. You turn the Christmas lights on with the kids and I'll be waiting out the back.'

'You mean just walk out?'

'I mean just walk out. Don't tell anybody. Be very naughty. Give them the slip!'

'But I've got the Loomba Trust reception—'

'I get you back for that. Promise.'

So that's what happened. Between three and four thirty I was down in Number 10 for the Christmas party for the Barnardo's children. I had taken on the presidency a year earlier, which was a great honour, a role I would continue for the maximum six years allowed. The Christmas tree ceremony over, I walked back in through the Downing Street front door, turned left, and pushed the button for the Number 11 lift. I didn't normally bother to take the lift up one flight of stairs. And this was no exception. I didn't go up, I went down. Down into the basement, through the comms office and out into the back car park where André was waiting. Nobody stopped me, nobody even seemed to notice. His flat is in Berwick Street, in Soho. Carole was already there, he said. He'd be waiting in the café across the road. But we didn't have much time, 'Half an hour, tops,' he warned me. It was a few minutes after five.

She was in a bad way. Very upset, very contrite, very tearful, not least because she had lost the baby. I told her that I wouldn't abandon her. That, as far as I was concerned, she had done no wrong. Did it do any good? I don't know. But we both had a cry and I think we both felt better. She showed me the contract that Ian Monk had negotiated with the *Mail on Sunday* for a weekly column. She pointed out the bit that said, 'Any reference to Mrs Cherie Blair shall appear only after prior approval.' She would never talk about us, she said. Then I had to go. Any idea that I wouldn't be found out was ridiculous, of course. I had been seen leaving on the security cameras. But at least they hadn't had time to follow us. They didn't know where I was going. It felt like a victory. When we got back André gave me a hug, then I opened the car door and walked in the way I'd left. I nodded to the uniformed officer on duty. He nodded back and picked up the phone. The prisoner had returned.

The next day it got worse. The Tories were calling for an inquiry. I couldn't stand it any more. I was just shaking. Alastair had had more questions through from the *Daily Mail*, saying I had been trying to nobble a judge. The law was my life! How could anybody think I could do such a thing? Yet Alastair was asking me as if it was a real possibility. I felt so angry that when they said they wanted me to make a statement, I agreed. They wrote it. That evening I was due to present the Partners in Excellence awards, which as patron I did every year, to organisations involved with affordable childcare and associated services, the venue being the Atrium restaurant just beyond the House of Commons. Fiona suggested that we use it as a platform.

The old gang were all assembled in Alastair's office: Peter Mandelson; Charlie Falconer, who was really nice to me, though he left early; Alastair and Fiona. Tony stayed out of it. When I got back from a charity function, I added in some stuff about Carole. Alastair wasn't happy but I didn't care. It was supposed to be my statement, after all. As I got into the car, Fiona sitting grim-faced beside me, I was thankful that the lovely Dave was driving. For once no Magic FM on the radio. From the moment we passed the barriers into Whitehall it began: flashlights against the windows of the car, the shouts of the photographers. Never before, or since, have I felt myself so hounded. I was their prey. It was that simple. Past the House of Commons, on to the Embankment, then finally we were there. The nice new 'tec opened the door, an arm from somewhere guided me in, the lights blinding me, the voices shouting, but I couldn't see. Once inside, I stood there shaking, checking to see if the microphone was turned on. It had been timed at nine minutes. Just another nine minutes and it would all be over. And these good people thought they were getting a speech on children and excellence. They are the ones I should be apologising to. All their hard work and they get this charade. A nod from Fiona, and I was on.

'In view of all the controversy around me at the moment, I hope you don't mind me using this event to say a few words . . . You can't fail to know that there have been a lot of allegations about me and I haven't said anything, but when I got back to Downing Street today and discovered that some of the press are effectively suggesting that I tried to influence a judge, I knew that the time had come for me to say something. It is not fair to Tony or the government that the entire focus of political debate at the moment is about me . . .'

Tony was at his weekly audience with the Queen, but he saw it later on the news. There was a moment, towards the end, when I nearly broke down, when I mentioned Euan having left home. What we'd wanted for him in Bristol, most of all, was that he would be safe, that he would be away from the press. He'd had all that furore over going to school, then there had been the drinking episode, and he'd gone to Bristol to get away from all that and now here he was, tangentially at least, caught up in this. I'd dragged my son whom I wanted to protect into the news; my girlfriend who had just lost a much-wanted baby was being hounded by the press. And on top of all this I had to try to keep going with all my official engagements and keep relatively calm at home so that the other children didn't get too upset either. All of that I could cope with, but the mention of Euan's name was the thing that tipped me over.

One day, a few months before the '97 election, Philip Gould told me that Tony was going on a long journey, and that neither his past friends nor the office could go all the way with him. The only one who could do that was me, and I needed to make sure I was by his side supporting him. I took those words to heart and vowed always to be there for him.

The worst aspect for me of the whole Bristol flats nightmare was that I had let Tony down. At the moment in his life when he most needed me, I was a drag on his energies rather than a source of support. Yet, however bad things had been, I never felt that he had abandoned me. For a quarter of a century we had been not only lovers but best friends. I always knew there would be things that Tony couldn't talk about, but I also knew that he would never lie to me, which was why I was 100 per cent behind him over Iraq and the threat Saddam Hussein represented to world order. His preoccupation with what he had to do, and the consequences for individual lives, both British troops and Iraqi civilians, weighed on him night and day, awake and asleep. In trying to get the Security Council of the UN to force Saddam to comply with its resolutions, he faced a titanic struggle. He was tireless in his efforts to persuade the Americans not to act unilaterally, while at the same time attempting to galvanise the rest of the world into action when it was clear that the language of diplomacy was no longer enough.

Although 2002 had undoubtedly been a bad year for me, whatever problems I had faded into insignificance compared to what he had on his plate. There wasn't one prime minister's wife who hadn't talked about how lonely it could be at Number 10, and I think this is particularly true for the Prime Minister himself. No matter how many advisers there are bringing up the rear, in the end everything rests with you. I was less lonely because of the children; family life meant I was rarely alone and through them I kept in touch with the ordinary rhythm of life, as indeed did Tony. As the years went by I had become increasingly conscious of just how good he was at his job, and how much he was respected throughout the world. Yet the job itself was so demanding and tough, I was determined that – as a family – we would do everything we could to make it easier for him, and make home a haven when he needed just to be himself.

I have never been happier to get on a flight out of the country. Magi Cleaver and I flew to Warsaw the next day for the Lord Slynn Foundation event. Not that there was any escape there. The flat saga had even reached Poland and the wives of both the President and the Prime Minister raised it with me, and couldn't have been more concerned. We were staying at the residence of the newly appointed ambassador to Poland, Michael Pakenham, one of Lord Longford's sons. That year I had given the first annual Longford Lecture on penal reform and so the Pakenhams were well inclined towards me, though they are decent people and I think they would have been nice to anyone in those circumstances. In fact they were delightful, and I was deeply grateful for their kindness in my hour of need. I remember Magi and me sitting down with them in their sitting room, tired after an exhausting itinerary – a legal speech and a charity visit – and turning on Sky News to see Peter Foster coming on and making yet more outrageous allegations. Even though Downing Street was denying them, Adam Boulton, a respected journalist, was reporting these claims as if they were true. I couldn't believe it. 'But if their case against me is that I should have had nothing to do with a convicted fraudster, why are they accepting his word?'

Following that splendid tenet of tabloid journalism, no smoke without fire, 'Cheriegate', as it was wittily dubbed, dragged on for weeks, until eventually they just got bored. The only positive thing to emerge were the letters I received in commiseration: the charities I was involved with, colleagues at the Bar and on the Bench, politicians from both sides of the House, priests and vicars, monks and nuns, friends and people I had never met and never would. I even got a kind letter from Prince Charles. Although, of course, I replied to them all at the time, they will never know just how much their support meant to me. The following gave me particular heart, from a barrister called Robert Flach:

I am I believe the oldest practising member of the criminal Bar and as I am about to reach the age of 80 it is perhaps impressive to say that this is the first fan letter I have ever written to anyone in my life. I have been absolutely appalled by the treatment which you have received in the media, when you have done absolutely nothing wrong. Let me tell you, in case you have not discovered this yet, that the Bar is a very bitchy profession with a great deal of gossiping during the many hours of waiting to which we are all, at times, condemned. Although your name, for obvious reasons, crops up in many conversations, I have never heard anyone speak ill of you in any way whatsoever. I have heard judges in whose court you sat as a recorder comment on the courteous and modest way in which you treated them. A young, female member of my chambers told me of her first appearance in the Law Courts when she was understandably terrified and an older lady spoke to her in the robing room and tried to allay her fears. She was so grateful although she did not know who you were until she saw your name on your wig box. You are universally respected for your ability, your manner and your integrity as well as your devotion to your clients.

Expressions of sympathy from such an extraordinarily wide spread of people made it just about bearable, just as they had after my miscarriage less than six months before. I felt I wasn't entirely alone. Eventually Peter Foster was deported. One of his more spectacular claims, worth including for its sheer audacity, was that Tony was the father of Carole's baby. He is now in prison in Australia, serving a four-and-a-half-year sentence for fraud. He was not even above forgery. A few months after he was deported he was in touch with the *Mail* again, sending them copies of fabricated emails purporting to show that I had tried to channel monies through an off-shore tax haven. He clearly had no idea of how little money we had. The *Mail*, naturally, demanded yet more answers. This time, thanks to Martin Kaye's earlier investigation of my entire computer system, Downing Street was able categorically to deny the whole thing. The *Mail* decided not to run the story. What people forget is that, by definition, conmen like him are plausible. Their stock in trade is their ability to make normal mortals believe them.

The reverberations continued to rumble around Downing Street. There were more cross-examinations by Hilary Coffman. There was a belief that Carole had taken clothes either for me or herself, without paying for them. I was required to contact everyone who had ever supplied me with clothes and get written assurance that the discounts I'd been given were standard for people in the public eye, that there had been no special favours. This I did. It turned out not to be sufficient. The new Cabinet secretary, Sir Andrew Turnbull, told me that I had to repay the discounts anyway. I refused. I wanted to know on what authority he was able to interfere with personal contracts I had made. 'You show me the law that says that I have to pay this back, and I will do it. Otherwise I will not.' Eventually a private secretary was assigned to investigate the whole business of the clothes. She told me that she would try to work out a better scheme, where the rules would be clearly set out. I had done my homework, and from ambassadors' wives to the Queen's ladies-in-waiting, nobody carried the burden of having to dress well for official duties without financial help and under such constant media scrutiny. As for other leaders' wives, they too expressed total disbelief that I didn't have a budget for formal occasions. A report was apparently written and presented, but, in spite of several requests, I never got a glimpse of it.

While all this nonsense had been going on, the situation in Iraq was becoming increasingly tense, involving Tony not only in telephone calls round the clock, but an endless series of bilateral talks, some of which I had to attend.

On 11 October we had flown to Moscow for Tony to see Vladimir Putin. The aim of the meeting was to persuade Putin that the UN needed to demonstrate unity so that America did not feel it would have to act unilaterally. It was the chance, Tony said, to show that in the new world order the UN did have power and that it could make things happen. That evening, I remember, Putin was at pains to point out that, far from being a convinced communist, he had always been a man of religious faith with a strong attachment to the Orthodox Church, but I was not entirely convinced. You sensed that the former KGB chief was still there under the surface. He has a very powerful presence – he's broad-shouldered and keeps himself very fit with judo. He puts a lot of value on physical strength, his own and Russia's. This is not a man you would want to cross.

The invitation to his private dacha was a sign of favour, and that night, apart from the interpreter, there were just the four of us. It was in fact a hunting lodge and Lyudmila, his wife, had never even been there before, their main dacha being outside St Petersburg. The meal was heavy in the traditional Russian manner: meat and no veg unless you count pickles. When it was over, Putin stood up and stretched.

'And now', he said, 'I want to take you wild boar-hunting.' By this time it was about half-past ten at night. Despair crossed my face. No one had said anything about hunting, wild boar or anything else, and I was dressed for dinner in high heels and a dress, and the temperature outside was well below freezing. Tony came to help me on with my coat.

'Buckle down, girl, and stop complaining.'

Lyudmila gave me a look: this wasn't her idea of fun either. Outside it was pitch-dark, and there was nothing I could do to prevent my heels from click-clacking on the concrete path, while everyone else was creeping along with exaggerated stealth. I was petrified. The machine-gun-toting Russian bodyguards were behind us, while our own protection officers were presumably somewhere behind them. At least I hoped so, in case we were about to be ceremonially assassinated. I didn't know whether to be more frightened of the various guns or the wild boar which I'd seen pictures of, and which I knew to be particularly vicious creatures. Putin led us down to a hide and was explaining the finer points of boar-hunting as he peered down the sights of a night-vision rifle. One day, I thought, I will tell my grandchildren about this. No doubt to their disappointment (but not mine) there would be no violent denouement to the evening. Not one wild boar was seen, let alone killed.

Russian hospitality is not for the faint-hearted. The next day we were told we were going on a picnic. Again the temperature was sub-zero, but it was very beautiful in a wilderness kind of way, with a huge lake and water birds everywhere, and everything glistening with hoar frost. A wild boar was being roasted on top of a huge roaring fire and, next to it, in a kind of bower, a table had been laid complete with white tablecloth and silver cutlery. Seeing that I was shivering, Putin ordered one of his soldiers to give me his greatcoat, not very different from the ones in *Dr Zhivago*. I was faced with one further practical problem. In order to cut the meat I had to take off my gloves, but if I took off my gloves the cutlery stuck to my hands. The wild boar was delicious, but the cold was so overwhelming that I can't say I really enjoyed it.

The meeting, however, was generally deemed a success. Tony felt that Putin had an understanding of where he was coming from, and that he wasn't just doing this as an acolyte of the American President, but because he wanted to make the UN work.

In December, immediately after the Peter Foster nightmare, we went on a similar mission to the Schroeders in Berlin. Gerhard Schroeder had come to power in 1998, and, as a social democrat and as a moderniser, there was a natural affinity. Doris his wife had been a journalist, although she looked very fragile, with short blonde hair, and I liked her. Unusually we were invited to their home, where we met her daughter from a previous marriage. Again the meeting was very convivial, with just the four of us. Gerhard assured Tony that while he had to tread carefully because of his own political position, he wasn't going to cause difficulties for the Americans in the UN. In the event, he, Chirac and Putin developed an alliance which ultimately did for Tony's attempts for unity. On 24 February 2003, the US, the UK and Spain sponsored a further resolution. France said it would veto the new resolution 'whatever the circumstances'. It was thus never ratified.

Following that evening with the Schroeders, Tony gave an interview just before Christmas with British Forces Radio in Germany. They, more than anybody else, knew that preparations were well under way for an invasion of Iraq. When asked about the final decision about whether to go to war, and how difficult this would be to make, Tony replied: 'These are the hardest decisions because you are aware that you are putting people's lives at risk and that is why we should never undertake conflict unless we have exhausted all other options and possibilities.'

And that is truly what he felt and had done, for months and months. At the same time as Tony was trying to make an alliance with the European leaders he was also talking with Chile, Cameroon and Angola, all of which were then on the Security Council, having conversations late into the night, desperately seeking to keep a united front, in order that Saddam Hussein would, in the end, back down. That was the message. That's why when Chirac said that he would not support the second resolution 'whatever the circumstances', all Tony's careful negotiating came to nothing, and he knew that if Saddam Hussein didn't back down, the Americans were going to go in anyway. And, that of course, is exactly what happened. George

Bush did offer him the way out, but Tony turned it down; he was determined that we would be there supporting America because he thought it was the right thing to do. He could not let Saddam Hussein get away with defying the international community and making his own people's lives a misery. So the die was cast. After that it was only a matter of time.

Then one evening, on 10 March, the secure phone line rang in the flat. It was the call Tony had been expecting. It was the Americans saying they were going in.

CHAPTER 29

Family Matters

Sometime in 2006, I was on Radio 4's *A Good Read*, and for my book I chose *Saturday* by Ian McEwan, which takes place over twenty-four hours on 15 February 2003, the day of the big anti-war demonstration. The atmosphere he describes is very evocative to me. McEwan's fiction often concerns the lives of ordinary people being torn apart by the aggressively unexpected, and I remember so well being in the centre of a storm. Tony was now the pariah and there were anti-Blair slogans everywhere. The kids were badly affected. To see their father portrayed as 'B-LIAR' every time they left the house was upsetting, to say the least. We shielded them as much as we could but it was difficult. They couldn't be wrapped in cotton wool. As all this was happening, we had a warning about a threat against Euan in Bristol. I had arranged to go down to see him for lunch on his nineteenth birthday, and I remember having to ring him up and needing to be very vague. There was a change of plan, I said. He should bring some clothes and meet me at a hotel in Bristol. Once he got there, I told him what the situation was, that there had been a threat, and that he had to go to a safe house until we found out whether the threat was real or not.

'But what about my party?'

'I'm sorry, but the police are insisting.'

Gary was the protection officer designated to stay with him. For the first few days the two of them were cooped up in this safe house, unable to go anywhere. After that Gary went with him until things quietened down. He obviously couldn't stay at the halls of residence, and with all the publicity about the flats, he couldn't stay in them either. Not only would he be in danger, but other residents would be endangered too. So all that was a total disaster.

In the meantime Carole had started doing a documentary with Peter Foster. As the woman making it was one of her clients, she thought this would be her vindication. It wasn't. Alastair was, rightly, dead against it. He and Fiona wanted her cast into the outer darkness. Tony, on the other hand, agreed that I could still exercise with her, as long as it was done well away from the public eye.

The Conman, His Lover and the Prime Minister's Wife was broadcast in February. From my point of view, watching this man who had created so much havoc in our lives was oddly gripping. I had said a brief hello to him once at the gym, but that was the only time I'd seen him. On the screen he came over as a complete shyster.

Sitting through that programme had an unforeseen effect on me, however. For the first time I found myself looking at Carole objectively and querying her judgement. She knew this man's track record, and staying with him for the sake of the baby no longer applied. Could she really not see what a liability he was? It was nothing sudden, but over the next few months I found myself backing away from her. I found myself going to the gym less often. As for my wardrobe, Angela and I managed all that ourselves with the designers I had now been working with for years.

Unfortunately there was one last chapter still to come.

Sometime that spring, Barnardo's press office got in touch with Fiona. They were launching a campaign in relation to child prostitution, they explained. *Marie Claire* was supporting the campaign and had asked Barnardo's if I – as president – could give them an interview, as part of which I would visit a project in Islington which dealt with fourteen- and fifteen-year-old girls. Naturally I said yes. A few days later the magazine changed its tune. It would prefer 'A Day in the Life' sort of piece, it said. Nobody was very keen – the access was unprecedented – but in the end it was agreed. The date chosen was 8 May, a day I wouldn't be in court – that wouldn't have been appropriate – but it would include a visit to Matrix and Barnardo's, and the Asian Women of Achievement Awards, of which I am patron, in the evening.

André came to do my hair that morning at eight o'clock. The *Marie Claire* photographer took some pictures as I left Number 10 on my way to the gym. Next stop Matrix, where I talked with some of the team – more photos – then it was back to Number 10 where we broke for lunch. We all agreed to meet up again at two p.m. before heading off to Islington and the Barnardo's project.

Around one thirty Carole popped up to the flat. I had seen her at the gym that morning and she'd suggested she come along before the afternoon session to make sure I was still looking all right. She had often done my make-up for photo shoots, so I said fine. The prohibition on my seeing her had lapsed, largely because I rarely saw her any more outside the gym. Shortly after she arrived, the custodian rang through from the Number 10 front hall. Was I expecting some people from *Marie Claire*? Yes, I was.

Carole and I were upstairs when I heard voices. Peering down from the landing, I realised to my dismay that while the writer and the photographer were there, Fiona wasn't, and that somewhere downstairs Leo was playing. Knowing what journalists are like, the last thing I wanted was them getting into conversation with my three-year-old son, or even seeing him. I had to act quickly to lure them away. 'I'm not quite ready for you,' I called out. 'You'd better come up.' Hurriedly I phoned down to Jackie and asked her to keep Leo in his room. I then phoned Angela and suggested she come up to the flat to be introduced: anything to keep them from wandering round.

They were early, they admitted, when they reached the bedroom. Carole quickly redid my make-up for the photo session that would follow downstairs. As the photographer raised her camera to take a picture, Carole put up her hand and said, 'No.' As soon as I heard Angela's voice, I took them down to the study to meet her, then suggested she might like to take them to see the garden. Anything to get them out of the flat. At that moment Fiona turned up. Except in relation to Iraq, I had never seen her so angry, her fire initially directly against poor Angela who she assumed – wrongly – had let these two women in. (The poor custodian who gave them access to the building ultimately got the blame.)

A few weeks later the magazine sent over a spread of the

photographs they wanted to use. I was horrified. It included the picture of Carole touching up my lipstick, even though her hand saying 'No' is clearly visible. Worse, there was a picture of our bed. We rang the magazine immediately, said we didn't want those particular pictures used, and that they constituted an invasion of our privacy. The editor's response was, Sorry but these are our pictures and we intend to use them. It turned out that Fiona hadn't agreed picture approval. It wasn't how Downing Street worked, she later explained. Usually she would be with the photographer so the situation wouldn't arise. Except, of course, this time she wasn't and it had.

The August issue of *Marie Claire* duly appeared in July 2003 and the picture of Carole retouching my lipstick became front-page news. 'Lippygate' was the tabloid's shorthand this time. I was really angry. It may be that it wasn't Fiona's fault, but nonetheless she had been in charge and I felt that, one way or another, she had truly landed me in it. It proved to be the last straw. When she left for the summer, she never returned. It was a sad ending. As someone who knew only too well the pressures I was under, because they paralleled her own with Alastair, she was invaluable. It's hard to imagine how I could have coped without her in those early years and I will always be grateful for that.

Meanwhile over at *Hello!* magazine, Carole was breezily commenting on various outfits that I had worn since Tony was elected, who the designers were and so on. Providing such information had been expressly forbidden by Number 10 right from the start, and she knew it. This was the moment I finally decided her naivety was less innocent than I had always believed. I had been a very loyal friend to her, but the time had come to call it a day.

'This is doing neither of us any good, Carole,' I told her. 'As long as you are linked to me, you are not able to be independent in your own right.' All in all, we thought it best to put some distance between us. Another sad ending.

Fiona's job was taken over by Jo Gibbons. She was quite a different character from Fiona and had no interest whatever in my charity work, so was perfectly happy for Angela and Sue to handle me on their own. From then on they did everything from organising my diary and charity events to sorting out my wardrobe and accompanying me, both in the UK and abroad, right to the end of our time in Downing Street and beyond. They have had to put up with a lot, but both have been wonderful. I couldn't have managed without them, and our little team suddenly started to work a whole lot better.

We had first met the Putins in February 2000. He was then the heir-apparent and this was a getting-to-know-you trip to St Petersburg, his hometown and powerbase. After a whistle-stop tour of the Hermitage, we were taken to *War and Peace*, a four-hour opera by Prokofiev. Refreshments during the two intervals had consisted solely of champagne and caviar. As I was then six months pregnant with Leo, it wasn't easy, and although the hotel was like an oven, outside was bitterly cold.

My next visit couldn't have been more different. It was the three hundredth anniversary of the founding of the city. In the short time since assuming the presidency, Putin had poured money into St Petersburg and totally transformed it, or so at least it appeared. Much of it, we later discovered, was no more substantial than a film set: the façades of the houses had been 'painted' and others disguised to make them look totally restored. It was the end of May and the weather was lovely – a few years later they actually sent up aeroplanes to disperse the clouds, so that the sun could shine for the G8.

The idea was to show St Petersburg in all its former magnificence and in that Putin certainly succeeded. The most extraordinary of the reconstructions I saw was the amber room in Catherine Palace. The original had dated from the early eighteenth century, a room completely lined with amber and semi-precious stones, but it had been looted by the Germans during the war and no trace of them has ever been found. In terms of the entertainment, expense was no object – ballet, fireworks, vodka and caviar wherever you looked. Rather surprisingly, I found I liked it. When our host saw me spooning some up, he hastened over.

'You don't want this stuff,' Putin said, removing my plate, and got me some Beluga.

In all it was a mind-boggling display of Russian power. Once again, I was grateful and amazed to have been granted a ringside seat to history, to fascinating people and incredible events.

Three weeks later the Putins arrived on their first state visit to Britain and I was down to entertain Lyudmila one afternoon. As we had been taken to see *War and Peace* in St Petersburg the first time we met, I arranged to visit the Royal Opera House in Covent Garden where we would be joined by an array of cultural people for lunch. On the Putins' arrival in London, however, I was informed through an aide that Mrs Putina would really like to go shopping. From what I knew of her, I judged that Burberry's might hit the spot, so arranged a discreet visit to their showroom just off Piccadilly Circus immediately after the lunch. Unfortunately, this being a state visit, transport had been provided by the Palace, and Lyudmila arrived at Downing Street in the royal Bentley, glass everywhere, designed to provide an unrestricted view of the occupants. Discreet it was not. The aide had been right, however; the opera wasn't her thing, but she perked up immediately we got to Burberry's. No sooner had we arrived in the showroom, than she stripped off down to her underwear. In the interests of diplomacy, I decided I had better keep her company. As she didn't have any money on her, I put her considerable purchases on my credit card. The next day I was informed that a large packet had arrived from Mrs Putina. She was repaying me in cash. I had never seen so many £50 notes. Our friendship was undoubtedly consolidated that afternoon in our knickers.

In those early days, Lyudmila Putina was very unsure of herself. Her husband had fairly chauvinistic views about the role of a wife. He had two basic rules, she confided: 'A woman must do everything at home' and 'never praise a woman, it will only spoil her'. Language was important to her; she had studied modern languages at Leningrad University's philology department and also spoke fluent German, the Putins having lived there for several years.

After the Berlin Wall came down, she told me that she feared for the future of Russian literature and language, hence her scheme. In 2002 she had visited the United States to take part in the second annual National Book Festival hosted by Laura Bush and she decided to replicate the idea. I promised I would support her and I did, going over to the launch with Laura and on two further occasions, when I met the First Lady of Armenia, Bella Kocharian, and the First Lady of Bulgaria, Zorka Purvanova. Without my support, Lyudmila later admitted, she didn't think she would have gone through with it. There's no doubt that her book festival gave a huge boost to her confidence and, I think, her status. As a thank you she gave us lunch in the state rooms of the Kremlin and an extraordinary private tour. By us, I mean my 'entourage': to whit, André and Sue Geddes. To his credit our ambassador, who was also invited, did not baulk at this unusual arrangement. We were taken high up on to the roof by the famous golden domes, from where we looked down at the cathedral totally restored by Boris Yeltsin after its ignominious decades as a public swimming pool, the cathedral having been razed by communist apparatchiks because they didn't want to look out on it.

July the eighteenth in 2003 was a momentous day for Tony. He became the first British Prime Minister since Winston Churchill to be awarded the Congressional Gold Medal by Congress for being 'a staunch and steadfast ally of the United States'. We were allowed to take several guests to the Capitol and I invited my half-sisters Jenia and Bronwen, who both live in America, and was able to introduce them to Laura and Hillary. The moment Tony walked on the stage, the whole of the auditorium rose and gave him the most extraordinary standing ovation. It would have been moving in any circumstances but coming, as it did, after all the heartbreak and negativity, it made my heart sing.

Washington was only the first stop on the itinerary: next came Japan, then Korea, China and, finally, Hong Kong. For once Alastair didn't come with us. He was increasingly disaffected and Fiona had made it abundantly clear that they both wanted shot of Downing Street, so the moment the occasion was over he flew back to London while we went on to Tokyo. We were all so cheerful, happy and laughing, and were just settling down to go to sleep when the first call came through. A comms person came forward from the back of the plane and handed Tony the phone. It was Downing Street: David Kelly, the scientist at the centre of the bitter row between Number 10 and the BBC, was missing.

The row centred on allegations broadcast by the BBC about the government report into Saddam's Weapons of Mass Destruction. The *Today* programme had claimed that Downing Street, against the wishes of the intelligence services, had deliberately inserted false information into a dossier. Number 10 had vigorously denied the allegations, subsequently repeated around the world, and demanded their withdrawal. The BBC, equally vigorously, refused. BBC bosses believed that David Kelly had told one of their journalists that this was the case – a claim shown at the Hutton Inquiry to be untrue. But that was all later. For now, for the past few weeks, Alastair had been involved in a hideous and very public shouting match with the BBC. They had called him a liar and he objected to that very strongly. The 'source' of the story had remained anonymous until the previous week. Then he had been named. Now he was missing. Within a few hours there was another call.

As I watched Tony hand back the phone, I saw him slump into his seat. From sitting upright he just crashed. David Kelly was dead, he said. His body had been found in woodland close to his home. It was awful. He decided there and then that there had to be an investigation and spoke to Charlie Falconer, now Lord Chancellor, from the plane to see which judge might be available. I have never seen Tony so distraught and I felt helpless to do anything. Eventually he spoke to Alastair – God knows what time it was for either of them – who had just arrived back in London. Alastair said he couldn't handle any more and he wanted out.

After a night in Tokyo in which he barely slept, Tony had a meeting with the Prime Minister while I visited a centre for disadvantaged children, where I found it hard to give the staff and the children the attention they deserved. We then flew by helicopter to Hakone just below Mount Fuji. The Prime Minister Mr Koizumi had long wanted us to have a traditional Japanese experience. And the Ryuguden Hotel certainly was that, with futons and sliding doors, and utterly beautiful, looking out over Lake Ashinoko, and surrounded by hot springs. Mr Koizumi was very unusual among politicians, especially Japanese politicians. He had a look of the young Richard Gere, and had a passion for Elvis and Cliff Richard, of all people, and I had brought him a CD that Cliff had signed specially.

It should have been a great trip. We realised soon enough that it was going to be quite the opposite. In the twenty-five years since I had known Tony, I had never seen him so badly affected by anything. At the Tokyo press conference, a journalist from the *Mail on Sunday* shouted at my husband: 'What's it like, Mr Blair, to have blood on your hands?'

Our next stop was Korea, where we had dinner with the newly elected President Roh and his wife. She was incredibly nervous, though once we got chatting, she gradually relaxed. They clearly had no idea what Tony was going through and I tried my best to keep up the small talk. At the end of the dinner when I admired her earrings, she immediately took them off and handed them to me. There are strict rules in Downing Street about gifts and anything worth over £140 has either to be paid for or deposited in the strong room, to be borrowed for special occasions. I couldn't possibly take them, I told her. But she insisted. They were not expensive, she said. They were made in Korea and she could easily get another pair, but this was her first official visit and she wanted to thank me for making it all so easy. I wear them all the time.

After a stay of only a few hours, we were on our way to Beijing, though I had just time to attend Mass where I prayed for David Kelly, his family, and for Tony.

Throughout the trip, Tony did his best to look cheerful for the sake of his hosts, but it was desperate. In Beijing we saw an installation of hand-sized terracotta figures by Antony Gormley. There is a photograph of the two of us taken that morning that I keep in my study: Tony crouching down among these thousands of tiny figures, me behind him, my arms around him, giving him the support he needed.

'You are a good man,' I told him, as we crouched there, the cameras whirring. 'And God knows your motives are pure, even if the consequences are not as you had hoped.' And it's true. Tony knew David Kelly was a loyal public servant driven to despair because of all the furore, caught up in something he could never have imagined.

At Tsinghua University in Beijing a group of students were throwing everything they could think of at him. As we were about to leave, one last voice rang out. 'Sing us a song!' From a Western perspective, this sounds like a very strange request, given the seriousness of the issues he'd been dealing with till that moment, but I have come across it often in the East – the home of karaoke. They already knew that Shanghai, our next stop, was linked to Liverpool and so they asked for a Beatles song. Tony kept saying no, then finally said: 'Ask my wife. She can sing.' The atmosphere was so tense, I would have done anything to lift the mood. I gave him a look, as if to say, is this what you really want? 'Whatever you like,' he said. Then added, 'When I'm Sixty-four.' So that's what I sang.

The rest of that tour couldn't have been over fast enough as far as I was concerned. We had lunch in Shanghai and then set off for Hong Kong. Although only a six-day tour, Tony seemed to age ten years and the stress was written on his face, however much he tried to keep up appearances. It wasn't fair he said, to take it out on these people who had put so much time and effort into the visits.

Back in London, Alastair was going to pieces and Tony spent half the time on the phone trying to calm him down: physically and emotionally he was exhausted. At least when we got to Hong Kong, we had a day's downtime inked in. Or rather, that had been the idea. However, a hurricane was on its way. If we wanted to get out, we were told, then it had to be now. The rest of the visit was cancelled and, as I always do if the crew will let me, I was in the cockpit for take-off. The wind was already getting up when the plane in front of us suddenly stopped halfway through its take-off.

'If we don't get the PM out now, he'll be stuck here,' the pilot said. 'I'm going to try.' As our speed increased, suddenly the brand new automatic warning system kicked in: there was a buzzing and lights flashed ABORT, ABORT, ABORT, and the plane swerved. The pilot looked bemused. 'That's the first time that's ever happened,' he said. 'I'm going to try again.' Even I was scared but this time we soared steeply into the air, over the end of the runway above a churning China Sea, banked, then headed for home.

As a postscript to David Kelly's tragic death, his widow and grown-up children came to visit us at Chequers. We wanted to say personally how very sorry we were about what had happened. It was clear to me that what had made Mrs Kelly's life even more intolerable was the behaviour of the press after he had killed himself, to the point of taking pictures through their front windows, utterly failing to respect their privacy at all.

Whatever else is going on, Balmoral is a fixed point in the prime ministerial calendar. Built by Queen Victoria in the valley of the River Dee, it's where the Queen and Prince Philip spend the summer and is probably the nearest thing they have to a private home. Guidelines on what to expect had been given to us that first year, in 1997, but Diana's death meant that we only went for lunch rather than the full weekend. Over the following nine years, however, the pattern remained constant. After flying up from Northolt to Aberdeen on the Saturday morning, we'd have lunch at the lodge with the Queen's private secretary who, from 1998, was Robin Janvrin. He and his

French wife were roughly the same generation as us, and had children of a similar age, so that was all very easy.

Balmoral itself felt almost like a film set the first time I went there. Everywhere you looked there were stags' heads and tartan and, being in the Highlands of Scotland, it was always cold – even in the first week of September. We usually stayed in what was known as the Prime Minister's suite, which was heated by a two-bar electric fire, not that dissimilar to one my grandma had in Ferndale Road. We had two rooms, one with a double bed, the other with a single. The big bed came complete with feather pillows which, unfortunately, I am allergic to, though later these were kindly changed. Beside the bed were two bells, marked 'maid' and 'valet'. The maid who was allocated to me that first year was very young, and kept curtsying and insisted on 'my lady'-ing me. 'Please don't call me my lady,' I implored, but this only flustered her more.

The atmosphere the first year we went was noticeably tenser than it was in subsequent years, understandably, as 1998 marked the first anniversary of Diana's death and William and Harry were both visiting their grandmother. Other members of the family were also in evidence. Prince Edward had just got engaged to Sophie Rhys-Jones, I remember, so they were there, as were Princess Anne and Princess Margaret, while the Queen Mother was a fixture until she died. I got the distinct impression that the oldest royal thought I didn't know the first thing about protocol. And she was right. The Queen herself was very approachable. She has never been anything other than gracious and charming and I admire her enormously. From what I saw she wasn't half as stuffy as some of her courtiers.

The visit always started with tea, a proper sit-down affair, with the Queen at the head of a large table in charge of an urn bubbling with water. She always made it herself, from putting the leaves into the pot to the pouring. To eat there would be cucumber sandwiches, bread, Balmoral honey and Duchy preserves and finally Dundee cake. It was all delicately done, and that first time I watched to see what other people did before daring to lift a finger, let alone a tea cup.

At six o'clock the Queen had her audience with her Prime Minister so I would go back to our room to get ready for the evening's barbecue, and Tony would join me later. Then came the moment of horror on that first visit when I discovered that my suitcase had been unpacked and everything put away in drawers or hung up. We were both puzzled by what turned out to be the traditional country-house practice of laying out the husband's belongings in the single room. Was he supposed to sleep there? we wondered. Or was he allowed to come and visit me in my double bed?

Bath done, suitably attired, we went downstairs. Saturday afternoons might change – the Highland Games at Braemar, for example, might be on the itinerary, depending on the date – but Saturday evening was always a barbecue. In the event of bad weather, it would have been switched to a formal black-tie dinner – and we always brought the necessary clothes – but, over nine years, it never happened. As it was, trousers and jumpers were *de rigueur*, so press reports about the Queen being shocked at my wearing trousers are pure invention. On that first visit when Tony and I arrived downstairs, it struck me that we had been invited into what was really a very private home. The Queen presumably didn't mind at all – and certainly must have been used to it – but I couldn't help feeling I was somehow encroaching. Yet everything looked very normal. The Queen was playing cards with the boys, and Prince Edward was tackling a crossword. Family life was just going on, and round the edges were us, the guests; not only Tony and me, but other people too.

At one point that first year Princess Anne came over and said something which included 'Mrs Blair'.

'Oh. Please call me Cherie,' I said.

'I'd rather not,' she replied. 'It's not the way I've been brought up.'

'What a shame,' I said.

My relationship with the Queen's only daughter went rapidly downhill and never recovered.

I never really got the hang of the protocol business in terms of what you called people and how you greeted them. Diana I called Diana. Charles I called Charles, and in fact would always kiss him, though I'm not convinced he really liked it. The Queen, however, was always Ma'am.

I would watch other people go through the rigmarole. That first weekend, Sophie Rhys-Jones was still clearly finding her feet with the protocol. Charles came in, she'd bob; Princess Anne came in, she'd bob. I decided I'd limit my bobbing to the Queen and the Queen Mother and leave it at that.

The highlight of the visit was undoubtedly the barbecue, though it was not remotely what I'd expected. The barbecue itself was an amazing design and I was so impressed that I asked where it came from. The answer was unexpected to say the least: Prince Philip had designed it himself, and in fact he very kindly gave us one.

The arrangements never changed. The Queen drove Tony and me across the moor and we'd arrive at about eight. Being so far north, it was still reasonably light, even in September. Prince Philip and his equerry would have gone ahead, and by the time we arrived at the little house where it was held, the grouse stuffed with haggis were already on the go. Not traditional barbecue fare, perhaps, but something I can highly recommend. Over the years it featured regularly on the menu, as did venison sausages. Plates, cutlery and salads in plastic containers arrived in a massive hamper on wheels, which was towed behind the Range Rover. Everyone had their job. That year Prince Edward was in charge of the first course and did a thing with prawns. The Queen laid the table, which was set up in the kitchen near a big wood-burning stove, and I helped her. There was no electricity, and as the light faded candles took over. There were no staff around at all; no one except the Queen's equerry. This is an officer allocated from one of the services, who spends a year or so in the post, fulfilling a role somewhere between private secretary, companion and looker-after, whereas the lady-in-waiting is more of an equal, a friend.

One unexpected pleasure was meeting Lady Susan Hussey again, the lady-in-waiting who had been so nice to me that first morning at Buckingham Palace in May 1997. When the Queen appointed her, she was only eighteen, daughter of the Earl of Waldegrave. This was in the late fifties, and up until then the Queen's ladies-in-waiting had been chosen for her. In 1959 Lady Susan married 'Duke' Hussey, but as he had been seriously injured at Anzio during the war – the Germans even repatriated him – the general consensus was that they could not have children. Almost immediately, however, she fell pregnant and the Queen said, 'Well, there's no accounting for God.' There was no question that this would prevent her from carrying on, and so Lady Susan has been a lady-in-waiting ever since.

Whatever members of staff are along, from the garden girls to the 'tecs and comms people, their role is to be invisible. Their instructions are, If you see the Queen, ignore her. This is her holiday and the last thing she wants is to be having to say hello to everybody. Only the principal private secretaries exist in this context. They would take it in turns to come and always stayed with Robin Janvrin and his wife, in the smaller lodge – in fact, where the Queen and the Prince stay when they don't want to open the big house – and then joined the assembled throng at the barbecue. I always looked forward to it: the drive, the meal, the informality. As the evening wore on, the light faded slowly and we'd all help clear up before driving back. It is just fabulous, wonderful landscape, completely empty, and the air is so clean.

Following the Queen Mother's death in the spring, that September I asked the Queen whether she would mind if we had a picture of Leo with her, and so we did. She is very good with small children and she liked Leo and Leo loved the dogs. I remember when he was about eighteen months old, the Queen was showing him how to throw a biscuit to one of the corgis. She told him that now they all had to have one, so he took a handful and flung them across the room and the corgis went wild.

'Oh,' she said. 'That wasn't quite what I meant.' But she wasn't remotely cross at the ensuing mayhem. By the time he was two and a half, he had learnt the words of 'God Save the Queen', and at the end of our stay he sang it to her on his own. Her Majesty was very gracious and congratulated him. All praise to Jackie who had taken a lot of trouble over it. Leo was really the person who broke the ice at Balmoral, and once he came along the whole atmosphere completely changed.

That first visit I was on edge the whole time, thinking, Oh my God, what *faux pas* am I going to make next? But over the years we had got used to one another. She was clearly very fond of Tony, and the last time we went I was really sad to think we would never go there again.

While the Queen is very approachable, I can't say the same about Princess Margaret, whom I met several times at Balmoral. One evening I was at the Royal Opera House for some gala performance and was talking to her about what we'd seen, when Chris Smith came over.

'Have you met Chris Smith, our culture secretary, Ma'am?' I asked.

She peered at him.

'And this is his partner,' I continued.

'Partner for what?'

I took a breath. 'Sex, Ma'am.'

She stalked off. She knew exactly what kind of partner I meant. She was just trying to catch me out.

Her niece Princess Anne and I similarly never found an accord. The reason, I think, was less our slightly awkward meeting when we were first introduced at Balmoral than her perception that it was me who was egging Tony on with the ban on fox-hunting, Anne having very strong feelings about the matter. She made it very clear to me when Tony and I attended a state banquet at Windsor Castle while the Bill was going through Parliament. Prince Charles and Prince Andrew, on the other hand, who also had strong views on the subject, were extremely civilised about it.

As for me and fox-hunting, animals have never really been a passion of mine, so what happens to the ruddy fox completely passes me by. It's people I'm interested in.

It was Lady Serena Rothschild who told me that I had this anti-hunting reputation. She was very pro-hunting herself, to the extent that she placed a fake fox's tail on my seat as a joke at a dinner party. I told her, on the contrary, that I had no strong views one way or the other. That circle, it seemed, genuinely thought it was me putting Tony up to it. I put her straight. 'My feeling is that there are far more important things to worry about,' I said.

Nevertheless that message did not get through to the pro-fox-hunting lobby, and in September 2004, my fiftieth birthday party at Chequers was stormed by a group of hunt supporters. The party had been due to start at seven thirty, but with protesters blocking the gates only Charlie and Marianna and Freddie Reynold somehow managed to beat the blockade. It looked as if we were in for a quiet evening.

Tony was in pessimistic mood. 'I warned you, Cherie. I told you we shouldn't have a party in our position.' We certainly hadn't had one the previous year for his fiftieth because of the Iraq war.

Eventually, after inviting the leader of the protesters in, Tony charmed her into seeing reason. They had made their point, he said, so perhaps now they could unblock the road. From then on his mood lightened considerably. Gradually the friends who had been diverted by the police to the Tesco car park in Princes Risborough started drifting in, but it was nine o'clock before the party got going. For many of our guests it was a strange experience: in their youth they were more likely to have been on a picket line than actually being picketed. In the end everyone agreed that this was one birthday party they would never forget, with Tony himself up with the band and having a brilliant time, letting his hair down for what seemed like the first time in years.

CHAPTER 30

Going the Distance

In September 2003, no sooner were we back from Balmoral than Tony was off again: this time to Berlin for talks with Jacques Chirac and Gerhard Schroeder on the rebuilding of Iraq. It was no wonder he always seemed so tired: no world leader before him had undertaken so much travelling. Next in the round of talks were the Aznars. At least they were coming to us. That evening over dinner the conversation again came round to his decision to stand down at the end of his second term in 2004.

A few weeks later, we were at Chequers as usual for the weekend. Tony had been down at the bothy – the police guardhouse where they had a small gym – exercising on the running machine, and he came back looking distinctly grey. He had a pain in his chest, he said. He didn't understand it: no matter how much effort he put in, he was short of breath and didn't seem to be getting any fitter. I said I was going to call the doctor. He told me not to be ridiculous, but I did anyway.

Dr Shaikh was the resident GP at the local RAF air base and he expressed amazement that the Prime Minister didn't have his own doctor to hand. I told him that he had probably been offered one but, knowing my husband, had just said no. Dr Shaikh arranged for him to go immediately to Stoke Mandeville hospital. I went with him, and promised I'd keep in touch with the garden girl who is supposed never to leave his side. At Stoke Mandeville they erred on the side of caution, saying they'd prefer to send him to London. The garden girl arrived at Hammersmith hospital shortly after we did and sat outside the consulting room throughout, with the prime ministerial red box. Tony's condition, the consultant explained, was an irregular heartbeat and this was usually cured by an electric shock. The procedure would take seconds, so we didn't need to involve John Prescott whose job, as Tony's deputy, was to take charge when Tony couldn't. Following the treatment, Tony immediately felt a lot better but thereafter made no effort to take the daily aspirin he'd been told to swallow as a precaution. Not surprisingly, therefore, a year later the problem returned. Now it was decided that an operation was necessary. Again it was something quite simple, though he would need to have a general anaesthetic, albeit for a matter of minutes. This time John Prescott would have to be involved.

The 2004 Labour Party Conference was just coming up, and Tony was determined to wait until it was over. In my view, the stress of having to write that speech was unlikely to improve matters, and I told him I'd rather they did it straight away. Again, he took no notice. I took matters into my own hands and fixed for him to go into hospital on the Friday after conference ended, which is usually a very quiet day.

In 1997, at his first Labour Party Conference as Prime Minister, Tony both promised and warned that his tenure would be a time of 'high ideals and hard choices'. Never was that truer than in Iraq. There were times when I faltered, when I was worried about the direction that things were taking in Iraq, and would have to remind myself that I did not have the overall picture that Tony did. But because I believed in his judgement I was prepared to put aside the doubts; I knew him and knew he would never do the wrong thing. He had enormous strength of conviction, a quality I had recognised very early on, and my job, as his wife, was to support him.

Although in 2004 conference voted 4 to 1 against pulling our troops out of Iraq, over the previous year the pressure on Tony had became increasingly intense. There was Iraq and there was Gordon. Gordon wanted to become Prime Minister so much, he failed to understand that, had he been prepared to implement Tony's programmes on internal reform – academy schools, foundation hospitals and pensions – Tony would have stood down, there is no question. Instead of which Tony felt he had no option but to stay on and fight for the things he believed in.

As the tension began to mount inside Number 10, Tony once again began to consider standing down and I felt helpless to do anything. Of course, such a close relationship in the hot-house atmosphere of politics was always going to be difficult. Gordon wanted to be leader and he had a perfect right to want to be. Yet my sympathies inevitably lay with Tony and I wanted him to go on his own terms. It was the effect that the constant attrition had on my husband, the man I loved, that coloured my feelings. I accept that I am not objective on this – and, frankly, it would be odd if I were. Nor am I blind to the many qualities Gordon has. But I was intensely loyal to Tony and resented any pressure being put on him.

This time at least there was a positive focus: the job of President of the European Commission needed to be filled by June. Tony had always been fired by the idea of Europe, and we started to talk about whether he should put his hat in the ring; I even went so far as to look up schooling possibilities for Leo on the Internet. In the end he decided to throw his weight behind the candidacy of José Manuel Barroso, the Prime Minister of Portugal, whom he admired, and who shared Tony's views on the future of Europe and was an ally of the US.

There had been a point, around the time of the debate on Iraq in March 2003, when Tony felt he might actually get pushed out. With the Tories onside he never believed the vote would go against him, but had there been a major Labour revolt, he believed he'd have had to resign. The idea of us being cast out in the wilderness with nowhere to live was terrifying to me, and I knew that, somehow or another, we had to buy a house in London, and this time Tony agreed.

My recent history with property-buying being so dire, Tony decided to ask our friend Martha Greene to help.

I first met Martha in 2001, through Carole, at the gym. Then, in 2002, she developed breast cancer and we became closer as a result. Martha is American, one of those who come to London when they're young and never leave. When I first met her she was running a restaurant called Villandry, which she had turned around. She had catered for our twenty-first wedding anniversary and she would also bring in supper for Tony when I wasn't there, and became a family friend. Tony and I put great trust in her ability with all things culinary and financial.

Where to start looking proved a bit of a conundrum. Tony had no wish to stay in Westminster, while I was determined that Leo wouldn't change schools. I also needed to be within hitting distance of chambers, and Tony wanted to be near the Heathrow Express. Connaught Square fulfilled all the criteria except one: price. Although it didn't have a garden, at least it looked out on one and by now we knew that, for security reasons, Tony would never be able to use it anyway.

For a middle-aged couple whose total capital couldn't even buy one flat in Bristol, let alone two, the purchase of a house of this size and price represented a major leap of faith. Yet we had to have something. If we had to move out suddenly from Number 10 we needed somewhere to go. I had to work, as did Tony. And three years on from 9/11 we were only too aware of the security implications of wherever we lived once Tony stepped down. The usual rules, drummed into me by my grandma, about cutting your coat according to your cloth, didn't apply. The answer was a mortgage the size of Mount Snowdon.

To raise this kind of money, Martha put together a business plan. In the long term Tony had 'prospects'. In the short term we still had to meet mortgage repayments. The rent we could obtain would not cover the whole mortgage. We also realised, again for security reasons, that at some point we would have to buy the mews house behind the original house. As Tony's income was fixed, somehow I would have to increase my earnings dramatically to cover the balance, hence the speaking engagements, which Martha arranged through her contacts in America.

As a barrister I am no stranger to making speeches and I particularly enjoyed speaking on women's rights. In America I would speak on these issues and other legal matters at conferences. Public speaking seemed an ideal way of doing something I felt passionate about while at the same time resolving a pressing financial situation.

While I still reject the idea that I had no right to do them, the speaking engagements proved disastrous from a PR point of view, particularly the series I did in Australia. I was just one 'item' on a road-show dinner, which included entertainment and an auction, and I was given a set fee, as were the four other performers on the

programme. The road show went to several cities and the idea was
to raise money for the Children's Cancer Institute of Australia, which
in the end it did. It was far from the disaster the British press made
out, however, and in fact the tour exceeded expectations. Altogether
the profit from the tour of Australia and New Zealand was
£350,000. This was the most money the charity had ever raised and
the whole tour was considered a huge success. It may be standard
practice in the charity world to be paid a fee for speaking, but it was
a painful lesson that 'standard practice' did not apply to me.

There was no doubt that in April 2004, with Gordon rattling the
keys above his head, Tony suffered a crisis of confidence as to
whether he was still an asset to the Labour Party. I remained determined that Tony was not going to resign, that he was going to fight
the next election and that he was going to win it, and in this I was
helped hugely by our closest friends in the Cabinet, especially Tessa
Jowell, Charlie Falconer, John Reid, Hilary Armstrong and David
Blunkett. Also the support of Patricia Hewitt, Alan Milburn and
Stephen Byers helped to persuade Tony that he had to stay on. It
wasn't just for the sake of his reputation, but for the sake of the New
Labour agenda – most importantly for the public services. As before,
when he had failed to get a seat, or when he was uncertain about
whether he would win the leadership, I reminded him that he needed
to 'pick himself up, dust himself off and start all over again'. Among
many others, I was convinced that if Tony failed to stand for a third
term, it would be seen as a response to the negative criticism of the
war. It would be read by history as a tacit admission of failure. I
worried that he was responding to a *Guardian*-type intelligentsia
who would never forgive him for Iraq even if he were to flagellate
himself in front of them, but who would just say, 'I told you so. We
should never have trusted him.' I always felt strongly that he should
not apologise for something he believed to be right. He could regret
the lives lost in Iraq but he should not apologise for taking the right
decision for the country.

By the time of the Party conference, Tony had decided on his strategy. In an interview with Andrew Marr, the BBC's political editor, on
the last night of the conference, he said that if he were elected he
would serve a full third term but would not serve a fourth. He also
explained that he had a heart flutter and that he would be having

surgery the next day. At the same time, Downing Street announced that we had bought a house in Connaught Square.

That Friday evening, after conference ended we made our way back to Hammersmith Hospital in White City. I stayed beside him until he grew woozy, then returned to his room and went down on my knees with my rosary and didn't stop praying until the garden girl came up to tell me that all was well.

When Matrix was set up, I'd been hoping that my former mentor Michael Beloff would join us. In the end he didn't, fearing we would be too left-wing. Michael and I remained friends, however, and sometime in 2002 he rang me with a proposition. How would I like to be involved in the London Olympic bid? I knew of his interest in athletics – it was one of the things we used to talk about back in the days of Gray's Inn Square. He had been a bit of an athlete in his youth and over the years had acted as a judge during the Olympics – a panel of international lawyers who act as a tribunal when there are queries and challenges to decisions. He had been talking to the sports editor of the *Daily Telegraph*, he said, who was involved with the British Olympic Committee. There was a theory going round that the International Olympic Committee had been won over by the charms of the Greek businesswoman who had fronted the Athens bid, the Athens Olympics then being imminent. Given my interest in athletics, perhaps I could think about it?

There were a few reasons I couldn't accept, I told him. First, given my position, it would make it too much of a government thing. Then, I would have had to give up my career, and as this was a paid job, the idea that I was taking government money would be manna from heaven for the tabloids. In short it was a total no-no, and Barbara Cassani was eventually appointed, replaced a year later by Seb Coe, who did a brilliant job. Their enthusiasm was infectious, however, and I volunteered my services wherever they thought I could be of most use, and I duly became an ambassador, along with Steve Redgrave and David Beckham among others.

Raising support for an individual country's bid among members of the International Olympic Committee – the people who make the ultimate decision – is complicated by a history of corruption, when 'sweeteners' of varying kinds and value would be used by the competing countries to 'buy' individual IOC members' votes. Ultimately what the IOC wants is a successful games. It needs to know the country itself is behind the bid. It needs to know that the infrastructure is there. It needs to know that the financial implications have been thought through, that hosting the games won't bankrupt anyone. Finally it needs to know that athletes from around the world will be looked after and welcomed. My job was to speak informally about all those issues to those who, either directly or indirectly, would have a say in the outcome. In short, I was on the hunt for votes.

Before each trip I made over the next two years, I would contact the British Olympic Committee, who always came up with someone whose ear was worth bending. Even during that brief visit to Korea, for example, I managed to meet the IOC delegate. The International Olympic Committee is a mixed bunch: athletes certainly, but far wider-ranging than that. Over the next two years my knowledge of field events increased dramatically: the votes of pole-vaulters and weight-lifters were as valuable as those of hurdlers and sprinters. I remember Sue trying desperately to contact the Mongolian delegate. It proved a successful, if unusual, encounter. He brought his granddaughter with him to interpret. Somehow she had heard of my interest in women's issues, so that was our subject of discussion.

It was surprisingly hard work, but to have a grandstand seat at the Athens Olympics in 2004 was sheer joy. Tony and I went to the opening ceremony, and I returned a week or so later with Jackie, who shared my enthusiasm for athletics, leaving Tony at the Strozzis' with Leo, Kathryn and her friend Bella. Jackie and I were there when Steve Redgrave won his fifth gold medal and Matthew Pinsent won his third. On that occasion we were in the VIP stand, sitting behind the Australian broadcasting people. I could see the rowers in the distance, but at the same time could follow it in close-up on their screen, where the statistics were also visible. The atmosphere was fantastic and at the end I went down to congratulate them. I knew them both, so how could I resist those open arms? Even if they were rather warm and sweaty, they are such nice people – not to mention those fantastic bodies.

Although the Paralympic Committee has only one vote, it exerts more influence than this would suggest, and it did us no harm that the Paralympic movement was started by the British at the 1948 London Olympics in response to the numbers of disabled servicemen who otherwise could not compete. In many ways the courage and spirit in the Paralympic movement is even more astonishing than that of the Olympics itself, and in September I returned to Athens for the Paralympics, and later built on this when I visited the Chinese Paralympic Association while on a trip to Beijing with Tony. It was headed by the son of the former leader, Deng Xiaoping. When Deng fell out of favour, his son was thrown from the top of a building by a revolutionary guard and broke his back. He has been a paraplegic ever since. He is a very powerful, intelligent man, and speaking to him was humbling.

The 1948 London Games proved important in another way, I believe. In Athens I talked to an Irish doctor who, working in London immediately after the war, found himself appointed as doctor to the small Irish team and, now in his eighties, is still involved. London's willingness to host the games at a time of such economic stringency was extraordinary, he said. Had this not happened, he felt the Games might never have re-emerged. Many older members, he thought, would know the circumstances but he also thought it would be worth reminding them, and indeed I did.

Without support from the government the London bid could never have got to the starting line, let alone the finishing post. And although my husband is not as keen on athletics as I am, he had been very pro from the beginning, reflecting not only on what it would mean to London and Londoners, but the impact it would have on young people, on sport in general and the country's self-belief. And then there was what is known as the 'legacy', not only for London's East End but for the country as a whole. For example, the proposals included the relocation of Olympic-sized training pools to other parts of the country. As a showcase for the country it's hard to imagine anything more globally visible.

For some years Silvio Berlusconi, the Italian Prime Minister, had been inviting us to stay as his personal guests, but we'd always declined. As Italy were key players in the IOC Tony felt that if he played his cards right there was a good chance we could get their three votes for London, so he had agreed to go on an overnight visit to Berlusconi's summer villa in Sardinia. Downing Street was naturally horrified, fearing bad publicity, but Tony was insistent. Berlusconi had stood with us over Iraq, one of the 'coalition of the willing', and if we could get the Italian IOC votes, then he would do it, he said, and 'Bugger the opprobrium'.

Although we were invited as a family, in the end only Tony and I went. We were to be in and out in less than twenty-four hours. Kathryn and Leo were not happy. As far as they were concerned, our holiday had already been disrupted by our disappearing to Athens, and now Mum and Dad were disappearing yet again.

Silvio Berlusconi never does anything by halves, and the yacht that awaited us in the harbour at Olbia put the Royal Yacht in the shade. And there was Silvio waiting for us. Suddenly I felt Tony tense beside me, and no wonder: our host was wearing what looked like a pirate outfit, complete with multi-coloured bandanna around his head.

'Oh my God,' he muttered, as we made our way across the gangplank. 'The office is going to have a fit.'

He was right. It had 'foolish photograph' potential written all over it.

'Whatever happens,' I said, 'I'll make sure he stands next to me.' I sighed. Not only did I have to give up time with my children, I had to make myself look ridiculous. No matter. Funny hats are a speciality of mine. 'At least,' I said, 'the boat isn't exactly public, and nobody knows you're coming.'

Famous last words. 'Now I am going to show you something of the island,' Silvio announced as we swooshed out of the harbour. This wasn't to be a beaches-and-headlands cruise, we realised, as the yacht raced into an enclosed harbour thick with small craft.

'Please excuse me for a moment,' our host said. 'I must just go below and change.'

Tony breathed a sigh of relief. Common sense had prevailed. But when Silvio re-emerged, minutes later, the only difference was the bandanna, which was now white to match the rest of his outfit. The quay was crammed. No way was this going to remain a private visit. There was no possibility that Tony could entirely escape the cameras, but I did as promised and a casual observer would have assumed I was besotted with our Italian host, as I never left his side.

Meanwhile the detectives were having kittens. Usually they send out an advance party to check out the security, but this excursion hadn't featured on the itinerary. The port was extremely well-to-do. Rather than ships' chandlers, it had luxury boutiques, into one of which we were propelled. Silvio wanted to buy me some jewellery, he said.

'It's very kind,' I protested, 'but I can't accept. It's not allowed. I won't be able to keep it.'

'What you mean you can't keep it! This is not from my government, it is from me. A personal gift of friendship, Cherie.'

'I'm really sorry, Silvio, but I can't.'

'Nonsense. Here. What about this?' He held up a really expensive piece of jewellery. I realised it would have been insulting to keep saying no, so I desperately started looking for something cheap while trying to explain that if he gave me anything over £140 I wouldn't be able to keep it anyway. It would go straight into the Downing Street vault.

'Well, this is lovely,' I said, pointing at an insubstantial looking piece of gold wire-work.

'No, no, no,' Berlusconi protested. 'This one is so much nicer. Trust Silvio.'

'Honestly, this is much more me.'

He clearly thought I was a mad woman.

Villa Certosa is as extraordinary as its larger-than-life owner. On our initial tour, we were serenaded by his personal guitarist-troubadour, and every so often Berlusconi would break into song – many of which it turned out he had written. Dinner too came with musical accompaniment, the grand piano being on a raft moored in the middle of a vast lagoon. I had never met Silvio's wife Veronica Lario before. She generally kept a low profile but Villa Certosa was very much her husband's project, she said. Their house in Milan was much more her domain.

After the meal we had limoncello from his own lemon groves, before once again music appeared on the menu. 'Do you play, Tony? Do you sing?'

'No. But Cherie does.'

Thanks, I thought.

Our host's face lit up. The pianist would accompany me, he said. Fortunately my expression was hidden in the dark. I opted for 'Summertime'. After a few bars he joined in. In fact he has a very good voice of the 'O Sole Mio' variety. Then Tony and I exchanged glances. We were ready for bed. It was not to be.

'But what about the concert?' he exclaimed. The evening's event was apparently the inauguration of a 400-seater auditorium carved out of the cliff. An orchestra had been flown in especially from the mainland, he said. Not to mention the soprano and the tenor. There was nothing to be done. Among the audience I saw the 'tecs, garden girls and comms people. I was glad I couldn't see their faces when Silvio demanded that I do a repeat performance of 'Summertime'.

The 'just a few fireworks' turned out to be one of the most magnificent displays I have ever seen, lasting at least twenty minutes and ending with 'VIVA TONY' emblazoned across the sky. So much for discretion. Tony was mortified.

The next morning was a bit lower-key. For me, a whole series of thalassotherapy pools, while Tony played football with Berlusconi and the detectives. The final hurdle was the masseur. My husband has a horror of male masseurs, but this was the masseur for AC Milan. 'Look, Tony,' I said. 'He does footballers. Believe me, he's not after your body.' Later he was forced to admit that it was a really great massage.

Was it worth it? As experiences go, it falls into the category of ultra-surreal. As for the IOC votes, Berlusconi promised nothing, and of course the IOC members are independent, but he said he would do what he could. We will never know for sure, of course, but for all his eccentricities, Silvio Berlusconi is a man who does what he says he will.

By 19 November 2004, the nine cities competing for the 2012 Olympic Games had been reduced to five and the following February the IOC evaluation team came to London. I was learning that every little helped: leading the delegation was the first Muslim woman ever to win a gold medal, and I was able to talk to her about how sport can improve the position of women. Another was a South African who had been involved in the anti-apartheid movement and we had no doubt that he was on our side. As part of our presentation, I talked them through our new legislation brought in to protect the Olympic five-ring symbol, which in terms of raising money for the games is a very valuable trademark. Some time earlier, I'd been asked by the 2012 Committee to join their legal team and was glad to be able to use my legal expertise in helping to make our case.

Horse Guards Parade being the proposed site for beach volleyball, where better to view it than from the balcony where the royal family watch the Queen Trooping the Colour every June? As it was just down the road from Downing Street, I was deputed to escort the delegation. The room behind the balcony includes Wellington's uniform and desk, and this was the first time I had ever been in there.

That night the Queen hosted a banquet for the evaluation committee at Buckingham Palace. The Palace had put on the most fantastic display related to the royal family's involvement over the years, including Princess Anne's riding gear – she was a member of the British Equestrian team in the 1976 Olympics in Montreal. It is hard to believe that such a wonderful evening could have been matched anywhere in the world. It ended as royally as it had begun, with the Queen's pipers piping them off.

'Come on, Mrs Blair. Let's go on to the balcony,' she said. So we did.

Finally, as the last notes faded away, she turned to me. 'I think that went very well, don't you?'

The 2005 election, held on 7 May, was a vindication of my belief that, whatever the press might say, the British public still had faith in Tony. A reduced majority perhaps – but hardly surprising after eight years in office – and Labour achieved a third successive term for the first time in its history. As for the Conservatives, although they had increased their presence in the House, their percentage of the poll was below 35 per cent for the third time.

On this occasion I made sure that I had no commitments in court and was able to take in fifty marginals, campaigning largely on my own as the Party wanted Tony and Gordon to be the story. It was a poignant few weeks for me as it would be the last time I would be campaigning for the Labour Party in the role of Prime Minister's wife.

A month after the election the London Olympic bid was agreed to be well in the running; behind the favourite – Paris – certainly, but higher than anyone could have anticipated. This was in large measure thanks to Seb Coe's energy and determination. Decision day would be 6 July in Singapore. As far as Tony and I were concerned, the timing was as bad as it could be. Only two days later Britain was hosting the G8 in Edinburgh, 7,000 miles away. I was hosting the spouse programme. The G8 leaders were due to assemble at Gleneagles on 6 July. The big question in the run-up to Singapore was, should Tony go? Some voices in Downing Street were saying no: Just before the G8, what is the point? Although by now Tony was used to long-haul travel, the constant crossing of time zones, grabbing sleep when you can, grabbing food when you can rather than when you need it, does nobody any good. The risk was that he would end up being tired and unfocused both in Singapore and in Scotland. The 2005 Gleneagles G8 was particularly important for Tony as, in addition to the usual heads of state involved, he had invited the leaders of China, India, Brazil, South Africa and Mexico – known as G8+5, as well as representatives from Africa and Asia. It was the first time, too, that the focus would be less on the issues of the day than on the future, namely Africa and climate change. We also knew that, as we needed to be back in Gleneagles before the first guests arrived, we wouldn't be able to stay in Singapore for the final vote. But then, neither would President Chirac, who we knew would be representing the Paris bid. Tessa Jowell, Minister for Sport and Culture at the time and passionately committed to the Olympics, was keen however.

I remember going through the pros and cons with Tony way into the night. I don't know what it was that decided him – perhaps the gut feeling that his presence could tip the balance, that we'd come so far it was really important to give it a final push. Or perhaps the sense that, if he didn't go and we lost it, he would always feel he could have made the difference. It was a bit like athletics itself. There is no point in competing if you don't want to win, even though you know you may not – and in this case, the odds were definitely against us. The risk of failure, however, has never led Tony to back down. He would rather stick his neck out and risk success, which ultimately is what makes him a great leader.

The roll-call of support in Singapore covered a spectrum unimaginable in any other world: from Princess Anne via Ken Livingstone to David Beckham, looking wonderful as only he can in an extraordinary white and silver track suit. As we approached the final furlong, we knew we were running neck and neck with Paris and, as this was the third time Paris had been in the last six, there was a real sense that its time had come.

The voting was done by a process of elimination. Round by round, the lowest-scoring country was eliminated. The dark horse was Madrid, who we knew would be heavily supported by Spanish-speaking South American countries, but should it go out before us, the feeling was that those South American votes would come to us rather than Paris.

Tony's determination not to leave a stone unturned – or in this instance, a committee member unspoken to – was extraordinary. Of about 110 IOC delegates, he was scheduled to meet forty. Sitting in adjacent suites, we divided them up between us, one every twenty minutes, while the London bid people kept tally and Ken dashed in and out. With my husband turning on the charm and determination as only he can, I was very happy dealing with the smaller fry – their votes were worth no less.

Over those two days of intense activity, I was constantly bumping into IOC members I had already spoken to over the preceding two years. Until now Tony had very little sense of what I had been doing behind the scenes: now he did.

People really wanted to meet Tony and were genuinely astonished that he was so approachable – very different from Jacques Chirac, whom I watched sweeping presidentially through the hall, not staying to mingle, there just to be seen, as if to say he was doing them a favour simply by turning up. Tony made people feel they were doing him a favour by letting him come along. There was a definite sense of the contrasting styles making a real difference. Chirac's final blunder may have been Paris's undoing: on remarking that British cuisine was second only in ghastliness to Finnish cuisine, he waved goodbye to Finland's two votes.

We flew direct from Singapore into Glasgow airport, arriving at Gleneagles at eight in the morning, when Tony went straight into a meeting.

The G8s move from country to country. In 2005 we had now come full circle and the Gleneagles G8 would be our second. The first, in 1998, was in Birmingham and had been a baptism of fire for me in terms of hosting the spouse programme. By then I'd had two examples to consider. First Hillary Clinton's G7 in Denver where, in addition to our ride in the train, the wives had been to a craft fair and had a group discussion. From that I knew we were all intelligent, interested and – on the whole – educated women. I was determined that when it was my turn, I would treat the ladies as though they had a brain rather than just a husband.

Three months later, Britain had hosted the annual Commonwealth Heads of Government meeting in Edinburgh. Again I was not impressed. Here were fifty women from fifty-two Commonwealth countries, many of whom operated like First Ladies. In Africa, in particular, the role is more like that of a queen: she can have real power, initiating and funding really important work, particularly in relation to women and children and disability. To discover that the Foreign Office only considered us worth a visit to a tartan factory, a cookery demonstration and a fashion show was, frankly, patronising.

For my first G8 I decided to give my wives a rather more serious programme. After dinner, a group from the Royal Shakespeare Company gave us 'Shakespeare's Women', which went down very well. Obviously Hillary Clinton and Aline Chrétien (Canada) had no problems. Nor indeed did Flavia Prodi. Like her husband, the Prime Minister of Italy, she was a university professor and her English was excellent, whereas Mrs Hashimoto and Mrs Yeltsin needed interpreters. Even so, I felt, better to aim high than be patronising.

The next day I had been given permission to use the royal train, and took everyone to Chequers for lunch. On the basis of sticking with what I knew, I invited Rosalind Higgins, then a professor at the LSE – later a judge at the International Court of Justice – to talk to us about international human rights. I don't believe I am the only wife of a leader whose husband expects her to be able to discuss things with him. In 2005, eight years on, my general attitude remained the same. We might be in Scotland but we'd be looking at the whole world.

After two days of non-stop campaigning, followed by a twelve-hour flight, I was shattered and jet-lagged. Sleep, however, seemed impossible: the vote from Singapore could come in at any time, so I decided to have a massage to calm down. Lying there, oiled up and generally not fit to be seen, I was finally drifting off to sleep when there was a knock at the door . . .

It was Gary.

'Mrs B? Just thought you'd like to know, we're in the last two—'

I lay there, the guy pummelling away, every muscle tensed. Finally another knock.

'Mrs B? I'm sorry to have to tell you, but . . . we've won!'

If I'd been stung by a swarm of bees, I could not have leapt higher. Pulling on my tracksuit, I hopped to the door and I was out before you could say Steve Ovett, running down the corridor, Gary laughing behind me, through the public areas to our suite and my wonderful husband.

We were both nearly delirious.

'It was all down to you,' I said when we finally stopped laughing. And it was true. However many representatives I was nice to, it was Tony who made the difference.

A moment of panic flitted across Tony's face.

'Oh my God,' he said. 'What am I going to say to Chirac?'

The relationship with Chirac was, in any event, strained because of Iraq. 'Whatever else we do,' he said wagging his finger and giggling, 'there must be no crowing!'

That night, the Queen was hosting the dinner. Towards the end of the first course, my Cliff-Elvis-loving friend Mr Koizumi leant across the table, waving his fork.

'What do think, Jacques?' he piped up, loud enough for everyone to hear, including the Queen. 'Very good food here!' At which he began laughing. I looked round at the various faces. Chirac's was a study in diplomacy. The Queen's in total mystification.

'I didn't say it,' Chirac explained to Her Majesty.

'Say what?' she countered.

Koizumi was in relentlessly high spirits throughout the meal, finally getting everyone to sing 'Happy Birthday' to George Bush, whose birthday it was.

As the evening was winding down, the Queen and Prince Philip caught my eye. 'Marvellous news, Mrs Blair,' she said quietly, giving Chirac a covert look.

'Of course,' said the Prince, 'I'm so old, I won't be here then.'

'Oh, sir, please don't say that. I certainly hope you will.' And I did. I was actually quite fond of the old boy.

'Well, one needs to be realistic,' added the Queen. 'It'll be for Charles and the boys, not for us.'

How terrible, I suddenly thought. How can we possibly have the Olympics without the Queen? She smiled, and moved away. Strange how things turn out. I found the idea that the Queen might not be there quite upsetting.

The spouses' programme was surprisingly royal, I realised. The following morning we were going to Glamis Castle, where the Queen Mother was born and brought up. In line with the G8's theme of Africa and climate change, I had arranged that trees be planted in the name of each of the ladies, mirroring a plan in Burkina Faso that encouraged the planting of income-producing trees.

The following morning, I was chatting to André as he was trying to restore some order to my hair, when his mobile rang. He listened, said nothing, then crossed to the TV and turned it on. It was his boyfriend, he told me, saying he was OK, but there had been some kind of explosion in London. I later found out he worked at Aldgate East – the scene of the first bomb. Like any other mother, my first thought was for the safety of my own children. I called Jackie, but couldn't get through on her mobile. The Downing Street phones were working however: Leo and Kathryn were fine. The detectives had already picked them up from school and they were on their way home. Next I got hold of Nick, who was in Oxford, and finally Euan in America. Although the two older boys weren't in any more danger than they had been a day or a week before, when something so terrifying strikes at the heart of all you hold dear, there's comfort to be found in just hearing the voices of your family. As the enormity of what had happened began to come through, I felt both angry and numb. These were streets I knew. The bomb on the Piccadilly Line was beneath Russell Square, where those first meetings about Matrix were held. The bus that was so callously targeted after the underground was closed was in Upper Woburn Place, where the old industrial tribunal building used to be.

The summit was to go ahead, it was decided. Otherwise the terrorists would be seen to have won. All the leaders immediately understood that Tony had to go down to London, leaving Jack Straw to chair the climate change session that morning.

My spouse programme went ahead, but the atmosphere was far from the one I had planned and expected. Among the guests I had invited that evening were Darcey Bussell, Anish Kapoor and Alexander McCall Smith, not only author of the popular The No.1 Ladies' Detective Agency series, but the emeritus professor of medical law and bio-ethics at Edinburgh University. We ended up discussing the finer points of moral philosophy.

One sad postscript and a victory for the terrorists. I had invited Chicken Shed, a theatre company that runs workshops for young people and children, including disabled children. For reasons of heightened security, I was told, Jo Gibbons had decided to cancel the performance and so they were not allowed to come in. I could hardly bear it. Although such terrible things had gone on that day, the idea that these special people had come all the way up to Scotland for nothing made me angry on their behalf.

That night I lay in a luxurious hotel, surrounded by every kind of security imaginable, and it was dreadful. I thought of all those hundreds, perhaps thousands, of people who tonight wouldn't sleep, because they had lost someone close to them. Someone they were never able to say goodbye to. To go from the euphoria of the previous day to this terrible tragedy was beyond comprehension.

CHAPTER 31

Benediction

When tragedy strikes, there's a profound need to make sense of it all. It wasn't long however before my 'what are we doing here?' turned into 'what am I doing here?' Increasingly I knew I needed to find my own voice.

One of the last conversations I'd had with Fiona in the summer of 2003 had made me acutely aware that something had to change. 'You have to go underground,' she said. 'Go back to being a mother and a barrister and nothing more. The press all hate you. They have all the cards and you will never win.' How could I do the things I wanted to if that was how she felt? But once my team changed, things gradually got better.

Decisions often emerge from negatives, and at least I knew now what I was not prepared to do. I was not prepared to spend the rest of my life worrying about what people thought about the way I dressed. It didn't matter in real terms, and it certainly didn't matter to me. What did matter to me, I increasingly realised, was helping other women find their voices. Women make up half the world's population and yet continue to be under-used at best, and at worst abused and defiled.

By the summer of 2005, Laura Bush and I had known each other for over four years and, although our politics were different, we were definitely friends – always delighted to see each other and catch up.

At the Gleneagles summit, Laura had proposed that I join her on a visit to Africa, immediately following the G8. She was going with her daughter Jenna to visit South Africa, where her other daughter, Barbara, had been working in an Aids clinic. They were then going on to a number of other countries before visiting Rwanda, and Laura asked me to join them. Having been involved with the International Criminal Court, I was interested to see what impact the Rwanda tribunal had made, and everyone – which is to say Tony and the Foreign Office – seemed keen that I should go, but then came the inevitable question: who was going to pay? Laura's offer of a lift on Airforce One was rejected as 'inappropriate' and, in any event, I couldn't do the whole trip as I had legal commitments. Obviously Rwanda was too poor a country even to think about paying. The Foreign Office said it wouldn't pay, Downing Street said, 'We don't have a budget.' So, after going round the houses, Sue was informed that 'Mrs Blair will have to pay'.

This was the final straw. 'You claim to want to highlight the cause of Africa, yet you won't back it up,' I told the private secretary concerned. 'And as for handing over two thousand pounds of my own money, for me and Sue to represent Britain, I am simply not doing it. I shall tell Laura Bush that I can't come because the British government doesn't think it sufficiently important.'

It was ridiculous. The UK was Rwanda's main development partner. Direct aid was running at over £34 million a year. On many levels it was a success story, an oasis of stability and economic growth, and if we wanted to have influence in the areas of concern – democratisation and human rights – then to visit at the same time as the First Lady of the United States made obvious sense. Not to go would have been such a wasted opportunity to fly the flag for Britain. In the traditional Downing Street way, the buck finally stopped at the Cabinet office, and Gus O'Donnell, Cabinet secretary and head of the Civil Service, decided that, after all, this visit should be paid for by the British government. Once that was agreed, everything fell into place.

I had to fly via Nairobi, and following the success of our Olympic bid, I decided to visit a project for young footballers in a local township. I took as many 2012 T-shirts and footballs as I could stuff into suitcases and, with a local hero by my side – the great marathon runner Paul Tergat – consolidated the message that the Olympics wasn't just about London, but about sport around the world, and its ability to lift the impoverished everywhere. That night, at a dinner at the Kenyan High Commission, I met both the Chief Justice and human rights lawyers and learnt at first hand about the rapidly deteriorating situation in the country which, at that point, was not generally known, and I left the next morning feeling thoroughly depressed. At the airport I realised the inroads China was making when I saw every sign translated into Chinese.

An idiosyncratic rendition of the national anthem greeted my arrival at Kigali airport and as the red carpet unrolled I realised I was in for the full state visit, with the President's wife there to greet me with her welcoming delegation. As for the British delegation, it was me, Sue and Ken McKenzie, our protection officer. Twenty minutes later the band struck up again, this time with the 'Star-Spangled Banner', as Airforce One whispered to a halt. The door opened and out poured fifty people, finally Laura and Jenna. Among my welcoming party was the British Ambassador, and all four of us squashed into his Range Rover while helicopters patrolled overhead, anything that moved having been commandeered by the American secret service, including fire engines. As for the ceremonial exit from the airport, we had no alternative but to sneak into the slip stream of the American convoy.

Our first stop was the Gisozi Genocide Memorial, where we laid a wreath before going into the museum itself. Set up with the help of the UK-based Aegis Trust, it presented the background and history of the civil war that had devastated the country and shamed the rest of the world. Over 800,000 Tutsis were murdered and a lesser number of Hutus. In most conflicts children are absolved of responsibility and are treated with compassion, but in Rwanda that was not the case. As with rape, infanticide became a weapon of war. Tutsis were like cockroaches, the propaganda went, and to eradicate them babies and toddlers were held by their legs and their heads cracked against walls. It is hard to imagine a more hideous example of a crime against humanity and Laura and I just stood in this room and wept. Later we met some survivors – mothers and rape victims – who even ten years on find it hard to talk about. As I know from my courtroom experience of sexual abuse, even within rape there are degrees of horror.

When Laura left, I stayed an extra day wearing my legal hat. The leaders of the genocide were facing trial at the International Criminal Tribunal for Rwanda in Arusha, in Tanzania, but the cases handled there were only the tip of the iceberg. Back in Rwanda there was a huge backlog of people waiting to be dealt with by the internal courts, but the system could not cope. The reality is far from simple. On numbers alone, it would take two hundred years to process each case currently before the courts. Put simply, it's not achievable justice. While those awaiting trial in Arusha were – rightly – receiving proper medical treatment for HIV/Aids, their victims, mainly women, who had been repeatedly and brutally raped, were dying before they could give evidence, unable to get similar treatment. While the Tribunal deals with the major perpetrators, Rwanda itself is pioneering a system for the 'lesser players', known as Gacaca courts, and I went to see one in operation accompanied by Janet Kagame, the President's wife, a tall, imposing mother of four in her forties.

The courts are based partly on traditional tribal methods of solving disputes, and partly on the Truth and Reconciliation Commission in South Africa; we watched as men accused of individual crimes of violence and theft were brought before a village gathering of what appeared to be many hundreds of people. My abiding impression was one of colour: the dresses of the women; the forest of umbrellas used as sunshades; and the accused who were dressed entirely in pink. Witnesses were called, the men answered and an appointed group of nine elders from the locality gave judgement. It all takes place within the course of a day. There is no capital punishment but, if found guilty, they can be sentenced to more then twenty years in prison. Rough justice indeed.

The idea behind the Gacaca courts is that the harm caused by the genocide was done to the community as a whole and so the community as a whole should judge what happens. For lawyers brought up on the common-law view of due process, there is some disquiet. Issues of bias and the rights of the accused come to mind. But what is the alternative? How do you heal a country after a civil war of such magnitude and horror? I'm not saying they have the answer, but it was both instructive and fascinating to talk about what works and what doesn't work. One thing is clear to me: on a scale like this, in a country as poor as this, the idea of trial by jury, or even a trial by a tribunal of three judges, is not really a practical possibility. Yet to throw up your hands and not deal with it at all is no answer either. Not to acknowledge these crimes leaves festering resentment. At least by giving these victims the opportunity to tell their stories, there is an acknowledgement of what they went through. It's very complicated and I can't pretend that I know the answer, but part of it must be to go along with the grain of the society concerned, to go along with a system that is already embedded in its culture, rather than imposing one from the outside. This is not an uncontroversial view, however. Following my visit I addressed an international law college in Geneva and it was clear from the response that not all the professors and students were willing to see this as a way forward. For some, due process was all.

Although the country has achieved more than would seem possible only ten years after the war ended, there remain huge unresolved problems, not least that of orphans. I was delighted to see, among the New Year's Honours in 2008, the name of Mary Blewitt, who set up SURF, which supports survivors of the Rwandan genocide. A British citizen and Rwandan survivor herself, she lost forty-two members of her family.

On my next visit to Rwanda, in March 2007, eighteen months after my visit with Laura Bush, I opened a survivors' centre, provided by the British government and run by SURF, which offers not only practical advice but training for trauma counsellors. Now that the country's immediate needs of shelter and food are beginning to be met, there is a real need for psychological counselling.

The focus of that second visit was a seminar of women parliamentarians from across the world, but particularly from Africa, of whom Ellen Johnson-Sirleaf, the President of Liberia, is a shining example, a true role model. To take up the reins of a country so devastated by war, with no infrastructure to speak of, is a huge task at any age, let alone at sixty-eight. I had been invited to speak on violence against women and, listening to other delegates, I realised how far we had travelled in the UK. In the Sudan, for example, there isn't even a word for rape. As a result of the war, women outnumber men six to four in Rwanda. One positive consequence is that 49 per cent of the MPs are now women, which inevitably changes the government's priorities. In stark contrast, the Kenyan delegate was one of only six women MPs in their Parliament. We heard how she had been trying to get through a law on wife-beating and rape for years, but the attitude in Parliament, she explained, was no different from that of the male population as a whole, and quoted an MP who said: 'It is well known that when an African woman says "no" she means "yes".'

The night of the official dinner was one of the most extraordinary of my life. Towards the end of the evening, the charismatic and legendary 'Princess of Africa', Yvonne Chaka Chaka, began to sing. Little encouragement was needed for the delegates to take to the floor and soon even the two presidents were dancing while I was handed the microphone to join in with 'No Woman No Cry'. And so, in spite of the difficulties women in Africa face, this was a joyous celebration of life, a spontaneous display of warm-hearted exuberance.

Among those dancing was the British Ambassador. I have met two kinds of diplomats in the Foreign Office: the establishment ones, the high-calibre people who do the high-class negotiating and end up in Washington and Paris, and the other kind who are never going to end up in Washington or Paris, and nor would they want to. These diplomats believe in getting their hands dirty and can make a huge difference to the way people in that country live or die. Jeremy Macadie fell into this latter category: jovial, languid and laid-back but really involved, and the Rwandans loved him.

The climbdown by the Cabinet office over that first visit to Rwanda in the summer of 2005 marked a turning point, not only in my relationship with Downing Street, but to some extent with the press. From then on I felt I was being given a hearing on issues I was highlighting, issues that increasingly related to women.

Every year Breast Cancer Care focuses on a particular area of concern, and in October 2005 it produced a report showing that within minority and ethnic communities we are still not getting our message across. Within the Muslim community, in particular, the taboo against discussing women's bodies makes it hard to achieve breast awareness so necessary for early diagnosis. With this in mind, Breast Cancer Care invited the Pakistani High Commissioner to share the findings. The problem was even greater in Pakistan itself, she said, and as a result invited me to visit her country early the following year with the aim of highlighting the breast-awareness message. Breast Cancer Care paid my travel expenses, and the Pakistani government agreed to pay for Sue's expenses, so the charity didn't lose money. The Foreign Office had also agreed that I could continue on to Afghanistan. I had maintained contact with the Minister for Women, and she was very keen for me to go to see for myself what was being achieved in the wake of years of Taliban rule.

Like all women with a growing family, the crunch comes when children start to leave home – and let no one underestimate how hard it is. Just as they have to learn to live without you, so you have to learn to live without them. Painful though it is, there are advantages. Whereas when I had four children at home I rarely went away for more than three days at the most, I was now able to take longer trips. By the time of my visit to Pakistan and Afghanistan both Euan and Nicky were away at university. For me at least it was never a case of out of sight out of mind – once a mother, always a mother – and I would speak to Leo and Kathryn every day, timing the calls so that they could tell me about their day. Even in the ten years since we arrived at Number 10, communications have totally changed. Now they know that, wherever I am in the world, I am always on the end of my mobile. There is something both surreal and grounding to find yourself in a truck negotiating a mountain pass, or smearing anti-mosquito cream on your arms in equatorial Africa, and having Leo on the line asking where I put his goggles, or Kathryn asking if she can borrow a pair of my shoes and, while I'm there, do I think black or brown mascara is better?

The two destinations of that trip early in 2006 to Pakistan and Afghanistan couldn't have been more different. Among the Pakistani middle class, gender is no barrier to high achievement, and the women I met included a general, three newly qualified fighter pilots and the governor of the central bank. They live in an entirely different world, however, from those who packed the refugee camps set up in the wake of the recent earthquake in northern Pakistan, and again in Kashmir where the women I met were completely covered up, so conservative was their culture.

Pakistan has the highest rate of breast cancer in Asia, partly due to environmental conditions but also because they don't examine their breasts. In the developed world 80 per cent of women going to the doctor with non-benign breast lumps have a grade 1 or grade 2 tumour, for which there are many good treatments leading to a positive prognosis. In Pakistan, by contrast, 80 per cent of the women presenting with lumps already have a grade 3 or 4 tumour. As a result the prognosis is not good and many can only be offered palliative care.

I talked to one woman sharing a bed with another woman, lying top to tail. She was crying. When I asked about her condition, she pulled aside her hospital gown and showed me a suppurating tumour on her left breast. She was forty-two with young children. She had only come to the hospital, the British doctor told me, once the pain and discomfort could no longer be ignored. There was very little they could do for her. In the UK, he said, they would never see a tumour like this, as it would never get that far without treatment.

I had been due to meet Madame Chirac in Kabul; however, Sue and I turned up at the airport to find that our flight had been cancelled. Luckily a UN flight was going there early the following morning and we were allowed to hitch a lift.

Kabul itself was extraordinary, and we drove in from the airport through a capital laid waste by war. The minister had arranged for me to visit the largest girls' school in the city where the age range went from five to twenty-one. There were 8,000 pupils, and in order to accommodate them all the school functioned on a shift system. Many classrooms were filled with rubble, and there was no glass in the windows, yet classes continued as they needed to make up for lost time. They were desperately in need of a science lab, the head told me, nor was there any games equipment. As for books, I saw girls reading dog-eared copies of low-grade Pakistani magazines and the Koran, and that was it. Accompanying us on the trip was a *Times* journalist, and on our return enough money was raised to provide six new classrooms and a science lab. A Swiss charity, called Smiling Children, has since taken up their cause and is providing training for teachers.

I knew there was an issue in Afghanistan concerning the appointment of women judges to their Supreme Court. Chief Justice Shinwari was an old-fashioned conservative who was claiming that women did not possess the necessary qualifications in Sharia law. Taking the bull by the horns, I raised it with President Karzai. He wasn't entirely surprised, and later that afternoon a group of women MPs told me they'd been bending his ear about this very subject for some time. Afghanistan's new constitution stipulates that one-third of MPs should be women, and they were already beginning to show their muscle. The men had wanted segregation in the debating chamber, but the women had simply refused, and MPs now sit alphabetically. Sitting literally beside each other, the men were obliged to notice the women's existence. The women told me that they were determined to challenge the idea that no women were qualified to sit in the Supreme Court, and they did. I later learnt that they had organised a campaign in Parliament and when President Karzai renominated Shinwari for chief justice in 2006, Parliament refused to accept him and a more liberal chief justice was appointed.

There is no doubt that the President is under enormous pressure from the conservative elements within the government, and one example of the concessions he is having to make on women's issues is with his own wife. Before the Taliban, she had been a doctor and now she is no longer allowed to work.

I was granted the rare privilege of meeting her. I knew from the President that she longed for a baby – an admission that astonished me at the time – and that he feared that she wasn't able to, and when I met her I sensed a real aura of sadness. When I discussed the implications of living in a city so inherently dangerous, she told me that it didn't affect her because she never went beyond the palace. She hadn't even been permitted to join Madame Chirac at that morning's opening of a children's hospital.

'It's not safe,' she explained.

'But surely, if it's safe for the French President's wife, it must be safe for you?'

She smiled and repeated, 'I just don't go out.'

On leaving I said I hoped that, one day, she could visit me in the UK. It didn't happen. But what did happen was that, six months after my visit, she became pregnant, and I hope that in due course she will find her voice and be able to play a bigger role in her country.

The role of leaders' wives is particularly important, I believe, in Muslim countries. When I was in Pakistan, the Prime Minister's wife gave her first public interview in which she used the word 'breast' and in so doing may have saved thousand of lives. The work being done by Sheikha Mozah in Qatar is a beacon for what can be achieved. Her Shafallah Center for disabled children is world-class, with facilities that put the West to shame. In my role as patron of

Scope, the UK charity that works for people with cerebral palsy, I addressed a conference at the Shafallah Center on the way forward for children with disabilities in the Gulf Region. There the battle is not about money, but removing the stigma of both physical and mental disability. In discussions with the families at the centre, a number of the young women spoke of how, as sisters of children with disabilities, their marriage prospects were considerably diminished, and this was one of the reasons families were prepared to keep these special children behind closed doors.

My colleagues from Scope could only marvel at the standard of the facilities available, yet were also able to share their expertise about inclusion and integration, and their belief that this is not only better for the children but is also a matter of basic human rights. Around 10 per cent of the world's population, or 650 million people, live with a disability. They are the world's largest minority. Their special needs have now been recognised in the UN Convention on the Rights of Persons with Disabilities, and I was able to speak about what the Convention meant, not only at the Shafallah conference, but on Al Jazeera TV. The UK was among the first countries to sign the convention when it was opened for signature on 30 March 2007 and Qatar followed in July 2007.

Over the ten years we were in Downing Street, I had access to people with real power to make things happen and I'm not ashamed to say that I made full use of it on behalf of the charities I was involved with. As an example, in April 2007 I visited both Qatar and Kuwait in my capacity as president of Barnardo's. Many people still think of Barnardo's as running orphanages, but in fact the last Barnardo's orphanage closed its doors in the early 1970s. Barnardo's' experience of disadvantaged children stretches back a century, yet it is always looking at innovation. Its mission today is to provide the services children need wherever and whenever they need them. Their main focus is keeping children with their families rather than removing them, and they run a huge number of schemes to help disadvantaged youngsters. I have been lucky enough to visit many of these, such as the Dr B's restaurants, where young people with disabilities learn practical skills in the catering industry, at a pace more suited to their ability. Not only do they learn to deal with the pressures of an 'ordinary' job, but the public learns to focus on what they can do, rather than what they can't. Children from other cultures face particular pressures, and Barnardo's has projects across the British Isles wherever there is a need, from an initiative with the Chinese community in Belfast, to supporting the children of asylum seekers in Manchester. It works with some of the most difficult children in our society, as I saw on my visit to the Islington centre which provides a safe haven for child prostitutes in King's Cross. What Barnardo's always needs is money, and in 2007 I was able to accept a cheque for them for £500,000 from the Kuwaiti government.

As I have seen everywhere I have travelled, women are tremendously resourceful. Not only do they keep their families together, they are a source of wisdom and strength, prepared to walk miles to fetch water, or carry their children to health centres where they know treatment is available. Yet, so often, these same women are at the mercy of unwanted pregnancies and sexually transmitted diseases. I remember visiting a labour ward with Salma Kikwele, the First Lady of Tanzania, and seeing a young girl, no more than sixteen, sitting by herself. Her baby had been stillborn. There was no chance of privacy here, either in birth or in death. We were being followed by photographers and there was no sense that perhaps this wasn't appropriate. We also saw the last push of a baby being born, and as the little girl was put on her mother's breast we were introduced. We were told afterwards that she was going to call her little girl Salma Cherie after us both.

Each culture brings its problems. In countries where sexual activity is rife, you have HIV/Aids. In those countries where young women are married as soon as they become sexually active, too early pregnancies result in fistulas – where the vagina is so torn that the bladder leaks into it. It is relatively easy to repair, but for young women in the middle of nowhere, treatment is not available and, often leaking and smelling, they are considered unclean and rejected by their families. We in the West don't even begin to understand.

My religion and my family are the two fixed planets which give my life meaning. Yet because my mother wasn't a Catholic, I can hardly claim to have been brought up in a conventional Catholic household. Perhaps as a result, my views and the Church's sometimes differ, usually for reasons of pragmatism. In the conventional sense, therefore, I cannot be considered a good Catholic, and indeed for a period in my twenties my attendance at church was sporadic, to say the least.

But once my children were born that changed and I have found that the weekly period of reflection that Mass affords me is incredibly important. After so many years the rituals are second nature to me and that, in itself, brings solace and reassurance.

The Pope is seen by Catholics as the successor to St Peter and to meet him is considered the ultimate benediction and, as my faith deepened following the birth of Leo, I hoped that Tony might meet him. The beginning of February 2003 was a hard time to be living in Downing Street. In the background were drums, and every time we went out it was to a chorus of jeers and shouts, of 'Blair Liar' and 'Blair Murderer'. We were all living in an atmosphere of enormous tension and stress.

One of Tony's foreign policy advisers was Francis Campbell, a committed Catholic from Northern Ireland, who also worked with Tony on multi-faith projects, and by this time he knew that Tony was genuinely interested in religion. Downing Street had been very resistant to the idea of Tony meeting the Pope; drawing attention to his dubious practice of going to church was singularly ill-advised, they decided. But, as the Iraq War loomed ever nearer, even they saw that such a visit might serve a diplomatic purpose as, apart from anything else, the Vatican had contacts with the Iraqi Christians, and Tony never gave up trying to find a diplomatic solution.

As religion was such a contentious issue, however, it was decided not to announce the visit until the very last moment. This meant that we couldn't stay in the embassy, so Francis arranged for us to stay at the Pontifical Irish College, which trains priests from Ireland. This solution also had its problems: not only was the Irish College very Catholic but there was the whole Irish dimension, the Catholic Church having always supported the cause of a united Ireland. Needless to say, it was the first time that a British prime minister had stayed there. We were originally put in the cardinal's room, but then the implications of a married couple sleeping in a cardinal's bed proved too much and we were moved next door.

As it was half-term we were able to take the children, apart from Nicholas who was on holiday. John Paul II was not only the pope but a major historical figure, and I was delighted that Sir Stephen Wall – Tony's chief adviser on the EU – Kate Garvey, and Gary and Nick from among the 'tecs, all of whom were Catholic, even if not practising, were able to join us, as well as Magi Cleaver.

A papal audience is a big occasion, whatever the circumstances, but, even so, my emotions ran away with me when I thought of how proud my grandma would have been. All those admonitions to behave, to learn my catechism, had not been in vain.

Francis had briefed us as to what was going to happen, but the reality was so awe-inspiring that I felt as wonder-struck as a child. The ritual had probably remained unchanged for hundreds of years. Once inside the walls of the Vatican, our private visit had become official and we were led by the gentlemen of the guard in solemn procession through wonderfully decorated corridors into the medieval heart of the Vatican. In those surroundings – the massive blocks of stone and marble – you cannot fail to be aware of history, but I was very conscious of just how historic Tony's coming here was. He was still a practising Anglican, though he had been going to Mass with the children for many years. I knew that Francis would have let this be known and my fervent wish was that he be allowed to take Communion, and under Francis's guidance I had written a letter to that effect, but whether it would happen I did not know. Nor did I know whether we would be invited to kiss the Pope's ring.

I had been brought up to venerate the papacy and all that it stood for. The feeling was so deep it was visceral, and part of me wondered if Tony realised just how momentous it was. Although he might not have realised it, the history he had learnt at school was Anglican history. For us Catholics the history of England was rather different: Elizabeth I was a bad queen and Mary Tudor misunderstood. It was as if all my life had been leading to this moment, leading down this endless succession of corridors and throne rooms. All these years, I thought, English Catholics had been in the minority and suddenly I felt that we weren't a minority any more.

Finally we reached the Pope's private chambers and realised that we were in the very heart of the Vatican, the room behind the balcony from where he blesses the crowds in St Peter's Square. While Tony was having his private audience with the Pope as Prime Minister, Vatican officials asked whether Leo would like to sit on the papal throne, which of course he did, though he was too young to appreciate the honour. After about twenty minutes, I was ushered in to join my husband. John Paul II was sitting on a chair, a very old man dressed in his papal white, frail and clearly very tired. He talked to me about my having Leo at such a late age, and what a good

example it was. Then everyone else in our group came in to be introduced, one by one. When it came to Leo's turn, the Pope stretched
out his hand for the ring to be kissed, and Leo simply handed up a
little picture he had done. We still have the most beautiful photograph of that moment, when the small child looks straight into the
eyes of the Pope, signed by John Paul himself. It is very precious.

His conversation with Tony probably lasted half an hour and the
question of Iraq did come up, he told me later. The Holy Father
made it clear that he was anti-violence but finished by saying, 'In the
end it's your decision and your conscience. It's your job to take these
decisions and, whatever you do, I'm sure you'll do the right thing.' I
know that Tony took a lot of comfort from that.

The press later reported that the Pope had given Tony a hard time.
That wasn't true. He actually gave him a very kind time, and as a
sign of favour we were taken to the Crying Room, the ante-room
where the newly elected Pope is left for a few minutes when he
realises the enormity of what has just happened and he cries.

While we were being shown some of the unseen corners of the
Vatican, and of course the magnificent Sistine Chapel and the cata-
combs, word came through that we were invited to join the Pope at
Mass in his private chapel the following day and that Tony would be
allowed to take Communion. That was another moment of pure joy
for me. Francis Campbell and I had chosen some English hymns just
in case and, as a thank you for their hospitality, we invited two sem-
inarians from the Irish College to join us, and also two from the
Scottish College and two representatives from the English College.
When we arrived in the chapel the following morning, the Pope was
already before the altar, hunched over in a chair, bent nearly double.
He had been praying for an hour, a nun explained in a whisper. He
seemed to me then such an extraordinary symbol. In spite of his
fragility, he was still pope, and you sensed no diminishing of his
power, as if within his weakness lay his strength, and when he stood
up and faced us, an enormous energy filled the chapel.

In my mind socialism and Catholicism have always been inex-
tricably connected. The liberation theology of the Young Christian
Students that so marked my girlhood was fundamental to my view
of politics: Christ as the radical feeding the poor. This was where
Tony and I had first come together, and this extraordinary man, from
the Polish working class, who grew up under the cloud of Nazism,

then communism, exemplified everything my husband and I believed in, political in the best sense of the word. Being given his blessing was of enormous comfort to us both.

Unlike the long-awaited audience with John Paul II, I had no expectation of meeting his successor Benedict XVI. Three years later, I was in Rome to address the Pontifical Council of Social Sciences. It was only after my talk was over that I was approached by an official from the Vatican.

'The Holy Father would like to meet you,' he said.

'But I'm not dressed appropriately,' I said. 'I haven't even got my head covered.' The protocol surrounding papal visits is very exact. As a woman from a non-Catholic country on an official state visit, you are expected to wear black. White or cream can only be worn by queens from Catholic countries. And here I was wearing cream.

He brushed my objection aside. 'The Holy Father won't mind at all,' he said. 'Just come along now and meet him.' So I did, together with my friends Sara Carello and Kateena O'Gorman from chambers. I spoke with the Pope for about twenty minutes, about Tony's proposed conversion to Catholicism, and also of his plans for a faith foundation for which I knew that he hoped for the Pope's support. I said that I felt my husband would very much like to discuss both matters with him and asked if it would be possible. He said, yes of course, and one of the last visits we made during Tony's premiership was to Rome to meet Pope Benedict. This time I was in a long black skirt, black jacket and mantilla, as custom decrees.

After that first audience with Pope Benedict, a photograph was published with me dressed in the cream outfit I had worn to give my lecture. The British press had a field day and, to her discredit, in my view, the former MP and Catholic convert Ann Widdecombe chose to join in the hullabaloo, saying, 'Who does she think she is? The Queen of Spain?' No. Just a Crosby girl who got lucky.

CHAPTER 32

Leaving

One great pleasure of the last ten years has been my chancellorship of John Moores University. JMU is a grouping of several famous institutions: the Liverpool Mechanical Institute, the Liverpool College of Art – where John Lennon famously studied – to name just two. In March 2002 Yoko Ono and I unveiled a statue of Liverpool's most famous son at the newly named John Lennon airport. When I introduced her to JMU's new vice-chancellor, Michael Brown, he said, 'You know that your husband used to go to our university.' She looked at him, and her eyes opened wide. It turned out that she'd been giving money to the wrong university all these years! She'd even endowed a scholarship in his honour . . .

My relationship with JMU began in 1997 when they offered me an honorary degree, confounding the aphorism from St Mark's Gospel that a prophet is not without honour except in his home town. To be honoured just down the road from where I grew up was for me the ultimate accolade. Two years later they asked if I would become chancellor, and I was delighted to accept. JMU has a great mission about access for young people whose families haven't been to university. In other words, for people like me. The role of chancellor is largely ceremonial, turning up once a year and awarding degrees and cutting the ribbon on the opening of new facilities and buildings.

Everything at JMU is wonderfully theatrical. Recipients of

honorary degrees have a gown designed and made by the fashion department which is unique to them. When I was installed as chancellor, a special fanfare was composed and played. At its best, education should be broadening rather than narrowing, and the range of degrees I present every year at JMU demonstrates this, from law and astrophysics to the LIPA, Paul McCartney's Institute for Performing Arts. After two terms as chancellor I was obliged to stand down, and my successor, Dr Brian May, famous virtuoso guitarist of the rock band Queen and less famous astrophysicist, is proof that academic excellence and popular culture are not mutually exclusive. My successor's appointment is highly appropriate: in addition to its well-known involvement in the artistic life of Liverpool – Phil Redmond of *Brookside* fame is an honorary professor – JMU has one of the most important astrophysics departments in the country.

I have been to graduation ceremonies at ancient universities but I can honestly say that John Moores is something special. Liverpool Cathedral, where the ceremony is held, is the biggest in the UK, so there is a real sense of occasion and it is always packed with the families who are, rightly, incredibly proud of their offspring who are often the first to make it through to tertiary education.

Fortunately, I was able to play more than just a ceremonial role and beneath the surface – perhaps more ugly duckling than swan – I was very involved. I supported them in every way I could, both at home and overseas. Education is the future, and JMU epitomises what can be achieved in harnessing the strengths of a local community. Its motto – 'Dream, plan, achieve' – sums it up. Thankfully my link with JMU is set to continue; as Chancellor Emeritus I fully intend to keep the link with JMU and help in whatever way I can.

The value of a good education can never be over-estimated, and nowhere more so than in areas of social deprivation. Less than a mile from Liverpool's central dock, I have visited Belvedere School twice in recent years. My first visit was shortly after Sir Peter Lampl and the Sutton Trust funded an experiment to allow access to this high-achieving school, not just to the lucky few who could pay the fees, but to girls from all over Liverpool who passed the entrance exam. By the time I returned, those same girls had completed their GCSEs, and results had shot up. The Girls' Day School Trust, to which group of schools it belongs, decided to go one step further and Belvedere became the first successful independent school to join the state system as an academy. The academy scheme has become a lasting legacy to Tony's determination to raise standards overall, rather than levelling down to achieve equality. Belvedere was founded in the 1880s, one of the first in the country to offer girls a well-rounded education. Once again, it is a pioneer, and I feel sure that in opening its doors to girls with ability across Liverpool, regardless of their background, it will prove a model for many other schools.

I visited Belvedere again within days of it becoming an academy and with me was Hilary Heilbron, daughter of Rose Heilbron, lodestar to that gawky young girl from Crosby who had ambitions to become a barrister in her image. Hilary is also a QC – and a good friend – and together we announced an annual scholarship in her mother's memory to enable young women from her old school to study law at university.

The Labour Party Conference in 2006 was my last as wife of the leader, and as I chatted to the stallholders for the twelfth year in succession, we all knew it: times they were definitely a-changing. For a start, there were no bracing photo opportunities in front of a lashing sea, be it at Blackpool, Brighton or Bournemouth. We were in Manchester. Not only that but our old friend Bill Clinton came along – proof if ever it was needed that leaving high office is not the end by a long chalk.

Then there was Tony's speech. After the pain of Iraq, it was greeted with a standing ovation, and no wonder. Even the arch-conservative *Daily Telegraph* called it 'the most dazzling speech of his career'. He urged the Party not to turn in on itself. We had grown so used to things only getting better, he said, that it was salutary to remember just how grim things were in the bad old days before New Labour. 'Take a step back and be proud,' he said. 'This is a changed country.' The challenges in 1997, Tony reminded us, were largely British, while the challenges before us now are largely global. What he didn't say was that he intended to be very much a part of it.

The biggest laugh came when he referred to me. 'At least,' he said, 'I don't have to worry about my wife running off with the bloke next door.'

In Gordon's speech the previous day he had said how he felt it had been a privilege to work with Tony. The news agency Bloomberg subsequently reported that I had been overheard saying, 'Well, that's a lie', and the press went for it like a rugby scrum after a loose ball. The truth is that whatever I might have felt, I never said it. It was as if the press had to have its 'Cherie-cross-behaviour-moment' and that was it – another Labour Party Conference tradition that has hopefully come to an end.

As for the manner of our leaving, I would have preferred to stay in Downing Street for another month, but that was entirely for practical considerations – the end of the school term would have been less disruptive, and I had also hoped that the house in Connaught Square might be ready for us to move into, but it wasn't. But Tony needed to resign his seat in order that a by-election could be held before the summer recess. He had been determined to go on his own terms and he had achieved that, and passed on the country in good shape to his successor.

Unlike previous tenants of Number 10, for whom leaving came as a shock and sometimes at barely twenty-four-hours' notice, our move was carefully planned. The packing itself took months: in addition to the accumulated possessions of ten years of family life, there was an entire room full of mementoes of government and charity visits. I must admit to being one of nature's hoarders and I found it hard to throw away these gifts which had been so thoughtfully given to us, many of them by children. We have them still.

As his last day in office Tony had chosen Wednesday 27 June. Children are not usually permitted to attend Prime Minister's Questions, but the Speaker gave special dispensation for Leo to come along as well as the older children (though Nicky sadly missed it due to floods in Oxford), to hear their father face the Leader of the Opposition for the last time. It was a wonderful House of Commons occasion: dotted around the chamber I saw many of Tony's colleagues – past and present – who had come to share this moment: Jonathan, Anji, Kate Garvey, Hilary Coffman, Sally Morgan among many. All so important to his years in power, all of them there to salute him and wish him well . . . When the House stood up to applaud, emotion got the better of me and I found I could barely see.

Leaving your home after ten years is always difficult, and we were all sad to leave, but in my case it was less the building than the people. Although inevitably there are comings and goings in any government-run organisation, among the non-political staff there is some semblance of continuity and over ten years the relationships that you build are not washed away like sandcastles with the next tide. Before walking out of that famous front door for the last time, we had first to walk out of our own front door, the door to the Number 11 flat that for a decade had formed the frontier between our home, with its scattered toys, aquarium, piano, Playstations, guitars, iPods, computers, board games and general family chaos (not to mention my collection of files and law books), and the tight-lipped centre of British political power, a frontier that far too many people seemed to think they could cross without knocking. There were times when all I wanted was to ram a bolt across the door and say Closed.

All that was now in the past. On the kitchen table I left a bottle of champagne, and presents for Sarah and the children: I wanted to show Gordon and Sarah the same kindness that the Majors had shown Tony and me. Then, pulling the door of the flat shut for the last time, we made our way, down and then up – there is no direct link between Number 11 and Number 10 on the first floor – to the state rooms, where the staff was already assembled. Tony made a speech thanking everybody for their hard work, and I made a short speech thanking everybody for being so kind and welcoming to us as a family. Then we were asked to wait while everyone else went downstairs to clap us out – the final tradition for all outgoing prime ministers.

As we stood waiting for the word to proceed, Tony walked across to the window and stood there motionless and alone for a few moments, gazing out over Horse Guards Parade for the very last time. Then, turning abruptly, he led us down that historic staircase lined with portraits of prime ministers where a space now awaited 'Tony Blair 1997–2007', into the hall and corridors below lined with all those familiar faces.

I hadn't anticipated how hard it was going to be to say goodbye, and how emotional. There had been times over the past ten years when the outside world had seemed a very hostile place indeed and the support of the people around me meant more than any of them will ever know. Garden girls, messengers, comms people, drivers, custodians, the 'tecs – over the years they came to be like an extended family, the only people in the world apart from my blood relatives who knew me as I really was: the Cherie they chatted to about family crises and joys; about relationships and careers; about parenting and children – not the Cherie they saw portrayed in the media. 'It's a good thing you've got a sense of humour, Mrs B,' I remember one of the 'tecs saying after a particularly unflattering photo of me appeared.

'Luckily the ability to laugh is one thing I've never been short of,' I replied. 'I'm a Scouser, remember. It's hard-wired, part of the DNA.'

After all the hugs, the embraces that were hard to pull away from, the bowed heads, the wrists raised to eyes to wipe away tears, the occasional ripple of subdued laughter, there came a moment when it was only the six of us, simply there as a family, standing in that hall with its familiar black and white chequered floor, the long corridor extending away towards the Cabinet room at the back of the building, looking at each other thinking, This is it. Then Tony straightened his back, took hold of Kathryn's hand and said, 'OK. This is the last time, guys, so let's get out there and do the business.'

Sitting there in the back of the Daimler, Tony stony-faced beside me, I stared out of the window as we passed the Cenotaph. He was right to be angry. Even though I had tossed my remark to the press light-heartedly – or so I thought – I didn't have the right. We had discussed it so often: leaving was to be on his terms and was to be done with dignity and grace, and what I had just done was neither gracious nor dignified. It was not my day, it was Tony's day. I knew it, and he knew it, and I sat beside him feeling both foolish and small. Then, just as the car turned into the Mall, he shrugged his shoulders, took my hand and gave me a grin, that infectious grin that I have never been able to resist. He grinned because he loves me. Because he knows that I just couldn't help myself. In the end, part of the reason he loves me is my unpredictable character. I am impulsive and he is not. I am the abrasiveness against which he can spark.

He didn't say anything, nor did I expect him to. When you have known someone for thirty years, a lot of things go unsaid, because you know each other so well they don't need to be said. Tony has a very quick temper which I have always suspected he inherited from his red-headed mother, but it flares up and is gone in a minute. When he says something unkind, I know he doesn't mean it. I know it's simply the tension talking. But when he asks me my opinion I know he wants to make up.

In all those years, whatever strain he was under, Tony never lost his temper either in public or with his staff. The one place where he could release his frustration and anxiety was at home. Even the children understood and learnt not to take it personally. He was under incredible pressure and if he was short-tempered, we knew he wasn't really cross with us. And we were more than happy to pay that price to have him at home as much as we did. Home was always where he felt happiest, one of the reasons we'd had an open house from the beginning of our marriage that continued into Number10. Why have a meeting in an office when you can have a meeting at home?

As the Victoria Memorial came into view at the end of the Mall, I saw once again the jubilant crowd of ten years before. I felt proud of him then, and I feel proud of him now. I remembered the vulnerable young man I first met, who had just lost his mother, and the resilience and determination that took him all the way to Downing Street and across the globe. But more than anything, I am proud of what he has achieved for us as a family. We went in there together, saw our kids grow up and our family expand, and we had come out the other side still happy and united, all of us, in our different ways, coming to terms with the weight of ten years of experience, and looking forward to the next phase of our lives.

ACKNOWLEDGEMENTS

First and foremost this book is about a family on a journey, so I could not have written it without the blessing of Tony and our children Euan, Nick, Kats and Leo, who know they are the centre of my life. My mother, my sisters (yes, all of them) and the wider Blair clan are always there for me, and I thank them for standing by me. I have shamelessly tapped into their memories for this project.

One question I'm always being asked is how do I keep so many balls in the air, and the truth is that I could not and do not do it on my own. There are many special people who have helped me on my way, some of whom are mentioned in these pages, some of whom are not. I certainly could not have coped without a wonderful group of women who keep my life ticking over and help care for the family, so thanks especially to Jackie and Maureen, but over the years to many others as well. Eternal gratitude, too, to Angela Goodchild and Sue Geddes, who together keep me organised and sane. To Martha Greene, who sorts out so many aspects of my life; to Hilary Coffman for her advice and support; to David Bradshaw for his speech-writing talents; to Faith O'Hara for her skill and understanding; and the unflappable André Suard for his patience, loyalty and unfailing good humour.

At work there is Amanda Illing and the great team at Matrix who have had to cope with the disruption to my practice caused by writing this book just when they thought they had got my full attention. As to all those who have been such an inspiration and help to me in my charity work, to name individuals here would be invidious, as they are legion.

I could not have got through ten years at Number 10 without my girlfriends, and I thank them wholeheartedly for all their support; you know who you are! I want especially to thank the wonderful staff at the Labour Party whose hard work got us to, and kept us in, Number 10; and all those at Downing Street, especially the events and visits department, who worked so closely with me on the Number 10 receptions, as well as overseeing our domestic and foreign visits. I am glad to have this opportunity to thank the unsung heroes of the corner of Whitehall I got to know so well: the IT and comms department who put up with my amateur interest in the subject of computers with such good humour. The garden girls and the 'tecs who, over all those weekends at Chequers and family holidays, became like our surrogate family – and not forgetting the drivers. David Heaton, the house manager at Downing Street, and all his staff who helped the house function twenty-four hours a day; and, of course, the wonderful switch, without whom Number 10 would cease to function at all. A big thank you to all the staff at Chequers – our refuge every weekend. As for my fears on arriving that first day at Number 10, they proved utterly groundless. I can guarantee that these loyal and hardworking people will serve every prime minister with the same dedication and professionalism they showed to us.

I should like to thank everyone at my publishers Little, Brown for their encouragement, advice and patience, especially Ursula Mackenzie, Antonia Hodgson and Vivien Redman. I couldn't have even contemplated it without your stalwart support. You had much more to do than would usually be the case, and I am truly grateful for all your hard work.

Finally I should like to pay tribute to Kate Jones, my agent, who first had faith in this book and whose vision and encouragement got me started then kept me going. While she read the early drafts, she never saw the completed version as, like so many other good people, she was taken by cancer far too young.

INDEX